RED SKELTON

THE MASK BEHIND THE MASK

Red Skelton's book says it all in A Southern Yankee *(1948), Skelton's greatest film.*

RED SKELTON
THE MASK BEHIND THE MASK

WES D. GEHRING

Indiana Historical Society Press
Indianapolis 2008

© 2008, 2013 Indiana Historical Society Press

Printed in Canada

This book is a publication of the
Indiana Historical Society Press
Eugene and Marilyn Glick Indiana History Center
450 West Ohio Street
Indianapolis, Indiana 46202-3269 USA
http://www.indianahistory.org
Telephone orders 1-800-447-1830
Fax orders 1-317-234-0562
Online orders @ http://shop.indianahistory.org

The paper in this publication meets the minimum requirements of American National Standard
for Information Sciences—Permanence of Paper for Printed Library Materials,
ANSI Z39. 48–1984

Library of Congress Cataloging-in-Publication Data

Gehring, Wes D.
Red Skelton : the mask behind the mask / Wes D. Gehring.
    p. cm. — (Indiana biography series)
Includes bibliographical references.
ISBN 978-0-87195-275-2 (cloth : alk. paper)
1. Skelton, Red, 1913-1997. 2. Comedians—United States—Biography.
I. Title.
PN2287.S395G44 2008
792.702'8092—dc22
[B]
                                        2008032320

To Cassie and my daughters,
Sarah and Emily

"Comedy is … "

laughing at this "cockeyed
caravan" instead of
turning on the gas,

realizing the "boy genius" was
no genius when it came to
homogenizing the Marxes,

wondering if a reference
to Carmen Miranda should
have occurred in *Brazil,*

hurting your sides instead
of those people talking
during Chaplin's "Oceana Roll,"

knowing Buster's "Great Stone Face"
still managed an Oscar load
of expression with those eyes.

being thankful for all the ways
in which Red Skelton brought
"I dood it" humor to the world.

—Wes D. Gehring

An earlier version of this poem first appeared in
Literature/Film Quarterly 23, no. 2 (1995).

Red Skelton: The Mask behind the Mask is made possible through the generous support of the Lacy Foundation/LDI, Ltd.

Contents

Valentina and Richard Skelton, a few years before his leukemia diagnosis.

Foreword

Red Skelton: My Dad Remembered
Valentina Marie Skelton Alonso

In early 1957 nine-year-old Valentina's younger brother Richard (then eight) was diagnosed with leukemia. Later that year, while the disease was in remission, the family did a great deal of traveling—an attempt to jam a lifetime of experiences into a few months. But Red, well aware of all the attention Richard was getting, wisely sensed that Valentina was feeling neglected. Thus, what follows is a special memory of a father-daughter date.

My first real experience of realizing how talented dad was happened when on a summer vacation in Honolulu, Hawaii, in 1957. He said, "There is a movie playing called *The Clown*, I'd like to take you to see it." So, dad and I went to the movie. We sat down with popcorn and soda. The show began. It was black and white and I realized that it was dad up on the screen. He was *The Clown*. The story was so sad it made me cry. I felt the pain of that clown and his sadness. At the end of the movie I turned to dad and said, "That was you on the screen." I gave him a hug and held his hand as we walked out of the theater. I realized my dad's talent then as a hero; I was taken by him.

I commend biographer Wes D. Gehring for researching my dad's life story, and for helping me to understand more about my father. Thank you Professor Gehring for writing this story for those young and old about one of America's distinguished clowns.

Preface

*After Red Skelton's hyperbolic tendencies had gotten him in trouble with
the fourth estate, the comedian would confess to a reporter, "That's my
trouble. If you want a good story—talk to me. If you want the facts—talk
to Edna [Stillwell, Red's first wife and manager]."[1]*

The above statement, a rare dropping of Red Skelton's public mask,
is easily the most significant admission made by the comedian in his
long career. It is the Skelton Rosetta stone, pivotal to deciphering the
apocryphal tendencies of this most gifted of comedians. Granted, a
common phenomenon of writing any biography is wrestling with that
most human of traits: "Like most people, he gave different accounts of
what he believed at different times."[2] But Skelton's propensity to reverse
reality to mold his own personal mythology went well beyond the
natural changes associated with that old movie montage cliché of pages
falling from the calendar.

Of course, Skelton's inventive inclinations towards his life story
put him in great embellishing company, including such diverse iconic
figures as Dizzy Dean, Ernest Hemingway, and Bob Dylan. Indeed,
biographer Marc Pachter has even articulated a key question for the
professional profiler to ponder: "How much can be learned about an
individual from the facts he invents about himself [?]"[3]

The full answer to that question, with regard to Skelton, lies in the
following pages. But it seems apropos to briefly note, without turning
it into a Freudian free-for-all, some seminal suggestions. First, probably
the greatest catalyst for his mythomania was seemingly quite simple—
the need to tell a better story. After all, what came easier for Skelton,
one of the greatest comic storytellers in the history of American
entertainment? Second, to borrow a page from literary scholar Jeffrey
Meyers, what follows is an insight about Hemingway that applies
equally to Skelton: "[He] combined a scrupulous honesty in his fiction
with a tendency to distort and rewrite the story of his life ... [There
was a] reluctance to disappoint either his own expectations or those

of his audience … he felt virtually forced to invent an exciting and imaginative alternative to commonplace reality."[4]

Here is how those comments are equally applicable to Skelton, an artist whose work brilliantly tells the truth through comedy (especially his attention to slice-of-life reality) but whose personal story seems to have been gerrymandered by Skelton to complement his comedy career. The diversity of examples ranged from Skelton's false claim that his grocer father was a famous clown and a college professor, to later deleting the sizable influence of Stillwell and legendary comedian Buster Keaton from his entertainment résumé.

Third, beyond telling a better story and suggesting Skelton was a total comedy auteur (having received no help, beyond the sentimental hook of a clown father), Skelton's embellishments were also about creating positive details for a black hole of a childhood. As the comedian's only surviving child, Valentina Skelton Alonso, recently told me, "My father was from a major dysfunctional family."[5] The following chapters include a number of bombshells, from Skelton's paternal grandmother operating a brothel in Washington, Indiana, (near Skelton's hometown of Vincennes), to the comedian's later strong belief that his biological mother was actually a prostitute who died in childbirth.[6]

Some might say why dredge up disturbing facts. Such critics would be fans of an earthy axiom by Skelton's favorite comedian, Charlie Chaplin: "The more you stir an old turd, the more it stinks."[7] But the justification for such thoroughness, beyond simply being a conscientious biographer, is that much of the controversial material to be found in Skelton's private papers was earmarked for a memoir he never got around to writing.[8] Skelton was not like film-noir writer Raymond Chandler. When a publisher attempted to get the novelist to write his memoirs, Chandler refused, saying, "Who cares how a writer got his first bicycle?"[9] Skelton cared about the details, and even had a researcher doing the legwork for his book.

One could say that Skelton was a self-made man who was not as well made as he might have been, but who (like all of us) was coping.

And despite those private demons, or maybe because of them, Skelton became one of *the* clowns of the twentieth century. No less a pantheon comedian than Groucho Marx called him "the logical successor to Chaplin."[10] Thus, besides exploring the mask behind the mask that was the private Skelton, this book also addresses his funny public persona, from his dual focus screen characters (fluctuating between antihero and smart aleck), to the troupe of buffoons through which he filtered his humor on radio and television.

Sadly, Skelton's bitterness over his television program being canceled by CBS has hurt his comedy legacy. He was an early victim of demographics. Skelton was dropped, despite high ratings, because his Nielsen numbers skewered too small town/rural and old. CBS was looking for a younger urban audience—an audience more likely to part with its money. In retaliation, Skelton kept his amazing twenty consecutive years (1951–71) of inspired television locked away from video viewers. Due to the network's perceived lack of respect, CBS would never again make a profit from Skelton's comedy—at least that was his reasoning. He even threatened to have the programs burned when he died. Consequently, despite being every bit as significant as Lucille Ball and Jackie Gleason, arguably early television's two most iconic figures (thanks to the broadcasting in perpetuity of *I Love Lucy* and *The Honeymooners*), Skelton's small-screen work is today largely unknown to younger viewers.

Skelton's acrimony towards CBS, to the point of flirting with destroying his greatest legacy, was a window into a less stable world the public seldom saw. But as his daughter Valentina shared in another interview, while "Dad was open and warm with fans, there was always a lot of secrecy going on with the family."[11] One could posit, as Steve Allen entertainingly does in his book *The Funny Men* (1956, including a chapter on Skelton), "I have never known a successful comedian who was not somewhat neurotic."[12] But after spending years researching Skelton for this book, as well as an earlier biography, I am convinced he pushed the envelope on this subject.[13] In fact, one of the signature lines of the brilliant but unstable wit Oscar Levant reminds me more of

Skelton: "There's a thin line between genius and insanity … and I have erased that line."

Fittingly, in later years Skelton was even fond of saying, "I'm nuts and I know it, but as long as I make them laugh they ain't going to lock me up."[14] In fact, I heard the comedian utter this mantra, or variations thereof, on several of his performing visits to Ball State University in Muncie, Indiana, times when I was able to interview and interact with Skelton.[15] Obviously, by this point it was largely done for effect. But after studying his private papers, and interviewing various family members, there is no doubt that he was often a tormented man. In short, Skelton fits, almost too perfectly, the stereotype of the tragic clown. One is reminded of the notable British clown Joseph Grimaldi (1779–1837) and the apocryphal story about his depression. Visiting an eminent doctor for his melancholia, the physician prescribed a night at the theater with the remarkable Grimaldi. After a pause, his patient hauntingly replied, "I *am* Grimaldi." Skelton could be called a modern-day Grimaldi.

Let me be quick to add, however, that this book is not limited to being a sad tale about a celebrity who was overly inventive about his private life. Though this is part of the portrait, given that these are components of Skelton's life, I am much more about celebrating the unique range of his comedy gift. This places me in agreement with Oscar Wilde's biting take on too many modern biographies, "formerly we used to canonize our heroes. … The modern method is to vulgarize them. Cheap editions of great books may be delightful but cheap editions of great men are absolutely detestable."[16]

I first came to Skelton as an elementary age class clown desperately in need of suitable material for my recess riffs and cafeteria cut ups. A television clown whose monologues regularly included the "team" of Gertrude and Heathcliff, video's only stand-up comedy seagulls, was more than user friendly for an underage wannabe comedian. Only decades later did I realize the army of youngsters for whom Skelton was providing material. Many have gone on to comedy acclaim. For example, in a 1999 *Rolling Stone* interview Steve Martin related a childhood memory very similar to mine. That is, when asked about the first time he was funny, Martin said, "Probably in the third grade ... I would watch Red Skelton the night before I came in and do his bits."[17] One should add that years before Martin first became famous as that "wild and crazy guy," with the fake arrow through his head, Skelton's Sheriff Deadeye character, the cowboy whose slipping holster often gave him a sissy-pants walk, frequently had a ten-gallon hat full of arrows.

Like the universality of Bill Cosby's later childhood-orientated inner-city stories, which still resonated with me (a midwestern small-town white kid), Skelton's all-inclusive comedy and pantomime cut across racial lines, too. This was first brought to my attention during a 2004 conversation with Cheech Marin of Cheech and Chong comedy fame. The comedian shared that as a youngster he "especially liked Red Skelton. There was a purity about him that shined through. And he had a great [comic] film career that no one [now] seems to know about."[18]

Soon after that, while researching an article on Richard Pryor, I discovered that this comedian had also "admired and imitated in grade school ... [all things in] the Red Skelton style."[19] And though Pryor later became controversial to conservatives for his adult language, so seemingly distant from Skelton's public image, one often forgets the poignant pantomime of which Pryor was capable *throughout* his career. For example, there is the touchingly inspired yet funny sketch about a deer at a watering hole, with hunters in the distance, showcased in the comedian's best performance film, *Richard Pryor–Live in Concert* (1979). One cannot watch a routine like this without thinking of Skelton's "Silent Spot," the pantomime section of Skelton's television program.

For another black comedian, the now underrated television entertainer Flip Wilson, Skelton's pièce de résistance was the sheer size of his one-man cast of comedy buffoons. A young Wilson had a practical epiphany: "the comedians who have done characters have had the longevity. Gleason, Skelton had characters to help them carry the weight on TV."[20] Flash forward to Wilson's hit variety program, the *Flip Wilson Show* (1970–74), and the young performer has a one-man troupe almost as imposing as Skelton's. Two of Wilson's most creative characters were the sassy Geraldine and Reverend LeRoy of the Church of What's Happening Now. Geraldine's enormously popular signature line, "The Devil made me do it!," was even reminiscent of Skelton's single best known catchphrase (by way of his "mean widdle kid" character, Junior), "If I do I get a whippin' ... I dood it!"

All in all, Skelton was not only a hugely influential comedian, he was, like Will Rogers, one of the profession's most beloved figures. Whereas many performers, such as Skelton's fellow Hoosier James Dean, generated a broad range of criticism—"He has been cussed, discussed, loved and hated"—Skelton's relationship with the public was one long mutual-admiration society.[21] His daughter Valentina "enjoyed how the room would light up when Dad came into it, and fans would surround him."[22] But ironically, as previously suggested, the private Skelton had many demons, making for the most full-blooded of biographies. Unlike one memorably savage review of an early Susan Sontag novel, "The tone is detached, the action almost nonexistent, and the characters do not lead lives, they assume postures," Skelton's life was more Eugene O'Neill meets Mack Sennett.[23] So be advised: the story that follows, like so many tales of genius, is a real roller coaster. And if it is true, as suggested by Henry David Thoreau, "That most men lead lives of quiet desperation," Skelton might have served as the axiom's poster child.

This study was made possible by a number of libraries and archives across the country: the Red Skelton Collection at the Lewis Historical Library in Vincennes, Indiana; the Red Skelton Collection at Western Illinois University in Macomb, Illinois; the New York Public Library's Performing Arts Library at Lincoln Center; the main New York Public Library at Fifth Avenue and Forty-second Street; the Margaret Herrick Library of the Academy of Motion Picture Arts and Sciences in Beverly Hills, California; the MGM/Red Skelton script material in the Cinema-Television Library at the University of Southern California in Los Angeles, California; the Museum of Television and Radio in Beverly Hills, California; the Television Academy in Beverly Hills, California;

the Vincennes Public Library in Vincennes, Indiana; and the Ball State University Library in Muncie, Indiana.

Numerous people helped make this book possible. Skelton's daughter, Valentina Alonso, granted me two lengthy informative interviews. Valentina's daughter, Sabrina, the comedian's only grandchild, also gave me a very helpful candid interview. Marvin L. Skelton, Red's nephew, did three insightful interview sessions with me. The comedian's widow, Lothian Toland Skelton, who donated the Skelton collection to the Vincennes University Foundation, answered a number of questions for my first biography of her husband.

Doctor Phillip M. Summers, president emeritus and project coordinator of Vincennes University, generously opened the Red Skelton Collection to me, even though the holdings are not yet fully cataloged and available to the general public. Two of his assistants, Billie Jean Primus and Jackie Bloebaum, were especially helpful. Indeed, Billie Jean's knowledge of the materials was invaluable. Robert "Gus" Stevens, of Vincennes College's Lewis Historical Library, provided invaluable advice and shared his own research on Skelton.

An interview and correspondence with Brenda Grant, the daughter of Carl Hopper (the apparent model for Skelton's Clem Kadiddlehopper) was a major plus. Correspondence with Janice Thompson Dudley, the sister of Red's first childhood sweetheart, provided an interesting window on his childhood. Earl Williams, a Skelton friend and former general manager of Ball State University's Emens Auditorium, provided background material on Skelton.

University of Southern California archivist Ned Comstock always goes out of his way to be helpful on my books. Western Illinois University Special Collections archivist Marla Vizdal also went the extra mile to assist me in my Skelton research.

Friends Joe and Maria Pacino provided both valuable research assistance and a place to crash when I was in the Los Angeles area. My department chair, Nancy Carlson, helped secure release time. Film historian Conrad Lane was always available for manuscript advice. Hoosier historian Dave Smith opened his considerable Skelton collection to me. As usual, Janet Warner logged time as my copy editor. The computer preparation of the manuscript was done by Jean Thurman.

A special ongoing thank you is in order for Ray E. Boomhower, Indiana Historical Society Press Senior editor. I am forever grateful to his support of my writing, from the pages of *Traces*, which he edits, to my earlier IHS Press biographies of Carole Lombard and James Dean. An award-winning historian himself, Ray is a wonderful facilitator for any biographer with a life to tell.

Mark Twain once wrote, "A successful book is not made of what is in it, but what is left out of it."[24] If I have accomplished that goal, the sheer volume of material I waded through might have given me some de facto assistance—short of creating a multiple volume *Encyclopedia of Skelton*, I attempted to keep it tight. I was reminded more than once of my graduate college mentor, film historian Richard Dyer MacCann, and the framed axiom in his office, "When in doubt, leave it out." My daughters, Sarah and Emily, avid students of film comedy, were patient and insightful when I frequently utilized them as Skelton sounding boards in the editing process. And an army of friends and family, especially my parents, were an ongoing rooting section for the project. Thank you one and all.

Prologue

It All Started with the Donuts

"Comedy is taking the everyday and slightly exaggerating it."[1]
RED SKELTON (1986)

Years before Red Skelton's phenomenal success on radio, television, and in the movies made him a household name, he was a struggling comedian in assorted live venues, from minstrel shows to Depression-era walkathons and vaudeville. But in the mid-1930s, this was all about to change. And it all came down to watching a man dunk a donut in a coffee shop.

As often happens in life, the catalyst for this memorable moment came out of desperation—Skelton needed new material. There are two variations, however, to the donut rescue. One story has the comedian tanking in a Montreal nightclub, the Lido, because on his initial visit to French Canada he overreached his talents, attempting to be a Hoosier Maurice Chevalier. But when Skelton fell back on his tired standard shtick, his exasperated wife/manager Edna Stillwell said, "'I could write stuff better than that.' Red's answer was, 'Why don't you?' also in sarcasm. But she did, and she has written his material ever since."[2]

The second take on how Stillwell came to create the sketches is born of triumph, not failure. Skelton is a smash success at the Lido club, and one night a representative for Montreal's top vaudeville house/film theater, Loew's Harry Anger, sees the act. Anger is bowled over and signs Skelton for an extended booking at Loew's. After a short exit to honor a prior Chicago commitment, the comedian is again headlining at Loew's, but Anger wanted all-new material. Skelton noted: "That floored me, but again it was Edna to the rescue. She said she could write 'em. I said, Well, now was certainly the time for her to display her hidden talent, if any ... So Edna took over my writing, and she's been at it ever since. And there's no better."[3]

These two 1941 reports were *both* credited to Skelton within a time span of three months. Such are the frustrations of a biographer. But as noted chronicler Paul Murray Kendall reminds fans of the genre, getting the "absolute truth" is nearly an impossible task. Instead, one must aspire for the "best truth."[4] In this situation the "best truth" would seem to be that in the mid-1930s (probably late 1935) when Skelton elevated his performance skills to "major league" status. This soon led to vaudeville's "A" bookings, all of which was dependent upon Stillwell's observational humor. (Critiques of Skelton's performances at Loew's begin to appear in the *Montreal Gazette* during 1936.) An additional "best truth" take occurs in yet another 1941 article that indicated Stillwell's initial writing "didn't seem funny to that experienced comedian, Red Skelton. 'But the customers laughed,' he said. 'Edna knew what she was doing. She kept on writing my material.'"[5] Fittingly, this latter article was amusingly titled, "Ex-Usherette [Wife] Leads Skelton to Success." And this title is hardly hyperbole. As a *Photoplay* essay from the following year stated, "There can be no story of Red Skelton without Edna."[6]

So where does the aforementioned coffee shop donut man figure in these preceedings? Well, the young, desperate-for-new-material couple were sitting in a Montreal diner when the eureka moment arrived. Skelton recalled, "Edna noticed a man at the counter dunking doughnuts in coffee and Edna said, 'There's our first routine.' Darned if the gal wasn't right … [what followed was] probably the best thing I've ever done.'"[7] Skelton biographer Arthur Marx (son of Groucho Marx), even called this donut epiphany the "exact moment when he [Skelton] quit being just another entertainer and crossed over to the ranks of the superstars.[8]

The donut-dunking routine that evolved from "slightly exaggerating" reality had Skelton inventively demonstrating various types of dunkers, from the petite to the sloppy, with several sorts in between. The other varieties included both the flamboyant dunker and the timid one who tries to dunk on the sly. But my favorite Skelton

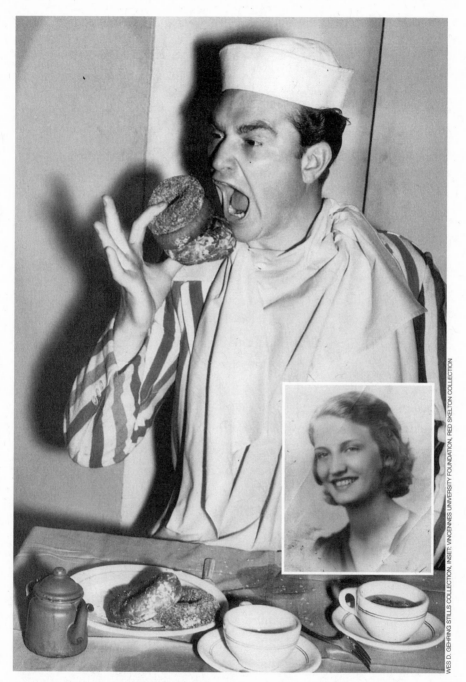

Red Skelton's donut routine—preparing to eat the "props" (circa 1938). INSET: *Edna Stillwell Skelton—Red's first wife and the creator of his career-making donut sketch.*

donut dunker is the most antiheroic, the poor person who miscalculates his pastry submersion time and dissolves the donut!

Drawing from period reviews, which sometimes suggest as many as nine dunker types by 1937, Skelton also further embellished the routine through making a big deal of dragging onto the stage a table, a large cup of coffee, and a plate of donuts.[9] After this comic setup, Skelton peppered his visual shtick with amusing verbal patter. One might label this a pioneering example of gross-out humor, since Skelton talked with his mouth full, occasionally "broadcasting" donut chunks in every direction. The comedian also became known for throwing several "sinkers" into the audience. Not quite gross-out Gallagher, the melon-smashing fanatic of fifty years later, but it was still groundbreaking comedy for the Great Depression. Appropriately, the *Milwaukee Journal* critic praised the merry mess of a routine as the "donut-dunking massacre."[10]

Despite the realistic foundation of Skelton's sketch, the ultimate over-the-top "donut-dunking massacre" nature of the routine reminds me of pop culture critic John G. Cawelti's description of the comic-laden mystery prose of Dashiell Hammett, where "'realistic' detail [can take on] a surrealistic flavor."[11] For film comedy guru Leo McCarey, a writer/director contemporary of Skelton and Hammett, starting with an anchor in reality is central to comic exaggeration: "Even in comedy of the most fantastic variety there has to be a could-be quality lurking around in every sequence. We may stretch the credulity of audiences to the breaking point one moment—but we have to snap right back into reality [for people to fully connect with the comedy]."[12] Thus, Skelton's donut sketch realistically started with one type of dunker, only to have the comedian amusingly pervert the situation. Red would then "snap right back into reality" with another "could-be" dunker that he would comically exaggerate, and so on.

Sixty years after the routine's creation Skelton confessed, "When I did the donut bit for the first time I had written on the tablecloth the next little piece of business I was going to do."[13] And during the initial performance history of the sketch he sometimes changed his personal prompter, depending upon the audience's response. Skelton claimed, "The first time, it ran, like, fifteen minutes [he chuckled]. The stagehand said, 'Hey, that's a funny bit but it's awful long.' So then I started cutting things out that didn't get the big laughs."[14]

This routine defined him for years. For example, when Skelton's career-making movie *Whistling in the Dark* (1941) opened, it was not unusual for critics, such as the *New York Journal American*'s G. E. Blackford, to footnote just who this new movie comic was by way of the sketch: "many know Mr. Skelton from his efforts to educate the amusement-seeking public as to the correct and modern and most efficacious manner of dunking a donut."[15]

Of course, for a vaudevillian such as Skelton, even in that medium's declining 1930s, a classic routine could fuel a career for years. Unlike the later "glass furnace" nature of television, where a nightly audience of millions metaphorically burned up countless material, a stage sketch played to just a fraction of those numbers. Moreover, with a vaudevillian only visiting a given city once or twice a year, positive word-of-mouth comments even gave legendary bits an added uniqueness.

Skelton's donut shtick also represented an entertainingly amusing subject for a series of advertisement-like articles. In 1938 *New York Daily Mirror* writer Robert Coleman turned mathematician as he documented that the routine necessitated the comedian eat *nine* donuts a show and vaudeville had him doing *five* shows a day! Is it any wonder that Coleman observed, "Red is a doughnut consumer. He slaughters doughnuts in wholesale lots."[16] Earlier that year the *New York Daily Mirror* film critic Blaud Johaueson also went the merry math route with regard to Skelton's famous sketch. Though her numbers were somewhat inflated, the article was titled, "Ate 12,000 and Each Made 'em Roar." Again crediting Stillwell as Skelton's writer, Johaueson posited that the "American public always gives a doughnut a laugh."[17] At the same time Skelton gave his own comic take on the subject to the *New York Daily News*, "Red Skelton, the doughnut-eating fool at Loew's State, says he has eaten so many doughnuts in the last few years that he swells when it rains."[18] Years later Skelton told me this avalanche of Great Depression donuts resulted in a more than thirty-pound weight gain.[19] When Hollywood eventually called to put the routine on film, in *Having Wonderful Time* (1938), the producing studio (RKO) put the comedian on a strict diet.

Sometimes the donut-related problems had nothing to do with the added poundage. Often it was difficult just maintaining the pastry supply. Skelton needed five to six dozen donuts a day; four dozen were for the show, with the extras covering the random hungry fellow vaudevillian, who would eat the "props." But shortly before one late 1930s Milwaukee opening, Skelton and Stillwell arrived at the theater to find empty donut boxes.[20] At first they thought it was a prank or overly ravenous performers. It soon became apparent, however, that the Skelton's Boston bulldog, Jiggs, had eaten more than sixty donuts. While the various stage acts on the bill fanned out in the neighborhood in search of "props" for Red's routine, the comedian took care of a very sick Jiggs. This was the same bulldog that figured in some later entertainingly hyperbolic Skelton stories. Skelton's daughter, Valentina, remembered how Jiggs would be somehow lowered out an upper story boardinghouse (where pets were not allowed) window for his late-night constitutional. One evening this allegedly caused a passing drunk to stumble back to a nearby bar and shout, "There's flying bulldogs out there!"[21]

The thankfully preserved sinker sketch of *Having Wonderful Time*, with a dieted thin Skelton, is a more streamlined look at the routine. Running right at three minutes, it features three dunker types: the cross-eyed variety, the society sort, and the sneaky dunker. Though not as outrageous as the review descriptions of the stage original, the movie take on donut dunking gives one a sense of the added business the comedian brought to the bit, from using a second tablecloth as a comic bib, to his ongoing patter: "Notice [coming out squeaky and high-pitched] how I hold the little creature [the donut], with the index finger. The pinky [finger] should always be out, that's so if you slip you won't go to your elbow [into the coffee cup]."

The athletic Joe E. Brown often comically focused on food in his films. Here he "costars" with some pie in Local Boy Makes Good *(1931).*

Naturally, one need not be a psychology student to see a certain irony in an eating routine being so popular during the Great Depression. Granted, funny films of all eras feature food sketches, from Charlie Chaplin stealing hot dog bites from a child in *The Kid* (1921) to John Belushi's instigation of the food fight in *National Lampoon's Animal House* (1978). Still, there are a plethora of eating-related sketches in Depression-era movie comedies. And the range is simply inspired, be it loopy Stan Laurel munching on wax fruit in *Sons of the Desert* (1933), or Chico and Harpo Marx pitting their combination peanut and hot dog stand against Edgar Kennedy's lemonade concession in *Duck Soup* (1933).

The proverbial golden spoon, however, for *the* Depression-era food-conscious clown would probably go to Joe E. "cavernous-mouthed" Brown. The comedian's first extended comedy scene in one of his definitive films, *Elmer the Great* (1933), is predicated upon his title character eating the largest breakfast on record—stacks of pancakes and ham, apple pie, gingerbread, donuts and jam, and assorted fruit (especially a comic favorite, the banana), while drinking coffee and a large glass of milk. But unlike a more typical comedy eating scene, such as when the Marx Brothers focus on pigging out in *Room Service* (1938), Brown's breakfast in *Elmer* has him talking away, too. He later amusingly confessed, this was no easy task, "even with my mouth."[22]

I dwell on Brown for a special food-related comedy connection to Skelton. Upon the release of *Elmer* a *New York World Telegram* article appeared titled "His Heavy (Eating) Role Fits Joe Brown Exactly." The piece revealed that the comedian "attributes his propensity for eating parts to the time when he would have appreciated them because of the scarcity of good [eating] fare in his days of initiation into show business."[23] This catalyst was equally applicable to Skelton. In fact, he told me as much on several different occasions when I was preparing my first biography of the comedian.[24] But for both Brown and Skelton, the lack of food factor predates their early apprenticeship as entertainers. Each of these funnymen had Dickensian childhoods, where a square meal was almost as rare as a new pair of shoes. Flash

A circa 1935 Skelton apes Claudette Colbert's leg shot from It Happened One Night *(1934).*

forward to the Great Depression, and millions of Americans were suffering through similar deprivation. Consequently, just as 1930s screwball comedies featured the escapism of watching the eccentric idle rich, the era's personality comedies often showcased another vicarious bit of voyeurism—a comic abundance of food. One could even liken the sweeping comprehensiveness of individual food phenomenon bits to Barbara W. Tuchman's definition of the biography, "The universal in the particular."[25]

"Success," as the old axiom goes, "often has many parents." While Stillwell was the author of the donut sketch, she might have been inspired by director Frank Capra's hit film *It Happened One Night* (1934), a pioneering screwball comedy with Clark Gable and Claudette Colbert. Where's the donut connection? Capra's movie has an auto camp scene in which Gable's man-of-the-people type briefly

A sleeping Robert Benchley, despite those loud Picasso-like pajamas, from the Oscar-winning How to Sleep *(1935). Benchley was a comedian who had a great influence on Skelton.*

demonstrates the appropriate way to dunk a donut to his debutante sidekick Colbert. It is a fleeting moment in a film that otherwise milks such scenes. But it might have planted an idea in Stillwell's mind.

What are the chances she even saw the film? Excellent. There is a period photograph of Skelton parodying another more famous *Night* scene—Gable's how to hitchhike routine. Paradoxically, for all the worldly wisdom of Gable's everyman, his tried and tested thumb is no match for Colbert's shapely leg. The aforementioned Skelton-spoof photograph has him exposing a less than lovely limb. But even without this *Night*-related picture of the comedian, it would have been hard to miss the influence of the Capra movie. *Night* is one of the seminal films in Hollywood history. And it was a box-office smash that would not go away, getting extended 1935 playing dates after that year's Academy Awards made *Night* the first film to ever sweep all five main categories—Best Picture, Director, Actor, Actress, and Screenplay. (This is something that has still only happened twice since *Night*—*One Flew Over the Cuckoo's Nest* in 1975 and *Silence of the Lambs* in 1991.) The Oscar overdose that came *Night's* way, followed by 1935 repeat business, approximates the genesis of the Skelton donut-dunking sketch.

Of course, one could argue that a whole "how to" mentality permeated 1930s comedy, from the hitchhiking and donut examples of *Night*, to Stillwell's proclivity for variations upon the signature donut sketch she created for Skelton. For example, another Stillwell routine for Skelton, which was also featured in *Having Wonderful Time*, had the comedian amusingly demonstrating the various ways people go up and down stairs. But the nominal 1930s comedy king of "how-to" humor was Robert Benchley. His first book-length collections of comic essays began to appear in the 1920s, something he complemented with drama reviews for the old humor magazine *Life* (before moving to the *New Yorker*) and the occasional comic lectures in vaudeville. One could argue that after the 1935 death of Will Rogers, Benchley soon assumed the mantle of America's favorite humorist.[26] He was certainly one of the most active. While the popular writing continued, he was increasingly active in film and on radio. Most germane to the Skeltons

David Letterman early in his television career (circa 1980), another Hoosier comedian whose early career was assisted by the writing of a woman with whom he was romantically involved.

were Benchley's acclaimed short films, such as his Oscar-winning (Best Live Action Short Subject) *How to Sleep* (1935).

Benchley had pioneered the live-action sound short with such brilliant early outings as *The Treasurer's Report* (1928, which he originally made a hit in 1920s vaudeville) and *The Sex Life of the Polyp* (1928). However, the plaudits generated by *How to Sleep* had Benchley doing assorted "how-to" films for years. As with the 1935 awards and re-issuing of *It Happened One Night*, *How to Sleep* was generating attention at approximately the same time Stillwell was creating the donut dunking sketch for Skelton. Moreover, the numerous observational routines that Stilwell soon penned for her husband were often reminiscent of Benchley's lecture or professorial style. Indeed, this Skelton-Benchley link is given a historically casual connection in a 1937 *Detroit Free Press* rave review of Skelton's donut sketch. On the same page that critic James S. Pooler praises the comedian's routine as a comic "lecture" is a review of Benchley's latest parody lecture, *How to Start the Day Right* (1937).[27]

By 1938 Skelton himself was accenting the professor slant with the press. *Pic* magazine, drawing upon the comedian's material, stated, "Professor Red Skelton, B. D. (Bachelor of Dunking), is currently delivering his lecture on 'Dunking As Art and Science' in the movies."[28] With a photo spread done at Maxwell House Coffee's "doughnuttery" on Broadway, Skelton had the comic last word, "'The field of dunking,' says the professor, 'has not yet been fully explored. And I for one think it's just as well.'"[29]

None of the previous professorial parallels need take away from the comic creativity of Skelton's partner. One could simply liken this Depression-era tendency for a "how to" humor to what the Germans call zeitgeist—the mood or spirit of a particular period of history. Regardless of the source of inspiration, this donut-dunking bit would lead the Skeltons to star status in 1930s America. (The sketch also brought Skelton some early fame back home in Indiana when the *Indianapolis Star* ran a Sunday feature titled "Indiana Boy's Doughnut Dunking Hit on Stage" in 1937.[30]) Ultimately, the Stillwell routines brilliantly bring an audience a slice-of-life silliness which, to paraphrase the much later *New Yorker* critic Hilton Als, was "not her world but *the* world."[31]

While Stilwell's writing made a unique contribution to Skelton's career, it is not unusual for celebrated comedians to be greatly assisted by creative women. For instance, today's most prominent Hoosier humorist, David Letterman, owes much of his success to his longtime companion and former *Late Night* head writer Merrill Markoe. Even her take on Letterman's style, what she labeled "perceived reality," is comparable to Stillwell making Skelton appreciate "slightly exaggerating" reality.[32] To borrow an insight from art critic Holland Cotter, "Sometimes a revolution is just a matter of altered perspective, changed position."[33]

Interestingly enough, a few years after Stillwell's writing and managing helped orchestrate Skelton's stardom, one of his eventual celebrated comedy contemporaries, Danny Kaye, came to owe his success to another writing/manager wife, Sylvia Fine. The description of Fine's relationship to Kaye, by the comedian's definitive biographer, Martin Gottfried, might just as well be describing Skelton and Stillwell: "The most important thing in Danny's life was to succeed as an entertainer, and for that he lacked not just material but a performing identity. Sylvia, as a writer, needed a medium. In Danny, she found a purpose, almost a maternal one: to use her gift to conceive and nurture the man of her dreams; to give birth to Danny Kaye."[34]

Ironically, the obsessive drive of both Stillwell and Fine ultimately soured their personal relationships with the comedy legends they helped to create, though Stillwell continued to manage and write for Skelton well into his second marriage. But that is getting ahead of the couple's donut changing beginnings. Now it is time for the rest of the story.

1

The Early Years

On the superiority of being a clown: "I mean, a clown's got it all. He never has to hold back. He can do as he pleases. The mouth and the eyes are painted on. So if you wanta cry, you can go right ahead. The makeup won't smear. You'll still be smiling."[1]
RED SKELTON, 1979

The pathos inherent in the above statement is fitting for comedian Red Skelton, born on July 18, 1913, into abject poverty in Vincennes, Indiana, with his thirty-four-year-old father having died the preceding May. The Dickensian childhood of Skelton (christened Richard Bernard), whose hair color gave him his nickname, included three older brothers—Joseph Ishmal (1905), Christian, (1907), and Paul (1908). Their overworked and overwhelmed mother, Ida Mae Skelton, widowed before she was thirty, struggled to make ends meet by taking in washing and cleaning businesses and homes. Paradoxically, one of Ida Mae's key jobs was cleaning a vaudeville house.

This has long been the accepted foundation to the Skelton story. But there is a darker side that has never before been told. Through the gift of the comedian's private papers to Vincennes University, some of which had been earmarked for the comedian's unrealized memoir, a more provocative tale unfolds. The central character in this real-life melodrama is Skelton's paternal grandmother, Ella Richardville (from which the comedian's given name of Richard comes.) In the late 1870s a teenaged Richardville went to work as a maid in the home of prominent Princeton, Indiana, attorney Newton Elmer Skelton. Richardville became pregnant and Joseph Elmer Skelton (Red's father) was born on September 14, 1878. The scandal ruined Newton's marriage and probably contributed to his premature death in 1880, when he was in his early forties. Joseph never knew his father. According to the researcher who uncovered these materials for the comedian's projected autobiography, "You won't believe it [Red] but you look exactly like … [Newton Elmer Skelton]—especially around the eyes."[2]

Richardville seems to have fallen through the cracks of time until October 1891, when her common-law husband, Joseph Earhart (sometimes spelled Ehart, or Eheart), was charged in court with "unlawfully selling to one James E. Reney, one quart of intoxicating liquor."[3] Presumably Richardville had been with Earhart for some time, because Red's father seems to have been named, or renamed, after him. (She also had a son with Ehart, Chris, Joseph's half-brother.) Joseph fluctuated between using the last names Skelton and Ehart.[4] His 1913 Vincennes obituaries listed him as Joseph Ehart.[5]

In December 1892 Ella married William Cochran, a union that produced court headlines over the next decade. For example, the following month Ella Cochran was indicted for "keeping a House of Ill-Fame," with one of the prostitutes, Beatrice Richardville, probably being her sister.[6] The brothel was in Washington, Indiana, another small town near Vincennes. This has special pertinence for Skelton, beyond helping to establish the roots of a dysfunctional family. Between autobiographical writings in the comedian's private papers, and various interviews with his daughter, Valentina Skelton Alonso, it can now be revealed that Skelton believed his mother was a woman named Lillian—the favorite prostitute in Grandma Cochran's brothel.

The prostitute Lillian doubled as the mistress of Skelton's father. But like most of the comedian's stories, there are various versions of the tale. The one commonality is that both Lillian and Ida Mae (the woman credited on Skelton's birth certificate with being his biological mother) gave birth within days of each other. But Ida Mae's child was stillborn, while Lillian delivered a healthy boy. Some accounts have Lillian dying in childbirth, others state she committed suicide. In either case, Ida Mae received Skelton as a replacement child.

When the comedian related this provocative take on his origins to Valentina, he seemed to focus on circumstantial evidence, such as "Why was I the only one with red hair and no resemblance to the other boys?[7] While Skelton makes similar comments in his private papers, he also claims to have proof, explaining why he always called Ida Mae "Mur"— "This was the name I gave ... [her] the instant she told me she was not my mother. For fifty-three years I gave her that title."[8] Though Skelton's use of Mur as a reference to Ida Mae is well documented through the years, both publicly and privately, he had always kept the reason quiet, except to a few family members.

Obviously, this is a topic that will merit more examination throughout the book, but first the rest of Ella's colorful story needs to be told. In May 1894 she was indicted for "receiving and concealing stolen goods."[9] In December 1900 Joseph Ehart (Red's father) testified

Skelton (the baby) with his adoptive mother, Ida Mae Skelton, and (left to right) his half-brothers Christian, Paul, and Joseph Ishmal.

under oath that William Cochran (Joseph's stepfather) shot and
wounded Christopher Ehart (Joseph's half-brother) with "premeditated
malice ... to kill and murder."[10]

Cochran was convicted the following year and received a two- to
fourteen-year sentence at State Prison North in Michigan City, Indiana.
Ella subsequently filed for divorce, which was granted in January
1903.[11] (At this point her occupation was listed as housekeeper.)
Though Cochran was now safely incarcerated, family brushes with the
law continued. These included multiple charges against Ella for selling
"intoxicating liquor without a license," a conviction for carrying a
concealed weapon against her son Chris (after the attempt on his life),
and an "assault and battery" charge against Ella and Joseph. Ultimately,
the ruling in the latter case went against Ella, with her son being found
not guilty.[12]

The court records on the assault and battery case are sketchy,
though it appears that Ella might have taken a guilty charge as a
plea bargain to get Joseph off. Regardless, it is quite the rough-and-
tumble family that has a mother and her oldest son taken to court on
assault charges. The situation was probably exacerbated by the fact
that Joseph was then living in a room at a local bar. Ironically, this
point of information is revealed by yet another court case. Almost
simultaneously with the assault case, Joseph was found guilty of the
rather vague charge, "obstructing the view of his saloon room."[13] (Not
surprisingly, the general consensus among Skelton family members is
that Joseph's premature death was brought upon by his alcoholism.[14])

While Skelton never knew his father, he maintained entertaining
memories of Ella and Ida Mae's mother, Elizabeth "Granny" Fields,
who often took care of him when her daughter worked. In yet another
folder of the comedian's autobiographical writings, he affectionately
said of the "notorious madam," "I don't think I ever referred to her a
'grandmother' ... when I talked to her. It was always 'Ella.' I wasn't
prompted to call her 'Ella.' She just had a dignity about her that called
every bit of respect one could give to her. She was kind and gentle."[15]

A young Skelton poses for a Vincennes photographer (circa 1919).

Though Granny Fields told entertaining Civil War stories, and her woodcarving husband, A. C. Fields, had artistic tendencies, the boy clearly preferred Ella. He found her more affectionate and generous with food—major factors for a neglected and underfed child. In yet another autobiographical musing, Skelton even flirted with the idea of doing a book on the two women. As the following pages will document, throughout Skelton's long career there would be periodic announcements about various writing projects, none of which came to fruition. The comedian tended to spread himself too thin on his many creative projects. But I also feel these pronouncements were Skelton's way of simply saying, "I like these people and/or topics." What follows is Red's tongue-in-cheek comment about a book on Ella and Granny: "I always wanted to write a book about my two grandmothers—one being an undertaker [a popular profession in Fields's family] and the other being a madam—and call it 'My Grandmothers—They Got You Coming or Going.'"[16]

Of course, over the years, the comedian's most public comments about family involved his father, with Red often claiming Joseph was a noted circus clown. Indeed, a *New York Sun* article from 1938, "Red Skelton of 'Having Wonderful Time,' Discusses His Hollywood Debut," went so far as to describe the elder Skelton as an "internationally famous clown."[17] This is a great story, but there is little or no evidence to support it. As Skelton author Wesley Hyatt later observed, "What we do know is that for a man [Red Skelton] who came across so open to the public, he was remarkably mysterious about his own history."[18]

The comedian's father had possibly been a minor circus clown sometime before he married Ida Mae Fields (April 13, 1905). Such a nomadic profession would explain how Joseph Elmer (born in Princeton, Indiana) might have met his Nebraska native wife. But if such a circus link existed, it was ancient history by the time of Joseph's death. His 1913 obituary headline observed, "North End Grocer Dies Suddenly," with no mention of any big-top experience.[19] Though one might argue that this small-town death notice was not particularly

detailed, the obituary did go so far as to mention his membership
in a series of lodges (Knights of Pythias, Moose, and Odd Fellows).
However, these organizations might represent a clue to Joseph's
entertainment roots. Years later, the only vague memory Ida Mae's half-
brother, Fred Foster, had of Joseph Elmer doing any clowning involved
"a Masonic organization."[20]

Away from the hoopla of big-city journalists, such as the *New York
Sun*'s Eileen Creelman (who conducted the aforementioned interview),
Skelton sometimes assumed a less romantic perspective on his father,
too. For example, when the comedian himself applied to join his
hometown Masonic Lodge in 1939 (quite possibly to emulate the
parent he never knew), "he listed his late father's occupation as 'grocery
man.'"[21] Plus, as early as 1908, the Vincennes city directory listed
Joseph Elmer Skelton's occupation as grocer. One should add that at
this point in time, being a grocer was a common occupation in small-
town Indiana. Neighborhood markets were found every few blocks.
If one also factors in the aforementioned court cases involving Red's
father, the window of time in which Joseph could have been a circus
clown, even in the best of circumstances, would have been very brief.

So why was Skelton often rather inventive about his father's past?
First, one does not have to be a psychiatrist to assume Skelton was
attempting to connect with a parent he never knew. This point was
reinforced by an interview I had with the daughter of Carl Hopper,
one of Skelton's childhood friends. Brenda Hopper told me that her
dad recognized that when young Skelton expounded about his famous
clown father, it was more a reflection of not having a father.[22]

Second, the clown connection Skelton credited to his father
probably came from the comedian's mother. Late in Skelton's life
he confessed, "Mom used to say I didn't run away from home [to
entertain]. My destiny just caught up with me at an early age."[23] That
is, Ida Mae allegedly waited to share any circus-related information
about Joseph with their youngest son until after Red had expressed
interest in entertaining. Ironically, there was even some hyperbole to
Skelton's telling of this story, too. He never "ran away from home" to

perform. The boy first went on the road, after joining a medicine show, with his adoptive mother's blessings. These were tough times for the Skelton family, and one less mouth to feed meant that much more for his siblings. Moreover, Ida Mae quite possibly received some modest reimbursement for her son's novice beginnings. Certainly, this was the case with many poor youngsters trying to break into show business. Comedian Joe E. Brown enjoyed telling people throughout his life that he was the only youngster who ever ran away to join the circus—with his parent's blessing![24] Appropriately, Brown's struggling family received a small stipend for young Joe's summer acrobatics with a circus. (Show business or not, "hiring out" children was long a common practice for poor families.)

A third potential take on this inventive yarn about his dad being a notable clown probably went beyond just filling in the blank spots with a unique father. Joseph Ehart (Skelton) and his clan were essentially hell-raisers, pure and simple. Skelton's cosmetically revisionist history made an embarrassing family tree go away. I am reminded of a line written by novelist F. Scott Fitzgerald, "So being born in that atmosphere [of people looking down on my family] ... I developed a two-cylinder inferiority complex."[25] Between all the poverty and scandal attached to Skelton's background, he probably had a V-eight inferiority complex!

A fourth possible explanation for Skelton's creative take on having a famous father might be called the *Big Fish* phenomenon, after the Daniel Wallace novel and director Tim Burton's brilliant screen adaptation of the same name. *Big Fish* is the story of a man whose oral history tends to have tall-tale tendencies. But as the man's son investigates this life, he finds it often loosely anchored in the truth. The title character, like all entertainers from the beginning of time, simply wants to tell a better story. I would posit, this is part of what drove Skelton's son of a clown perspective, though Joseph quite possibly did amateur entertaining. Red was a great clown, and making his father into a famous funnyman creates a better story. In writing over two dozen books, the majority of which are about entertainers, I have seen

Charlie Chaplin created his famous Tramp character in 1914, the year after Skelton's birth. Chaplin was always the *comedy model for Skelton.*

countless variations of this *Big Fish* tendency, starting with Charlie Chaplin.[26] Unlike the conclusion of Rainer Maria Rilke's famous poem, "Archaic Torso of Apollo," which posits: "You must [literally] change your life," Skelton and others merely reinvented themselves.

What makes Skelton's creative take on his personal history all the more poignant, however, is the degree of genuine love that the comedian generated for the father that he never knew. With such passion in mind, the young narrator of *Big Fish* observes in the novel, "I think, that if a man could be said to be loved by his son, then I think that man could be considered great."[27] On this level, if no other, Joseph "could be considered great." Skelton had more than been the good son.

Still, there was little time in the comedian's early years for pondering career choices of a long-departed father. Poor was all Skelton knew as a youngster, and he attempted to reframe these dire beginnings into something positive. The aforementioned Brown's populist take on early survival could just as well have been Skelton's childhood mantra: "I began life as an undernourished baby who grew into a gaunt, too-thin ... boy; it was a fact that disturbed me not the slightest. Most of the kids in my family and neighborhood were equally thin. And if it was a hardship, it was good conditioning for the [tough performing] life I later knew."[28]

Skelton did all he could to help his financially struggling family. "My family was hungry, and I had to make money somehow," he recalled.[29] His odd jobs started at age seven with the street-corner sale of newspapers before and after school. Like a brash Tom Sawyer, Skelton said he "soon learned to sass the customers so that they bought papers to get rid of him."[30]

Skelton enjoyed this huckster gamesmanship, though the original catalyst remained the quiet desperation of poverty. While earning pennies racking balls in Kramer's Pool Hall, Skelton collected discarded decks of playing cards. Demonstrating his flair for art early, he doctored the cards into "new" novelty deck items. As survivor Skelton proudly noted in 1941: "I worked [sold the cards to] the gullible citizens of the [nearby] towns right on the main streets."[31] Like a young Thomas Edison, Red also sold sandwiches on the local passenger train. But again, Skelton played the huckster. Years later he confessed, "I put a lot of ham and lettuce outside the sandwich [hanging from the sides] and nothing in the middle."[32]

Fittingly, for someone attracted to show business, young Skelton also regularly attempted to sneak into Vincennes's Pantheon Theatre. Invariably booted from this movie mecca, the boy often gravitated to Pauline DeJean's candy shop, which was in the same building. DeJean's nephew, Joe O'Toole, knew Skelton from these days. Consistent with the young con-artist character previously described, O'Toole remembered Sketon "as a kid who was always on the lookout for a new gimmick to scrounge a nickel or dime from anyone whose attention he could divert."[33] Still, O'Toole found Skelton to be a resiliently entertaining fellow, who was using a sardine can lid to cover a hole in the sole of his shoe—an experience Skelton no doubt tapped into later with the creation of his greatest comedy character, the tramp Freddie the Freeloader.

Giving up on sneaking into the movies, Skelton later fed his fascination for film by ushering at Vincennes's Moon Theatre. His other odd jobs ranged from washing dishes at a diner to crating boxes in a department store. Like his comedy idol, Chaplin, young Skelton sometimes simply sang and danced on street corners for small change. The comedian later told me he never had stage fright—it was only difficult when he did *not* have an audience.[34]

Like later children of the Great Depression, Skelton never lost his appreciation of a dollar or creative ways to earn one. In 1979 *Village Voice* writer Ross Wetzsteon did an affectionately telling piece on the comedian titled "Red, the Renaissance Goof." The article keyed upon the market for Skelton's clown art, both original oils and reproductions on limited edition plates and in coloring books. The comedian comes across as without ego and constantly peppering the conversation with comedy. For example, when Wetzsteon asks about the genesis of his art, Red responds, "Have I been painting all my life? Not yet!"[35]

What strikes me most about the piece today is how effectively Wetzsteon captured the childlike excitement Skelton still felt about a profitable project, all those decades removed from his childhood poverty. (To borrow a phrase from Skelton's youth, such schemes never failed to make him feel "full of beans and conceit.") I had experienced similar displays of Skelton's entrepreneurial enthusiasm during his many appearances at Ball State University for concert dates. Always modest about his talents, he genuinely enjoyed sharing information about his profitable creative projects, as if he could not believe his good luck. And there lurked a degree of that little boy huckster. Note the comic honesty he shared with Wetzsteon, when discussing the price of his limited edition culinary line: "Fifty-five dollars a plate. I made $200,000. I wouldn't give you a nickel for them myself, but people seem to like them."[36]

Skelton, the later millionaire who often carried huge sums of cash as an adult—yet another legacy of his early poverty—suffered through numerous childhood travails. Many were consistent with being poor: hand-me-down patched clothing, taunts about his wrong-side-of-the-tracks existence, and an attic bed that often had snow on the quilt when he awoke in the winter. Schoolwork was also a challenge for Skelton, not to mention more kidding from children over his mismatched attire and red hair. One rare bright spot for the boy, however, at Vincennes's William Henry Harrison Elementary was the patriotic principal and teacher James S. Lassell. His creative extrapolations on the meaning of each word in the "Pledge of the Allegiance" later became the foundation for Skelton's acclaimed 1969 recording of the "Pledge."[37]

Paradoxically, part of the grief young Skelton experienced came at the hands of the older boys he came to see as his half brothers. The future comedian was several years younger than the trio, and was babied by both "Mur" and his grandmothers, who often cared for the boys when Ida Mae worked. Red later claimed that the boys continually told him he did not belong. Whatever the reason, whether it was antagonism towards a redheaded outsider, or typical older siblings roughhousing the youngest, Joe Ishmal, Chris, and Paul gave a whole new meaning to the phrase "tough love." Their pranks included dragging their brother by a rope behind an early motorcycle, and pitching him into a rock quarry lake. This nearly resulted in Red drowning when the boys made a game of not letting him out of the water. A dark comedy reframing of these "brotherly" misadventures could claim they helped prepare Skelton for his future slapstick tendencies as a clown. (Unbeknownst to his later fans, Skelton's lifetime of pratfalls eventually resulted in his need to wear leg braces.)

Ironically, the antics of Skelton's brothers might also have been borrowing from Mack Sennett, the self-proclaimed "King of Comedy" in the 1910s. A brief examination of his pandemonium style turns up some parallels with the Skelton boys' pranks. First, Sennett's speeding Keystone Kops, in paddy wagons and motorcycles, reduced human beings to so many comic mechanical figures. By metamorphosing these people into inanimate objects, as they bounced and fell from racing vehicles, it was easy to laugh at them because they had ceased to be real. Second, in the simple story world of Sennett cinema, the perfect ending was to have one's comedy conclude in a body of water. Even a Sennett character comedy, like the short subject *The Rounders* (1914, with Charlie Chaplin and Fatty Arbuckle), closed with this duo going under in a sinking rowboat. Thus, one could argue that maybe Red was not the only Skelton youngster who was a student of early screen comedy.

Regardless of one's take on the pranks of Joe, Chris, and Paul Skelton, young Red was a much more compassionate child than his brothers. This is borne out by his early relationship with the aforementioned Carl Hopper. The Hoppers were north Vincennes neighbors of the Skeltons. Both families were poor and comprised of male children. Carl, two years younger than Red, suffered from a severe hearing loss that caused many to consider him not quite "all there." Later, ear surgery and a hearing aid helped Carl achieve a normal and successful adult life. But he suffered through a childhood of cruel putdowns over his difficulty in communicating with those around him. His hearing loss also resulted in a high-pitched voice and a tendency to comically butcher the language—both of which opened young Carl up to further peer ridicule. Despite this childhood mean-spiritedness, Carl remained a remarkably upbeat farm boy with a good sense of humor that often involved talking to himself and a fixation with hats.

Skelton doing an Oliver Hardy imitation (circa 1945). Both comedians drew humor from observing people in childhood.

Through an interview with his daughter Brenda Hopper, and correspondence, the Hopper family remains strongly appreciative of Skelton's rare friendship for Carl, in what was often a sea of cruel faces.[38] Nicknaming him "Kadiddle," possibly playing upon the slang definition of "diddle" (idling away one's time) and combining it with Carl (Carl-diddle equals Kadiddle), Skelton always included him in any childhood activities. Given Skelton's clowning nature, even as a boy, he occasionally did an affectionately spoofing impersonation of his friend. But Carl was never bothered by this parody. In fact, he was proud to generate such attention from his friend.

What makes this story fascinating today, besides Skelton's compassion for a handicapped child, is how Carl was probably

Chaplin (right) and Fatty Arbuckle in Mack Sennett's The Rounders *(1914), explore the comic possibilities of water.*

the catalyst for Skelton's pivitol early comedy character—Clem Kadiddlehopper.[39] While Skelton never officially acknowledged the connection, the Hopper family remains proud of the obvious parallels between the two figures. Here are the common links: unschooled mumbling rural rubes, inordinately happy, derailers of the language, high-pitched voices, fans of their own jokes, and wearers of signature hats (a trait that applies to most of the comedian's characters). When one considers these obvious ties, plus the similar names, it is hard to deny Carl as an inspiration for Clem.

Like the evolution of Skelton's classic donut dunking routine chronicled in the prologue, with the initial catalyst an anonymous coffee shop diner, drawing from reality takes nothing from his comic gift. As noted earlier, Skelton's style is anchored in exaggerating the everyday. And during Red's aforementioned Indiana concert dates, he repeatedly referred to Kadiddlehopper as his most "Hoosier-inspired" character. While no reference was ever made to Carl, the comedian implied it went back to observations he had first made as a child. I am reminded of how Oliver Hardy of Laurel and Hardy fame also used to reminisce about drawing from people he had watched as a boy in his mother's boardinghouse.[40] Most entertainers, particularly comedians, have similar tales to tell. Indeed, Chaplin and W. C. Fields both learned this practical side to voyeurism firsthand from mimicking mothers.[41]

Of course, since Skelton's Kadiddlehopper occasionally said something surprisingly insightful, one could also pigeonhole this rube in the most universal of comedy types—the wise fool. Through the centuries, a mask of incompetence allowed the comic fool to safely state unpopular truths. For the student of American humor, Skelton was born just after the heyday of a movement known as the Literary Comedians.[42] This school of comedy drew much of its entertainment from rubes known for their misspellings and hyperbole.

Interestingly, shortly after the birth of Skelton, a carryover of the Literary Comedian rube found great success in the writing of Ring Lardner. His emergence as a national humor presence came from a series of *Saturday Evening Post* short stories later collected in book

Carl Hopper, the Skelton childhood friend who was the apparent model for Clem Kadiddlehopper.

Skelton as Clem Kadiddlehopper (circa 1960).

form as *You Know Me Al: A Busher's Letters* (1914).[43] The pieces, a
fictional correspondence from a rookie Chicago White Sox pitcher
(Jack Keefe) to a hometown friend, chronicled the comic misadventures
of an amusingly self-centered rube in the Major Leagues. Keefe is
barely literate, and again the humor comes from misspellings and
exaggeration. But Lardner peppered his prose with an inspired ear for
dialogue and American slang. He did not so much take the air out
of the national pastime as just remind us it was part of the human
comedy, too.

Why is this important to Skelton and the evolution of
Kadiddlehopper? During Skelton's formative years Lardner's rube-
orientated humor cast a huge shadow on American comedy, from the
Keefe pieces to later Lardner diamond tales such as the celebrated short
story "Alibi Ike" (1915), and the play *Elmer the Great* (1928, coscripted
with George M. Cohan). Moreover, Lardner's baseball rubes are from
Indiana. Keefe begins his correspondence from Terre Haute, long a
popular place name for humorists in search of funny sounding towns.
Elmer starts in the small Hoosier town of Gentryville. And despite
Lardner's early 1930s death, his legacy continued for years, fueled in
part by the very popular Joe E. Brown film trilogy, *Fireman, Save My
Child* (1932, from Keefe-like material), *Elmer the Great* (1933), and
Alibi Ike (1935).

Another conceivable Indiana-based literary rube who might have
impacted Skelton's Kadiddlehopper is Kin Hubbard's Abe Martin,
whose comic axioms were syndicated in hundreds of newspapers
throughout the United States during Skelton's youth. No less a
humorist than Will Rogers believed that Hubbard was "the funniest
man in America."[44] Martin was more cracker-barrel philosopher than
fool (Kadiddlehopper was often simply "crackers"), but there are small-
town Indiana parallels, especially since Martin became progressively
more antiheroic through the years.[45] For instance, "Th' first thing a
feller does when he's held up is change his mind about what he used t'
think he'd do," is something Kadiddlehopper might have said, too.[46]
In addition, one cannot help noting the close proximity of Skelton

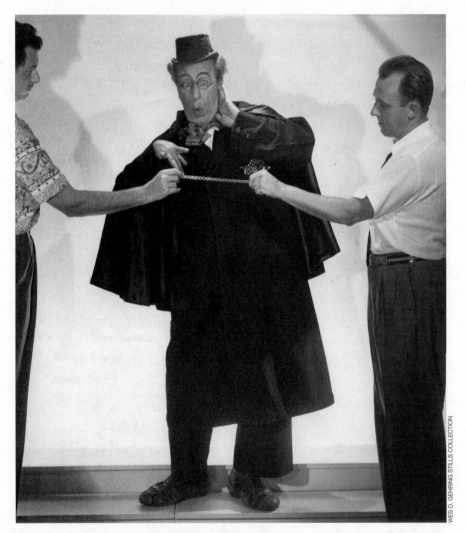

An undated Ed Wynn appearance on Skelton's hit CBS television program.

and Kadiddlehopper's poor Vincennes to Abe Martin's down-home base in Brown County, Indiana. In either case, they are throwbacks to an earlier, harder time. As Martin once opined, "Beauty is only skin deep but it's a valuable asset if you're poor or haven't any sense."[47] *New York Herald Tribune* media critic John Crosby even placed Skelton's Kadiddlehopper in a timeframe that paralleled both the original Literary Comedians and the Hubbard/Martin formative years: "Clem Kadiddlehopper is a rustic of rococo design not seen in these parts since the 1880's."[48]

Besides these hypothetical takes upon the creation of Skelton's Kadiddlehopper, one must add a final pertinent entertainer the comedian claims to have met during his childhood—Ed Wynn. A vaudeville headliner before he was twenty, Wynn first started appearing in Broadway's acclaimed *Ziegfeld Follies* in 1914. His comedy persona was known as the "Perfect Fool," a country rube with a high-pitched voice, an unbelievably happy nature, and a propensity for funny hats. Wynn rode this loopy character to a lengthy stage success, as well as later triumphs on radio, television, and the occasional movie. One such inspired late-career appearance of his "Perfect Fool" was when Wynn was cast as the somewhat befuddled fairy godfather to Jerry Lewis's title character in the film *Cinderfella* (1960).

As the aforementioned description of Wynn's "Perfect Fool" suggests, there are definite parallels with Skelton's later Kadiddlehopper. In addition, both characters could run a broad range of emotions, from a slapstick over eagerness to please to a propensity for pathos. Also, Skelton and Wynn enjoyed taking their alter ego off the stage, such as unexpectantly popping up in the audience before a show, or somehow managing to be at the door to shake the surprised hands of exiting fans. During the 1930s Skelton even had a baseball sketch where he ran from the stage to the back of the theater to catch an imaginary baseball. Fifty years later, Skelton sometimes got on the public-address system shortly before curtain time to provide comically nonsensical traffic reports. Besides amusing and further endearing themselves to their public, it was good business—fans never knew where they would surface. (This practice was not limited to Wynn and Skelton. For example, Brown sometimes worked the box-office window of his stage show.)

So when did young Skelton meet Wynn? Here the story gets a little murky, not unlike the claim that the comedian's father was a clown. Skelton's age at the time varies from reference to reference, ranging from seven to fifteen. The comedian himself has often contributed to the confusion with conflicting stories. But in the mid-1980s he actually gave a newspaper reporter a specific year (1923), something he had rarely, if ever, done.[49] This would have made him approximately ten years old.

The story begins with Skelton selling newspapers in front of the theater where Wynn's stage show was booked. A stranger asked the youngster, "What do you do for excitement in this town?" The boy politely replied, "Well, sir, we've got a big show coming into the theatre tonight. You could go to that." When the stranger asked him if he was going to attend, Skelton said he had newspapers to sell. The man then bought all his papers, to ensure that the youngster saw the show. Years later Skelton concluded this anecdote by adding, "I'll never forget how surprised I was that night to see that the guy who had bought all my papers was the star of the show."[50] The event proved so memorable that Skelton decided that night he would become a comedian, something the boy shared with Wynn after the show, as he thanked the performer for making it possible.

The only problem with the story is that there is no evidence of a Wynn stop in Vincennes during the time periods cited. Poring over period publications, in which a visit by someone of Wynn's status would have generated sizable coverage, I have yet to find documentation of the event. In fact, a prominent Vincennes University historian has confided to me privately that he feels the Wynn connection should be assigned to Indiana folklore. I am not prepared to go that far, though chronicling this as another Skelton example of the aforementioned *Big Fish* phenomenon is tempting.

The case for a Skelton-Wynn connection is also damaged by the fact that Skelton does *not* include the story in early high-profile chronicles of his life. In late 1941 he authored (probably dictated to first wife Edna Stillwell Skelton) a five-part autobiography that ran in the *Milwaukee Journal* under the title "I'll Tell All."[51] No mention of Wynn occurs. Six years later, when Skelton was profiled in the prestigious *Current Biography*, Wynn is again missing in action.[52] For such a seemingly significant event, it seems odd that the story only surfaced in the 1950s, in conjunction with one of Wynn's guest appearances on Skelton's television show. In fairness to Skelton, he does bring the Vincennes visit up with Wynn on the program. But when I presented this television evidence to my doubting Vincennes University historian, he had a simple rebuttal—the vacuous look in Wynn's eyes during the segment suggests a polite acquiescence instead of an actual memory.

Personally, I am convinced a visiting vaudevillian showed a special kindness to young Skelton, the sidewalk newsboy. Whether or not it was actually Wynn will probably forever remain a mystery. But the story deserves a special addendum. It first surfaced at a time when Wynn's career was on the skids. Besides Skelton helping out the veteran performer with several guest appearances on his long-running television show, Skelton was especially supportive when Wynn struggled with a breakthrough dramatic part on the watershed CBS anthology series *Playhouse 90*. Undoubtedly, this experience paved the way for Wynn's Oscar-nominated Best Supporting Actor performance in *The Diary of Anne Frank* (1959). Consistent with the great compassion Skelton showed for both friends and fans throughout his life, an embellishment of a childhood event (with Wynn penciled in as the hero) sounds like something the benevolent Skelton would do for a special colleague going through a tough time. In writing an earlier biography of Skelton, and spending time with him, I saw countless examples of thoughtful, innocent fabrications.[53] He signed autographs to strangers, "To my dear friend," so that people would later have "bragging rights." On one of his Ball State concert date visits, a fan requested that he meet with the man's dying mother, a longtime fan of the comedian. Skelton immediately acquiesced, requesting only that there be no publicity. And when he met with the woman, the comedian waxed poetic about what a wonderful mother she had been. Skelton was forever the thoughtful embellisher. I am convinced this trait lies at the heart of the Wynn story. As Abe Martin once noted, "It's purty hard t' be interestin' without embellishin' th' truth a little."[54]

While Skelton was later in a position to tweak his biography, there was no fooling anyone when he was a poor youngster. One of the most painful results of this situation was losing his first teenage girlfriend, Velma Thompson of Vincennes. According to Velma's younger sister, Janice Thompson Dudley, the girls' parents broke up the romance with Skelton because he "had no future."[55] One can hardly blame the Thompsons. Besides Skelton's impoverished background and his family's checkered background with the law, he was then working for "Doc" R. E. Lewis's Patent Medicine Show, which traveled small-town middle America selling a magic bottled elixir. The youngster who had showed huckster traits in earlier money-making schemes had graduated to working for a seasoned con artist.

A funny-sad story of Skelton conning the con artist ("Doc" Lewis) comes out of this period. The youngster gave Velma a set of spoons when she and Janice were "at the railroad station seeing [off] Red and the Medicine Show."[56] Skelton had no money for gifts, but Lewis's show sold candy as well as "medicine." And this former "Cracker Jack"-like product had "A Prize in Every Box," an added selling point for financially strapped customers. Janice later hypothesized that Skelton was probably in charge of stuffing the candy boxes, which gave him the opportunity to "liberate" six spoons for his girl. But why spoons? Janice later observed, "I would think that just maybe Velma had found a spoon in an earlier box of candy and remarked to Red how much she liked it. And to impress Velma he gave her six spoons."[57]

Given that tough times were the only kind of times young Skelton knew, he forever tried to see the funny side of life, not unlike his early signature character Kadiddlehopper. And as the aging Skelton was "always on," the boy was a constant kidder, too. Carl Hopper remembered Skelton as a practical joker, once picking up a playmate's dachshund (wiener dog) between two pieces of bread and pretending to hawk this hot "dog."[58] Another classmate, Dorothy West Hagemeier, recalled Skelton doing a headstand on the train tracks topped off by spinning around. She also added that he made funny faces, as if to "turn his whole face wrong side out." For Hagemeier and the other students, "He was only there to make you laugh."[59] She might have added that Skelton had a head start with his locks, which Hagemeier called "the

Vincennes's Velma Thompson, Skelton's first sweetheart.

reddest hair I've ever seen in my life." Of course, some classmates were *not* fans of Skelton's jokes. During elementary school, Norma Grubb sat in front of the boy earmarked for comedy greatness. She described Skelton as "mean," because he would forever dip her pigtails in the inkwell on his desk.[60]

As with many class-clown types, such acting out did not play well in school, so Skelton often simply skipped school. His Uncle Fred later recalled that Red was the least academic minded of Ida Mae's four sons. The comedian eventually dropped out of Vincennes's Clark Junior High School when he was thirteen or fourteen, depending upon the source. This would date his early exit as 1926 or 1927. (His first wife, Edna Stillwell, later helped him earn a General Education Development degree, as well as encourage his comedy-related study.) Skelton's formal education might have gone differently had there been more elementary teachers such as Andria Ross, who supported Skelton's performing aspirations and even critiqued his halting attempts at writing comedy. Fittingly, he could also be amusingly brash about chiding her, if he felt Ross's comments were too brief: "You didn't read a word of it, did you?"[61]

Even with an army of Rosses, however, Skelton's formal education probably would have suffered due to his unstable family environment. His overworked, widowed "Mur" (who the boy saw as an adoptive mother), could provide little adult supervision. Skelton's private musings, both in his autobiographical writings, as well as the occasional verbal revelations, suggest his half brothers flirted with what another age would call juvenile delinquency. There were frequent moves in and around Vincennes, presumably for cheaper lodgings or to avoid overdue rent. And young Red's food and clothing were often provided by various members of the community, from his sometimes employer at Kramer's Pool Hall to local songwriter Clarence Stout, Skelton's first important show-business mentor.

Maybe the best gauge of this dysfunctional family is documented by the Vincennes Public Schools records for 1923 and 1924.[62] A parent or guardian is supposed to provide the name and birth date for each student in a household. Shockingly, none of the four Skelton boys' birth dates from 1923 are a match for those listed for 1924. What is more, the spelling (misspelling?) of Ishmal and Christian changes, while Red is noted as Richard one year, and Bernard the next. In addition, Skelton was struggling with school at a time when popular culture often suggested education was overrated. No less a humorist than Hubbard observed, "Seems like ever feller that makes a success o' anything never knowed nothin' when he went t' school."[63]

If academies represented the nadir of life for Skelton, the zenith was when the circus visited Vincennes. His Uncle Fred later related, "If a circus came to town, you could always bet on finding Red there—and usually he got in by doing jobs like watering the elephants."[64] Beyond the ongoing distraction a circus continued to exert on children, during the preradio and pretelevision days of Skelton's youth, a circus visit was like being transported to another, better, world. As Indiana's James Whitcomb Riley, arguably America's most popular poet of the late nineteenth century, wrote in "The Circus-Day Parade": "how the boys behind [the wagons], high and low of every kind, marched in unconscious capture, with a rapture undefined!"[65]

Like young Skelton, humorist Hubbard remained obsessed with the circus throughout his life, for example, "Th' trouble with walkin' in a [circus] pe-rade is that life seems so dull an' colorless afterward,"[66] or, "It's purty hard t' think that ever' thing is fer th' best when it rains on circus day."[67] Skelton's fellow screen comedian Brown later described his childhood enchantment with the circus in terms Skelton would have undoubtedly seconded: "I was fascinated by the gaudy [circus] colors everywhere. The sound of the band and the noise of the happy, laughing, crowd was the most beautiful music I'd ever heard."[68]

Although people of all ages need a steady flow of approval for mental and physical well-being, a disenfranchised youth such as Skelton badly needed the instant and repeated validation that comes through the positive response of an audience. Building upon a knack for being funny, not to mention how wonderful that laughter feedback made him feel, the boy knew in his bones entertaining was for him. This was where the arc of his life began. Moreover, the statement that Skelton's father had been a clown (whether true or not), probably helped make it seem like a more attainable goal, as well as being a way to reconnect with a parent he had never known. One can also argue that "myths are tales we tell over and over to help make sense of the world."[69] And just as claiming his father was a clown helped young Skelton make sense of a chaotic youth, attempting to be a clown maybe made the future less frightening. With that in mind, Skelton was about to begin an apprenticeship in the lowest rungs of the performing arts.

2

Clarence Stout and Other
Early Skelton Mentors

*"If that boy [Red Skelton] ever gets his foot inside
the gates of Hollywood, they'll never get him out."*[1]
CLARENCE STOUT, CIRCA 1929

A popular perspective on the catalyst for young Red Skelton
wanting to be an entertainer posits either the influence of a father
(Joseph Skelton), who was a clown, and/or the chance encouragement
of comedian Ed Wynn during a stop in Vincennes, Indiana. Both of
these "facts," however, are of dubious origins. When the elder Skelton
died (1913) shortly before Red's birth, he had long been a grocer and
a former lineman for the telephone company. Equally vague is Wynn's
alleged early 1920s Vincennes visit, which has yet to be documented,
though it is quite possible that some touring vaudevillian showed a
kindness to young Red.

What is clearly on record, however, is the encouragement Skelton
received from three Vincennes natives: Father Henry Doll, local YMCA
director Ray Beless, and musician/songwriter Clarence Stout. Doll
was for many years the assistant pastor of the Saint Francis Xavier Old
Cathedral parish, for which he staged an annual Boy Scout Circus.
Costumed youngsters doubled as all the animals, while other boys, such
as Skelton, played the clowns. Beless also produced a seasonal YMCA
circus that both showcased the acrobatic gym skills of Y members, and
allowed comic kids such as Skelton to play clowns. Stout put on local

minstrel shows and variety programs, always reserving a featured spot
for the young Skelton.

The encouragement and performing opportunities provided by
these three men meant the world to Skelton. Decades later a childhood
classmate of Skelton's, Dorothy West Hagemeier, remembered an
unexpected encounter with him when the comedian had made an
impromptu visit to Vincennes to see Doll. Hagemeier was acting as a
guide at the historic Old Cathedral when Skelton suddenly appeared
in the doorway. The comedian was then headlining at the Indiana State
Fair in Indianapolis and had impulsively decided to visit the priest. But
this went beyond mere reminiscing. It was shortly after the 1958 cancer
death of his son, Richard, and Skelton wanted some special time with
the supportive priest from his youth. Unfortunately, Doll was gone.
When Hagemeir asked Skelton if he wanted to see another priest, the
comedian replied simply, "No I just came to see Father Doll."[2]

Though this favored hometown religious leader had immediately
come to mind in Skelton's time of grief, the Vincennes entertainment
mentor who had the greatest effect on his show business career was
Stout. There are four good reasons to give Stout this unique status.[3]
First, while Doll and Beless simply dabbled in the arts, Stout was a bona
fide performer who wore various hats: musician, composer, producer,
and director. And it was important for young Skelton to actually see
someone actively engaged in show business. (Plus, Skelton's later drive
to compose music was probably inspired by Stout's example.) Second,
though choosing to maintain his Hoosier home base such as Indiana
humorist Kin Hubbard, Stout had had success at a national level. One
of his compositions, "O Death Where Is Thy Sting?" had been featured
on Broadway in the celebrated *Ziegfeld Follies* (1919). The acclaimed
black entertainer Bert Williams had elected to perform this song. A
friendship developed between the two men, with Williams nicknaming
Stout "Hoosier Boy."[4] Unfortunately, Williams's unexpected death
from pneumonia ended their plans for later collaborations. But with
relationship to Skelton's future in comedy, one should add that the
Williams-Stout pairing on "O Death Where Is Thy Sting?" was rooted

Clarence Stout (center) at the Vincennes, Indiana, premiere of Skelton's Whistling in the Dark *(1941).*

in humor. That is, the song title comes from a satirical member of a congregation quizzing his pastor. After hearing in the sermon that hell is full of vampish women, whiskey, gin, and dice, he comically asks, "O Death Were Is Thy Sting?"

Still, despite the loss of a well-placed connection in Williams, Stout continued to sell songs to such major music publishing houses as Mills Music Company, Leeds, Bob Miller Company, and the Handy Brothers.[5] Though no famous standards were forthcoming, Stout's tunes were reliable sellers that earned him a living. His other show-business friendships included singer/songwriter W. C. "Father of the Blues" Handy and comedian/singer Jimmy "Schnozzola" Durante, who later featured a Stout song on his television program, *The Jimmy Durante Show*.

A third reason for the significance of Stout's mentorship to Skelton involved the professionalism of Stout's productions. Though Skelton greatly appreciated his clowning opportunities in Doll's annual Boy Scout Circus and Beless's seasonal circus, these entertainments had the more amateur ambience of a school play. In contrast, Stout's elaborately produced minstrel shows were on a par with the vaudeville acts that regularly visited Vincennes. Although minstrels have long since become politically incorrect, this particular variety show format was a cornerstone of American popular entertainment from shortly after the Civil War until the Great Depression. Thus, as with Skelton's medicine show background, this minstrel tie had the boy experiencing the last hurrah of a staple from a bygone era.

A fourth, and final, reason for the importance of Stout's assistance embraces fatherly ramifications. According to Stout's widow, Inez, young Skelton first came to her husband's attention when he saw the boy performing at Vincennes's Fifth and Main streets, "dancing and clowning to coax nickels from passersby."[6] The address was fitting for a budding young performer, since it was the site of the Pantheon Theatre, where Stout played in the pit band. The Pantheon, which opened in 1921, was a most imposing period structure. The theater had seating for 1,200 people and featured a motion picture screen, an elaborate stage, and a $16,000 Wurlitzer organ in the orchestra pit.[7] Across from the Pantheon was the more modest Moon Theatre, where Skelton later worked as an usher and all-around troubleshooter for the owner.

Whether Stout was most moved by young Skelton's poverty, the quiet desperation in his "dancing and clowning," or a combination of the two, is unclear. Regardless, the boy became like a son to this Vincennes entertainer. When the newly famous Skelton later made his triumphant 1939 hometown return, local press coverage documented the comedian's closeness to Stout. The *Vincennes Post*, after noting that Skelton and his first wife, Edna Stillwell, would be houseguests of the Stouts, added that the comedian "will need no directions from his hostess as to how to find the light in the hall when he goes up to bed because many hours were spent in the Stout home when he was a boy. He [also] picked up his first dancing steps from the Stout's daughter, Miss Frankie Stout, now a popular dancing teacher here."[8]

The Skeltons' thank-you letter to the Stouts, following this 1939 homecoming, revealed an obvious sense of family. Written by Edna, who handled all the couple's correspondence, it reads like a bride's first nervous encounter with her mother and father-in-law: "I was scared to death of what you were going to think of me—maybe when you knew me better [they'd already been corresponding] you wouldn't think I was a suitable person for Red—and since Red thought so much of all you … that would have been a calamity … I was counting on you folks."[9]

Clarence and Inez's appearance at the Vincennes train station, however, immediately put Edna at ease. She described the Stouts as "the sweetest, kindest faces I have ever seen," and called the visit "one of the happiest times of our lives—and that isn't just a lot of talk—I seemed closer to being home than I've been in years—I've added my love (and I'm sure it's equal) to Red's for all of you."[10]

The Skeltons' 1939 homage to the Stouts was not limited to private letters. During Vincennes's official reception for the comedian, Skelton went out of his way to honor this surrogate father. As the town's toastmaster added Skelton's name to a list of illustrious homegrown heroes, Skelton stopped the proceedings: the comedian "reminded the toastmaster that he had omitted mention of another Vincennes boy who had achieved fame. He introduced Clarence A. Stout ... [and] declared that he [Red] owed to Stout much of his success, for it was he who encouraged him to develop his talents as an entertainer."[11]

So how was the young Skelton used in Stout's productions? The veteran entertainer chronicled his discovery of Skelton to an MGM (Skelton's home studio) official in a 1947 letter: "I started Red out and gave him his [initial] chance on any stage back in 1929, when he was 15-years-old, and I was producing shows. His very first stage appearance was as one of the end men in a minstrel show and I had him do an impersonation of [Jazz Age legend] Al Jolson doing 'Rainbow 'Round My Shoulder.'"[12]

Refreshingly, period publications back up Stout's claims, as well as representing Skelton's earliest known critical notices. The *Vincennes Commercial*'s rave review (May 14, 1929) of Stout's *Minstrel-Revue* had the following praise for his protégé: "Red Skelton got a big hand with [his spoof of Jolson's] 'There's a Rainbow 'Round My Shoulder'; he had to come back for three encores."[13] But even this was not enough for the audience. The local critic added, Skelton did an encore "and imitated Al Jolson with [another of his signature songs] 'Sonny Boy.' He really got a hand for the number; Red may not be God's gift to Vitaphone [the preeminent sound system of the day] but he can certainly do some high-powered impersonating."[14] The *Vincennes Sun* reviewer was in agreement, calling the teenager's Jolson spoof one of the revue's "highlights."[15]

Though today Skelton's comedy genius is not associated with impressions, like most comics (from young Stan Laurel doing Charlie Chaplin to a beginner Jim Carrey doubling as everyone), Skelton excelled early at mimicking. Jolson's over-the-top demonstrative performing style would have been an impressionist's fantasy, from his footlight singing intimacy with an audience to belting out "My Mammy" (yet another Jolson standard) on one knee with his white gloved hands clenched before him. While Jolson was best showcased in the 1920s on the Broadway stage, period film fans around the world had been mesmerized by his musical numbers in the groundbreaking *Jazz Singer* (1927). This influential first talkie, though essentially a silent film with sound/singing sequences, briefly escalated Jolson to the status of show business's highest profile performer. Consequently, Skelton's spoofing of Jolson made good entertainment sense, given that he was then the most topical of targets. In addition, the Jazz Age Jolson often sang in blackface, given the frequent minstrel nature of his music, such as the aforementioned "My Mammy," and the Stephen Foster composition "Old Folks at Home," popularly known as "Swanee River." Jolson later even starred in 1939's *Swanee River*, a biography film of Foster, whose music (including "O Susanna," "Camptown Races," and "My Old Kentucky Home") was often featured in minstrels. Since Skelton's first show business appearance was in Stout's *minstrel* show, this was yet another reason for young Skelton to mimic Jolson.

Skelton's proclivity to do imitations of specific personalities had all but disappeared by the time of his long-running television show. But Skelton's 1940 MGM screen test featured a performer who still spoofed entertainers. The movie was a casual compilation of the comedian's best vaudeville material, including his career-making donut sketch. But for MGM viewers, *the* hit routine in the test was Skelton's impression of how various period stars die in their movies, such as James "Cagney still running after he had been shot, running on his buckling legs, on hands and knees and finally on his chin."[16]

Skelton's Cagney spoof only modestly caricatured the actor's major critical and commercial hit *The Roaring Twenties* (1939), in which Cagney's fatally wounded gangster somehow keeps running and staggering away from a shoot-out. Just as Jolson was a good first impression for young Skelton, Cagney was an inspired choice, too. Cagney's dying *Roaring Twenties* gangster was already bordering on self-parody; Skelton brilliantly embraced what seemed like an open invitation to comically derail Cagney. Skelton's other "dying" parody targets in this MGM test included the swashbuckling Errol Flynn and the grandfatherly Lionel Barrymore, then an MGM star. Conveniently, Skelton's success on the top rung of 1930s vaudeville had given him

an ongoing cinema tutorial, since his stage work was in support of
first-run movie houses throughout metropolitan America. (As a final
footnote to the screen test, this in-house MGM movie was so popular
with VIP guests and studio insiders that one period article about the
phenomenon was titled, "Skelton Out of the Closet: Red Skelton's Film
Masterpiece Has Never Grossed a Dollar."[17])

A neglected aspect of Skelton's involvement in Stout's 1929
Minstrel-Revue involved his participation in a sketch titled "Memories
of the South." Again, the comedian's work is praised by local critics,
but what makes the routine of more interest today is its source
material—Harriett Beecher Stowe's groundbreaking 1854 abolitionist
novel *Uncle Tom's Cabin*.[18] Though its racial stereotypes are now seen as
politically incorrect, the book's then radical antislavery message greatly
contributed to the moral climate that resulted in the Civil War. In fact,
upon first being introduced to Stowe, a tongue-in-cheek Abraham
Lincoln is alleged to have affectionately chided the author, upon her
visit to the White House, "So you're the little woman who wrote the
book that made this great war."[19]

Though neither Stowe nor *Uncle Tom's Cabin* are mentioned
by name in reviews of the Stout sketch, the characters noted are
clearly from the novel. Stowe's book was a poplar source for morality
plays well into the twentieth century. And the Stowe-Stout-Skelton
connection clarifies a misperception in the comedian's forever vague
personal accounts of his early performing career. Stout took his theater
troupe on the road to play other small-town dates in Indiana and
neighboring states. But Skelton's later accounts of this minstrel and
Stowe-related work, starting with the serialized memoir that appeared
in the *Milwaukee Journal* in December 1941, date the comedian's
blackface entertaining as occurring *after* his employment by "Doc"
Lewis's Medicine Show and the John Lawrence Stock Company.[20]
Unfortunately, other Skelton biographers, such as Arthur Marx, have
seconded this later minstrel/*Uncle Tom's Cabin* chronology.[21]

Once again Skelton finds himself in the awkward position of
contradicting himself—crediting Stout as his beginning mentor and

then pushing their collaboration back on his entertainment timeline. But if the previously cited Stout documentation (correspondence and critiques of 1929's *Minstrel-Revue*) were not enough to weight the chronology in the mentor's favor, another passage from a previously cited Stout letter cinches it. In 1947 correspondence with music publishing executive Lou Levy, Stout stated: "The following year [1930] he [Skelton] had a chance to go with a Med[icine] show, and I urged him to take it and get more [performing] experience."[22] This later medicine show time frame reinforces the spoon story cited in chapter one of a teenaged Skelton giving his first girlfriend, Velma Thompson, a set of spoons lifted from the "Cracker Jack"-like boxes of candy he was in charge of preparing for "Doc" Lewis. This approximates the 1930 date earlier noted by Stout.

Before exploring other early Skelton performing experiences, there needs to be some closing comments on the unique relationship between Skelton and Stout, the parentlike mentor he affectionately nicknamed "Professor" and "Doc." Whereas, Doll and Beless simply provided pioneering entertaining chances for the youngster, Stout gave Skelton invaluable starter tips on "selling" a routine, general comic timing, and an ongoing sense of stage presence. Moreover, while Stout immediately recognized that the youngster "outdid the show's [1929] veterans in a specialty art," the Jolson parody, he also advised Skelton never to get a big head.[23] Years later Skelton demonstrated that he had learned such lessons well. After a series of personal stage triumphs, the comedian assured Stout in a 1937 telegram: "my hat [size] is still seven and one-eights and I haven't forgotten you or the old gang."[24]

As one would expect of a fatherly adviser, Stout's life lessons to Skelton often went beyond show business, from the importance of perseverance to racial tolerance. While the former principle is self-evident, the latter bears fleshing out. Skelton was a child in the most bigoted of eras, one that saw the 1915 rebirth of the infamous American racial hate group the Ku Klux Klan. Ironically, for the entertainment-bound Skelton, born in 1913, a motion picture helped fuel the resurrection of a Klan whose origins dated from post-Civil

War Reconstruction. The film in question was pioneering director D. W. Griffith's *Birth of Nation* (1915), a groundbreaking technological achievement that romanticized the origins of the Klan. But as Griffith's definitive biographer, Richard Schickel, has so movingly observed, "high artistic vision does not necessarily correlate with a similarly elevated social vision."[25] Coupled with this, Indiana was a hotbed of the KKK resurgence that peaked in the early 1920s.

Historian Richard Hofstadter has linked the revival of the Klan and other reactionary developments of the 1920s (such as antievolutionism) to what he calls "status politics." For example, "in the boom years of the 1920s ... millions of small-town and rural 'native stock' Americans, alarmed by the ascendancy of the country's pluralistic urban culture, had embraced the organized bigotry of the Ku Klux Klan and flocked to the punitive crusades of anti-evolutionism and Prohibition."[26] With regard to the Klan, only the 1925 second-degree murder conviction of Hoosier Klan leader D. C. Stephenson and its resultant political fallout (including an Indianapolis mayor and a local congressman going to jail), helped curb the Klan's growth, both nationally and in Indiana.[27]

Even a cursory examination of period literature from Skelton's hometown reveals the Klan's high profile. For example, an early 1924 issue of the *Vincennes Morning Commercial* showcases a large ad for a "Ku Klux Klan Initiation."[28] More chilling still is the casual inclusion of the rally's location, complete with its KKK-directed misspelling—Knox Kounty Klan Park. As if the KKK's blasé appropriation of a park were not disturbing enough, the nonchalant enticement, "Public Invited," suggests this was the most natural thing in the world, which it then undoubtedly was.

The black friendships of Skelton mentor Stout long predated the older man's songwriting ties with such memorable African American entertainers as the aforementioned Williams and Handy. Stout's color blindness was born of grade-school baseball with young minority classmates. "His interest in the songs of the Negro was credited to this. And the Negro's song style influenced his early works [musical compositions]," a Vincennes newspaper noted upon

Stout's death.[29] Because of Stout, Skelton was both long cognizant
of black contributions to the popular arts and a vocal proponent for
racial equality. Even as late as 1996, the year before Skelton's death,
the comedian spoke out passionately against racism: "I could never
understand it [racism], myself. I tried to make friends with everybody
… blacks were treated not as human beings. Let's put it that way …
and in some parts of the country it's still that way now, which is sad. It's
sad."[30]

    If the world according to Stout had not been enough to totally
convince Skelton about the wisdom of racial harmony, there were
two other factors that no doubt helped shepherd the boy towards that
philosophy. First, like Stout, Skelton had black classmates. And given
the extreme poverty of the youngster's family, Skelton often had more
in common with the disadvantaged plight of these African American
children. Indeed, the future comedian sometimes received assistance
from minority mentors. Local black barber Dudley Miller often gave
the child free haircuts because Skelton's "widowed mother was having
a hard time."[31] Second, Skelton also accepted both help and musical
tips from veteran Vincennes minstrel man Gabe Jackson. This talented
black entertainer, a friend of Stout's, taught Skelton how "to finger a
few chords" on his (Jackson's) instrument of choice—the ukulele.[32]

    One should also note that while the image of white performers
wearing blackface in minstrel shows is now offensive, black entertainers
(such as Vincennes's Jackson, or the celebrated toast of Broadway,
Williams) appeared in minstrel shows, too. Granted, this could be used
to demonstrate the then limited performing opportunities available
to African American entertainers. But it is a little known, ironic fact
that the genesis of the minstrel show dates from blacks in the pre-Civil
War South. Plantation slaves created an early form of the genre as a
satirical take on both white masters, and on house slaves (as opposed
to field slaves), for taking on the refined airs of the whites. And as
pivotal cultural historian John Strausbaugh notes, "However shameful
we [now] find it, blackface has played a large and integral role in the
formation of American popular culture," especially as the minstrel

filtered into vaudeville.[33] Strausbaugh also movingly adds, "the question of whether minstrelsy was White or Black music was moot. It was a mix, a mutt—that is, it was *American* music."[34]

Consistent with that, Stout was a true populist who, to borrow a later phrase from the Reverend Jessie Jackson, had a veritable "rainbow coalition" of friends. Stout could also appreciate a good comic send-up of racism. A much repeated story involved one of Stout's periodic Chicago get-togethers with Handy. Accompanied by his wife Inez, Stout had the opportunity to pitch some songs to Handy as well as to socialize with the legendary blues giant. On one visit the two men found themselves in a downtown Chicago bar. A racist bartender said to Clarence, "That will be fifty cents for you, and five dollars for him [pointing to Handy]."[35] Handy, by this time a very successful entertainer/composer, lackadaisically took a twenty dollar bill from his pocket (much more than a week's salary for most Americans at that time), and blasély placed it on the bar. "Keep the change," he said to the amazed bartender. Life lessons such as these helped mold Skelton into a color-blind adult and ongoing spokesman for racial tolerance.

The comedian's kinship with black performers is best demonstrated by two documents in Vincennes University's Red Skelton Collection. The first is a 1967 letter he had written to black comedian Godfrey Cambridge after the young performer had appeared on Skelton's television show. What makes the correspondence especially pertinent, in addition to Skelton's generous praise for a minority entertainer, is how Skelton eventually drew a direct line between Williams and Cambridge: "There will be many volumes written about you [Cambridge] in years to come praising your unmistakable wit, acting ability and practical wisdom. Each time I see you perform, it's a pleasure ... We, as gentlemen of the [clown's] cap and bells ... are giving to our generation the love of a great profession as did Ed Wynn and Bert Williams in their day."[36]

The second example of Skelton's lifelong affinity to African American performers born of Stout's pioneering liberalness can be found in a 1958 telegram Skelton received from Sammy Davis Jr. after the comedian's young son, Richard, died of leukemia: "Once when I was going through a trying time you helped me with these words 'when chosen people are in doubt with every talent God can bestow upon them, they are sometimes called upon for still greater service in his behalf' and your great loss will give infinite courage and heart to others throughout the world."[37]

Thoughtfully, Skelton did not forget Stout in later years, periodically visiting the aging entertainer in his Vincennes home during the 1950s. Stout's grandson, Douglas Wissing, fondly remembered those memorable visits when Skelton "would show up in a vast car and disappear behind the pocket doors [that slid into the walls] of my grandfather's wainscoted [home] office, which was hung with hundreds of autographed publicity photos of show business greats, and not-so-greats, from the 1920s to the 1940s."[38]

While Skelton's entertainment career, and arguably his life in general, was most affected by Stout, other early performing influences merit inclusion. Most logically, this began with the woman formerly seen as Skelton's mother, Ida Mae Skelton. Though she was often absent working multiple jobs to support the family, Ida Mae's half-brother, Fred Foster, remembered her in terms that applied equally to the later comedian, "good natured, ambitious and, above all, clever."[39] More importantly, she always encouraged her youngest adopted son's clowning tendencies. For example, when he eventually left home to perform, she made him a comic wig and gave him her blessing.[40] Add to this Ida Mae's apparent embellishment of the iffy clown background of Skelton's father (stories that obviously further inspired an impressionable child), and Ida's show-business effect on Red was significant. (Despite his later belief that Ida Mae was not his biological mother, he publicly gave her that title throughout his life.)

The musical talents of Skelton's brother Paul Skelton, the youngest of the comedian's three older brothers (five years his brother's senior), also contributed to Red's desire to be a performer. In fact, Red dreamed of teaming up with his brother. Even a lifetime later he sadly reminisced, "I wanted Paul to go into show business with me because he played piano. My mother played piano [too]. But he didn't want to go into show business, so I went in alone. I wish he had gone with me."[41] This quote also movingly suggests how obsessed young Red was with entertaining. Any talent, such as simply playing the piano, was equated in his eyes with a basic production for use—entering show business.

As an addendum to Red's fondness for Paul, their connection was not just about closeness in age and performing skills. They had shared a poor family's misadventure that had nearly cost the older brother his life. The two boys had been responsible for procuring winter coal by whatever means possible from passing trains. This was a typical scenario for impoverished midwestern families of a bygone era. Ohio-born comedian Joe E. Brown kept his family in heating fuel as a child by making faces at passing train firemen, provoking them into throwing coal at him! (This was the first time young Brown realized his "cavernous" mouth could be an advantage.)

Red and Paul did not, however, obtain coal in the rubber-faced manner of future funnymen. Showing much more moxie than Brown, the Skelton boys actually boarded a local train at the Vincennes water stop. When the fireman briefly left the engine and coal car unattended, the two hurriedly filled their two sacks with coal. They then hid themselves between cars until the train started moving again. Since being poor often meant not only living on the proverbial "wrong side of the tracks" but also near the tracks themselves, the train soon passed by the latest Skelton family shack. Paul and Red then tossed their sacks from the moving train and jumped.

Though this was not exactly *The Great Train Robbery* (1903), the Skelton family routine of snitching coal was a time-honored system, having been passed down from older brothers Joseph Ishmal and Christian. Paul and Red became equally adept at the task—until Paul slipped. The boys' normal train hiding place was between the coal and baggage cars, but one night Paul lost his footing and fell beneath the train. The only thing that saved him was a protruding metal bar the boy desperately held onto, plus young Red putting himself in harm's way to grasp Paul, too. Somehow they held on until the next stop, a neighboring small town. As the old axiom suggests, "desperate times demand desperate measures." The ongoing challenge that passed as Skelton's childhood probably made the long shot odds of succeeding in show business all the more palatable.

While piano-playing Paul neglected to team up with Red as a performing duo, the youngest Skelton did get a sibling boost by borrowing one of his older brothers' birth certificate. Through the years the comedian confided to countless people, including this author, that his underage entry into show business eventually necessitated using "a phony birth certificate showing I was born in 1906 so I could go to work."[42] Paradoxically, while actresses often shave years off their real age, the ongoing application of 1906 (instead of Skelton's actual 1913 birth) often resulted in profiles making him older.

Of course, one could posit the further irony that none of the comedian's brothers was born in 1906: Joseph (1905), Chris (1907), and Paul (1908). But then, that is par for Skelton's sketchy handle on his personal history. More problematic are the aforementioned timeline troubles one encounters when attempting to date Skelton's relationship with one final early pivotal mentor—the frequently cited "Doc" R. E. Lewis and his Patent Medicine Show. Ultimately, however, the significance of this individual is more important than the exact chronology. Given Lewis's huckster persona, it is more than likely that he helped inspire Skelton's later comic character San Fernando Red. Certainly, Lewis has been described in terms equally applicable to San Fernando—"as slippery a pitchman and charlatan as ever mesmerized an audience of Kadiddlehoppers."[43] Even when Lewis admonished young Skelton to work faster, the old con artist maintained a smooth W. C. Fields-like huckster patter: "Here, hurry out with some more [bottled medicine]. Don't be the innocent means of depriving these wonderful people of an opportunity to purchase glowing health for such a minute sum."[44]

Beyond the boy's fascination with this figure, Lewis represented an endless tutorial on showmanship. Like the later song "Razzle Dazzle," featured in the musical *Chicago* (2002), Lewis knew that if the product one was "selling" (be that a client on trial or a bottle of patent medicine) was without merit, it was necessary to dress up the proceedings with entertainingly mindless "razzle dazzle." Consequently, after starting as a do-everything medicine show "gofer," Skelton graduated to performing in both comic and dramatic sketches, as well as singing and playing his ukulele. (Given that a teenaged Skelton learned how to play the ukulele from the aforementioned Stout friend Gabe Jackson, this is more evidence that Skelton's medicine show days occurred later than the comedian remembered.)

Young Skelton's most memorable moral learned during his association with Lewis occurred at the beginning. Between the boy's natural enthusiasm and Lewis's demand for speed, Skelton accidentally took a spectacular fall into the audience while retrieving patent medicine bottles from a makeshift stage. Once it was clear that Skelton had survived this impromptu slapstick symposium, the crowd gave him an appreciative round of applause. His chance pratfall was an epiphany for the future comedian, as he punningly observed in 1941, "I went on falling for crowds, and if you'll pardon a little boasting, they've been falling for me … [for] years now."[45]

Lewis further underscored the importance of this providential pratfall by having Skelton orchestrate a similar "accident" for every new audience, though they worked on minimizing the number of "Hot Springs System Tonic" bottles that were broken. (This cure-all elixir was largely composed of water, sugar, and Epsom salts.) The second entertainment lesson Skelton drew from the incident, beyond the popularity of pratfalls, was that the funniest things were spontaneous, or at least seemed that way. Mistakes and/or accidents were regularly scripted into his later long-running television show. Indeed, Skelton sometimes added to an ongoing rocky relationship with his writers by relishing jokes that misfired so that he could seemingly ad-lib a variation of "I told the writers that wasn't funny."

While Skelton sometimes dated his entertainment exit from hometown Vincennes as early as the age of ten, this was an exaggeration. Though there *might* have been some random summer performing experiences of a preteen nature, Skelton was still very much a Vincennes citizen as late as 1929, the year he turned sixteen. Besides, the aforementioned local reviews for Skelton's appearances in the Stout-produced minstrels, there are also periodic 1929 Vincennes newspaper notices for Skelton's clowning in local circus shows. For example, the *Vincennes Sun* highlighted the teen's comic confrontation (dressed as señorita) with a bull (costumed boys) in a front-page story about the YMCA circus.[46]

As noted earlier, Skelton's first significant touring was under Stout's guidance when the veteran Vincennes composer took his minstrel show on the road in 1929. Past accounts of Skelton's apprentice performing activities have also included stints with the John Lawrence Stock Company, a Mississippi stern-wheeler showboat, and a touring circus.[47] While sketchy Skelton accounts implied these just noted activities covered years of his post-Vincennes life, it now appears they involved, at most, several months. That is, Skelton met his pivotal first wife, writer/manager Edna Stillwell, in 1930, when he was a beginning burlesque comedian and she was a head usher with a gift for comedy.[48] Yet, Skelton had allegedly already logged his time with the various just noted performing groups. And this is less than a year removed from his minstrel touring with Stout. The numbers do not add up, even if these assorted activities were really just summer jobs. (To recycle a pivotal Skelton quote, "That's my trouble. If you wanta good story—talk to me. If you want the facts—talk to Edna [Stillwell]."[49])

What this means, besides Skelton's weakness for embellishing his life story, is that his Vincennes mentors, particularly Stout, represented much more of an entertainment foundation for the comedian than has ever before been fully recognized. Moreover, examining Skelton's initial performing experiences also reveals that essentially all his struggling on-the-road time really came during the early years of his show business partnership/marriage to Stillwell. And just as the discovery elevates the importance of Stout in this chapter, the disclosure increases the already significant debt Skelton owed to his guru to success—Stillwell.

3

First Wife Mentor: Edna Stillwell Skelton

"If it weren't for her he'd [Red Skelton] be a bum. That's exactly what he [Skelton] said ... Edna did it all. Red insists she did."[1]
FREDERICK C. OTHMAN

When Red Skelton and Edna Stillwell married in June 1931 she had just turned sixteen, and he was a month shy of eighteen. They had met the year before and it was *not* love at first sight. He was the self-proclaimed "youngest comic in burlesque" and she was the sassy head usherette at Kansas City's Pantages Theatre, a vaudeville house. Skelton was appearing at a nearby burlesque theater, the Gaiety. But vaudeville was a step up on the entertainment chain, and the young comedian hung out at the Pantages, ever available if an act failed to appear. Ironically, when Skelton's opportunity came, he was at the Gaiety. The balcony box stooge for one of the Pantages acts did not show and a desperate stage manager pressed Skelton into vaudeville service. It was left up to flashlight-bearing usherette Stillwell to both lead Skelton to his box and flesh out what was expected of him.

The bored and sometimes "drunken" heckler and/or disruptive audience member is a special treat for the student of comedy, since this bit of stage shtick is as old as the theater itself. Filmed examples stretch from Charlie Chaplin's *A Night in the Show* (1915) to those old men Muppets who sabotage *The Muppet Show* from their balcony perch. Chaplin's short subject expands his disruptions to two characters: a drunk in the auditorium (Mr. Pest) and a tipsy blue-collar type in the

balcony (Mr. Rowdy), with the latter figure frequently in danger of
tumbling to the main floor. Skelton would have known some version of
this sketch, since variations of the routine had been playing vaudeville
houses for years. Chaplin had done two stage tours of the United
States for Britain's famed Fred Karnó troupe dating from 1910 to 1913.
Thanks to Chaplin, an earlier version of *Show, Mumming Birds* (also
known as *A Night in an English Music Hall*) was the company's most
popular property.[2] But even after comedy film pioneer Mack Sennett
discovered the English comedian in 1913 (the year of Skelton's birth),
another Karno troupe continued to crisscross America with *Mumming
Birds* in its repertoire. Copycat variations of the sketch proliferated
throughout show business, including comedian Joe E. Brown's inventive
later take on the material in his popular film *Bright Lights* (1935).

Regardless, the version of this routine playing the Pantages in 1930
was ineffective for budding comedy critic Stillwell—a fact she shared
with young Skelton as she led him to his balcony debut. Given her lofty
criteria, she was also neither a fan of Skelton's vaudeville baptism under
fire, nor his subsequent subbing opportunities at the Pantages. The
comedian's standard routine, after graduating from audience heckler,
was heavy with slapstick—opening with a spectacular fall "into the
orchestra pit and coming up with a bass drum wrapped around his
neck."[3] Skelton later observed that after taking the fall he would yell at
the orchestra from the pit, "'Wise guys! Movin' the stage on you when
you're not looking.' And then I get [back] on the stage and I say, 'Why
don't you fill that in, that hole.' And then [I go] into my act."[4] The
hard to impress Stillwell went so far as to encourage her boss, the stage
manager who had retrieved Skelton from the Gaiety, to fire the young
comic. The more forgiving manager had the perfect comeback: "I don't
have to fire him. He'll probably kill himself falling into the orchestra
pit."[5]

In a serialized 1941 autobiography for the *Milwaukee Journal*,
Skelton revealed that Stillwell's initial reservations about him were
much broader than he had ever imagined: "She told me since that she
didn't like my act, nor the way I dressed, nor the way I talked."[6] Not

surprisingly, when Skelton attempted to date her, he received a "freezing brush-off."[7] With the young comic still on a burlesque circuit that also included Saint Louis, Indianapolis, South Bend, Chicago, Toronto, and Buffalo, Skelton and Stillwell parted company for several months.

The two next met at the El Torreon Ballroom in Kansas City. While some things had not changed, such as the city and Edna's icy demeanor towards Skelton, both teenagers were now in different jobs. Stillwell was the El Torreon cashier and Skelton was the master of ceremonies for a walkathon at the ballroom. Walkathons were a new quasi-sadistic entertainment born of the Great Depression. The walkathon (also known as the danceathon) involved dozens of couples in a competition to be the last duo standing. With no time limit, the event could go on for weeks as the couples staggered around a dance floor fighting the exhaustion that eventually weaned their numbers down to a winning pair. (Competitors were allowed one ten-minute break per hour for food and bathroom needs.) Colloquial comedy of the time nicknamed the walkathon the "fallen-arch marathon."[8] But the phenomenon was a first cousin to all those Depression-era endurance "entertainments," such as the six-day bicycle race, which was also the subject of a popular period film comedy starring Brown, titled *6-Day Bike Rider* (1934). The walkathon/danceathon would be immortalized in film by the much later screen classic *They Shoot Horses, Don't They?* (1969).

Since Great Depression deprivation was ultimately about people finding a way to endure, audiences of the 1930s were often drawn to events that replicated the need for survival skills—a microcosm of their lives. As poetic as that sounds, walkathon entertainment frequently involved audiences savoring the collapse of competitors and the funny/sad sight of the partner attempting to keep them both upright. In addition, since there were never enough of these minitragedies, walkathons needed a master of ceremonies to keep things lively. Skelton's ten-hour shift as master of ceremonies involved nonstop patter—a running commentary punctuated with jokes, comic songs, impromptu impressions, his signature pratfalls, kidding encounters with contestants, and whatever other distractions he could conjure up. Skelton once "borrowed" a mounted policeman's horse and rode it around a walkathon dance floor just to keep an audience involved. Decades later I complimented him on the seamless comedy flow of his two-hour-plus concerts. His response was that compared to a walkathon shift, his one-man show stand-up dates were ever so easy.

Skelton had moved to walkathon duty after a change in burlesque closed many theaters. With tough times and the added difficulty of finding paying customers, burlesque had moved from peppering its parody format with sexual innuendo to outright striptease acts. Local blue laws in midwestern cities often then closed these theaters, making the once dependable burlesque circuit an iffy proposition for comedians such as Skelton. Moreover, in the days before air conditioning, burlesque and small-market stage productions often shut down during the summer. But walkathons initially proved to have a year-round popularity.

Some later accounts of the eventual Skelton-Stillwell romance have Stillwell actually being a contestant at a walkathon where Skelton was the master of ceremonies.[9] Though the often sizable winning purse might have attracted the teenaged girl, further research suggested that this is more hyperbole by the always inventive comedian. Neither Skelton's aforementioned serialized autobiography nor Stillwell's own reminiscing article, "I Married a Screwball" (1942), make any mention of her competing during the walkathon.[10] When dealing with the comedian's personal life, I am reminded of an observation on baseball by *New York Times* sportswriter John Branch—"where the history runs deep and the folklore deeper."[11]

Regardless, the forever persistent Skelton eventually won over the icy Stillwell with his walkathon comedy. "For four weeks I tried to thaw her out," Skelton noted. "Then one night from the stage I tossed a joke at which she laughed. It was her first smile for me, and I moved in fast, taking her out occasionally."[12] Ironically, the budding romance next had to cope with the fact Stillwell lived on the distant outskirts of Kansas City. Accompanying her home, they "embarked on what he [comically] claims was a streetcar ride that went from Kansas City to somewhere

Ann Miller (left), Skelton, and Arlene Dahl in Watch the Birdie *(1950). Miller was a longtime friend and frequent Skelton costar.*

near the Ohio State line."[13] Stillwell later recalled a joking marriage
proposal tied to those long streetcar trips: "After about three months,
he [Skelton] said one night, 'Why don't we get married and save me all
this travel?"[14]

Despite all the faults Stillwell initially found with Skelton, they
did have a number of things in common. First, neither had known
his/her father. While the elder Skelton had died before his son's birth,
Stillwell's dad had abandoned the family while she was still a baby.
Second, both teenagers had worked from a young age to help support a
struggling household. Third, though Stillwell never thought of herself as
a performer, even after later stooging for Skelton in their stage act, both
youngsters were drawn to show business. Stillwell eventually found her
entertainment gift to be writing comedy. Fourth, each was driven to
succeed, with Stillwell channeling her talents into remaking Skelton
into a star. Fifth, as in most teenage marriages, there was also a certain
growing-up together factor, too.

While Stillwell was the younger by nearly two years, hers was
the dominant personality. Stillwell's mission to remake her husband
was not limited to show business. As noted earlier, she had initially
disliked everything about him, from Skelton's act to his general lack
of education. Just as she eventually wrote him better material, she also
undertook a sort of home-schooling mission. Indeed, when the couple's
late 1930s budget could afford it, their nonstop life-on-the-road
existence included a tutor. Undoubtedly, this helped Skelton's sense of
self confidence. For example, Skelton's childhood Vincennes friend,
Dorothy West Hagemeier, remembered that schoolwork was a challenge
for the comedian. There was a building across from their school
called the "Dummy House," for poor students and/or troublemakers.
According to Hagemeier, "He [Skelton] spent a lot of time there but he
was anything but dumb."[15]

In 1938 George Bernard Shaw's celebrated play *Pygmalion* was
inspiringly adapted to the screen. While Stillwell's makeover of Skelton
during this same decade does not approach Shaw's transformation of
a Cockney guttersnipe into a lady (the later basis for *My Fair Lady*,
1964), she represented a finishing school for the comedian. With her

support, Skelton eventually passed a high school equivalency exam and even took some college extension classes. Plus, careerwise, Stillwell's writing of material such as the groundbreaking donut sketch placed their act on vaudeville's top rung.

Though the couple's relationship was often that of a teacher to a student, a better analogy was parent and child. As Stillwell comically observed even before their marriage, "I ... discovered that he needed a guardian angel. Or at least a guardian."[16] Skelton's longtime friend and film costar, Ann Miller (*Watch the Birdie*, 1950; *Texas Carnival*, 1951, and *Lovely to Look At* 1952), later recalled that "Red did everything Edna said. She was like his mama. And he called her Mommie."[17] (Appropriately, Stillwell's nickname for him was Junior.) Skelton's later explanation was that he was actually calling Stillwell "Mummy," an outgrowth of her cold, disapproving, mummy-like (à la ancient Egypt) stare when he made a mistake. But even this qualifies as having a sort of *Mommie Dearest* tone to it—a reference to actress Joan Crawford's domination of daughter Christina Crawford. Regardless, Miller was hardly alone in describing the Skelton-Stillwell relationship as like that of a parent and child. Powerful Hollywood newspaper columnist Hedda Hopper noted in a 1946 article, "At his [Skelton's radio] broadcasts Edna stands in the wings where he can see her. During a show recently, he glanced at the place she usually stands and she was gone. She'd just stepped out for a smoke. 'But,' said Red, 'I almost got panicky. After the show, I told her, 'Don't ever do that to me again.'"[18] What makes the comments of Miller and Hopper doubly amazing, with regard to Stillwell's mothering mastery of Skelton, is that both the actress and columnist are describing a period *after* the Skeltons' divorce—when the former usherette continued to manage and write for the comedian. Stillwell's own description of her post-divorce relationship with Skelton was "a kind of nurse maid to an adult."[19] One would assume she had exercised even more control during their marriage, which lasted from 1931 to 1943.

These developments, however, are getting ahead of the story. In 1931 Skelton and Stillwell were like many young Great Depression couples, struggling to get by. Physically, the Skeltons were also

Gloria:
There's
no limit to
my admiration
for your
work, and
you—
Best wishes
Edna Skelton

A sexy publicity still of Edna Stillwell Skelton (circa late 1930s).

reminiscent of the then phenomenally popular newspaper comic strip duo *Mutt and Jeff,* where skinny Mutt towered above his short pal. Similarly, the gangly six-foot-three Skelton towered over the petite Stillwell. Adding to the dissimilarity was Skelton's carrot-topped head, versus Stillwell's blonde bob, though she colored it brunette in later years. This comic contrast was pertinent to their act, since Skelton used his wife as his theater stooge later in the 1930s. While not having to pay an assistant was probably the biggest reason for Stillwell doubling as her husband's sometime sidekick, an amusing physical difference is always a plus in a comedy act.

Fittingly, for someone not immediately taken with Skelton's talents, Stillwell's initial stooging for Skelton was as a heckling audience plant. She loved to yell, "Take him off!" Stillwell later explained, "I like to holler, and it fed him lines, anyhow."[20] Though Stillwell's writing forte was yet to be discovered and she was never comfortable as a performer, her stage appearances were still enough of a plus to merit being singled out. For example, *Variety*'s review of Skelton's March 1937 booking at the Capitol Theatre in Washington, D.C., noted, "Skelton, after some [comic] patter, brings on Edna Stillwell. Girl makes pretty foil and gets by with [musical number] 'Sing, Sing, Sing.'"[21]

Of course, this Capitol booking chronicled a time from the couple's later vaudeville heyday. Their early 1930s beginnings had been less than secure. Skelton was still a former burlesque comic trying to make it in the world of walkathons. Indeed, Skelton's mother-in-law had originally objected to her daughter marrying a burlesque comedian. (Stillwell later comically wrote, "Red didn't help matters much by telling her that he was going to reform and become a dope-peddler."[22]) Following the walkathon phenomenon from city to city, Skelton became confident enough as a master of ceremonies to eventually ask for a percentage of the gate instead of a straight salary. But consistent with his childlike nature, he naively accepted promoters' box-office numbers, even if they were watered down. This is when Stillwell first came into her own as Skelton's money manager, negotiating contracts that also made her the cashier (as she had been back at Kansas City's El Torreon Ballroom), so

she could check on the attendance figures. Eventually, Stillwell worked
Skelton's weekly walkathon income up from seventy-five dollars to five
hundred dollars—quite a raise for someone who had to borrow his
three dollar marriage-license fee from his bride.[23]

As good as these numbers were for the Great Depression,
walkathons were not always steady work. Plus, one never knew when
they would end. There was inevitably down time between engagements.
Moreover, the Skeltons' on-the-road expenses ate up most of their
money, as they had to pay for food, lodging, and transportation to the
next walkathon city. Early in the Skeltons' marriage, when they were
just hoping for that seventy-five dollars a week, they often had to get
creative to survive. Consequently, Skelton fell back on the huckster
skills he had employed as a child in Vincennes, where his numerous
schemes included doctoring old playing cards and selling them as new
novelty decks.[24] When the couple found themselves stranded in Saint
Louis, Skelton created a fog-preventer for car windshields. All this
amounted to were slivers of soap wrapped in recycled tinfoil taken from
discarded cigarette packages. But it was not so much the product as the
comedian's ability to "sell" anything on a street corner—briefly recalling
the shakedown skills of "Doc" Lewis, the medicine man salesman for
whom Skelton had worked as a child. Stillwell stooged as the eager ice-
breaking first customer and lookout for any patrolling street cops.

While Skelton could play the classic wheeler-dealer confidence
man, à la his later San Fernando Red character, the comedian's real
personality was still that of a man-child who could not handle money.
Ironically, despite Skelton's proven con-artist skills, he was a sucker
for competing scam artists, too. In addition, Skelton was also an easy
touch for any sob story involving a handout. And after a lifetime
of impoverishment, any extra money would, to borrow a popular
Great Depression era phrase, "burn a hole in his pocket." Befitting a
husband she called Junior, Stillwell put Skelton on a modest allowance
and handled all money matters. Even years later, after their divorce,
Skelton's checks had to be cosigned by manager Stillwell. This was both
a safeguard to protect the comedian from bad investments, and simply

an exercise in basic bookkeeping—Skelton was bad at keeping records of his purchases. *If* he wrote anything on his check stub, it would be something goofy, like "None of your business."

What proved even more exasperating to Stillwell was that for much of their long association Skelton refused to be concerned about money. Or, as she phrased it, "He's allergic to financial worries."[25] Undoubtedly, part of this was a product of his never having had anything, yet always somehow getting by. Skelton's real-life personality seemed fueled by the central characteristic that attracts us to most personality comedians— the resiliency factor. Yet, the financial freedom with which Stillwell gifted her boy/man (today's "kidult") by playing purse-strings parent became a strain on their relationship.

Another minimelodrama for Stillwell involved Skelton's proclivity for pets, an outgrowth of both his overgrown youngster nature and the unconditional love animals tend to give caretakers, something a formerly attention-starved Skelton could appreciate. Their menagerie often included multiple dogs, as well as "once a duck, and a polar bear cub they used in their act."[26] To say Stillwell was in charge of pet "damage control" was to state the literal truth. When the aptly named polar bear cub, Snowball, got loose in a hotel dining area, a Mack Sennett-like scenario ensued. What Skelton most recalled was Snowball chasing the waiters. "They were pretty fast afoot but so was the bear," he remembered. "They'd cut and twist among the tables like a halfback running a broken field but they couldn't shake Snowball. ... There was considerable furniture and glassware smashed in the melee and no doubt a few nerves were shattered but I think the hotel people were severe [in their angry response]."[27]

Besides playing diplomat over these pet problems, Stillwell also had to be a fast-talking arbitrator for those occasions when Skelton allowed his walkathon comedy to take on destructive surreal silliness. For example, during a Minneapolis competition he invited a contestant to sing a song on stage. As the contestant launched into his rendition of "Singin' in the Rain," Skelton had a comic epiphany—simulate a raining backdrop to see if this sudden "storm front" would derail the wannabe warbler. Skelton began by squirting the contestant with a seltzer bottler, just as Harpo Marx had tried to quiet a blaring radio in the film comedy classic *Duck Soup* (1933). When that did not faze the singer, the comedian doused him with a couple buckets of water—still nothing. But egged on by an appreciative crowd, Skelton moved to his comedy coup de grâce—spraying him off the stage with a fire hose. This was such a hit with the audience that Skelton then decided to turn the hose on the crowd. Though this topper greatly pleased the dry portion of the audience and Skelton, "It was a [comic] riot—one of the best I've ever seen," the walkathon "manager was all in favor of killing me … over the piffling matter of the organ under the stage which … was not waterproof."[28]

According to Skelton, however, the initial anger and follow-up intermediary skills necessitated by Stillwell following the funny fiasco with the organ "was nothing" compared to the ire and draining diplomacy exhibited by his wife when he "chopped down [the legs of] a rare and very expensive piano at [a walkathon in] Atlantic City."[29] Such chaotically surreal comedy was possibly influenced by the often absurd movie milieu of the Marx Brothers, a film comedy team then at the height of its popularity. Skelton's antics also anticipated by decades the comically violent showmanship of pioneering rock 'n roll musicians, such as Jerry Lee Lewis once setting his piano on fire during a finale performance of his signature song, "Great Balls of Fire."

Like the "thrill comedy" actions of silent film star Harold Lloyd, forever synonymous with the *Safety Last* (1923) sequence where he hangs from the hand of a skyscraper clock, Skelton was also happy to put himself in harm's way for comedy's sake. At one competition he rode a midget bicycle along the railing of a balcony overlooking the auditorium stage. After taking an unplanned fall and nearly going over said railing, he decided to begin the next night's festivities by hanging from a beam over the stage. This proved such a hit that the following evening Skelton noted that he "planted a dummy dressed like me on the beam, called to the crowd again, then pushed the dummy off into space. People fainted all over the establishment and once more it

Myrtle Farrell —
My very best
wishes to you.
Sincerely,
Red Skelton.

When he was not making goofy faces for comic effect, Skelton was quite handsome, and his wife Stillwell, for a time, was billed as his sister.

was only Edna who saved me from being torn limb from limb by the powers that were."[30]

Of course, all these Stillwell to the rescue stories merely reinforce the parent-child dichotomy of the Skelton marriage. Still, the surface has merely been scratched. Skelton had several other little-boy tendencies, such as a 1941 *Photoplay* article chronicling that "he will have absolutely nothing to do with that newfangled invention called the telephone."[31] Between Skelton having no experience with a phone during an impoverished childhood, and a later mistaken booking experience in adulthood, Stillwell was the only "telephone operator" in the Skelton household. If Stillwell did not answer the phone, the comedian simply let it ring. Skelton's allowance from his wife also often went to childlike purchases, such as the acquisition of an extensive toy train set. The adult Skelton tended to buy youth-orientated items in collectable bulk as if to be poignantly making up for a childhood that never was.

Given the mother-son relationship that defined the Skeltons' marriage, it should come as no surprise that Stillwell later used her husband as the "inspiration for the [all-important 1940s] radio character of Junior. I had to watch him [Red] the way Junior's mother had to watch Junior, or he's bound to get into mischief. He has the same approach to life: 'If I dood it, I get a whippin' ... I dood it!' He even calls me 'Mummy.'"[32] While Stillwell's creation of this pivotal figure, second only in Skelton's large cast of characters to the much later Freddie the Freeloader, will be fleshed out later, suffice it to say that this accomplishment rivals her penning of the donut-dunking routine. What's more, both were born of simple observation. But instead of an eating act being drawn from a stranger at a coffee shop, Stillwell simply had to sketch Junior from, to paraphrase humorist James Thurber, "her life and hard times with Red."[33]

What makes this revelation all the more fascinating now is that while Skelton is far from unique in essaying a man-child comedy persona, his seems to have been actually drawn from a real-life case of entertainingly arrested development. *New York Times* film critic Manohla Dargis opened her review of the Owen Wilson comedy

You, Me and Dupree (2006) with a sweeping reference to the lengthy
tenure of the boy-man in cinema: "The movies have long nurtured
the arrested development of the American male, serving as a virtual
playpen for whom Peter Pan isn't a syndrome but a way of life."[34]
But in a lifetime of writing about personality comedians, often in the
man-child mold (of which Wilson is a current prime example), I have
rarely seen such a close correlation (as in the Skelton case) between
performer and persona. Naturally, popular culture literature often
enjoys blurring the line between fact and fiction, reinforcing a natural
tendency by viewers to confuse screen characters with the performers.
With the possible exception of director Frank Capra's description of
the close parallels between comedian Harry Langdon and his "kidult"
persona (which Capra helped shape), however, the Skelton scenario is
strangely unique.[35] Perhaps this dependent relationship would explain
why the comedian tried to erase Stillwell from his later life. Seymour
Berns, Skelton's television producer in the 1960s, recalled, "When I first
went to work for Red, he used to give Edna a lot of credit for getting
him where he was. But as the years went by, he blotted her out of his
consciousness. Finally Red reached a point where he would barely
acknowledge that she had ever existed."[36]

Despite Stillwell's early controlling nature, or maybe because of
it, the Skeltons often quarreled as a young couple. At one point she
even left Skelton on the road and returned home to Kansas City. But
that seemed to have been precipitated by the comedian giving a pretty
waitress some free passes to the walkathon he was then headlining—a
very naïve thing to do when one's wife is the cashier. Skelton, however,
was lost without Stillwell and showered her with long-distance
communications. Besides, his was a little boy's approach to anger:
"He never stays mad longer than two consecutive minutes and can't
understand other people who keep on being mad when he isn't."[37]

Still, Stillwell stayed away for months. For a young woman who
never wanted children, she was probably coping with the fact that she
had married an oversized kid. So why go back with Skelton? When
one reads some of the letters she later wrote to Skelton's Vincennes
mentor Clarence Stout and his wife Inez, Stillwell sounds like the most

supportive of spouses. Paradoxically, given the reason for their early
separation (Stillwell's jealousy over a waitress), one letter from 1937
reveals just how much was later asked of her for Skelton's success. She
confessed in a postscript about new publicity stills: "I'm known as
Red's sister instead of wife. Our mgr. recommends it—he's right too, it
does make a difference, and we don't care just so he becomes a big, big
comic—Love, Edna."[38]

The same letter also reveals Stillwell's casually warm style. After
several affectionately detailed pages she observed, "Gee—this isn't
a letter it's a visit."[39] There is genuine "aw shucks" charm to her
correspondence that makes one think how appropriate she was writing
comedy material for such an "aw shucks" Hoosier humorist. In
addition, her engaging conversational style has a disarming directness,
even if she is revealing a personal weakness. One such example from
a 1939 letter to the Stouts is especially pertinent, given Stillwell's
established controlling nature and their early arguments: "Before I go
there's one more thing, Red is always warning me about it too—he says
that I'm too much of a worry-wart about [my perfectionist comedy
writing] work and that many times because of it I am rude. So, please if
I was at anytime during our visit won't you forgive me?—I really didn't
mean to be. Honest."[40]

With this later documented dedication, from playing sister to being
a driven comedy collaborator, one has to assume Stillwell returned to
Skelton, after their trial separation, with a new purpose. Providentially,
shortly after their reunion Skelton's move from walkathons to
nightclubs and vaudeville gave Stillwell the opportunity to demonstrate
her importance as a writer in elevating his comedy game. One has to
add, moreover, that despite any frustration associated with being a
surrogate parent to a man-child husband, Stillwell appreciated that
Skelton shared her ambitiousness. Plus, when his comedy gift did
not involve fire hoses and chopping down priceless pianos, Stillwell
admired her husband's comic aggressiveness to sell funny—funny she
would soon be writing. Indeed, given the immediate positive impact of

Stillwell's sketch material for Skelton and her given outspokenness (such as criticizing his act even before they dated), one can assume she was giving Skelton comedy tips from the beginning.

One another footnote as to why Stillwell returned to her caretaker marriage might be stating the obvious—period pictures document that Skelton was a handsome young man. When this goofy, carrot-topped comedian wasn't making with the rubber-faced plasticity synonymous to the comic arts, Skelton had matinee-idol good looks. Stillwell indirectly acknowledges this in a 1937 letter, confessing it is good for business if people think the young comedian is single. Even twenty-odd years later, the entertainer/comedy critic Steve Allen wrote of Skelton: "His face, too, is his fortune. An attractive face in repose, it becomes a true mask of comedy."[41]

One is also tempted to think that Stillwell hoped, even during the volatile early days of her marriage, that teaming up with this diamond-in-the-rough comic might coalesce into one of those survivor success stories that helped define the Great Depression, from a down-and-out boxer nicknamed "Cinderella Man" (James J. Braddock), to an underdog nag of a horse called Seabiscuit. I am also reminded of a similar take on *the* Depression-era book, Margaret Mitchell's *Gone With the Wind* (1936). Cultural historian Conrad Lane reminds us, "Mitchell always contended that survival was the major theme of the book ... it is easy to see why survivors of the Great Depression found so much with which to identify."[42]

This was the era of second-chance populism, a film genre forever associated with director Frank Capra and such comedy classics as *Mr. Deeds Goes to Town* (1936) and *Mr. Smith Goes to Washington* (1939). And with Stillwell being the planning "big picture" person in the Skelton-Stillwell marriage, she was the one most likely to see the second-chance potential in Skelton's comedy career. Besides, it offered the excitement of show business. Her best other job offer from a man was a conscientious uncle wanting her to assist him in his undertaking business. With hindsight, her return to Skelton seems quite predictable.

Whether or not she sensed the amazing Depression success story they themselves were about to become, Stillwell's 1930s correspondence documents the early furor: "Our manager has already signed the contracts [to appear on Rudy Vallee's career-making radio program]— you can well imagine how excited we are."[43]

Early Star Status: Memorable 1937

"We open at Loew's State Theatre in New York City. It's the one and only big vaudeville house there, and ... we have never played the big city before—we're scared too but darn happy about it."[1]
EDNA STILLWELL SKELTON

The previous chapter closed with Red Skelton on the verge of major stardom, and some hypothetical thoughts on how much his comedy guru first wife, Edna Stillwell Skelton, might have anticipated this development. Of course, the flip side to such seer suggestions (which would help explain why she stayed in a challenging marriage), is an old axiom from the most unlikely of sources, "gonzo" writer Hunter Thompson. His New Journalism reporting, which made the writer a pivotal part of the story, was fond of the line, "Buy the ticket, take the ride."[2] So maybe Stillwell simply felt she had bought the marriage "ticket" and now was on the metaphorical "ride." Regardless, after Stillwell created the famous Skelton donut sketch, theirs was the proverbial overnight success. Although Skelton had served an apprenticeship in medicine shows and minstrels, and some brief less-documented stops in tent shows, on a riverboat, and in a circus, when he met Stillwell he was still in the lowly position of burlesque comic. And the early years of their marriage reflected the tenor of the Great Depression times—Skelton was a master of ceremonies for walkathons. Skelton's performing dues had been paid.

Stillwell's mid-1930s donut routine and other reality-based writing helped Skelton segue his skills into vaudeville, the next rung on the entertainment ladder. By 1937 Skelton received rave reviews throughout the country and parts of Canada. Indeed, the comedian's first significant 1937 engagement in the United States (at the Capitol Theatre in Washington, D.C.) had the *Variety* reviewer praising a "Canadian lad" (Skelton), who "socked home enough heavy comedy in his emceeing to win solid front [praise] from critics and even the high school girls."[3] (The seminal donut sketch had been written for an extended 1936 engagement in Canada, and initially some stateside critics thought Skelton was Canadian.)

Word of mouth on Skelton coming into this key engagement was high, a fact noted by *Washington Post* critic Nelson B. Bell: "[Skelton] proves himself worthy of all the nice things that were said about him before his arrival in Washington. He is an elongated young man, endowed with tremendous versatility and that ingratiating sort of personality that makes everything he does seem perhaps better than it is."[4] *Variety* underlined, however, that the donut sketch was central to Skelton's success: "without [the] doughnut bit, which wows 'em, Skelton might have been overshadowed [but] through no fault of his own."[5]

The Capitol Theatre ads for the comedian heralded "'RED' IS HERE! That NEW dynamic personality you've excitedly awaited: RED SKELTON, six feet two of entertaining dynamite."[6] Impressively, when the comedian lived up to all this hoopla and was held over for a second week, Stillwell was able to provide him with two more slice-of-life sketches. Continuing the "how to" magic of the donut routine, the new material comically explored how different people go to sleep and how late theater patrons try to find their seats in the dark. *Variety*'s follow-up review, while noting the "two [new] pantomimes are obviously hauled out of the reserve bag," went on to praise them, even calling the sleep routine "hilarious."[7]

Sounding more like a Skelton press agent than a reviewer, Bell heralded the comedian's holdover week by revealing, "Skelton, who has scored so resounding a hit ... seems to be going places.... RKO-Radio [studio] has a 90-day option of his services."[8] The RKO deal ultimately led to Skelton's supporting role in a feature film released the following year, *Having Wonderful Time* (1938, where he reprised his donut sketch, as well as a routine on how various people navigate staircases). Stillwell's observational material remained a cornerstone of Skelton's repertoire for the remainder of his career. For example, in recently viewing a signature collection of Skelton's later television series authorized by his estate, an undated episode from sometime in the 1950s had the comedian demonstrating how different people seat themselves at a soda fountain counter, which segued into a comic take on how customers add sugar to coffee and then into the various ways a straw is used/abused when eating ice cream.[9]

In 1937 Skelton followed his smash engagement at the Capitol with two equally successful Canadian bookings at Montreal's Loew's and Toronto's Shea theaters. Once again, he could do no wrong. *Variety's* Montreal coverage stated, "Skelton has some new gags and sketches about at level of former performances here but house [audience] will take anything from him."[10] The *Toronto Daily Star* said of Skelton's opening at the Shea, "For the laugh spots on the bill the management has reached out and plucked … a fun favorite in these parts in the person of 'Red' Skelton, the clown prince."[11]

The comedian's Montreal booking also gave Skelton a chance to use the mimicking skills that had made him such a hit impersonating Al Jolson back in Clarence Stout's minstrel shows. This time around Skelton shared the vaudeville stage with British actor/impressionist Owen McGiveney, whose act was comprised of quick-change dramatic episodes from Charles Dickens. A special audience favorite was his abridged *Oliver Twist*, where McGiveney played six different characters in a miniplay called "Bill Sykes." In the more literary sensitive 1930s, this bit of high art in a normally low-art medium (vaudeville) went over very strongly. Fittingly, the *Montreal Gazette* had kudos for both Skelton and the Dickens aficionado: "McGiveney dominates the show this week and only the resourceful Red Skelton seems able to make himself remembered besides."[12] Where did the comedian's mimicry skills come in? *Variety's* review of the same engagement answers the question—Skelton's close for the show, and the vaudeville bill in general, was a "clowning imitation of McGiveney's act."[13]

One should note that an added responsibility of a vaudeville master of ceremonies was not only to keep the program running smoothly but also make it seamless, dovetailing one act into another. Translation: Skelton often needed to play a quasi-second banana to every act on the bill, as well as performing his own sketches. Skelton's gift for wearing all these hats also sometimes assisted an off night for individual performers. A *Variety* review noted that one night the crowd was not fully responding to McGiveney's Dickens routine. But after some creative mimicry on Skelton's part, the British actor was given an encore. Such showmanship skills further documents why Skelton was so popular with audiences *and* entertainers.

Skelton's banner year continued through nonstop bookings in the East and Midwest in which he polished the latest Stillwell-authored sketches but wisely anchored the act to the donut routine. When Skelton performed at Milwaukee's Riverside Theatre, a local critic summarized the situation in the following manner: "Red Skelton is back in town.... This year's show is entirely new except for the doughnut dunking massacre, which he repeats only because the audience demands it."[14] Stillwell's 1937 writing touch assumed a comically feminine slant in a Skelton sketch where he pantomimes a woman putting on makeup. The comedian so effectively inhabited the part that he performed variations of the bit for the rest of his career. The routine is best showcased in two later Skelton films, *Bathing Beauty* (1944) and *The Fuller Brush Man* (1948). But by then Stillwell had further embellished the sketch by having Skelton pretend to wiggle into an undersized girdle. (Appropriately, one of Skelton's earliest entertainment parts, back in his Vincennes youth, was playing a señorita in a local YMCA circus production.[15])

In a role that rivaled her writing activities, Stillwell also coached her husband from the wings—"he would rely on her hand signals, adjusting his jokes to the audience reaction."[16] Stillwell's behind-the-curtain directing continued through Skelton's 1940s radio days and into the early 1950s, even after their marriage had ended she continued to serve as his head writer/manager.

Just as Stillwell-authored observation pantomime approach was a constant through Skelton's television series (1951 to 1971), there were several additional 1930s performance nuances that also would not change for the rest of Skelton's career. Then and later, the comedian enjoyed laughing at his own material, a phenomenon generally frowned upon by other comedians. Thus, a 1937 critic for the *Philadelphia Inquirer* observed, "[Skelton] enjoyed his demonstration of 'dunking' doughnuts just as much as did the audience."[17] There are, however, several explanations/justifications for this response, beyond the comedian's pat answer, "Why should I be the only one not getting the joke?" First, there was a greater preponderance of 1930s comedians who laughed at their own observations, starting with arguably the decade's most beloved humorist, Will Rogers. Second, entertainer/comedy critic Steve Allen posited in the 1950s, "A great many comedians, especially those who have worked, as Red has, in vaudeville, employ the giggle device as a cover-up and a come-on. In a big theatre it sometimes takes a second or two for an audience to absorb a joke and respond to it. Lots of comedians fill that empty spot with some sort of nervous mannerism. George Burns and Ken Murray wiggle their cigars, Bob Hope pretends to be sailing right into the next sentence, although he rarely says more at such times than 'I-uh' or 'but I really.'"[18]

Beyond Allen's practical explanation of the "giggle device" as a bridging and/or pump-priming technique by the comedian, I would also argue for a more aesthetic answer. I draw this position from an unlikely source, a production memoir of director Stanley Kubrick's *Eyes Wide Shut* (1999) by the film's coscripter Frederic Raphael. The writer complained that this dominating/domineering director was "so guarded" that he substituted "grumbly little noises" for laughter. Why? Raphael's explanation was, "Laughter is loss of control."[19] For me, Skelton's "loss of control" laughter made audiences feel closer to him, like he was simply one of them. Though I do not think Skelton ever sat down and postulated this all out, I believe he intuitively recognized the logic in his laughter—a response as natural as the reality-based pantomimes penned by Stillwell.

Another constant in Skelton's act was a propensity for old jokes. One of his many hobbies involved collecting joke books. And like many comedians, he maintained (by way of Stillwell) a joke file. As a fan of Mark Twain, Skelton probably enjoyed a certain quote from Twain's time-tripping novel, *A Connecticut Yankee in King Arthur's Court* (1889). At one point in the title character's travel to the distant past, he must sit through the humorous speech of the court comic, Sir Dinadan. The Yankee amusingly observes: "I think I never heard so many old played-out jokes strung together in my life.... It seemed peculiarly sad to sit here, thirteen hundred years before I was born and listen again to poor, flat, worm-eaten jokes that had given me the dry gripes when I was a boy.... It about convinced me that there isn't any such thing as a new joke possible."[20]

Skelton's remedy for resurrecting such "worm-eaten jokes" seemed to be a combination of high-octane enthusiasm and his post-joke "giggle device." And throughout Skelton's career, he made it work. For example, the *Variety* critic covering his July 1937 Capitol appearance noted, "[The] lad puts 'em across even if they're corny by giving plenty."[21] When Skelton moved his act to New York City the following month, crowds and critics continued to find his old jokes Teflon-like: "Some of Skelton's puns are ultra sour and many of his lines are ancient, but he's generally a very funny buffoon who rates the big hand he gets."[22] (To put Skelton's puns from the 1930s in perspective, the then very popular Marx Brothers often peppered their pictures with puns.)

Flash forward to Skelton's first season (1951–52) on television. *New York Herald Tribune* critic John Crosby was still praising the comedian's ability to sell an ancient joke: "'Skelton can prattle along indefinitely, spitting out unrelated [old] jokes with an air of such vigorous humor that, I'm forced to admit, he carries a large part of the audience along with him by sheer determination. It's a gift not to be taken lightly,' I wrote once upon a time.... (If Mr. Skelton can repeat the jokes, I ought to be permitted to repeat the observations.)"[23] Many years later, a television rerun of the comedian's HBO special, *Red Skelton's Christmas Dinner* (1981), produced this positive but familiar sounding *Variety* review: "Freddy the Freeloader ... brings home a family message in a corny but good-natured style ... Skelton's sweet temperament and pure delight in his own antics make this a happy holiday entry."[24]

As a footnote to the high-powered enthusiasm with which Skelton sold old material, what critic Crosby likened to "sheer determination," one could also add a propensity for self-deprecating humor. Though the comedian was doing this from the 1930s on, the best extant example dates from a 1962 episode of his television series. First, Skelton pitches a bad pun about not wanting to "give himself away," noting: "I did that the other day. I jumped on the scales and got a weigh." After a pause, while his "giggle device" helps generate audience laughter, he adds: "You don't hear jokes like that any more ... and aren't we lucky?"[25]

Should one credit, or blame, Stillwell for Skelton's old joke tendencies, since she wrote the comedian's sketches? A Stillwell letter written to an early Skelton mentor in 1937 suggests otherwise. Stillwell created the pantomime sketches but was "not so good on quips & [verbal] gags.... But it doesn't matter 'cause Red's a whiz on those."[26] Ironically, while Skelton effectively sold the old shtick throughout his long career, what he is most celebrated for today is the pantomime.

Regardless, the young comedian never lost sight of the Depression-era dream he was living as a performer. Fittingly, the Hoosier humorist told an Indianapolis audience during his breakout year, "It's a silly way to make a living [dunking donuts] but it's better than working."[27] Yet, Skelton tried to improve himself. Just as he had enhanced his educational skills by traveling with a tutor, Skelton worked with other entertainers to polish his performing skills. Stillwell's late 1930s correspondence documents that Skelton was working on both playing the piano and dancing, including getting suggestions from the great Bill "Bojangles" Robinson, creator of stair-tap routine.[28] When Skelton and Robinson shared the bill at Chicago's Palace Theatre in mid-1937, the dancer was still riding the huge critical and commercial successes of three 1935 films: *The Little Colonel* (with Shirley Temple), *In Old Kentucky* (with Will Rogers), and *The Littlest Rebel* (again with Temple). Robinson was always generous with his time and talent, and appreciated the fact that young Skelton was asking for help.

If playing New York City's Loew's State Theatre was one of Skelton's watershed events for seminal 1937 (as suggested by the Stillwell quote that opens this chapter), at least three other events that calendar year rivaled the booking in importance. First, and most obvious, he was a critical and commercial smash in New York. But this success went beyond excellent notices and solid box-office numbers. This triumph resulted in a rave review in the all-important "New Acts" portion of *Variety*, the entertainment industry bible. The review stated: "[Skelton] is a young comic whose chances appear exceptionally strong. He has an easy, affable manner of working, quickly ingratiates himself and is pretty well equipped with material.... He's not going to have any trouble at all getting along in this or any other town, either on stage dates of this character, in picture houses or on nitery [nightclub] floors."[29]

Second, Skelton's stockpiling of 1937 critical kudos resulted in an invitation to appear on a popular coast-to-coast radio program, *Rudy Vallee Varieties*. This would be Skelton's first exposure to a national audience. Vallee had started his career as a popular singer, the first to be labeled a "crooner." His signature song, initially performed with his trademark megaphone, was "The Vagabond Lover," which doubled as the title of Vallee's first feature film (1929). Vallee's active singing career with his Connecticut Yankees orchestra and periodic screen roles enabled him to have a highly influential program on radio. The hook for the show, beyond Vallee himself, was a showcase for promising new performers. Radio historian John Dunning credits Vallee's program with being the "most important show on the air in the early to mid-1930s, so influential that a young unknown talent could rightly consider a booking there the break of a lifetime."[30]

Vallee's awareness of Skelton would not have been limited to the latter's superlative *Variety* notices. Skelton's active vaudeville stage schedule literally had Vallee and his orchestra frequently following the comedian into several 1937 bookings. The two performers even had a Canadian connection. Vallee was born in Vermont, attended the University of Maine, and had a soft spot for performing in Canada, and Skelton first came into his own with the donut routine while playing Montreal. Appropriately, a jubilant Stillwell wrote to Clarence and Inez Stout about the upcoming Vallee program: "Please would you listen in, and if you like it, drop us a line and let us know. This [booking] is definite, our manager has already signed the contracts—you can well imagine how excited we are—*Don't forget*, please let us know."[31]

The Vallee opportunity would mean little if the comedian did not go over, however, like everything else Skelton did in 1937, he was not to be denied. His guest spot that August proved so popular that Vallee had the comedian back twice more that year. Stillwell's letter to the Stouts might have tipped Skelton's hand as to the material the comedian would use on Vallee's program. That is, Skelton made his humor synonymous with Vincennes. A pleased critic for the hometown *Vincennes Sun-Commercial* proudly wrote, "From the beginning of the program Skelton cleverly wrapped his jokes around Vincennes."[32] Rating front-page coverage, the article was titled, "'Red' Skelton Tells of City in Radio Debut."

Vallee's radio show, also known as the *Fleischmann's Hour* (his sponsor), was tightly scripted, making this an odd fit for Skelton, a pantomimist with a proclivity for ad-libbing. The reason so many Vincennes references made the program was because Skelton strayed from the script. This did not win any points with the control-conscious Vallee, whose accidental dropping of the sacred script (or an exasperated tossing of copy no one was following) resulted in Skelton's best off-the-cuff line, "Rudy's ad-libs are scattered all over the floor."[33]

Skelton biographer Arthur Marx makes much of Vallee's frustration in his profile of the comedian.[34] But just as Skelton was playing to the program's studio audience with his ad-libbing, it seems more logical that the veteran Vallee was doing the same with his demonstrative response to Skelton. Moreover, one could also argue that Skelton's Hoosier humor was hardly a surprise to his radio host. After all,

Vallee had also booked his favorite Indiana-born performer, Joe
Cook, to appear on the same program with Skelton. One should
quickly add here that Cook was *not* a newcomer looking for a break.
Born in Evansville, Indiana, Cook logged time with a medicine
show and was part of a minstrel act. Cook's big break came in 1923
when he was featured in Earl Carroll's *Vanities*, a popular variation
of the *Ziegfeld Follies*. Cook's versatility often had him billed as a
"one-man vaudeville," though comedy historian Henry Jenkins's
description of Cook as the "nut comic" is more telling.[35] One might
liken Cook's signature Broadway stage production, *Rain or Shine*
(1928–29), to a Marx Brothers-type show, with Cook's character being
a zany, fast-talking huckster along Groucho lines. Despite this "nut
comic" moniker, Cook was such a beloved performer that another
characterization of his persona, "contagious good-naturedness," sounds
positively Skelton like.[36]

So what brought Cook to Vallee's youth-orientated variety hour?
The comedian was such a Broadway fixture that he became a regular
guest on Vallee's New York-based program in 1930. He stayed with
Vallee until the mid-1930s, then becoming the headlining radio comic
on first the *Colgate House Party* (1934–35), and later the *Circus Night
in Silvertown* (1935). Cook also found time to become a regular guest
on the *Al Jolson: Shell Chateau Program* during 1935 and 1936. The
following season it became the *Joe Cook: Shell Chateau*. For the 1930s
listening audience, the presence of this figure represented guaranteed
comedy entertainment. I belabor the Cook-connection here, because he
had a soft spot for fellow Hoosiers. Thus, his favored status with Vallee
quite possibly had something to do with Skelton's breakthrough radio
booking.

This hypothesis is given added credence by the nature of what
transpired on Skelton's first Vallee appearance. The two Hoosiers
proceeded to kid each other's Indiana hometown. Skelton comically
called Cook's Evansville a "suburb of Vincennes." (Though both
are located in southern Indiana, Vincennes is strictly a small town,
while Evansville qualifies for city status.) The end result, as reported

by another front-page *Vincennes Sun-Commercial* article, was a radio rating bonanza: "Red made a big hit with his wise-cracks and bantering comedy ... A deluge of fan mail has brought him back to the program again."[37] While history has not recorded a breakdown of the return addresses on that devotee correspondence, it is safe to assume that the majority came from Indiana.

Whether or not Vallee and/or Cook had consciously set out to create some sort of Hoosier hullabaloo with Skelton, they had succeeded. The *Vincennes Sun-Commercial*'s front-page headline for the return comedy bout between the two Indiana buffoons boldly stated: "Red Skelton to Pursue Feud with Joe Cook on Air Tonight."[38] In that age, radio feuds were big business. The year before Skelton and Cook went at it, radio comedy giants Jack Benny and Fred Allen had begun their famous feud. Although they were close friends in real life, Allen had initiated this entertainment battle royal over Benny's mediocre violin skills, an instrument that was part of Benny's persona. For instance, Allen noted, "When Jack Benny plays the violin, it sounds as if the strings are still back in the çat."[39]

Significantly, by 1937, after Allen and Benny had been lambasting each other from their separate shows, the two staged a much ballyhooed showdown on March 14. Benny guest starred on Allen's program, with all nature of barbs being tossed. When Benny discussed his ad-lib skills, Allen cracked, "You couldn't ad-lib a belch after a Hungarian dinner." Benny answered, "You wouldn't dare say that if my writers were here."[40] The two comics continued their friendly feud until Allen's 1956 death.

Shortly after the memorable March confrontation of Benny and Allen, another popular comic feud developed on Edgar Bergen's *Charlie McCarthy Program*. Also known as *The Chase and Sanborn Hour*, the program starred ventriloquist Bergen and his smart aleck dummy/youngster, Charlie McCarthy. The feud, possibly inspired by the then current Benny-Allen rating bonanza, involved the comic clash of McCarthy and Bergen's regular guest star, W. C. Fields. (Fields' legendary antiheroic persona was tied to a love of alcohol, footnoted by a red, bulbous nose, and a hatred of children.) The Fields-McCarthy

verbal exchanges are celebrated today as classic examples of American
radio comedy during its golden age. Especially funny lines included
Fields describing McCarthy as a "woodchigger's snack bar" and a
"woodpecker's pin-up" or McCarthy's "Is it true, Mr. Fields, that when
you stood on the corner of Hollywood and Vine forty-three cars waited
for your nose to change to green?"[41]

Obviously, with both these radio feuds taking off in early-to-mid
1937, the Skelton-Cook confrontation on Vallee's show must have
seemed a natural for the late summer and autumn of that same year.
The Skelton-Cook follow-up for Vallee was a hit, too. Consequently,
Skelton was invited back for a third appearance. This successful radio
exposure probably helped make it possible for Skelton to be featured
on the 1939 Chicago-based radio program *Avalon Time*, which will be
addressed in the following chapter. But beyond that, the Vallee coast-
to-coast radio spots kept his name out there in entertainment circles.
Just before Skelton's second Vallee guest appearance, career-making
reporter/radio personality Walter Winchell discussed the comedian's
film future in his widely syndicated newspaper column, On Broadway:
"'Red' Skelton, the RKO 'find' will get two Gs per [$2,000 a week]. He
is better described as a gentile Milton Berle."[42] This was just one more
bit of 1937 documentation that Skelton had arrived.

Before leaving the subject of Skelton's visits to Vallee's program,
one should note the boost it gave to Stillwell as a performer. Previously,
she was an often unbilled stooge for their vaudeville stage act; initially
she had even been encouraged by Skelton's manager to play down their
marriage so as not to distract from any potential Skelton sex appeal.
But by Skelton's second Vallee guest spot, Stillwell emerged as nearly an
equal performing partner. In fact, for the sake of all Skelton's newfound
hometown-focused humor, Kansas City-born Stillwell became a
Vincennes native, too. This development especially pleased an unnamed
critic for the *Vincennes Post*, who happily also recorded one of the
couple's joint routines for Vallee: "Recalling their days together in the
old school house here, he [Red] reminded her of the way she used to

look over his shoulder and copy his answers. 'Yes,' responded his wife cynically, 'and then we BOTH flunked!'"[43]

This tardy recognition of Stillwell occurred in NBC's Chicago studios, where Vallee had temporarily taken his New York-based radio program on the road.[44] Vallee's visit to Chicago might be taken as yet another example of Skelton's rise in 1937 entertainment circles. That is, Skelton was then performing at the Chez Paree's nightclub, which was to be immediately followed by a six-week booking at the Palace Theater. A quick follow-up to Skelton's hit first appearance on Vallee's program would have been impossible without the host taking his show to Chicago.

Vincennes press coverage of this event also sketched out Skelton's ongoing close ties with hometown mentor Stout. The veteran entertainer's daughter, Frankie Stout, had been in Chicago for some dance classes. Since much of this time coincided with the Skeltons' bookings in the city, Frankie stayed with the couple in their Seneca Hotel suite. The young dancer had her own studio back in Vincennes, and through the years Skelton had always generously credited Frankie with giving him his first dancing tips, back when they were both youngsters.

A fourth pivotal event for Skelton in 1937 involved a trip to Hollywood to shoot a supporting role in *Having Wonderful Time*. This was pretty heady stuff for a youngster who still felt like a bit of an impostor. Shortly before the film's 1938 East Coast opening, Skelton confessed to a *New York Sun* critic, after crediting this movie break to his appearances at Loew's State Theatre: "I may seem kind of smart-alecky out there ... [on the stage]. But, gee, I don't feel like that. Sometimes I wonder how long they'll stand for it. I've got a feeling that some day they'll just come around to the back and say, 'All right, Skelton, that's enough. You've had your fling. Now go on away. We've had enough of you.'"[45]

Besides this "I'm not worthy" mindset, which was probably intensified by the widespread poverty of the Great Depression, the workaholic Skelton also had difficulty coping with the seemingly casual pace of filmmaking. Once again, Stillwell played mother hen, later observing, "Nobody explained to him why he had to be on the set at 9 a.m. and stay on call, when they might not use him until 3 in the afternoon. So he would just wander out. I don't know how many times I found him up in Hollywood Boulevard when I thought he was at work; I must have sneaked him back into the [RKO] studio at least fifteen times. Finally, I had to go to work *with* him to make him happy."[46]

Skelton's take on this easy twelve-week movie commitment, which began after the comedian's late summer bookings in Chicago, sounds like the honest hardworking midwesterner that he was: "Why, I didn't really earn one penny of that [$2,000 a week] salary out there [in Hollywood]. I do more work than that just for an audition or a free rehearsal."[47] Still, with vaudeville largely being reduced to stage shows in support of large city movie palace screenings, Skelton realized film needed to be part of his future. Regardless, his *Having Wonderful Time* costars, Ginger Rogers and Douglas Fairbanks Jr., were very helpful in showing him the movie ropes. Plus, Rogers had even given the comedian some tips on one of his many hobbies, photography.

The final key event to Skelton's magical 1937 involves a cumulative factor—the comedian's numerous acclaimed appearances that year at the Capitol Theatre in Washington, D.C., brought him to the attention of President Franklin D. Roosevelt's White House.[48] Roosevelt's fascination with the entertainment industry and its potential to aid charitable causes dated from at least World War I. On April 14, 1918, Roosevelt, then the assistant secretary of the navy, had joined movie stars Charlie Chaplin, Douglas Fairbanks Sr., Mary Pickford, and Marie Dressler in a huge war-bond rally in Washington, D.C.

Roosevelt, a later victim of polio, subsequently turned his annual January birthday celebration into a charity fund-raiser for infantile paralysis. And across the nation schoolchildren also collected money through the March of Dimes program. Because of all Skelton's 1937 Capitol Theatre attention, the comedian acted as the master

of ceremonies at the president's Birthday Ball for four consecutive
years (1938 to 1941).[49] Besides the prestige this would bring to any
performer, it must have been yet another "pinch me, I'm dreaming"
moment for Skelton, the former poverty-stricken kid from Vincennes
hobnobbing with a president! What is more, after the comedian's 1940
Birthday Ball duties, a very impressed Mickey Rooney went out of his
way to give Skelton's movie career a major assist.

One might summarize the amazing turn of events that passed for
Skelton's 1937 by linking the year to one of the iconic Hollywood
landmarks—the famous huge letters/sign, "HOLLYWOODLAND"
overlooking the city from the foothills (the "LAND" portion of
the lettering was removed in 1949). I have always much preferred

Skelton and the thoughtful star Ginger Rogers in Having Wonderful Time *(1938).*

the term Hollywoodland over Hollywood. Most American success
stories, whether in or out of the entertainment industry, are not
really about any geographical place. Instead, as a more recent
critic has metaphorically observed, "It's about a state of mind, and
'Hollywoodland' suggests a state of mind. The pursuit of stardom
[whatever the field] is not restricted to Hollywood. You could call
America Hollywoodland. Everybody wants to be a star."[50] In 1937
Skelton was beginning to live everybody's dream.

5

Roller-Coaster Years: 1938–40

"A funny thing about Red—he has had to try everything twice to succeed at it. The first time he emceed walkathons, he was a flop ... the first time he tried vaudeville, he didn't make the grade.... And the first time he tried the movies, he didn't go over."[1]
EDNA STILLWELL SKELTON, 1942

Edna Stillwell Skelton, Red Skelton's first wife and writer/manager, was overly critical of her husband's first feature-film appearance. What she might more specifically have noted, however, was that *Having Wonderful Time* (1938) flopped. Indeed, Skelton's supporting role as an entertainment director at a summer resort was one of the better features of this Ginger Rogers and Douglas Fairbanks Jr. romantic comedy. The *New York Times* called Skelton "faultless," and credited his "Itchy" character with being "the irrepressible master of ceremonies."[2] Detail-conscious *Variety* focused on the signature routine that had gotten Skelton the role: "Richard Skelton, as the chief of entertainment, gets some honest laughs from an exposé of doughnut dunking."[3] While the picture still plays pleasantly enough today, the complaint at the time was that a boisterous ethnic play about a Jewish "borsht belt" summer camp, which was a hit on Broadway, had been completely emasculated. The *New York Times* diplomatically addressed the issue at the top of its review: "There was nothing genteel about Arthur Kober's 'Having Wonderful Time' and—bless its folksy heart—there was nothing gentile either. But RKO-Radio's film version ... is both."[4]

Hollywood's often Jewish-dominated powerbrokers were reluctant to adopt Hebrew-orientated stories to the screen. They were sensitive to how an ethnic slant would play in America's conservative "white-bread" heartland. But in their defense, period censorship was equally conservative. In fact, in her autobiography Rogers blamed the latter for the picture's problems: "At the insistence of the Hays Office [Hollywood censorship], the ethnic Jewish story was played by a decidedly gentile cast. As a result, the film was not nearly as funny as the play and, understandably, was nowhere near as successful."[5]

Interestingly, Rogers also believed that Skelton's supporting role should have been larger. Her brief but highly complimentary comments about him in her memoir were as follows: "A very funny up-and-coming comic named Red Skelton made his film debut; unfortunately, much of his antic inventiveness ended up on the cutting-room floor."[6] These comments meshed with earlier accounts of Skelton's donut sketch running much longer than this movie's approximately three-minute version. While the film also showcased another Skelton routine (on various ways people go up stairs), the comedian had numerous other "how to" bits, one or more of which was presumably filmed but not used.

As a footnote to Rogers, the man who earlier teamed her with Fred Astaire, Pandro S. Berman, produced *Having Wonderful Time*. When Berman visited New York during August of 1937 to obtain the movie rights to *Time*, he had caught Skelton's comedy act at Loew's State Theatre. But this was hardly a lucky coincidence as critics were lining up to praise of Skelton's stage act. For example, *Variety* best summarized the situation: "[The] comic scores every time."[7] Though one might not normally think of Berman as a comedy scout, his first principle of entertainment, including the Astaire-Rogers musicals, was to look for humor.[8]

Despite Skelton's personal triumph in *Having Wonderful Time*, which thankfully preserved (albeit abridged) his classic donut routine for comedy history, the picture was unable to launch his movie career. The Skeltons' disappointment over this fact undoubtedly colored her broad panning of the picture in general. While Hollywood had initially overwhelmed Skelton, Stillwell had absorbed the town's most basic rule—"You are only as good as your last movie." In an early 1938 letter to Clarence Stout, Stillwell described a couple bracing for failure: "Now the dirt—the picture [*Having Wonderful Time*] still hasn't been released and won't be until May [the opening would drag out to June], but day after tomorrow Red's [RKO] option comes up—which they must either pick up or refuse; naturally we are hoping for the best *but* don't expect it!"[9]

As implied in Stillwell's letter, the movie's delayed release had not been a good sign. In a period when Hollywood's turnaround time for a film was exceptionally brief, *Having Wonderful Time* had been on the shelf for months. Indeed, a movie Rogers shot after *Time*, *Vivacious Lady* (1938), eventually opened six weeks *before* the summer-resort comedy.[10] Nevertheless, Skelton, whose RKO option had not been picked up, put on a brave face when he talked to *New York Sun*'s film critic Eileen Creelman shortly before the picture's East Coast opening: "I'm going to be the first in line at the [Radio City] Music Hall tomorrow. Even going to pay for my ticket, so they can't throw me out [if it doesn't go over]."[11] The interview was peppered with this sort of self-deprecating humor, which often dovetailed into a poignancy that was antiheroically endearing. For instance, here is Skelton's funny/sad confession about the "nerve-racking experience" of first viewing himself on the big screen in a studio projection room: "[It was] like seeing a photograph of yourself that you know is terrible, and then having everyone else say it looks just like you—and 'what a good picture you take.'"[12]

Skelton may have been able to compartmentalize the fact that he was still funny in a film that failed. Though he remained very much in that "kidult" phase at this point of his career, with a motherlike Stillwell directing his personal and private life, one must never minimize the painful vulnerability a comedian forever fights. Years later, Skelton became almost mawkish in his description of this phenomenon—the potential absence of love from an audience. "A clown is a warrior who fights gloom," he noted. "When deafening silence [greets] his gestures, the agony comes. [It is] the loneliness of a lover saying good-by, a prelude to death.... There is no medication to relieve the pain, no understanding to wrap the wound in. He stands there and bleeds."[13]

At least Skelton experienced the *Having Wonderful Time* opening in New York, where he was more of a known stage commodity, and generated some positive attention, including the previously noted high-profile piece in the *New York Sun* and being singled out for praise in New York reviews of the picture. In contrast, the critique from the film industry's insider newspaper, the *Hollywood Reporter*, briefly undercut Skelton's performance, though never mentioning him by name: "[The film] could stand some extra story footage in place of some lengthy and extremely unfunny antics by a supposed camp comic."[14] The publication's failure to even note Skelton's name was consistent with its coverage, or lack thereof, during the time (autumn 1937) Skelton logged in the film capital for the *Time* shoot. Only one brief Skelton -related piece appeared, shortly before shooting commenced. But the short news item did reveal a possible explanation for the surprisingly vitriolic nature of the later *Hollywood Reporter* review reference to Skelton. The gifted screen comedian and popular Hollywood personality Jack Oakie was originally to have shared comedy duties on *Having Wonderful Time* with Skelton.[15] The fact that newcomer Skelton somehow usurped this beloved film insider might have colored the later critique—bad notices have often been born of much less.

Portentously, when Skelton attended *Time*'s New York opening at the prestigious Radio City Music Hall, the film broke just as the comedian first appeared on the screen. "Out of the ensuing blackness and above the murmurs of the audience came Skelton's exclamation: '!*~z! Those cutters [movie editors] are still working on [deleting] me!'"[16] Once again, even during adversity, Skelton was good for an ad-lib. But this time, the disgruntled comic dropped his normal ban on salty language.

The movie's negative fallout, however, was several months away. Initially, there were several positives that came from being in a Hollywood feature film. First, Skelton's two thousand dollar a week

RKO salary for twelve weeks, twice the amount he earned from his stage work, briefly gave the Skeltons some financial freedom. This enabled the workaholic couple to do the unthinkable—take a vacation. Thus, shortly before Thanksgiving of 1937, Skelton sent a postcard to Stout, "I'm down in Mexico trying to throw the bull!"[17] Besides being yet another example of the comedian's weakness for bad puns (à la "shooting the bull") and a general reference to Mexico's love affair with bullfighting, the phrase "trying to throw the bull" had a Vincennes connection, as well. Back in 1929, when Skelton was not quite sixteen, he had played a Mexican señorita in a comedy sketch for his hometown YMCA circus. The routine involved a comic confrontation between the in-drag Skelton and a pair of actors in a bull costume.[18]

Another immediate positive that came out of the film experience was the added confidence it brought to Skelton's stage presence. In February 1938 the critic for the *Cleveland Plain Dealer* made the following assessment of the comedian's stage act: "Skelton's recent trip to Hollywood ... was apparently a valuable educational experience. The young doughnut dunking champion ... has improved at least 60 percent. He displays much more assurance ... [and] times his daffy quips more expertly."[19]

Of course, added confidence can sometimes lead to new creative enterprises that do not pan out. After not making any professional miscues in breakout 1937, the Skeltons overextended themselves by putting together their own vaudeville troupe in early 1938. This involved an East Coast orchestra (Enoch Light), sixteen chorus girls, and five different acts. Unfortunately, according to one of the Skeltons' letters to Stout and his wife, Inez, the troupe immediately ran into booking problems: "you see we have some contracts for Red alone which still must be played out and those particular dates can't afford to buy the whole show—so our manager is trying to book the show in two and three day stands (to keep them all together) while we finish up his old contracts."[20]

Ironically, even when the Skelton troupe hit its critical and commercial stride in 1938, there were still problems. In Skelton's later (1941) serialized *Milwaukee Journal* autobiography, the comedian stated, "We broke house records everywhere and lost about $1,500 a week. It was all very thrilling to me but one day Edna sharpened up her pencil and said: 'We've dropped $5,000 in three weeks. We spent too much. Breaking box office marks and losing money proves we're in the wrong end of the business. We quit.' We did."[21]

Skelton's career roller-coaster ride returned to solid ground with a series of late 1938 radio bookings on country singer Red Foley's *Avalon Variety* program. Skelton's rustic humor, especially as personified by an early version of the comedian's Clem Kadiddlehopper, meshed so effectively with Foley's country format that Skelton soon became a regular on the show. Given Skelton's radio experience with Rudy Vallee, the comedian felt better prepared in tailoring his material to a *listening* audience.

In a later oral history for the New York Public Library, the comedian explained the process. On the first Vallee program he had attempted a radio version of his famed donut routine. But while the studio audience loved it, Skelton felt the listeners at home were disappointed. Consequently, by the second Vallee broadcast Skelton attempted "picture-oriented jokes," such as, "[A] lady says to her little boy, 'You pulling that cat's tail?' 'No, I'm not pulling the cat's tail. I'm holding on. He's doing the pulling.' Well, you know, that's a picture. The people can picture this. So that's how I established all my jokes on radio."[22]

Interestingly, this classic pulling the cat's tail bit was later used verbatim for his Junior character (the "mean widdle kid"), on both the comedian's next radio program, the *Red Skelton Show* (1941–53), and his similarly titled television series. A bratty child seemed especially appropriate for an imaginative radio audience. At this point in Skelton's career, he believed his strongest radio character was his early take on Kadiddlehopper. Noting that he always did radio jokes that "the audience could see," Skelton added, "That's why they liked Clem. They could see this idiot. [Then going into Clem character, the comedian began the sing-song patter that might be entitled Clem's theme:] 'Du-du-du du-du-du.'"[23]

The positives coming by way of Skelton's association with the *Avalon Variety* program quickly mushroomed. As late as December 1938 Skelton was merely an impromptu featured guest. In fact, according to a telegram to the Stouts at this time, a last-minute booking on the program necessitated canceling an early Christmas visit to Vincennes: "Will be on Avalon Cigarette program Saturday night, seven [o'clock, broadcast out] of Cincinnati. This spoils our [planned] visit but we still love you."[24] Yet by early 1939, Skelton had reached nearly costar status with Foley on the program. And after the country singer refused to leave Cincinnati when the program moved to Chicago in March of that year, Skelton essentially inherited the show. Though his ratings for the rest of the season were only so-so, he was competitive with other veteran broadcasts, such as Robert Benchley's *Old Gold Program*, the *Jack Haley Program*, and George Jessel's *For Men Only*.[25] Most important for Skelton, he had a nationally broadcast show.

Coming back full circle to the Stillwell quote that opens this chapter, Skelton seemed to do his best the second time he attempted something. Dissecting this observation further, his wife and head writer for both the *Avalon* program and the comedian's more celebrated 1940s radio series felt this meant that her husband was "somebody who has to be happy [or comfortable] to be a success."[26] The *Avalon* show was a Skelton shakedown cruise for the hit radio program he had in the 1940s.

Stillwell was a resiliently upbeat populist at heart, which could be capsulated in her expression, "everything usually happens for the best."[27] One might apply that philosophy more specifically to the *Avalon* program in two ways. First, in a big-picture perspective, *Avalon* not only allowed her husband to get used to his own coast-to-coast program, it also provided her with a tutorial on writing and producing such a broadcast. By the time of Skelton's next radio series, Stillwell exercised an amazing amount of control on both the program and other writers' access to her husband/star.

Second, applying her "for the best" philosophy to a more personal take on the sudden significant emergence of *Avalon* in their lives, canceling their Christmas stopover in Vincennes resulted in a February 19, 1939, visit that became a celebratory return for the prodigal entertainer. Feted by the town fathers, the comedian also brought his vaudeville troupe to the local Pantheon Theatre for five shows. And it had become a regional media event even before that Sunday, from Skelton periodically noting the forthcoming return on his *Avalon* program, to front-page coverage in the local newspapers, such as the *Vincennes Post* headline: "City Prepares Homecoming for 'Red' Skelton."[28]

While the broad local print coverage of the event offers a wealth of information, one can see the community pride simply in the newspaper headlines, from the *Vincennes Sun-Commercial's* "City Greets Red Skelton, Famous Entertainer At Reception Sunday, Civic Dinner Monday," to the *Post's* "Vincennes Takes Delight In Honoring Popular 'Red' Skelton."[29] Moreover, as yet another local article noted, "'Red's' coming to Vincennes has been one of the most talked about attractions that the Pantheon has had."[30]

Fittingly, Skelton and Stillwell stayed at the Vincennes home of early mentor Stout. The Stouts had joined much of the town in meeting the couple at the local train depot that Sunday morning as the couple came in from Cincinnati (still the site of the *Avalon* program). While there were nonstop activities for the next two days, ranging from performances to civic honors (including Skelton being made an honorary Vincennes fire chief and a member of the Junior Chamber of Commerce), the Stout home was a meeting place for a steady stream of Skelton friends, fans, and relatives. The *Vincennes Post* chronicled the first night's happy gathering: "This jolly group enjoyed dinner and the air was blue with talk of 'old-timers.'"[31]

The most pivotal Skelton relatives on hand included his grandmother, Susan Fields, who often played babysitter for young Red when his widowed adoptive mother was at work, and the comedian's brother, Paul Skelton. Of Skelton's three older brothers, Red was closest in age and temperament to the piano-playing Paul. Neither the comedian's siblings nor his mother still lived in Vincennes. But Skelton remained fiercely loyal to family, regularly sending money to his only surviving parent (Ida Mae Skelton) and having his brothers manage various Midwest businesses in which he had invested. By 1941 these included both a small bakery chain and a dry-cleaning chain. Red, ever the superstitious and/or pessimistic performer, was allegedly using the investments as a safety valve. That is, according to a period piece in the *New York Times*, he felt "if things ever get tough out in Hollywood it won't be a case of being 'back home and broke.'"[32]

As is befitting of all heroes, whether historical or contemporary, Skelton's honored-son status provoked many testimonials. One would have been right at home in Carl Sandburg's epic mythic-making biography of Abraham Lincoln, as it involved Skelton's honesty and work ethic as an employee at Theodore Charles's Moon Theatre. Besides being an usher, the future comedian was responsible for cleaning. While addressing these latter duties, the youngster had found a box-office sack of coins under a back step in the theater. (A small-town movie ticket for a child then cost no more than ten cents.) Some time before Charles had placed the bag in this natural hideaway and promptly forgotten about it. The comic paradox of the story, however, was that while the businessman was touched by Skelton's honesty (especially given Skelton's impoverished background), he was more impressed that the boy was the only worker whose thoroughness in cleaning had uncovered this secret cubbyhole. The same issue of the *Post* that included this "feel good" story on the front page also boasted a greeting advertisement to Sketon from the Moon Theatre owner and his wife, accompanied by a Skelton picture, with the following caption: "RED, WE WELCOME YOU BACK HOME! Mr. & Mrs. Theodore CHARLES."[33]

The manager of the Pantheon Theatre, Adler Lyons, the Moon's much larger rival, assumed a more wryly comic position on the visiting comedian, since Skelton and his road show were *not* appearing gratis at the Pantheon: "I have thrown that boy out of the theatre at least 3,000 times and now I'm paying him money to come back."[34] As noted earlier, Skelton had always been very forthright about his money-making schemes. And this paying Pantheon booking, during the comedian's homecoming, definitely demonstrates another example of Skelton's moxie about money. (This tendency was undoubtedly further reinforced by his wife's often shrewd financial abilities.)

Regardless, if there were a metaphorical Rosetta Stone on Skelton discovered by some comedy archeologist it would be that all stories eventually lead to pathos. Thus, once one gets by the cockeyed compliment nature of Lyons's comments on Skelton, the Pantheon manager reveals an underlying mournfulness to his tale about the comedian. Those "3,000 times" Lyons tossed Skelton out of the theater were *not* about punishing a poor kid for sneaking into the movies: "It was a regular nightly duty for months to be sure 'Red' had left the premises before closing up after the last show to make sure he wouldn't get locked in all night."[35] I later asked the comedian about this statement, Lyons's irony laced with pathos. I wanted to know if it meant the sheer magnetism of the theater was responsible for holding him, or if he hid there simply because it was a warm sanctuary during winter months when his home was a cold, drafty rental shack.[36] Unfortunately, I never really got a straight answer. Skelton had a way of ignoring a question he did not like. And while he had often expressed his love of *any* theater setting, I also believe that the then luxurious Pantheon would have been preferable to an attic bed where he often awoke to find snow on his quilt. But to tell me that would probably, in Skelton's mind, somehow reflect badly upon his beloved, overworked adoptive mother. Of course, biography, unlike a detective story, is a genre where one has to sometime live without exact answers.

Along more amusing lines, one could argue that Skelton's noteworthy Vincennes visit produced a second star—Stillwell. Sifting through period press coverage I was reminded of President John F. Kennedy's (1961) tongue-in-cheek comment about being eclipsed by his beautiful wife on a state visit to France: "I am the man who accompanied Jacqueline Kennedy to Paris and I have enjoyed it." Skelton had inadvertently encouraged Stillwell's elevated status by her more prominent position in the act when they had both been guests on Vallee's radio program a few months earlier. Then add the fact that Stillwell was an extremely attractive, leggy blonde, whose physical attributes were showcased in a provocative publicity pose that ran in the *Post* on the day of the couple's arrival, and one has another reason for all the local interest in her.[37] Indeed, Skelton's secondary placement in said picture suggested that Stillwell was the star and he was the stooge. Her sex appeal is also implied in a visit the couple made to a journalism class at Vincennes's Lincoln High School. When Skelton asked the students what they would most "like to know," the "unanimous answer" was: "We would like to know how you met your wife." Appropriately, even the front page *Vincennes Sun-Commercial* article covering this academic stop has a slightly suggestive title, "Red Goes Back to School, but Not to Study."[38]

Befitting Stillwell's status as Skelton's writer, she was not just another pretty face. She was quick to respond verbally to comic situations. For instance, on one of Skelton's radio broadcasts he claimed to have last left Vincennes barefoot. Consequently, among the gifts that the comedian received from the town fathers were "a pair of very serviceable though hardly becoming ... shoes." While a surprised Skelton looked on, Stillwell responded, "He'll wear them to his next [radio] broadcast."[39] The *Post* undoubtedly spoke for most of the comedian's hometown when it observed that "Mrs. Skelton was practically a 'native daughter' by the time she said her 'good-byes.' Vincennes warmed immediately to her gracious and cultured charms. All agree she was the girl for 'our boy.'"[40]

While Skelton's vagabond vaudevillian lifestyle had kept the comedian away from Vincennes for years, the special homecoming celebration and his steady radio work in Chicago changed all that. When Stillwell wrote a lengthy thank-you letter to the Stouts following the Skeltons' triumphant visit, she promised they would make regular pilgrimages back—a fact that is borne out by later press coverage. The same correspondence hinted at a modest degree of normalcy made possible by the *Avalon* show: "We are going to have a lot of our stuff brought on from the coast [California]—such as, our dog, car, books and a lot of other knickknacks. I think they would be nice for Red—he misses the dog so."[41]

Biographer Hermione Lee feels that the greatest challenge to a profiler is "trying to see the life and the work as part of a total pattern."[42] But for Skelton the man-child, equating work with play was the only pattern in which the comedian felt comfortable. Like a hungry man going after a waffle, the long deprived young comedian embraced life and entertaining as fully as possible. Since, according to Stillwell, Skelton was "allergic to rest and quiet," she often channeled his high energy into a mutual drive to succeed.[43] For the eternally optimistic couple, the vast world of entertainment was as simple and straightforward as the alphabet, with just as many possibilities. When Skelton was not contracted for a second season on *Avalon* (where the new rustic comedian was Cliff Arquette, later famous for his Charley Weaver character), Skelton successfully returned to what was sometimes called "new vaudeville"—stage show support of first-run feature films.

Though Skelton's notices were again strong, he was not immune to rough spots, most specifically, the forced retirement of his signature donut sketch. He had been doing the routine for three years, and a *Variety* review of a September 1939 engagement in Chicago voiced a common complaint: "The disappointment is Skelton, with this moth-eaten vaud routine. The donut dunking bit, which used to get laughs, failed to connect at all with [the] audience."[44]

Once again, however, it was Stillwell to the rescue. By early 1940 she had fashioned a new routine that became more synonymous with Skelton than the donut sketch. Now famous as the "Guzzler's Gin" routine, the bit has Skelton parodying a television announcer doing a gin commercial. (New York City's 1939 World's Fair had made the "new" technology of television a hot topic.) With each commercial break, Skelton's announcer downs a generous portion of the product, getting progressively more drunk. Best showcased in the *Ziegfeld Follies* (1946), Skelton also periodically performed the sketch on his long-running television program. His original pitch for the gin had him claiming, "No bad aftertaste, no upsetting of the nerves. Just a nice, smooth drink." But as Skelton's character gets ever more entertainingly hammered, the advertising copy is eventually reduced to the single drawn-out word: "Smoooooooooooooth!" To this day it remains the most diverting of routines, as well as being a special favorite among my college students when I lecture on personality comedians.

Although Arthur Marx's biography of Skelton makes a case for the sketch having been lifted from Fred Allen's radio show, that two-person routine involved an announcer being coached by a radio director.[45] Skelton's commercial spoof was strictly solo, interspersed with the comedian doubling as the program's featured talent, an amusing professorial poet. That is, when Skelton was not getting ever more looped pitching and sampling the gin, his poet was reciting such "weighty" verse as: "I bought my girl some garters; bought at the five and ten; she gave them to her mother; that's the last I'll see of them."

What is more, the Allen radio routine was strictly a verbal bit, while Skelton's sketch is inspiringly embellished with Stillwell's patented pantomime, which has become Skelton's greatest legacy. (That is why Skelton is playing a television announcer.) This verbal shtick involves everything from the comedian gradually assuming the general demeanor of a drunk to the amusing problems he has with props, such as the coat sleeve that swallows his arm. If Stillwell's routine is stolen, then someone might claim Lucille Ball's revered "Vitameatavegamin" sketch is lifted, too. Part of the *I Love Lucy* episode "Lucy Does a TV Commercial" (first broadcast May 5, 1952), the Vitameatavegamin bit had the comedienne getting increasingly inebriated as she rehearses and samples an alcohol-laced vitamin product. Paradoxically, of these three drinking routines, Ball's take is by far the most famous. Maybe the secret is not being first but most frequent, through syndication *I Love Lucy* has been on continuously for more than half a century.

Fueled in part by "Guzzler's Gin," Skelton's stage notices in 1940 approached the sterling reviews immediately following the American introduction of the donut sketch in 1937. For example, here is *Variety*'s take on the comedian's appearance at New York City's Paramount

Skelton doing his "Guzzler's Gin" routine (circa 1941).

Theatre, emceeing a bill that also featured Frank Sinatra: "Red Skelton clicks mightily with various takeoffs, from the opening 'pigeon-toed jitterbug' … to his finale 'television announcer' interlude. Latter is a howl all the way … Gets progressively drunk as the commercials come and go, and at the end is paralyzed [drunk]. Audience eats it up."[46]

Earlier in 1940 Skelton scored critical success as the emcee of a birthday party/infantile paralysis charity ball on behalf of President Franklin D. Roosevelt in the nation's capital. According to the *Washington Post*, this particular installment of the annual White House-sponsored bash drew twenty thousand people, with an army of entertainment celebrities motoring among celebrations at eight area hotels and two movie theatres.[47] While Skelton's favored status with Roosevelt had made the comedian a regular at these gatherings since the late 1930s, this festivity paid special Hollywood dividends for Skelton.

Skelton's Washington, D.C., emcee duties had him interacting with a who's who of movie stars, including America's top box-office favorite of 1939, Mickey Rooney, a position he retained through 1941.[48] Rooney was equally popular with the president, especially after his affectionately comic impersonation of Roosevelt in MGM's *Babes in Arms* (1939, with Judy Garland). Thus, Skelton and Rooney's paths kept crossing during the charity activities of 1940, and the young actor was impressed with Skelton's casual comedy style, such as Skelton interrupting a White House birthday toast with the warning, "Careful what you drink, Mr. President. I once got rolled in a joint like this."[49] (Besides charming Roosevelt, the line was a favorite with Skelton, too. Years later, when I repeated it during a keynote address honoring the comedian, Skelton smilingly nodded, as if to imply, "I can't believe I was brash enough to say that."[50]) Consequently, according to Skelton, Rooney promptly told his MGM studio boss, Louis B. Mayer, "There's a guy [Skelton] at the White House, funny as can be. You ought to get him."[51]

Normally, the recommendation of a box-office favorite such as Rooney would be more than enough to give Skelton a second chance at Hollywood, especially with Mayer having almost a father-son relationship with Rooney. But Skelton also had another filmland insider who was a fervent fan, the tempestuous, temperamental Mexican dancer/actress/singer Lupe Velez. A former nightclub performer who broke into movies as an exotic addition to Laurel and Hardy's short subject *Sailors Beware* (1927), Velez soon heated up the screen as Douglas Fairbanks Sr.'s leading lady in *The Gaucho* (1927). Her intermittent screen career in the 1930s was often overshadowed by a stormy marriage to Tarzan star Johnny Weissmuller, with their public quarrels often spilling over into the scandal sheets. The title of one of her later popular pictures, *Mexican Spitfire* (1940), perfectly captures her persona for period fans.

So, how does Velez connect to Skelton? And what kind of clout would she have in Hollywood, since she was not in a box-office league with Rooney? The "Mexican Spitfire" costarred with Skelton for part of his April 1940 booking at New York City's Paramount Theatre. Skelton's comedy impressed Velez, especially when his stooging for her helped flesh out a thin act, or, as *Variety* put it, "[Velez's] informality [is] making it appear that she lacks an act. That's true enough but she overcomes it pretty well on sheer vivacity and personality."[52] Skelton later observed, "She was going with [two-time Oscar-winning MGM director] Frank Borzage at the time. She got him on the phone and she says, 'There's a guy here that looks like a turkey [with his red hair]. You got to put him in a movie.'"[53]

With such strong support from Velez and Rooney, Skelton shot an MGM screen test later that spring with Borzage overseeing the production. The test might have been labeled "Red's Greatest Hits," since it included everything of note in his repertoire, from his career-making donut-dunking sketch to the comedian's then new "Guzzler's Gin" routine. But Borzage was a tough audience, despite the production crew being bowled over by Skelton's broad comedy. The director wanted something different, edgier. This was the catalyst for a demonstration of yet another facet of the brilliant Skelton-Stillwell partnership. When comedy brainstorming, she had the ability to endlessly pitch ever-more inventive sketch ideas to her husband. His gift was to zero in on a rich suggestion and create something memorable.

Though Skelton never complained publicly about Lucille Ball's "Vitameatavegamin" 1952 television sketch, he was unhappy about how closely it mirrored his "Guzzler's Gin" routine.

With Borzage, however, they worked this game as if Stillwell's many pitches were actually old bits of theirs. But in fact, she was merely trolling for something groundbreakingly different with which to inspire her husband's ad-libbing abilities. She hit a home run with her suggestion that Skelton do his parody of how various film heroes die. Pretending to be merely reminding her husband, she then sketched out some basic scenarios using James Cagney, Errol Flynn, Lionel Barrymore, and others. Given this instant outline, the amazing Skelton ad-libbed himself into a movie career.

For Borzage and everyone else who saw Skelton's test, the dying heroes routine was the best bit in the film. Skelton's MGM compilation proved so popular with various studio insiders, it was soon called "The busiest strip of film in the whole film capital."[54] Plus, this never-intended-for-release test later prompted the tellingly titled article, "Skelton Out of the Closet: Red Skelton's Film Masterpiece Has Never

Skelton later costarred with Mickey Rooney in Thousands Cheer *(1943, with Virginia O'Brien).*

Grossed a Dollar."[55] MGM signed the young comic, and his first movie for the studio, *Flight Command* (1940), was directed by Borzage.

Marx's biography of Skelton adds controversy to the comedian's second shot at Hollywood by suggesting Velez's recommendation might have been sexually driven. The claim is that she was having an affair with the comedian during their joint appearance at New York's Paramount Theatre.[56] Marx's evidence is sketchy at best, though Velez was infamous for bedding anything in pants. While such an indiscretion might have occurred, especially since the Skeltons divorced in 1943, Marx's claim that the dalliance occurred in the actress's dressing room, between stage shows, is most unlikely. During the comedian's working hours, even in the early years after the Skeltons' divorce, the then very insecure Skelton always wanted the still manager/writer Stillwell nearby. Moreover, at the time of the alleged affair, Skelton's wife had become a high-profile part of their stage act, too—guaranteeing that she would be ever present. An example of this added visibility can be found in the aforementioned positive Paramount review of Velez, which also noted, "[Skelton's] Best bit finds Edna Stillwell, credited as his writer, also stooging for him in a magic sequence. Miss Stillwell, incidentally, has quite a personality of her own."[57] Even when the Skeltons traveled west in the summer of 1940 to shoot his MGM screen test, the comedian was so nervous and superstitious that he insisted his wife also be included in the film. Strangely enough, the normally gossipy Marx missed a provocative coincidence in his circumstantial scenario about an affair between Skelton and Velez—Stillwell and Borzage later had a real romance. Briefly married, their union ultimately failed because Stillwell was still so involved in managing her former husband's career. Interestingly, one could rightly argue that Skelton's alleged involvement with Borzage's "Mexican Spitfire" later helped fuel a relationship between the director and Stillwell.

Regardless of such conjecture, certain very definite Skelton facts exist from this period in 1940. His stage act was so popular that the comedian was setting "house records in leading cinema theaters in

New York and other cities, including Chicago and Washington."[58] Skelton's live material, which often ran long, was in such demand that movie houses in these large urban settings were forced to cut back on their short subject programs (including cartoons, newsreels, and travelogues). Although strong recommendations from Rooney and Velez undoubtedly helped make Skelton's second chance at Hollywood a possibility, MGM power brokers might have taken note of all the superlative Skelton notices from New York and other eastern outposts. After all, when one studies the Academy of Motion Picture Arts and Sciences' clipping files from the 1930s and 1940s, reviews from the many New York daily newspapers of that era clearly dominate.[59]

Naturally, barring any future revelations about the newspaper subscription habits of Mayer, this suggestion remains simply scholarly speculation. One might best end the chapter with a notice bemoaning the inevitability of Skelton's Hollywood success: "The resourceful Skelton is in his second and final week on the Earle [Washington, D.C.] stage before a Hollywood screen test. Whether he's mocking people in a drug store or kidding with amiable Edna Stillwell, 'Red' is so refreshingly pleasant a comic that it would be a shame to have the films nab him away from the variety houses."[60]

6

Major Stardom: Movies, Radio, and a Touch of "Hope"

"We're all put on earth for a purpose, and mine is to make people laugh."[1]
RED SKELTON

A popular axiom among writers is: "I became an author because books gave me such happiness." One could extrapolate a comparable maxim from this for Red Skelton—he became an entertainer because comedy gave him amazing joy. Indeed, such an insight also provides another explanation/defense for Skelton's mildly controversial habit of often laughing at his own material. Regardless, the comedian had been knocking on the door of major stardom since his breakout year of 1937.

During a late 1940 hometown visit to Vincennes, on the eve of another watershed entertainment year, there was an added confidence to his comments. Discussing his just completed supporting part in *Flight Command* (1940), Skelton told the *Vincennes Sun-Commercial*: "If light comedy is all you can do, well and good, but if you can show that your talents are more diversified and that you can play really serious roles, all the better. I am glad for the opportunity this picture has given me."[2] But before one could ask what became of our Hoosier humorist, Skelton, with amusing nonchalance, then stated to another hometown journalist, "Of course, I'm already the second-best comic … Who's first? Well, the last time I counted up, there were 29 guys claiming that position."[3]

In a third Vincennes article from this visit, the comedian's writer wife, Edna Stillwell Skelton, provided a diverting interview about their new home and lifestyle in Tarzana, California. A bemused Stillwell confessed that Skelton and a "buddy" took three weeks to build a garage that a contractor claimed was a job of "two or three days." But in fairness to her carpentry-challenged husband, she said the West Coast had not affected Skelton's hometown citizenship: "Out there they swear that he's hired by the Vincennes Chamber of Commerce. He even brags about Indiana weather—and that's a capital offense in California."[4]

Fittingly, for an entertainer later synonymous with patriotism, Skelton's aforementioned *Flight Command* was a flag-waving affair about American military preparedness, while World War II already raged in Europe. For modern viewers, the picture now seems a fairly pedestrian affair about navy flyers, especially when one factors in a melodramatic subplot involving star Robert Taylor and his commander's wife, played by Ruth Hussey. But unlike the poor reception accorded RKO's *Having Wonderful Time* (1938), *Flight Command* was a critical and commercial hit. *Film Daily* called the movie "one of the best of the 'Service' yarns turned out of the Hollywood mill to date."[5] And the headline atop the *Hollywood Reporter*'s review told the same story: "MGM's 'Flight Command' Clicks From All Angles."[6]

Skelton acquitted himself admirably in *Flight Command*, but the modesty of the part did not always merit much attention in reviews. Given his status as a popular stage star in New York, Skelton's best notices, though brief, appeared in New York newspapers. The *New York Post*'s comments were most reminiscent of the comedian's earlier hometown remarks about not being just a comedian: "Skelton's ... skirmishes with the camera, while not allowing him an opportunity to perform the vaudeville acts that have made him a famous comic, reveal that he can act."[7] In contrast, the *Brooklyn Eagle* provided a more typical take on the comic: "What little comedy there is falls to Red Skelton as a wise-cracking lieutenant."[8] The *New York Telegram* assumed a patriotic posture as it democratically included him with the picture's more prominent stars: "It's nice to know, in the end … that the Naval Air Service is manned by such clean-cut, upstanding, clear-eyed fellows as Robert Taylor and Walter Pidgeon, and even Dick Purcell and Red Skelton, who came along for comic relief."[9]

After the years of touring, landing a movie contract allowed the Skeltons to really put down roots at their Tarzana home in the San Fernando Valley. Combining their two first names, the couple comically christened their place "Redna Rancho." It soon became a depository for the comedian's many eclectic collections, which included photography equipment, electric trains, autograph books, police badges, and various real guns. And this says nothing about an ever-growing collection of live dogs. By 1942 Edna observed, "One more [dog] and we'll be able to get a kennel license."[10]

After *Flight Command*, Skelton's next MGM assignment was another supporting role in the B movie *The People vs. Dr. Kildare* (1941). Though this was the most prestigious of all the Hollywood studios, famous for its tag line, "More stars than in the heavens," MGM's greatest regular source of income came from its popular B-movie series, such as the Doctor Kildare films. Though not quite in a league with the studio's phenomenally profitable Andy Hardy series (with Mickey Rooney as the title character), the Kildare movies had a large loyal following. The basic formula for the Kildare series had an earnest young Lew Ayres as the title character, with veteran Lionel Barrymore as an entertainingly curmudgeon mentor. Consequently, giving Skelton a chance to play comic relief in *The People vs. Dr. Kildare*, however small his hospital intern part, was a great opportunity for a young screen comedian.

One could liken B movies to the upper echelons of baseball's minor leagues—a place to get an actor ready for the majors. For example, at the same time MGM was grooming Skelton for better things, it was also promoting Skelton's vaudeville comic friend, "Rags" Ragland, who soon costarred with the Hoosier in several films. What follows is the *Hollywood Reporter*'s period take on that preparation: "To familiarize him with work before the camera, MGM has assigned 'Rags' Ragland to a small role in 'Ringside Maisie.' After that brief bow, he goes into a top comedy role in MGM's 'Honky Tonk,' Clark Gable-Lana Turner feature."[11] Shortly after Skelton's supporting appearance in *The People vs. Dr. Kildare*, the *Hollywood Reporter* printed an abbreviated version of the Ragland slant for Skelton: "MGM spotlights Red Skelton in its newest 'Dr. Kildare' film as part of his star build-up there."[12]

Despite being well into the series, *The People* was another affectionately received hit. The *New York Daily News's* Wanda Hale said, "The Kildare pictures are like grandma's pies. They never fail. It is gratifying that the latest [installment] on view at the Criterion Theatre keeps up the good work established in the beginning and sustained throughout the series."[13] Ironically, the *Hollywood Reporter* found Skelton and fellow comic Eddie Acuff too funny for a serious series: "[The screenwriters] give quite a bit of [comic] business to Red Skelton and Eddie Acuff as interns who replace the ambulance driver formerly played by Nat Pendleton. This is in addition to the laugh lines assigned … [series regulars]. It is a little too much fun for a well-managed hospital."[14] Once again, leave it to an East Coast critic to give Skelton unadulterated praise for *The People*. The *Baltimore Evening Sun's* Gilbert Kanour, who had been a fan of Skelton's many acclaimed stage appearances at nearby Washington, D.C.'s Capitol Theatre, stated, "Red Skelton again shows that he is one of the screen's up-and-coming clowns."[15]

The "up-and-coming" assessment reflected the thinking of MGM, too. But the young Hoosier, who was twenty-seven when he shot *The People*, also had a way of innocently exasperating studio chief Louis B. Mayer. Most incomprehensible to Mayer was Skelton's refusal to talk on the phone. The comedian was somehow disoriented by a disembodied voice coming out of the receiver. Even after Mayer realized this new contract player had not suddenly "gone Hollywood" on him, something the MGM boss had frequently seen in his long studio tenure, the older man struggled with Skelton's telephonophobia. Mayer, a bear for common sense, finally vented, "Well—but—God dammit—if you don't answer the phone how do you get any business done?"

"That's what Edna's for," Skelton answered.

Of course, debater-at-heart Mayer was not derailed by this goofy answer. Sensing a basic weakness in Skelton's response, the Hollywood veteran asked, "Young man, just let me ask you one more question. Who answered the telephone before you met Edna?"

An embarrassed but innocently honest Skelton then paid his writer/wife the ultimate compliment: "Before I met Edna, no one ever called me."[16] For once, Mayer was speechless.

Another Skelton bugaboo for the MGM chief was a more normal problem—he wanted his new comedian to lose weight. Just as RKO had put Skelton on a diet prior to shooting *Having Wonderful Time*, during the heyday of his donut-dunking (and eating) period, Skelton had again gained thirty-plus pounds. While one could still blame the donut sketch, which Skelton had pulled out of retirement to perform as part of his act at the then mushrooming number of California military bases, a bigger culprit was simply Skelton's poor eating habits. Growing up in southern Indiana's Vincennes, close to the Kentucky border, meant Skelton relished such tasty, but rich, Southern dishes as fried chicken, fried potatoes, pork chops, grits, biscuits and gravy, and so on. Plus, what is more common than a formerly impoverished individual putting on weight once his metaphorical ship has come in?

Granted, the Skeltons had become very familiar with success before this second chance at Hollywood, however, in contrast to their former hectic "new vaudeville" multiple-shows-each-day schedule, the couple's initial relocation to the film capital involved a great deal of free time. If this were not enough to contribute to a weight gain, the couple also did a great deal of socializing in the early 1940s. By the 1950s Skelton became almost reclusive, but in the comedian's Hollywood beginnings there was lots of partying and nightclubbing.

An all-purpose film factory such as MGM had a simple answer for fat—the studio gym. Thus, Skelton lost *some* weight. But playing the "wise fool" in real life, Skelton had another easier way to seemingly drop pounds. The comedian bought pricey, slightly oversized clothing. Then, when the powers that be would ask about his dieting/exercising,

Skelton quickly showed off the baggy pants and roomy sports jacket. It was an effective scam, because Skelton, the perennial huckster, later told me he was still getting away with this oversized clothing routine in the late 1940s.[17] But the comedian never warmed to working out. Here is one of Skelton's favorite jokes from late in life: "I get plenty of exercise carrying the coffins of my friends who exercise."

As a footnote to why Skelton eventually veered from being a party person to a recluse, beyond a later marriage and children, was that Skelton soon tired of the always "on" one-upmanship practiced by entertainers. Moreover, Skelton felt this lack of sincerity was especially strong among comedians. Eventually, he divorced himself from hanging out with fellow funnymen. Interestingly, a period joke on the subject survives from another midwestern family-orientated comedian such as Skelton, Joe E. Brown. What further connects the joke's heartland humanism to Skelton and Indiana is that Brown chose to tell it to an Indianapolis audience while on tour with the play *Harvey*. His setup for the story involved four film comedians who met regularly, but their conversation was simply an excuse to try to top each other. Brown then stated: "Mostly, they didn't listen to what anyone [else] was saying, for they were so intent on what they were going to say next. Anyway, one day one of them finished a story, there was automatic laughter and another said, 'You may wonder why I'm so quiet, but today I had news that has just about knocked me out. My father and I were very close. We corresponded regularly until I came out here and then I sort of drifted away. Today I heard—he died last night.' The man paused for a second, and immediately another comic burst in with, 'If you think that's funny, listen to this.'"[18]

While Skelton's shrinking from comedians was still a few years off in the early 1940s, the huge success of what is sometimes listed as his next vehicle, a star turn in *Whistling in the Dark* (1941), made him the envy of screen clowns everywhere. To clarify, the film industry then was still many years away from a movie opening simultaneously across the country. Regardless of when a 1940s picture premiered on the East or West Coast, it routinely took *months* to reach small-town markets.

Consequently, filmographies from this era are often dated from when a movie opened in the country's most important market—New York City. (The *Hollywood Reporter* even regularly ran capsule reviews from the then many New York daily newspapers.)

In 1941 Skelton appeared in three pictures: *Lady Be Good, Dr. Kildare's Wedding Day*, and *Whistling*, which was also the order in which they were shot.[19] *Lady* was an A production musical comedy orchestrated by the legendary lyricist/producer Arthur Freed (including *Singing in the Rain*, 1952), with Skelton in support. *Wedding* was yet another installment of the Kildare series, and this time Skelton's comic relief intern had more to do. But long before either *Lady* or *Day* was ready for release, MGM was so impressed with the young comedian that it decided to star him in *Whistling*—what might be labeled a B+ feature. The studio was not shy about this epiphany moment, either. The story made the front page of the *Hollywood Reporter*, under the headline "Skelton 'Whistling' First MGM Break."[20] Then, with the impressive slam-dunk completion of *Whistling*, the studio leapfrogged the movie past *Lady* and *Day* to open first in pivotal New York.

So what is this pivotal picture all about? *Whistling* is a comedy thriller, inspired by two like-minded Bob Hope hits for Paramount (*The Cat and the Canary*, 1939, and *The Ghost Breakers*, 1940), and had Skelton playing a radio murder mystery expert kidnapped by real killers. The leader of a fake religious cult (Conrad Veidt, the eerie somnambulist from the German Expressionistic classic *The Cabinet of Dr. Caligari*, 1919) needs a perfect scenario for a murder his organization is about to commit. Naturally, Skelton's underdog character is elected for the job.

The headquarters for the cult is a spooky old mansion with sliding panels, secret passageways, and a creepy housekeeper—the same haunted-house scenario used in the aforementioned Hope pictures. This means that the formula upon which both Hope and Skelton rose to film stardom was clown comedy meets parody, spoofing a mystery thriller setting. Initially, this might not seem so earth shattering. After all, personality comedians and parody were not, even then, a new movie mix. Be it cross-eyed comic Ben Turpin spoofing sexy Latin-lover Rudolph Valentino in the pun-titled *The Shriek of Araby* (1923), or Stan Laurel and Oliver Hardy having trouble *Way Out West* (1937), clowns and parody were an established happy equation. But what made the Hope and Skelton variations something different was their new type of hyphenated hero, one who could fluctuate between the most cowardly incompetent of comic antiheroes and cool, egotistical wise guy. Or, to comically paraphrase, they can talk the talk but they almost always trip on the walk.

If this dual personae sounds familiar, Woody Allen, the greatest film comedy auteur of the modern era (post-1960), has also affectionately highjacked the Hope dual personality persona. Allen freely admitted this in his cinematic tribute to Hope, *My Favorite Comedian* (1979): "There are certain moments in his older movies when I think he's the best thing I have ever seen … [But] it's hard to tell when I do [him], because I'm so unlike him physically and in tone of voice, but once you know I do it, it's absolutely unmistakable."[21] Along similar lines, Skelton was also a huge Hope fan. As late as 1948, *Photoplay* critic Maxine Arnold stated, "[Skelton] laughs so loud at Bob Hope's pictures that those around him suspect him of faking it."[22]

Unlike the undersized goofy-looking glasses character to which Allen alludes, both Skelton and Hope had the typical good looks of a leading man—that is, when they were not comically contorting said features. This fact actually assists the duality of the antihero/smart-aleck persona. The viewer more readily accepts the witty repartee of what appears to be a handsome hero. Conversely, when the Hope or Skelton character then suddenly metamorphoses into a cowardly antihero, the comedy payoff is again greater, because one expects the typical leading man to stoically soldier through whatever movie misfortune occurs.

Credit for this unique evolution of a still very modern comedy character (such as Owen Wilson's cowardly cowboy in *Shanghai Noon*, 2000) clearly belongs to Hope. But with Skelton's persona already predisposed towards being an antihero/smart aleck anyway, and because MGM placed him in the Hope-like *Whistling in the Dark* so closely

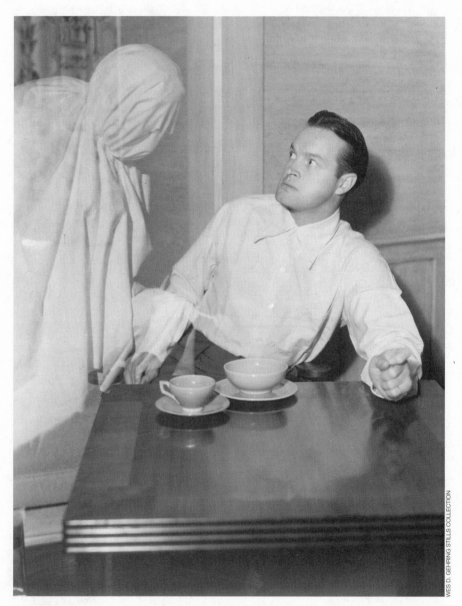

Bob Hope and an unwanted guest in Ghost Breakers *(1940).*

A poster advertising Skelton's star-making film Whistling in the Dark *(1941).*

after the ski-slope nosed comedian's screen ascendancy, Skelton's movie
future as a star was all but assured. The studio irony here is that during
Hollywood's golden age (the 1930s and 1940s), MGM was hardly the
best place to be a comedian. Indeed, the studio was actually better at
derailing the careers of funnymen. For example, when MGM took away
Buster Keaton's creative autonomy at the start of the sound era (the late
1920s), the studio's actions contributed to self-destructive tendencies in
the legendary comedian's personal life. Paradoxically, MGM is credited
with resurrecting the Marx Brothers' screen fortunes in the mid-
1930s. But it was at a cost—the studio homogenized the team, taking
away their iconoclastic edge. Comedy connoisseurs prefer the chaos-
producing purity of their earlier Paramount pictures.[23]

Fittingly, the Hope movies from which MGM drew their *Whistling
in the Dark* model were from Paramount, too. The latter studio is where
that era's pantheon comedians W. C. Fields, the Marx Brothers, Mae
West, and Hope—with and without his "road picture" teammate Bing
Crosby—made their best films.[24] In the case of Skelton, MGM deserves
credit for successfully launching the career of a major comedy talent.
Later in the decade there were questions as to whether the studio was
fully utilizing the Hoosier's talents, but there is no doubt MGM's plan
for Skelton was brilliant.

The link to Hope, moreover, is not some analogy spun by Monday
morning academics. MGM's Hope plan for Skelton was common
knowledge in the film industry. This awareness even leaked into early
Whistling reviews. For example, here are the opening comments from
the *New York Morning Telegram* critic: "The talk is that the MGM
studios fondly believe they've discovered another Bob Hope in the
personality of a lad named Red Skelton ... it would appear that this
belief is not altogether unjustified."[25]

If MGM had had any second thoughts about the strategy of
opening *Whistling* on the East Coast, ahead of two previously
completed Skelton movies (in supporting roles), an early sneak preview
critique from the *Hollywood Reporter* alleviated any anxiety. This
film capital insider publication served notice that a special talent was

emerging. Under the review headline, "Comic Hailed as Bright New
Star," the *Reporter* also predicted happy days for the studio: "Obviously,
MGM had only one purpose … [here:] showcase in a modest package
the comedy talents of Red Skelton. So well is this objective achieved
that one look at the film should bring 'radiant' smiles to the faces of
MGM executives and all their [theater] exhibitors, 'Whistling in the
Dark' brings to light … a really comic trouper named Skelton who
needs merely a couple of good pictures to zoom right up to the top.
He's dynamite with an audience."[26]

When the New York reviews for *Whistling* validated the picture,
MGM turned loose an advertising blitz that resulted in some amusingly
supportive coverage from the *Hollywood Reporter*: "Large [New York]
ads in the gazettes [newspapers] have been proclaiming Red Skelton
as the new comedy sensation and 'Whistling in the Dark' as a riot.
Sometimes, such advertisements turn out to be slightly fanciful. This is
not one of those sometimes. Skelton IS the new comedy sensation; the
flicker [movie] IS a riot, and the reviews were NOT written by Metro's
[MGM] press department—although they might well have been."[27]

New York World Telegram reviewer, William Boehnel, an earlier fan
of Skelton's vaudeville work, waxed the most poetic about Skelton.
Under the headline, "Red Skelton Terrific in Funny Picture," Boehnel
wrote: "Meet a new star. … He's terrific, as those of you who have seen
him in stage shows probably know, because it's been a long time now
since the screen provided such a fresh, unaffected, bubbling clown."[28]
New York Mirror critic Edith Werner was amusingly complimentary
about everyone involved in the production. But by zeroing in on
Skelton *and* his director, S. Sylvan Simon, Werner was anticipating a
collaboration that produced some of the comedian's greatest pictures
(including 1948's *The Fuller Brush Man*): "Anyone who has anything
to do with 'Whistling in the Dark' can pat himself on the back.
Director Simon and star Skelton can take two pats and a pinch on
the cheek, too. For they have concocted a gusty dish with laughs and
thrills galore."[29] The *New York Times's* Bosley Crowther added, "To the

cheerfully swelling list of bright new film comedians you may add the rosy name of ... Skelton. For Metro [MGM] has really turned up an impressive young Bob Hopeful in the person of this jaunty chap."[30] As Crowther's comic reference to Hope might suggest, several newspapers played punningly with Skelton's ties to the ski-nosed funnyman, such as *PM*'s inventive title for its *Whistling* review: "Meet Red Skelton, Hope of the B's."[31] But credit the *Brooklyn Daily Eagle* with quickly moving past the seemingly obligatory pun (calling Skelton "Metro's great white Hope") to a spirited differential defense of the Hoosier: "Red Skelton isn't aping [Hope]. He had a Hope-like style long before it was profitable to be like Hope. He [Skelton] is just coming into his own, and he came the hard way."[32]

Though these complimentary and often comic *Whistling* reviews were cognizant of a comedy star being born, they were short on specific examples of content. Consequently, what follows is a *Whistling* illustration of Skelton's dual-focus personae, which fluctuates quickly from smart aleck to coward. One of the cult thugs growls at Skelton's character (Wally), "Quit stalling ... You get in my hair!"

Wally's quick response is equally gruff, "Yeah, well, I'll tell you something!"

The mobster's comeback is an even tougher, "What?"

An abruptly meek Wally submissively replies, "You could use a shampoo."

More frequently, however, Skelton's *Whistling* transformation, from wise guy to antihero, occurs in the single reading of a line. That is, he starts out bravely but dovetails into a confession of cowardice. When a woman member of the cast asks him if he is a man or a mouse, Skelton replies, "I'm a man ... but tell me if you see a cat coming." On another occasion, he seemingly comforts a female costar by observing, "To show you it's perfectly safe, I'll let you go in first." And after some broad slapstick (a comic fall down a short staircase), he breezily notes, "Don't worry about me ... because that's what I'm doing." Like a junior psychiatrist, Skelton's smart aleck/coward even coins a comedy credo grounded in amusing logic. The catalyst for this insight is a complaint from a costar about always making with the smart remarks. He replies, "If I don't crack wise, I'll crack up."

Beyond the delivery of witty lines, Skelton's breakout performance in *Whistling* is also bolstered by his propensity for physical and/or visual comedy, especially the plasticity of his clown face. Handsome in repose, a sudden metamorphosis creates numerous comedy countenances, a humor take upon a *Dr. Jekyll and Mr. Hyde* scenario. This is best illustrated by *Whistling* borrowing from Skelton's "Guzzler's Gin" vaudeville routine, where he plays a television announcer getting progressively more drunk while he samples the sales product during each live commercial break. In *Whistling*, the heavies pose as potential sponsors for Skelton's in-film radio program. Their product is a liquid vitamin drink that is heavily laced with alcohol. The response of Skelton's character exactly mirrors his reactions with "Guzzler's Gin"— involuntary comic contortions of his face and upper body, wheezing, accompanied by an eye-popping countenance, and the transformation of his voice to a throaty whisper.

This creative incorporation of bits from Skelton's stage act into *Whistling*'s story seems to have played well with the comedian's vaudeville fans. For example, in critic Wanda Hale's rave review of *Whistling* in the *New York Daily News*, she observed, "Skelton doesn't have to be introduced to New Yorkers who get around."[33] But Skelton was in such an inspired comedy zone throughout *Whistling* that newcomers to the comedian seemed equally impressed, too. The critic for New York's liberal period newspaper *PM* amusingly stated: "[Skelton] recoils from reality with the matchless horror of a man trapped in a subway ladies' room. He is strictly a find, and finding him in *Whistling in the Dark* was a pleasure."[34]

Bear in mind, the entertainment excitement generated by *Whistling* in New York was being replicated throughout the nation. This might best be demonstrated by the review from the *Washington Post*, which Stillwell included in one of her husband's scrapbooks: "Conceding something to the enthusiasm of Washington audiences over their

Skelton's gift for physical comedy is showcased in a box-and-baggage routine in Doctor Kildare's Wedding Day *(1941).*

'adopted son' in any of his merry manifestations, the rambunctious Red would be a hit in any man's theatre in 'Whistling in the Dark' ... Here in the National Capitol, where he launched his 'big time' [stage] career, a crowd that overflowed the most capacious picture theatre in town almost tore down the house."[35]

What was Skelton's response to all this New York praise? Skelton's statement managed to be comic, as well as utilize one of the city's landmarks: "Hope my head fits when I try to get back to New York through the Holland Tunnel."[36] More importantly for the comedian was MGM's response to all that hoopla over *Whistling*. By October 1941 the studio had signed Skelton to a new long-term contract, with a promise to star him in the big-budget musical comedy *DuBarry Was a Lady*, which had recently been a Broadway smash.[37] (The *DuBarry* adaptation occurred in 1943, with Skelton co-starring with another redhead, Lucille Ball.)

Ironically, according to MGM's Legal Department Records, the comedian's salary was only raised from $1,250 to $1,500 a week.[38] Moreover, this was substantially less than his RKO pay for *Having Wonderful Time* (1938)—$2,000 a week. Still, $1,500 a week was a *fortune* in 1941. In addition, there was the prestige of working for MGM—the Cadillac of Hollywood studios. Skelton was rubbing shoulders with such box-office stars as Clark Gable, Spencer Tracy, Judy Garland, and Skelton promoter Rooney. Plus, there was simple job security. As early as 1938, the comedian had seen that even the "new vaudeville" (stage shows in support of movie palace screenings) was ending. "If you are going to stay in show business, you have to go out there [Hollywood]," Skelton observed[39] Coupled with this practical side was the fact that Skelton had been flirting with film for some time now. Besides *Having Wonderful Time*, there had been periodic short subjects, often shot in New York. Occasionally promising, such as the Warner Brothers's short *Seeing Red* (1939), nothing had come of these attempted forays into film. The comedian was feeling a certain quiet desperation about the movies. But most importantly, the Skeltons were ready to settle down after years of being on the road.

The comedian's two movies whose East Coast releases had been delayed, *Lady Be Good* and *Dr. Kildare's Wedding Day*, only further bolstered Skelton's stock with MGM. Skelton's supporting player reviews were so strong they might have been lifted from his *Whistling* notices, a movie often alluded to in these critiques. This was the *New York Daily News's* take on Skelton in *Wedding*: "Skelton, recently catapulted to stardom [by *Whistling*], does some of his funny vaudeville tricks [such as a slapstick routine involving a phone booth and numerous parcels], which caused his studio to sit up and take notice."[40] And the *New York Times's* review of *Lady* stated, "Red Skelton keeps popping up at random moments to remind the audience that he is a very, very funny fellow."[41]

True to form, Skelton remained self-deprecatingly comic about his sudden emergence as a film star. Late in 1941 he confessed, "That must be somebody else, I thought, and I still think so, for, as I've often said, Edna and I came to Hollywood solely because she had a pair of slacks she wanted to wear under a mink coat."[42] Surprisingly enough, Skelton's abrupt 1941 stardom would not be limited to the movies. In October of that year he also found comparable success on radio with his own coast-to-coast NBC comedy program. The following passage from Jim Knipfel's much later comic memoir, *Slackjaw* (1999), might have been penned with the young workaholic Skelton in mind: "[His life had] become one long slapstick routine—like living a Marx Brothers movie, except without quite so many musical numbers."[43]

Skelton relished all the activity, and if truth be told, the comedian preferred radio over the movies, because he and Stillwell controlled the program. At MGM, he was merely a hired hand, albeit a well-paid one. He had, however, managed to get something by MGM. His studio contract allowed him to have a radio program *or* a television show. The former clause was standard studio fare for the time. In fact, because so many major screen clowns from this era had programs, they are now often referred to as the "radio comedians," even when discussing their movie work. *But* the television clause was something new. The small screen was years away from being considered a threat to the film

industry. Skelton's contract loophole, however, became controversial
by 1951, when his television show made its debut on NBC. By then
Hollywood was in an outright war with the new medium over viewers.
Studios routinely barred major stars from appearing on the small
screen, let alone hosting their own show.

Why was Skelton so sage about the small screen? In sifting through
a mountain of material on the comedian, there is no pat answer. One
might assume it was partly an outgrowth of his high-profile New
York stage work at the end of the 1930s. The city was then a hotbed
of interest in the new technology, and this was further fueled by New
York playing host to the 1939 World's Fair. As a further addendum,
the comedian took part in an early pioneering TV broadcast during
this period. Fittingly, his celebrated "Guzzler's Gin" routine, about a
television pitchman, dates from 1940.

One can sense Skelton's well-informed enthusiasm about television
from an early 1946 interview/article with the comedian for the *Long
Beach Press Telegram*. Noting that "television is here, and I'm trying to
learn all I can about it," he insightfully added, "Television will produce
an entirely new line of talent, just as [motion picture] talkies revised the
list of silent stars."[44] This was Skelton's wish for a future television show,
"I'd like to appear in one scene as Clem, then go through a door and
come out as Willie Lump-Lump."[45]

Of course, Skelton's affinity for television might simply be a product
of that comic axiom, "No more things should be presumed to exist
than are absolutely necessary."[46] Translation: the simplest explanation
is usually correct. Maybe Skelton the vaudevillian plainly saw the
appropriateness of television as a showcase for the variety program
format that spawned him. After all, during the early 1950s, television
was sometimes jokingly referred to as "vaudeville in a box." Regardless,
MGM's new cinema sensation was about to become a radio star, too.

What gives Skelton's triumph on radio a certain consistency with
his emergence as a movie personality was the presence again of a Hope
factor. Just as MGM saw the wisdom of applying Paramount's parody
mix of the comedy thriller and Hope's antihero/smart-aleck persona to

Skelton's *Whistling in the Dark*, NBC Radio had even more reason to accent the two comedians' connection, as the network produced both programs starring the comedians. Moreover, to maximize the link, NBC put the comedy shows back-to-back on Tuesday nights, with Hope providing the lead-in for Skelton. Besides the legitimate parallels between both comics, it was simply good business for NBC to promote the connection, given that *Radio Daily*'s annual poll shortly crowned Hope the number one comedian of the airwaves.[47]

Interestingly, the *Radio Daily* poll offered another indirect tie to the Hope-Skelton link. While Hope had won the "best comedian" title, funnyman Jack Benny had received the "best airshow" award. A popular component of Benny's program was gifted black comedian Eddie "Rochester" Anderson. Though Rochester played the valet and general man Friday, Benny was the comic antihero. Hope was a fan of their teaming, and tried to obtain Anderson to play his sidekick in *The Ghost Breakers*, the year before Skelton's radio program came to NBC. When Anderson proved unavailable, Hope used popular black comedian Willie Best in the film. Flash forward to the initial cast of Skelton's new airshow, and one finds the young black comedian "Wonderful" Smith. As with Benny playing antihero to Rochester, Smith's specialty was comically hassling Skelton, a character type handled years before by Stillwell. Radio historian John Dunning stated that Smith's spot on Skelton's program helped make him 1941's "Negro comedy find of the year."[48] Granted, Skelton's mentorship by Vincennes's Clarence Stout probably predisposed Skelton to work with black talent. But the Benny-Hope influence here seems hard to deny.

The radio reviews for Skelton's new program were very positive. *Variety*'s comments were typical: "Much more costly entertainments would have been pleased this season to have done relatively as well on their inaugural program as did Red Skelton.... It was a very enjoyable bit of comedy and music that, if able to maintain the level, should find lots of listeners."[49] Skelton managed to more than "maintain the level." The comedian's Hooper radio ratings for a typical week that season (1941–42) clobbered the competing numbers of such show business legends as Bing Crosby, Burns and Allen, Eddie Cantor, Fred Allen, Rudy Vallee, and Kate Smith.[50] The handful of stars, besides Hope, that bested Skelton are among the most notable in this golden age (1930s and 1940s) of radio: Edgar Bergen and Charlie McCarthy, Fibber McGee and Molly, Jack Benny, and Frank Morgan and Fannie Brice. Plus, Skelton was almost in a dead heat with the latter duo—the incomparable character actor Morgan (the title figure from *The Wizard of Oz*, 1939), and the multitalented Brice, whose signature character, Baby Snooks, undoubtedly influenced Skelton's Junior figure.

While the basic components of Skelton's radio program are fully fleshed out in the following chapter, suffice it to say this medium allowed him more creative control. Though there were many parallels with the Hope persona, radio (more than the movies) gave Skelton a better platform on which to differentiate himself from Hope. Most specifically, there was the growing number of Skelton characters, starting with an early variation of his seminal silly figure, Clem Kadiddlehopper. This was an area in which Hope did not even attempt to compete.

Along related lines, the senescent Skelton liked to imply that having a densely packed psyche (all those comedy characters) probably made him a little crazy, but as long as he was making money, he was safe from the people with nets! Skelton would have undoubtedly enjoyed the following story from the modern screwball classic, *America's Sweethearts* (2001). In the picture, an actor (John Cusack) on a press junket is upset that he did not receive a large luxurious suite in the hotel. Instead, Cusack simply has a small bungalow on the grounds. But when he reminds the publicist that his ex-wife costar (Catherine Zeta-Jones) has one of these grand suites, he is told she has an entourage. Cusack's Skelton-related rebuttal: "I am a paranoid schizophrenic. I am my own entourage."

Whether, however, one sees Skelton as a comedy entourage or a single multifaceted clown, the twin triumphs of 1941, MGM's *Whistling* and the NBC radio program, put him on the entertainment map. And as is still typical of American society, when major success elevates the individual to a new chapter of his life, the public is interested in his past. Consequently, a five-part autobiographical series by Skelton ran in the *Milwaukee Journal*, segments of which were picked up by newspapers across the United States.[51] While Skelton's memoir musings can sometimes become apocryphal, as has been noted earlier in the text, the main thrust of the *Journal* story was a fundamental truth: "in his most fantastic moments before the cameras, he never portrayed a story more amazing than his own."[52] Skelton's public fame soon reconfigured his private life.

7

War Year Complexities: Radio and Redefining Red's Relationship with Edna

*"Mrs. Skelton said that she could work with her husband
but could not continue living with him."*[1]
NEW YORK TIMES

Red Skelton's World War II period (1941–45) was arguably the most volatile time of his lengthy life and career. The previous chapter documented the comedian's rise to major star status via the motion picture *Whistling in the Dark* (1941), and his new radio program, the *Red Skelton Scrapbook of Satire*, or simply the *Red Skelton Show*, which made its debut in the fall of 1941. The war years were all about change for Skelton—something the comedian never handled well. This state of flux involved a divorce, a broken engagement, war service, a nervous breakdown, and a new marriage.

This chapter focuses on what, for Skelton, was his greatest 1940s creative outlet, radio, and the restructuring of the comedian's most significant and complex relationship with first wife and pivotal mentor Edna Stillwell. The added control the Skeltons exercised in radio (as opposed to the movies) made the airways a medium in which Skelton could separate himself from his comedy contemporaries. But this represented a basic irony. Given the comedian's expressive rubbery face and gift for pantomime, he was foremost a *visual* comedian. Of course, radio was full of such paradoxes. For example, one of the few radio programs to initially top Skelton's show in the ratings starred ventriloquist Edgar Bergen and his smart-aleck dummy Charlie McCarthy.

The ticket for Skelton's great success on the airwaves was tied to creative comedy characters. Before examining these figures and other basic components of Skelton's radio program, one must address a major intangible—Edna Stillwell. Thus far, the Stillwell revealed in letters and comic articles has been a sympathetic, compassionate, funny, and seemingly regular person. Yet there was a tendency to be controlling and single-mindedly driven, such as her admission in correspondence to Clarence and Inez Stout that this concentrated focus could make her appear rude.[2]

When one polls Skelton's other radio writers, however, they seem to have primarily known the darker Stillwell. Nineteen-year-old Benedict Freedman observed, "Edna wouldn't let any of the writers see each other. She resented [writer Jack] Douglas trying to assert himself and dominate Red with his ideas ... I guess because she had been the one who guided Skelton to where he was ... So the first script conference was actually the last script conference where the writers and Edna and Red all got together and made suggestions."[3] Another writer, Sol Saks, explained what then evolved: "She [Stillwell] gave you a script, and you went home and rewrote the script with your lines—the same story with your lines—handed it in. And then in two weeks you might hear your lines."[4] Besides Stillwell's own written contribution to said script, she acted as chief editor, responsible for the final copy.

These controlling workaholic tendencies also say much about a Skelton marriage that was then unraveling. But to back up to a positive: their union was forged with the goal to put him on top. Though Stillwell was definitely the master sergeant in this game plan, man-child Skelton was a willing comedy soldier. This is best demonstrated by two statements Stillwell shared in a 1942 *Silver Screen* article while the Skeltons were still a couple. The first demonstrated her drive: "One of the reasons why I married him was that he was an ambitious kid—even if he was a screwball."[5] The second observation showcases Skelton's similar motivation. The comedian had been encouraged by various people to try golf, because he worked too hard. Stillwell remembered: "But one day we were out on a course, when he paused in the middle of a swing and said, 'Mummy, do you like this? Let's go home and write gags!'"[6]

Working, performing, and traveling together as nomadic vaudevillians in the 1930s, the Skeltons were a team to reckon with, but Skelton's success at MGM essentially retired Stillwell. Granted, she still advised her husband. In fact, Skelton never agreed to a film script without his wife reading it first and giving the story her okay. The comedian then had Stillwell read the script aloud to him, then it was all downtime for her as Skelton went off to film the movie. (True to Stillwell's good instincts for her husband, she was the first to recognize just how effective he would be in *Whistling in the Dark*.)

Consequently, with the movie portion of Skelton's career minimizing Stillwell's involvement, it is no wonder that she strongly reasserted her control on Skelton's new radio program. Moreover, one could argue that as the wheels came off the marital wagon, she might have become more of a martinet in their professional relationship. Furthermore, Stillwell, and Skelton's two future wives, were each intensely protective of their "kidult" husband. What others saw as controlling, these custodial spouses saw as safeguarding, even to masochistic extremes. In a later profile of Stillwell, she was described as Skelton's "advisor, script writer and business manager—and by her own admission sometimes acted as a 'whipping boy' for temperamental outbursts. 'It's better for him to blow off steam at me than at the sponsors,' she explained."[7]

So what happened to the Skeltons' marriage? They succeeded. Stillwell had masterminded them to the top. But while she remained relentless, Skelton wanted to play. This does not justify the comedian's straying eye; it merely helps to explain the phenomenon. Of course, it was also compounded by that age-old Hollywood story—the temptations available for a young film star. Skelton, however, was not stupid. He recognized, at least in the 1940s, how vital Stillwell was to his success. She continued to orchestrate his professional life for a decade after the couple's divorce. As novelist William T. Vollman has observed, "Any decent biography is a work of drama."[8] And there was no more complex relationship in all of Skelton's long life than the one he had with Stillwell.

The dissolution of the Skeltons' marriage, however, was still in the future when Skelton's new radio program was a runaway hit during the 1941–42 season. The show's winning format underwent little change during the war years. But prior to addressing the comedian's characters of country bumpkin Clem Kadiddlehopper and the "mean widdle kid" Junior, one should note the program's important supporting cast. In addition to black comic Wonderful Smith, who acted as a Skelton antagonist, the comedian's most significant assist came from Ozzie and Harriet Nelson, today famous for their long-running television sitcom *The Adventures of Ozzie and Harriet* (1952–66), which began on radio in 1944.

Even then, the Nelsons were well-known in their own right, Ozzie as an orchestra leader and Harriet as a singer and actress who had been appearing in films since the Fred Astaire-Ginger Rogers picture *Follow the Fleet* (1936). Eventually Harriet focused on being the main vocalist for her husband's orchestra, billed under her maiden name Hilliard, which is how she was credited on the Skelton program, too. Ozzie had a talent for comic musical numbers, one of which still holds the record for the longest title of a charted song, adding to its humorous charm: "I'm Looking for a Guy Who Plays Alto and Baritone, Doubles on a Clarinet and Wears a Size 37 Suit" (1940). Such novelty numbers were an important part of Skelton's radio program from the beginning. Indeed, *Variety*'s review of the comedian's debut show offered its first detailed praise to one such comic duet by the Nelsons: "Especially cute was the parody on the song 'Good-Bye Now,' in which, first, what the departing guests really said and, second, what they would have liked to have said was sung by Ozzie Nelson and Miss Hilliard."[9]

While Ozzie occasionally surfaced in a Skelton radio sketch, Harriet was a regular. She doubled as both Clem's girlfriend, Daisy June, and as Junior's mother. Just as Skelton had worked hard as a vaudeville emcee to "sell" each act on the stage bill, he was equally supportive of his radio performers. More than thirty years later, Ozzie could still get emotional about Skelton's cheerleader tendencies. When the Nelsons performed one of their novelty numbers during the latter portion of each radio program, Skelton regularly stationed himself so the studio audience could see him "laughing uproariously." To Ozzie it said, "These people are my friends. I like them and I enjoy what they do and I hope you do, too."[10]

Besides being an inspired comedy complement to Skelton's standard shtick, the Nelsons had several factors in their favor for making Skelton's radio program. First, according to Ozzie's autobiography, the show's sponsor, Raleigh Cigarettes, was strongly behind their signing.[11] As a relatively new brand, it made marketing sense to have one's product associated with fresh *young* talent, be that Skelton or the Nelsons. Second, after frequent joint appearances at charity functions, the Skeltons and Nelsons were already friends. Third, Skelton, the perennial Hoosier booster, enjoyed the fact that Ozzie's novelty number "I'm Looking for a Guy" told a musical story set in Indiana.

A fourth and final wild-card factor in the Nelsons making the show involved their ties with comedian Joe Penner (1904–1941). Though Penner's star had faded by the time of his heart attack death at only thirty-six, he had been an entertainment sensation only a few years before. Like Skelton, he had first come to national prominence by way of guest appearances on Rudy Vallee's radio program, which was a showcase for new talent. In the autumn of 1933 Penner had his own coast-to-coast program and was the top-rated comedian after Eddie Cantor on the airways. This popularity culminated in Penner being named radio's outstanding comedian of 1934.[12] Penner's program that all-important inaugural season on the air had also featured Ozzie Nelson's orchestra, with Harriet Hilliard. Plus, Harriet had later appeared with Penner and Milton Berle in the movie *New Faces of 1937*.

Why would the Nelsons' association with Penner be important to Skelton? Early in Skelton's career he idolized Penner. And as is often the case with heroes, a young Skelton also borrowed material from Penner.

Former Great Depression-era entertainer turned Hoosier politician Paul Cooley had an entertaining story about that Penner-Skelton connection. Cooley was a close friend of Herman Lewis, the brother of Doc Lewis, Skelton's medicine-show mentor back in the 1920s. The Lewis family enjoyed keeping tabs on the star they first knew as a fresh-faced youngster. According to Doc Lewis, as reported by Cooley, "One time [during the early 1930s] in Saint Louis Red sat in a vaudeville theatre balcony and copied all of Joe Penner's act out in longhand."[13]

Besides such youthful borrowing of Penner's jokes, Skelton also seemed to assume certain mannerisms of this comic. For example, when Skelton had his breakout review in *Variety*'s "New Acts" section, the critique called him "a little Joe Penner-ish at times with [demonstrative] hands, cigar [prop], and gestures, but it doesn't spoil his work."[14] Also like Penner, Skelton was his own best audience, leading and/or pump-priming the crowd with his laughter.

More importantly, however, a central component of Penner's act quite possibly influenced Skelton's most popular radio character—Junior. For reasons hard to define, Penner's pet phrase, "Wanna buy a duck?" made him the proverbial overnight success. And he was a master at milking a line: "Wanna buy a duck? ... Well, does your brother wanna buy a duck? ... Well, if you *had* a brother, would he wanna buy a duck?"[15] Though this was his signature line, with fans across the country sending Penner every manner of duck (including real ones), the comic had a gift for coining other popular catchphrases, such as "You nah-sty man!" and "Wo-o-oe is me!" and "Don't ever DOOOO that!" The latter line would appear to anticipate Junior's famous catchphrase, "I dood it!" With this variation of a Penner bit, tied to a bratty kid (Junior), Skelton had an expression that was just as much of a national sensation as the earlier "Wanna buy a duck?"

Junior's tag line, moreover, had "legs," a show business term for staying power. Introduced on Skelton's radio program in 1941, the following year various newspapers, such as the *Los Angeles Herald Express*, borrowed the phrase to describe Colonel James Doolittle's surprise bombing raid on Tokyo, "Doolittle Dood it."[16] (Stillwell saved this headline in one of Skelton's scrapbooks, as well as a follow-up photo of the comedian posing with the "Doolittle Dood It" front page.[17]) In 1943 Skelton starred in a hit movie titled *I Dood It*. Throughout the 1940s Junior and his signature line remained Skelton's most popular radio character. Initially retired when Skelton moved to television in 1951, because it was felt seeing a middle-aged man playing a youngster would not work, the comedian soon revived Junior for the small screen.

Paradoxically, despite Skelton's Penner connection, which probably contributed to the Nelsons joining Skelton's radio family, Skelton was still frequently compared to Bob Hope. The Hope link was further encouraged by NBC, the network for both comedians, which scheduled them back-to-back on Tuesday night. Both comedians did an opening monologue that focused on topical events of the day, just as both later did on television. Though Skelton was not in a class here with Hope, no one else was, either. Still, Skelton was better than most monologists, as evidenced by the *New York Times* periodically recycling his jokes, such as the comedian's crack about four days of Los Angeles thunder storms (1944), "The Southern California housing shortage is now relieved—houseboats are the answer, firmly anchored to keep from bumping against City Hall."[18]

Following the monologue, Ozzie and Harriet performed, including comic banter between the duo and Skelton. The third and final segment of the thirty-minute program was devoted to Skelton's comedy characters. His ensemble of zanies was still evolving in the early 1940s, but the two main stars were Junior and Clem Kadiddlehopper, both of whom resurfaced on his later television show. A distant third figure in the early days of his *Red Skelton Show* was Willie Lump-Lump, a comic drunk, whose pet expression was an inebriated, "Aw, sheddap!" Borrowing from his celebrated "new vaudeville" sketch, "Guzzler's Gin," Skelton often used Ozzie as a straight man in these radio routines.

Though most comedians depend, to a certain degree, on topical material (as best exemplified by Hope), Skelton's material, whether character-driven or in his monologue, often had a more generic universal component to it. For example, here is a Skelton radio bit ostensibly about staying in shape: "The craziest things happen when you're jogging. There was a guy up ahead of me running along, so I caught up to him and [nearly out-of-breath] said: 'Jogging? Health?' He said: 'Prison—escape'"[19]

As demonstrated by the "Doolittle Dood It" headline and the *I Dood It* movie, Junior was the key character of Skelton's wartime radio show. Stillwell had created this figure based upon the personality of a husband whose youth had yet to move toward its extended expiration date.[20] Verna Felton, who played Junior's radio grandma following World War II, later addressed the character's universality. After crediting Stillwell's modeling of Junior on Skelton, the radio actress shared an insightful Stillwell story about her husband: "She said he told me, looking sheepish, 'that all men are little boys at heart.'"[21]

The persistence of the character in Skelton's lengthy career means Junior rivals in significance the signature routines Stillwell originated

Skelton as Sheriff Deadeye with film star Alan Ladd, whose greatest film was the classic Western Shane *(1953). Although this photo is from Skelton's television years, both of these stars found 1940s success because of creatively driven wives.*

earlier—the donut-dunking sketch and "Guzzler's Gin." Having said
that, though, Junior was certainly influenced by two then already
existing and phenomenally popular child-inspired radio characters:
Fanny Brice's "Baby Snooks" and ventriloquist Edgar Bergen's dummy
Charlie McCarthy. Like these precursor types, Junior's extended tag
line—"If I dood it, I get a whippin' ... I dood it!"—is grounded in a
smart-aleck mentality.

Though Snooks and McCarthy came into their own on radio in the
late 1930s, the addition of Skelton's Junior in 1941 helped make the
war years the airway heyday of the child impersonator. While this trio
of radio rascals were known for their precocious lips, Junior did seem
to build upon Snooks and McCarthy. Snooks's mischief often resulted
in a spanking, with her comic crying just as frequently putting a close
on Brice's radio routines. Along related lines, Junior invariably signaled
a near conclusion to his routine by acknowledging the "whippin'"
that would soon be forthcoming. And while McCarthy had more of
an acid tongue than Snooks, radio historian Arthur Frank Wertheim
suggests, "[Junior] was much more rude and mischievous ... [:] 'Oh, I
wish I had left you at home,' his Mummie scolded. 'Oh, no you don't,'
Junior replied. 'Because by now I coulda had three rooms *completely
wrecked*!'"[22]

Skelton was also able to occasionally apply a semblance of his
antiheroic/smart-aleck screen character from *Whistling in the Dark*
to Junior. For example, here is a radio routine where Skelton's "little
brat," lost in a department store, segues into an example of this comic
dichotomy:

"Mommie, Oh Mommie! Where's my Mommie?"

The store's floorwalker replies, "There, there, my little boy, are you
lost?"

"Whatja think ... I sprouted from a crack in da floor?"[23]

Ironically, when Stillwell filed for a divorce at the end of 1942,
the two artists were so synonymous with Junior and the little brat's
"Mummy" that period publications sometimes bemoaned the split
as if the duo really were these characters. *Screenland* author John R.

Franchey wondered if "'Junior' [had] lost for keeps the good offices of
the second-best 'Mummy' he ever knew, a 'Mummy' who had gotten
him out of a jillion jams, out of the depths and doom into which great
comedians have a habit of sinking."[24] Though Franchey ultimately put
a positive spin on the divorce, titling the article, "Ex's Can Be Friends,"
the piece must have hit a nerve, because Stillwell included the essay in a
Skelton scrapbook.[25]

Skelton's other primary comic alter ego during his radio war years
was Clem Kadiddlehopper. Kadiddlehopper was Skelton's oldest
character, seemingly based, in part, on a childhood friend. This figure
had even greater visibility than Junior during the course of Skelton's
long career, given later questions about seeing (on television) a middle-
aged Skelton play a bratty kid. (Radio and the need for imagination
also enhanced Junior's often surreally silly quality, such as the sketch
where he is tempted to throw a bottle of ink into an electric fan.)

Clem's character on radio was initially employed as a singing cab
driver. While this might sound like an odd occupation for a rural
rustic, ultimately it is an imaginative choice. The stereotypical cabbie
is nothing short of the proverbial magpie—gabby. So one has a ready
excuse for Clem's nonstop verbal riffs and singing, especially when
one could argue that Kadiddlehopper's definitive line is his *humming*
simpleton anthem, "Du-du-du du-du-du." Even more importantly,
driving a cab ties directly into a basic component of personality
comedy—a picturesque (on the road) nature produces a potential
nonstop comedy catalyst of various locations and/or new characters
(represented by the various cab fares).

While many of Skelton's later comedy characters are inherently
fools, such as his punch-drunk boxer Cauliflower McPugg and the
antiheroic cowboy Sheriff Deadeye, Clem is the closest to humor
history's classic fool. Like the traditional court jester of medieval
Europe, Kadiddlehopper occasionally segues into the "wise fool" mode,
when an insightful observation pops out in the midst of all his comic
idiocy. And this simpleton norm acts as a safety valve—such a fool

cannot be held responsible for the seemingly random biting insight. That is, they would not seem bright enough to devise it on their own.

Skelton's radio studio audience received an added bonus after the broadcast. The comedian gifted them with a postprogram, where he "put on a wilder, more abandoned, and possibly more hilarious show during the half hour that follows his regular show."[26] Early in Skelton's radio career he had done a preprogram warm-up act, but the always full-tilt funnyman had only succeeded in "knocking out both himself and his audience by the time the scripted broadcast got started."[27] This bonus performance also allowed Skelton to do some of his patented pantomime that could never be used on radio. "Guzzler's Gin," part verbal, part visual, was a special favorite. (Skelton invented his own term for this type of routine—"verba-mimes," where "I'm [Red] talking while I'm doing all the miming. But you're doing two things at once."[28])

At some point in the after-show Skelton introduced Stillwell, often bringing her out to jointly perform one of their old vaudeville routines. The following description of a Skelton and Stillwell sketch dates from shortly *after* their divorce: "Then and there they began a routine which brought down the house, Edna playing straight man, catching dialogue, rigging up laughs for Red, sparring verbally, and in the end, [Edna literally] carrying Red off the stage on her back to the delight of all hands.'"[29]

So where does their ongoing professional glue come from, following the disconnect of their private life together? Five years after the divorce, a *Photoplay* profile of Skelton's radio producer/writer ex-wife provided this insight: "You'll always find her sitting on the top step in the [radio] control booth where Red can check her reactions as the show goes along. [Skelton added,] 'Edna's my confidence. As long as I look up and see her I figure everything is all right. She'll never lie to me or flatter me. And you have to have somebody you can believe!'"[30]

This same *Photoplay* article had the former couple still seeing themselves as the "Skeltons, Incorporated," a caring professional "combine too strong for filmland to fathom or to break."[31] This "us against the world" philosophy had even been present when Stillwell made her court appearance to finalize the split. In a *Los Angeles Times* piece entitled, "Red Skelton Waits Outside Court as Wife Divorces Him," the comedian explained his presence thus, "I just wanted to see that she got along all right."[32]

In the same amiable spirit, Stillwell's testimony regarding Skelton's apparent infidelities was reframed along the lines of a comic story— consistent with her comedy writing profession: "Mr. Skelton reversed the usual order of behavior for men. Most men leave home early and come home late. He went out late and came in early."[33] When the judge asked if the comedian had ever explained these absences, the *Times* article noted an even more amusing comment: "'Once he told me that he had been waiting at [the corner of] Sunset and Sepulveda for the signal to change.' Even the judge smiled at that one."

As sophisticatedly civil as their divorce and ongoing work relationship would be, Stillwell's staying power went beyond Skelton's need for her support and honest advice. There was a guilt factor tied to what she had meant to his career. The year before Stillwell filed for divorce, she saved one of Skelton's elaborate "I'm sorry" notes. Below a detailed caricature of himself, he had written, "For Mummie [—] Each man is given God's best wish for happiness. I like a fool belittled his gift to me. You. Love, Red."[34]

Thus far the inherent parent-child factor in the relationship has simply been addressed comically (from the catalyst for "Junior," to a motherly caretaker). But consider the psychological ramifications of man-child Skelton divorcing the surrogate mother represented by Stilwell. Even if she had not been so central to his ongoing success, it makes perfect psychological sense to keep her in the picture. A complete break might have been devastating. I am convinced that the nervous collapse he later suffered in the army was brought on, at least in part, by his separation from Stillwell.

Another component to Skelton's man-child identity was being a romantic—writing love letters to each of his *three* wives. Between all Stillwell meant to him, and being spouse number one, her romantic pedestal seemed to soar highest. *Chicago Sun* columnist Sidney Skolsky wrote upon the 1941 release of *Whistling in the Dark*, "When you see the picture, notice Red Skelton in his love scenes with Ann Rutherford. He has his fingers crossed. Skelton said: 'My Wife [Edna] is the only girl I love, and when I have to make [movie] love to anyone else I keep my fingers crossed."[35]

That same year *Family Circle* magazine author Kitty Callahan chronicled Skelton's touching anniversary note and gift to Stillwell. When the couple married, Skelton had been so poor he had to borrow two dollars from his bride for a license. Skelton's anniversary card said, "Here's the two bucks for the license and a little memento [a new car] of the greatest day in my life."[36] What makes these article insights all the more poignant is that Stillwell saved them in the scrapbooks she maintained for Skelton. Consequently, one does not have to be a psychiatrist to understand how a total break from such a celebrated love might have been more than Skelton could have handled at that time. (Decades later, after Stillwell had long been out of his life in even a professional capacity, he coped by not coping at all—her existence was all but denied. And woe to any innocent interviewer who made the mistake of bringing up her presence and/or influence.)

Given the sad nature of any marital split where the two partners were once so intertwined, friends and colleagues were initially in denial. This phenomenon was often encouraged by Skelton's actions. Syndicated movieland gossip columnist Louella Parsons reported on the couple performing for servicemen at the Hollywood Canteen, shortly after Stillwell filed for divorce. She noted Skelton's opening comments, "Now, boys, I would like you to meet my wife. She writes all my stuff and is my severest critic."[37] To this Parsons added her own personal plea, "I hope Red and Edna are back together, for two people who get along so well should never have been separated."[38]

Along similar mixed messages from Skelton, the comedian acted as an emcee for a Hollywood charity baseball game between leading men and comics shortly after the Parsons piece appeared. Like a time-tripping return to his walkathon days, Skelton was constantly "on," involving himself in nearly every comic diamond development. In the midst of all the craziness he yelled, "Is my [writer] wife in the audience?

I'm running out of material."[39] This appeared in a *Movieland* magazine article with the provocative title, "Why the Skeltons Parted," yet paradoxically, the piece noted more reasons (such as the aforementioned Skelton quote) why the two should stay together. (The Skeltons' performances of their old vaudeville routines were so popular at army camp shows that the soldiers' request for a joint picture of the duo was still being honored by March 1943.)[40]

Thus far the focus has been on Skelton's need to have Stillwell be a continuing presence in his life. What of her needs, especially after the humiliation of her husband's apparent indiscretions? Earlier in the book I suggested that while the Skeltons both were driven to put Red on top, this was even more her mission. Everything about their divorce and ongoing professional partnership further reinforced this perspective. Indeed, according to Stillwell's own courtroom testimony, though she made light of Skelton's carousing, she made it clear "she remained at home pecking away at the typewriter in pursuit of her duties as his business manager and official gag writer."[41]

To Skelton's credit, he had given Stillwell the chance to artistically shine when her best other Great Depression-era opportunity was to be a mortician's assistant for her uncle. Moreover, though Skelton was the star to the general public, within the entertainment community his ex-wife was a luminary nearly on par with the comedian. So why should Stillwell sacrifice this power and prestige to some little sexy starlet that had caught Skelton's eye?

The wannabe actress in question was Muriel Morris, also under contract to MGM. The leggy, beautiful blonde had had small unbilled parts in several of Skelton's films. Given the comedian's interest and pride in all things Hoosier, the fact that Morris's family was, like Skelton's, from southern Indiana (Evansville), probably assisted the relationship. In a more macabre coincidence, given Stillwell's mortician connection, Morris's late father was a casket manufacturer! After that era's one-year waiting period before a divorce became final, the comedian and Morris planned an April 1944 wedding.[42] Morris, however, underestimated Skelton's ongoing ties to his first wife.

In a *Los Angeles Times* article titled "Red Skelton Practically Left Waiting at Altar," the comedian confessed, "What a jolt. I was never so surprised in all my life."[43] Yet, was it really that big a surprise? The day after the *Los Angeles Times* piece appeared, a *Los Angeles Examiner* article revealed, "To Hollywood circles, the answer to the problem [broken-off wedding] seemed to be the dictum laid down by Miss Morris before she called off her proposed marriage to the comedian. 'Choose between your ex-wife and me!'"[44] A modest self-deprecating Skelton said, "I'm sort of a [comic] Frankenstein created by other people [like my first wife], and Muriel—who is really wonderful—and some others find it hard to understand things which are absolutely necessary in show business."[45] The same *Examiner* article also had Stillwell comically underlining the professional nature of her ties with ex-husband Skelton, "All I'm supposed to do is handle business; and I mean business."

Although both Skelton and Stillwell eventually married others, the "Skelton Incorporated" pact that they maintained for years after their divorce was a mixed bag—a rousing success professionally, but a stressful distraction for each of their subsequent marriages. Preceding these new unions came a series of very popular wartime Skelton pictures.

8

War Year Complexities:
Movies, Military, and Marriage

"We're both quick-tempered but quick to forget. It's different now [since our divorce]. If we argue, I can leave and go home or he can say so-long and shut the door."[1]
EDNA STILLWELL SKELTON, 1943

Because radio did not necessitate that the star memorize a script, have costume changes, and be aware of camera blocking (where to stand and look), there was much less preparation time for each program—as opposed to the later overwhelming demands of television. This gave airway performers the chance to balance a film career with radio. So while Red Skelton was becoming one of the most popular 1940s figures of the "crystal set society," he was moving towards a comparable status in cinema. And Hollywood production had never been in a greater boom period than during America's involvement in World War II. In fact, box-office numbers were so great that the increased production and extended theatrical runs meant movies were stacked up for extended times. To illustrate, MGM's *Ziegfeld Follies*, in which Skelton contributed his classic "Guzzler's Gin" sketch, was shot in 1944 but not released until 1946.

MGM, as the most powerful and prestigious of Hollywood's studios, had a very ambitious slate of movies in production. Unfortunately, this was not necessarily a good thing for the individual comedy artist. Indeed, as addressed in the previous chapter, MGM's control-conscious, overproduced tendencies were not favorable for personality comedians. Film historian Leonard Maltin went so far as to suggest MGM "offered everything money could buy except respect for individual comic genius."[2] Thus, even after Skelton's star-making turn in *Whistling in the Dark* (1941), he was under-utilized or misused in such war year pictures as *Maisie Gets Her Man* (1942), *Panama Hattie* (1942), *Du Barry Was a Lady* (1943), *Thousands Cheer* (1943), and *Bathing Beauty* (1944). Before addressing these still often entertaining Skelton misfires, Skelton's most comedian friendly outings during the war deserve prime attention.

Fittingly, given the significance of *Whistling*, Skelton is best showcased during this period with that movie's two sequels: *Whistling in Dixie* (1942) and *Whistling in Brooklyn* (1944). The *Whistling* follow-ups put Skelton's character, radio sleuth expert, Wally "The Fox" Benton, in new settings—down South and the wacky world of Brooklyn. In addition, both sequels built upon two key components that drove the original picture. First, Skelton's Benton is in the dual persona popularized by Bob Hope in *The Cat and the Canary* (1939) and *The Ghost Breakers* (1940). Second, this personality comedy can also be pigeonholed as a film parody of the mystery thriller genre. Both components complement each other, since nothing acts as a better comic catalyst for a fear factor than scary situations. Skelton was not alone in building upon the split Hope persona in a scary setting. Simultaneous to Skelton's seminal *Whistling in the Dark*, Bud Abbott and Lou Costello released *Hold That Ghost* (1941).

Whistling in Dixie involves investigating a spooky old Southern mansion and an equally creepy Confederate fort, where a flooded dungeon almost becomes the comic's crypt. These are hardly the backdrops Benton had in mind when he requested two weeks off from his popular murder mystery program. Skelton's radio character is so stressed out that the mere mention of murder sends him into a comic meltdown similar to the rubber-faced contortions synonymous with his "Guzzler's Gin" routine. The *New York Time's* review embellished the phenomenon further: "As he is faced by danger, his knees clatter, speech becomes difficult, and his eyes show a pronounced tendency to cross."[3]

Skelton's original getaway game plan had him honeymooning with his radio companion (Ann Rutherford). But their marriage is put on hold when her sorority sister friend (Diana Lewis) requests their assistance on some strange developments in Dixie. The story that unfolds is entirely mounted as a Skelton vehicle, although he receives excellent comedy support from his vaudeville friend "Rags" Ragland. Ragland frequently costarred with Skelton at MGM during the early 1940s, including the first *Whistling* picture. In *Dixie* Rags plays twins, a gangster gone straight and a fugitive killer. As the reformed former figure, Ragland effectively mixes slapstick and silliness, such as his comic reply to Skelton's question, "What are you, a moron?" "Yes, and we're organized."

Like most popular culture comedies, *Dixie* is also a compendium of current events played for laughs. These range from finding yet another way to incorporate Skelton's then trademark line from radio, "I Dood It," into the plotline, to including a gag reference to the previous year's monster hit, *Here Comes Mr. Jordan* (1941). "I Dood It" becomes the punchline for a thrill comedy scene set at the Confederate fort.

"Rags" Ragland (right) tells Skelton and Ann Rutherford that Guy Kibbee is overtired from lifting mint juleps in a scene from Whistling in Dixie *(1942).*

Skelton's character discards a lit cigarette that burns a guillotine-like trip rope and our hero almost loses his head.

Jordan, later remade as *Heaven Can Wait* (1978), is a fantasy comedy about a good-natured athlete "spirited" off to the next realm ahead of schedule. Until an earthy replacement body can be found, said athlete must get by in phantom form. Earlier in 1942, the release year of *Dixie*, Hope had included a running gag about Jordan in the *Road to Morocco*, with the comedian doubling as another "spirited" character himself. Though Skelton's *Jordan* reference in *Dixie* is more modest, it was no less funny. When Skelton's character runs into a door he wisecracks, "I thought I was Mr. Jordan."

Skelton's notices for *Dixie* were a series of raves. The *Hollywood Reporter*'s banner headline proclaimed: "MGM 'Whistling in Dixie' Full of Audience Howls: Skelton Picks Up Note of First Hit."[4] *Variety* stated: "While Skelton gained stature in recent pictures, this is his first comedy entirely dependent on him to score a laugh hit. He comes through in fine fashion and … 'Dixie' is headed for sturdy box office

WES D. GEHRING STILLS COLLECTION

Bob Hope's "how-to" approach in The Road to Morocco *(1942) probably influenced Skelton's bookish take in 1948's* A Southern Yankee *(see frontispiece).*

returns."[5] *Variety* proved psychic; *Dixie* made a profit of $542,000—an amazing amount given that the average ticket price then was twenty-seven cents.[6] (The original *Whistling* picture had been considered a major commercial hit with a profit of $219,000.[7])

Though it is now popular to bemoan a lack of creativity in the film capital with punning axioms such as "Hollywood, where all films are created sequel," Tinsel Town has always returned to popular profitable series pictures. But surprisingly, even before *Dixie* proved to be such a hit, MGM bought the original story rights to a second *Whistling* sequel—*Whistling in Brooklyn.*[8] In fact, the *Dixie* production had only recently wrapped, suggesting that MGM was confident of both its box-office potential, and a continued interest in the *Whistling* series, well before *Dixie*'s release.

The third *Whistling* installment for Skelton's radio sleuth Benton takes him to the wilds of Brooklyn, what the *New York Times* comically referred to as "A Hollywood Safari into Darkest Flatbush."[9] The film opens with a scary seascape and a dead body—yet another murder

A guillotine almost gives Skelton darkly comic problems in Whistling in Dixie *as Rutherford (right) and Diana Lewis look on.*

victim revealed to the authorities by way of a series of letters to a Brooklyn newspaper and always signed "Constant Reader." Once this ripe-for-spoofing setting is established, the story returns to a familiarly funny *Whistling* local—Benton broadcasting in a radio studio.

This particular program has Skelton's character playing both his whodunit wizard and a comic Nazi with a Hitler mustache. The mustache is obviously for the movie audience, which brings up the irony of visual-orientated Skelton being a real-life radio star—the Hoosier comedian had an underappreciated verbal gift, too. As radio historian Arthur Frank Wertheim has noted, Skelton "was an exceptional voice imitator who made the character *sound* funny."[10]

The comedy catalyst for much of what follows Skelton's radio Nazi is provided by Skelton's screen sidekick Ragland, returning this time as Benton's chauffeur and wannabe press agent. Ragland tells a reporter that Skelton is the "constant reader." When this news bulletin turns up on the radio, the delightfully dopey Ragland takes it as a publicist's coup and proudly appropriates Skelton's tag line—"I dood it!" But a less happy Skelton soon finds himself pursued by both the police and the gangsters responsible for the murders.

In the earlier *Whistling* installments, Benton struggled to stay on the airways. In this Brooklyn chapter, he is more of an established radio personality, with Benton's lines sounding like something the real Skelton might say. For example, when Benton is surrounded by what he takes to be autograph hounds, the comic observes, "If Bob Hope and Jack Benny could see me now." At another point, Benton makes a casual reference to Skelton's Willie Lump-Lump character. When Benton dresses down Ragland for making people think he is the "constant reader," Benton adds the further advice, "Next time you get a publicity idea, give it to [Jack Benny nemesis] Fred Allen."

The *Whistling in Brooklyn* entertainment factor escalates proportionately when the proceedings relocate to New York's most bonkers borough, a verdict seconded by the *New York Times*: "By far the funniest moments in this broadly slapstick excursion are when Red, hiding behind a flowing beard from a gang of killers, somehow or other gets into [Brooklyn's] Ebbets Field, into the uniform of the Battling Beavers and is pushed onto the pitchers mound against the Dodgers."[11] Skelton's visit to the ballpark, home to "dem bums" (as the Dodgers were then affectionately nicknamed), was to prevent a murder. Providentially, since Skelton needed a disguise, the Dodgers were playing an exhibition game against a Jewish all-star squad from that era, whose players wore full beards.

Of course, in poker parlance, connecting Brooklyn and "dem bums" to a comedy is what would be called "lay down" material—an automatic winning hand. Unlike the longtime winning tradition of New York City's two other major league franchises during this era, the "Bronx Bombers" (New York Yankees) and Manhattan's New York Giants, the Brooklyn Dodgers had forever represented an exercise in comic futility. For example, later the same year that *Brooklyn* opened, director Frank Capra established a madcap tone to another Brooklyn-

WES D. GEHRING STILLS COLLECTION

Skelton (seated) will not be moved as he and Brooklyn Dodger opponent Billy Herman, a fellow Hoosier and future member of the National Baseball Hall of Fame, act in a scene from Whistling in Dixie.

based comedy thriller, *Arsenic and Old Lace* (1944), by beginning the picture with a slapstick melee at Ebbets Field. A questionable call had the Dodgers (also known as the "Daffiness Boys") going into a comic attack made against their rivals and the umpire.

In Skelton's *Brooklyn* one gets that same sort of instant comedy association with the Dodgers. Ragland observes, "I wanna git there [Ebbets Field] before they throw out the first umpire." At the same time, Skelton's character is explaining the murder he and Rags will attempt to thwart, adding that a riot will then be initiated among the Dodger fans to cover the murderer's escape. When someone questions the difficulty of starting such a riot, Skelton responds, "not in Brooklyn. All you have to do is just say boo."

The film provided the added bonus of featuring several Dodger stars in cameos, starting with manager Leo Durocher, a future Hall of Famer synonymous with the line, "Nice guys finish last." Consistent with his nickname, "Leo the Lip," Durocher's best quip in the picture occurs after first seeing Skelton's bearded mug: "I never forget a face but this time I'll make an exception." During the production, Durocher and Skelton played comedy one-upmanship, starting with the manager giving the comedian a joke book, the cover of which featured a picture of Skelton's rival, Hope.

Consistent with the fact that Skelton's character is forced to pitch, the comedian proceeds to hit the first three batters—future Hall of Famers Billy Herman, Arky "Arkansas" Vaughan, and Joe "Ducky" Medwick. Naturally, the beanings produces a threat from Durocher, that era's most entertainingly angry high-profile manager: "Don't worry. You'll be up to [the] plate. We'll take care good care of you." Skelton's responding comic pun moves from antihero to wise guy in two lines, "I didn't mean to hit him. 'Dodger,' [the] guy [Billy Herman] can't even duck."

The extra attention accorded Skelton's leadoff batter (Billy Herman) during *Brooklyn* was probably a result of Herman's Hoosier connection. The star player was from New Albany, Indiana. The comedian was an ongoing booster for all things Hoosier and people from the nineteenth state. Consistent with this philosophy, Herman is also more prominently featured than any other ballplayer in *Brooklyn* press kit and lobby-card material.[12]

Given that *Brooklyn* was obviously geared, in part, toward attracting baseball fans to the film, a series of diamond trades after the shoot but prior to the picture's release, had MGM nervous: "What to do about it has the [studio] boys stumped ... [concerned as they are by] the inevitable howls of the baseball fans, especially the Flatbush contingent."[13] But given that this was a comedy, and numerous journeyman Dodgers were already doubling as Skelton's Battling Beavers teammates, the fact that a few Brooklyn stars had moved on (such as Medwick becoming a New York Giant) was eventually deemed no problem by MGM.

Back in a time when there was no question that baseball was the national game, *Brooklyn*'s diamond fans also included most critics, with some reviewers even going back to the film's entertainingly chronicled shoot from the previous year. For example, the *New York Herald Tribune*'s positive critique included Skelton's tongue-in-cheek telegram to MGM, when on-location shooting at Ebbets Field produced freezing weather and spitting snow: "Local newspapers are all dated April. Please confirm time of year and if correct, send long underwear."[14] *Variety* said the "Baseball sequence, with Skelton as a bearded player, ... is surefire."[15] The *Los Angeles Examiner*, under the headline "Red Skelton Comedy Corn, but Hilarious," raved about the "wild sequence with the genuine Brooklyn Dodgers."[16]

As with the earlier *Whistling* installments, *Brooklyn* was a commercial hit. The profit margin, however, was greatly reduced, compared to the first two pictures, because of *Brooklyn*'s location work and the expanded baseball player cast. The production cost, at $856,000, was more than three times the *Whistling* original, and greater than twice the amount spent on the *Dixie* sequel.[17] MGM's sometimes over-production of Skelton's films frequently became a detriment to his comedy. Thankfully that was not the case here. (Tentative plans for a fourth movie in the series, *Whistling in Hollywood*, were made but not realized.)

In addition to Skelton's *Whistling* trilogy, the comedian's other best war-era pictures were *Ship Ahoy* (1942) and *I Dood It* (1943). The latter film was Skelton's first remake of a Buster Keaton movie (*Spite Marriage*, 1929), and will be addressed in the next chapter, which explores the influence of this silent comedy giant upon Skelton. *I Dood It* appropriates Skelton's defining line from his radio character "Junior" as the title (for no particular reason, besides marketing). In a film that mixes personality comedy with the then hot topic of war-related espionage, MGM maintained the Skelton thriller-spoofing connection established with *Whistling in the Dark* by making his *Ship Ahoy* character a mystery writer.

The picaresque, or on-the-road quality, is also utilized in *Ship Ahoy* to maximize new settings and characters for comedy. Skelton meets his costar, dancer Eleanor Powell, on an ocean liner bound for Puerto Rico. The movie originally had a different destination and title, *I'll Take Manila*. But in the early days of World War II Japan had similar designs on the city, and the destination of Skelton's picture was changed from the Philippines to Puerto Rico.

Powell's character has been hoodwinked by enemy agents to sneak a magnetic mine prototype out of the United States, believing she is actually working for the Allies. Naturally, Skelton and Powell eventually put two and two together, with time out for comedy, dancing, and romance, before the enemy is thwarted. Powell became a frequent costar for Skelton during the war years, as well as arguably representing cinema's greatest woman dancer. Skelton also shared screen time here with several veteran performers, including the incomparable Bert Lahr (the *Hollywood Reporter* calling Lahr's performance "the funniest he has been since he portrayed the Cowardly Lion [in *The Wizard of Oz*, 1939]."[18]) Lahr plays Skelton's man Friday, who, between his patented double-talk shtick and the inspired belief that he is God's gift to women, threatens to steal every scene he is in.

For comedy contrast, the demonstrative Lahr is romantically teamed with pretty character actress Virginia O'Brien, whose comic specialty was deadpan patter and songs, earning her the nickname

Skelton clowns with Eleanor Powell and Tommy Dorsey for a publicity still from the film
Ship Ahoy *(1942).*

"Miss Red Hot Frozen Face." If this begins to sound like a variety show—and I have not yet mentioned Tommy Dorsey's Orchestra (with Frank Sinatra, and Buddy Rich on drums)—one should note *New York Journal American* critic Rose Pelswick's description of *Ship Ahoy*: "a large scale musical that indicates the return of vaudeville to the screen."[19]

This was Skelton's first picture to appear after the United States's 1941 entry into World War II. And Pelswick's "return of vaudeville" observation was a prophetic description of much of the Hollywood product that occurred during the war years. Unfortunately, as this chapter will soon demonstrate, Skelton sometimes became lost in MGM's full embrace of this variety-show mentality. But it is *not* a problem on *Ship Ahoy*. As *Daily Variety* stated, "Skelton has a wide latitude to extend himself in new routines and socko gags."[20] Moreover, he has great rapport with Lahr, whether they are coping with Skelton's story-related hypochondria ("a medical student could walk around me just once and get a medical degree"), or getting drunk in the wine cellar hold of this nautical nightclub.

As if maximizing his respite from a hit radio program, Skelton's *Ship Ahoy* character is at his best with the visual comedy: Skelton's signature slapstick falls, the rubbery facial expressions, an amusing wrestling match with a deck chair (he loses), and his drawn-out attempts to lift the *magnetic* mine (hidden in a suitcase) after it comes in contact with the *metal* deck. This satchel gag was Skelton's most praised bit in the film's reviews, from the *New York Post* calling it "hilarious," to *Showman Trade Review* labeling the routine a "scream."[21] Nevertheless, for the Skelton aficionado, the pivotal scene is the comedian demonstrating the dying star material he and Edna Stillwell improvised for his MGM screen test in 1940 that inspired the article, "Skelton Out of the Closet: Red Skelton's Film Masterpiece Has Never Grossed a Dollar."[22] This *Ship Ahoy* variation on the MGM test includes Skelton doubling as dying gangster Edward G. Robinson in *Little Caesar* (1930), talking away as if he has not been mortally wounded, and comically croaking as tough guy George Raft, slowly tossing his iconic coin, à la *Scarface* (1932).

As the review snippets suggest, *Ship Ahoy* was a critical success, which undoubtedly helped fuel the picture's strong box office. The *Brooklyn Daily Eagle*'s critique headline might have been a summary for several of these notices: "'Ship Ahoy' at Capitol a Fast, Funny Show."[23] Along similar lines, the *New York Daily News*' title promised an "Abundance of Fun, Rhythm at Capitol."[24] The *Hollywood Reporter*, as it was frequently wont to do, published an article capsulizing many of these positive notices, including a *Record* statement that called Skelton "'a real find' and saw him [as] a potential rival to Bob Hope ... [the film is] 'Fast, Fresh and Funny."[25]

Even the rare *Ship Ahoy* pan, such as Lee Mortimer's *New York Daily Mirror* review, was downright apologetic about being out of step with the masses—the *radio* masses: "As far as I'm concerned, he didn't dood it. I mean the sensational Red Skelton. And the rest of the film is about on par with his futile attempts at humor. But don't get me wrong. I know I'm in a minority. Millions of people are hysterical over [radio's] Red Skelton. 'Ship Ahoy' will undoubtedly make money ... plenty [of fans already] went to see the naughty boy Skelton."[26] Several *Ship Ahoy* reviews also referred to Skelton as the airway's "I-dood-it man."

As suggested earlier, Skelton's other war-period pictures, *Maisie Gets Her Man, Panama Hattie, Du Barry Was a Lady, Thousands Cheer*, and *Bathing Beauty*, failed to fully capitalize on the comedian's multifaceted skills. The *Maisie* movie casts Skelton in comedy support of Ann Sothern's title character, a popular figure in a series of B films. Sothern's Maisie was consistently out of work at the onset of each installment of the series, yet as modern critic Robert Bianco suggests, "there was a lively, buoyant spirit to her film persona that was always hugely enjoyable."[27] In fact, period critics were frequently after MGM to upgrade the Maisie series to an A category, as the studio had done with Mickey Rooney's Andy Hardy pictures.[28] Be that as it may, *Maisie Gets Her Man* did not, as insightfully noted by the *Hollywood Reporter*, "stack up with its excellent predecessors."[29] Worse yet, Skelton was miscast as an abrasive wannabe performer who was subject to stage fright. Still, Skelton was riding such a wave of popularity that he often garnered good notices despite weak material. The *New York Daily Mirror*'s Edith Werner observed, "every bit of [Skelton] mugging was greeted with [movie audience] chuckles. Red hasn't much to do.... But whatever it is, he 'doods it' slick and with a twinkle."[30]

Skelton's follow-up film, *Panama Hattie*, has an upscale Maisie aura to it, as Skelton is again teamed with Sothern. Critics frequently drew parallels with the Maisie movies, from the *New York Post*'s Archer Winsten stating, "You can't help thinking of Maisie as soon as the attractive Ann Sothern goes into her Maisie act," to the *Brooklyn Citizen*'s Edgar Price noting the film "might have been called 'Maisie in Panama.'"[31] But unlike the Maisie series, *Panama Hattie* was a big budget A picture, with a then sizable $130,000 having been spent on just the screen rights for this former Broadway hit.

While the *Hollywood Reporter* predicted major box-office numbers for *Panama Hattie*, most other publications expressed a biting letdown over the film adaptation.[32] For example, *The New Yorker* review included the darkly comic riff, "the picture needs a certain something. Possibly burial."[33] Such criticism, and disappointing revenues, were hardly unexpected, since the picture had been finished and shelved for nearly a year, as MGM attempted to fix the film. Not surprisingly, this too became grist for comic criticism cracks. The *New York Times* observed, "'Panama Hattie' was finished last fall. At several sneak previews, it cast a great pall. Metro [MGM] revised it, with scissors and pen, but it couldn't put 'Panama Hattie' together again."[34]

More than one publication suggested the adaptation was a victim of censorship: "'Hattie' isn't even a shadow of her former [provocative Broadway] self.... Blame it on the Hays [motion picture censorship office] ... all the racy dialogue has been eliminated."[35] And given its already thin story (title character Sothern entertains in a Canal Zone nightclub), the studio was forced, in the words of *Variety*'s review, to turn *Panama Hattie* into "glorified vaudeville."[36] A variety show format was also indirectly encouraged by Sothern, who initially battled the assignment, and then fought illness during the production.

The resulting "hodgepodge," to quote *Newsweek*'s review, is not without some charming interludes, such as another classic deadpan number from O'Brien, or Lena Horne's sexy rendition of "It Was Just One of Those Things" (the best Cole Porter song retained from the play).[37] The picture receives low marks here because Skelton, as one of three sailors on leave (with Ragland and Ben Blue), is lost in this variety show shuffle. As the *New York Times* complains, "the usually irrepressible Red Skelton is so held in check … that his favorite expression, 'I dood it,' is this time an idle boast."[38]

In two of Skelton's three remaining wartime pictures, *Du Barry Was a Lady* and *Bathing Beauty*, he is often brilliant—when he is on-screen. Unfortunately, however, an MGM variety show mindset often has him playing a supporting role. The 1943 *Du Barry* screen adaptation had been the prestige picture promised to Skelton back in 1941, after the major hit status of *Whistling in the Dark* caused MGM to renegotiate the comedian's contract. Like *Panama Hattie*, *Du Barry* had also been a racy Broadway musical comedy hit that featured Cole Porter songs

Skelton brings slapstick to the French court in DuBarry Was a Lady *(1943).*

WES D. GEHRING STILLS COLLECTION

and stage star Ethel Merman. MGM's soon to be legendary musical producer, Arthur Freed, faced the same censorship challenge on *Du Barry* that he had on *Panama Hattie*—tone down the language without destroying the spirit of the material. For some critics, such as the always censorship-conscious Edgar Price of the *Brooklyn Citizen*, the screen version was a disappointment: "The Hays office, no doubt, was responsible for blue-penciling the play's original off-color dialogue."[39] *Variety*'s critique comically concurred: "'Du Barry's too much of a lady now."[40] *Newsweek*'s review opined a similar slant, noting that Lucille Ball's title character, "in the Ethel Merman role, is both willing and attractive but her Du Barry is much too much the lady for her own good."[41]

In fairness to the screen *Du Barry*, however, the film is an often entertaining Technicolor variety show, particularly when Skelton's nightclub hatcheck attendant is drugged into a dream sequence where he is France's King Louis XV. The *New York Journal American* comically encapsulated this time-tripping transition in the title of its *Du Barry* review: "Skidding into History on a Mickey Finn."[42] (This time machine-like segment might have been the catalyst for the later dream sequence by Donald O'Connor, in Freed's celebrated musical *Singin' in the Rain*, 1952.)

Regardless, the best thing about the *Du Barry* sojourn back in history, Hollywood style, is that Skelton's screen time does increase. Coupled with the inspired lunacy of Skelton doing his comic shtick in the height of eighteenth-century French fashion, is his amusing nonstop smart-aleck attitude, such as the comedian's comment while chasing Ball on the world's largest bed, "This isn't a love affair; it's a track meet." When Skelton is not essaying this Hope-like wise guy, he is drawing upon his own greatest hits repertoire, such as Skelton's patented "Fox" howl from the *Whistling* films, or recycling signature bits from his radio program. When Skelton's King Louis is wounded by an arrow to the behind, his response is suddenly that of his "mean widdle kid" Junior: "My widdle back, my widdle back!" And though most of Porter's songs are again missing in action (as occurred with *Panama Hattie*), the two redheads (Ball and Skelton, in brightest Technicolor) perform a rousing rendition of the composer's delightful "Friendship."

Although Skelton was frequently off camera for long stretches of *DuBarry*, he did receive some excellent notices for the picture. The *Hollywood Reporter* stated, "Red Skelton is a riot as Louis, the hatcheck boy who dreamed of himself as king," while the *New York Times*'s pantheon-like praise claimed, "[*DuBarry*] permits Mr. Skelton to be as funny as he has ever been in films."[43] For today's viewer, the movie is now most memorable for its teaming of the two redheads who later dominated early television comedy. (As a Technicolor footnote, this was the film in which Ball *first* acquired her trademark hair color. Paradoxically, Skelton's naturally red hair had to be dyed a shade that did not clash with her new coloring.)

The year after 1943's *Du Barry*, Skelton is again absent for long periods of time in another MGM Technicolor extravaganza, *Bathing Beauty*. The picture's working title was *Mr. Co-Ed*, since Skelton plays a songwriter trying to salvage his marriage by following his bride back to the girls' college where she teaches. Finding a loophole that only a movie script could invent, Skelton becomes a student to save his marriage. Given the variety show mindset of the MGM war years, it was a foregone conclusion that Skelton would have to share time with a host of talented support players. But what knocked him from *Mr. Co-Ed* title character to secondary *Bathing Beauty* status was the casting of beautiful swimming sensation starlet Esther Williams as his screen wife.

Sometime during the 1944 post-production, MGM decided that the shapely Williams could herald a new subgenre, what might be called an aqua-musical category, in which grandiose water ballet numbers, in brightest Technicolor, reminded viewers of Busby Berkeley choreography, gone under the sea. Overnight Skelton's *Mr. Co-Ed* became Williams's *Bathing Beauty*, and Skelton, who had just entered the army, was in a state of shock.

Williams, who had won several swimming events at the U.S. Nationals in 1939, had been brought along so slowly by MGM that many had all but forgotten the girl who might have been an Olympic

star had the Games not been canceled in both 1940 and 1944 due
to the war. Her screen debut in *Andy Hardy's Double Life* (1942) had
made title character Rooney gaga—a phenomenon that seemingly
also described the state of MGM officials while a rough cut of *Bathing
Beauty* was being assembled. Though the usurping of Skelton on the
picture undoubtedly had him thinking of the tag line of comedy
contemporary Jimmy Durante, "What a revoltin' development," the
studio had correctly "read" the sexy attraction that was Williams.
The *New York Times* blushingly observed, "Miss Williams' talents as a
swimmer—not to mention her other attributes—make any title the
studio wants to put on it [*Bathing Beauty*] okay to us."[44]

Sadly, while previous MGM musical epics had still produced
critical hosannas for Skelton, despite reduced screen time, the often
Williams-obsessed critical reception of *Bathing Beauty* frequently
minimized Skelton's involvement. For example, after *New York Morning
Telegraph* critic Leo Miskin bluntly noted, "There is only one reason …
why anybody should go to see a picture called 'Bathing Beauty'—the
acres of exposed epidermis." He condescendingly referenced Skelton's
tutu scene (the movies' funniest sketch) by stating: "getting back to
Brother S [Skelton] and his ballet skirt, as if anybody's interested."[45]
One finds the same attitude in the *Brooklyn Daily Eagle's* review, which
only gets around to the film's original star in the third paragraph, as an
afterthought: "Red Skelton, by the way, is there, too."[46]

After MGM's insightful placement of Skelton in the Hope-like
Whistling films, the studio was wasting him in its overblown variety
shows. Granted, Williams's water ballet films eventually elevated her
to a top ten box-office star by the end of the 1940s (a status never
reached by Skelton).[47] But conversely, any lesser clown might have been
assigned to play her romantic co-star.

Ironically, despite Skelton's second-class status on *Bathing Beauty*,
the picture showcases two of the comedian's most inspired sketches.
The first is the aforementioned ballet routine, which was created by the
great Buster Keaton. The former silent film star had been reduced to
being a gag consultant at MGM. The sketch's pièce de résistance was

a bit Keaton had borrowed from his father, vaudevillian Joe Keaton. Skelton finds himself in a girl's ballet class, with one leg horizontal to the bar. The comically martinet instructor commands the comedian to seemingly defy gravity by lifting his other leg to a parallel position with said bar.

Amazingly, Skelton briefly seems to defy the laws of science (with both legs horizontal to the ballet bar) before taking one of his amazing patented pratfalls. Just as Joe Keaton's use of the bit was a hit on stage, Skelton's rendition is a tour de silly, too. The sketch is so memorable I often use it as a classic example of slapstick for my college seminar on American film comedy. As noted earlier, such violent physical comedy over a lifetime easily documents why an elderly Skelton was forced to wear leg braces to support permanently weakened limbs.

A second neglected watershed Skelton sketch from *Bathing Beauty* is a variation of a routine originally devised for the comedian's 1930s vaudeville act by Stillwell. The bit involved a woman's morning preparation ritual, and drew upon everything from putting on makeup to a wrestling match that passes for trying to get into an undersized girdle. While this routine, like the ballet number, first existed as an autonomous sketch, both bits are effectively incorporated into the *Bathing Beauty* story by way of the fact that Skelton's character is playing a student at a girl's school.

Despite the general neglect of Skelton by both his studio and most reviewers, a few critics recognized the uniqueness of Skelton's contribution to *Bathing Beauty*. The *Hollywood Citizen News*'s Lowell E. Redelings said, "It is his antics—in cold retrospect—which are the entertainment gems."[48] Redelings also entertainingly chronicled the added comedy generated by the audience's response to Skelton's previously highlighted *Bathing Beauty* sketches, noting that the extended ballet bit "caused a young lady behind me to become hysterical with laughter ... [while Skelton's woman-in-the-morning] scene had the audience roaring, this eyewitness included."[49]

New York Herald Tribune critic Otis L. Guernsey Jr. was similarly supportive of Skelton, while taking a potshot at MGM: "Audiences

TOP: *An army courtship starring Skelton and Georgia Davis (circa 1944).* LEFT: *A circa 1944 photograph of young Hollywood starlet Davis, soon to be Skelton's second wife.*

apparently are supposed to care a good deal more about what the heroine is wearing than whether Skelton gets her in the final reel."[50] *New York World Telegram* reviewer Alton Cook seconded this line of thinking in even stronger prose: "All the details of this picture have been given pleasant attention except that one matter of material for Red. He must have wonderful control over his temper.... They [MGM] seem to have an idea.... that Red's admirers are so smitten with him his presence itself is enough to keep everyone happy."[51]

Skelton's frustration over what might have been with *Bathing Beauty* was abated, in part, by his induction (May 25, 1944) into the U.S. Army, one month before the East Coast opening of the picture. While one might have assumed his brief appearance in the previous year's *Thousands Cheer* (1943, MGM's wartime salute to the army) would be Skelton's closest brush with the armed forces (beyond military camp shows), the comedian's divorce from Stillwell made his draft status 1-A.

Romantically, his bachelor years had been a bust. After starlet Muriel Morris called off their marriage at the eleventh hour, he was briefly but seriously involved with contract player Lynn Merrick, whom he had met on a war-bond tour. But she was not interested in marriage. Quite possibly, she, like Morris, was put off by Skelton's ongoing professional relationship with his ex-wife. Indeed, friends of the former couple were convinced, right up until Skelton's marriage to twenty-three-year-old MGM starlet Georgia Davis (March 19, 1945), that the comedian would reunite with his first wife. Although Skelton had tried to win Stillwell back, she preferred their new arrangement.

Davis later described her husband's unhappiness at this time: "He hated the bachelor existence he was leading, [and he] was mixed up. He'd struggled for years, and what did it add up to?"[52] Not surprisingly, her description of Skelton sounds like earlier comments by Stillwell: "He is a madcap clown, with an appealing helplessness and kindness that opens your heart."[53] Paradoxically, the new couple's first meeting had not gone well. Friends of the comedian had brought the actress to a 1944 party at his home. Skelton later confessed, "Because I am a comedian who is always 'on,' I started to kid her [Davis] by saying,

'Look, I just had that sofa reupholstered, so how about removing your feet [one of Davis's legs was curled under her]? Let's keep the seat neat. Are you a real redhead or can't you stay out of trouble? How about those freckles? Sincere or something out of a box of confetti?'"[54]

"Miss Georgia Davis arose to her full height, looked me straight in the eye and observed, 'Mr. Skelton, I think you are the rudest man it has ever been my misfortune to meet.' And she stalked out of the house with most of the male members of our dinner party trying in furious pursuit to explain that I was a corny character who meant no wrong but who had to play Bogart now and then," Skelton said.[55] Such began the fiery relationship of two volatile redheads.

The perennially insecure Skelton, his comically aggressive come-on to Davis notwithstanding, was immediately taken with the spunky auburn-haired beauty. Couple this with the added vulnerability Skelton was feeling during these wartime bachelor years, and he was quickly into marriage-proposal mode. But Davis, once she got past her "rudest man" assessment of Skelton, wanted to take the romance slowly. Consequently, theirs was largely a service courtship, with Skelton entering the army early in the relationship. Given that the comedian entertained stateside troops from June 1944 until March 1945, furlough possibilities with Davis were available.

That being said, Skelton was one busy private. By opting to serve as a regular soldier (with field artillery duty/training at California's Camp Roberts), he inadvertently set himself up for double duty—a soldier constantly asked to entertain. Eventually the strain would be too much, and he entered special services as a performer. Still, his easy-going nature and desire to please resulted in too many one-man shows, with a nervous breakdown occurring shortly after being shipped to the Italian war zone in early 1945.

One can see danger signs, however, in Skelton's press-clipping banter shortly before going overseas. For example, here is his comic take on always being tired since entering the service: "I think I know why the Army keeps you so darned busy all the time. If it didn't, every guy in camp would be falling sound asleep. I've actually seen fellows so tired that they have gone asleep standing up. And that's no gag."[56] In a military hospital article titled "Everyone's a Kid is Basis for Skelton's Philosophy," the comedian also revealed a positive fatalism: "Everything that ever happened to me or anybody else has happened for a reason … though I may never know it. Good is going to come out of it because out of everything springs some good."[57]

One need not equate this with some simplistic happy-face mindset. Skelton was quite capable of using his army experience to address some unpleasant truths. In a *Hollywood Press Times* piece "GIs Perplexed Red Skelton Reveals," the comedian documented an embarrassing irony rarely hinted at in history books: "When the war is explained to a GI 'as a war to defeat the forces that enslave Catholics, Jews and other people,' the GI answers, 'but we have those forces in our country, so why are we fighting?' Among the wounded there is no race, creed or color; civilians re-stimulate prejudice when the boys return. If we could raise one generation in which mothers would say to their children, 'all people are equal,' America would be a long way towards democracy."[58]

These were truly brave comments to make in 1945, reflecting, in part, the color-blind legacy Skelton learned from his Vincennes mentor Clarence Stout. I am aware of only one other World War II entertainer who expressed similar embarrassment over hypocrisy on the home front—the comedian Joe E. Brown. Best remembered now as the aging millionaire of *Some Like It Hot* (1959) who falls for Jack Lemmon in drag, during the war Brown repeatedly noted how servicemen were disappointed by the shameful placement of Japanese-Americans in interment camps.[59] (Skelton's advocacy tendencies towards GIs was also demonstrated by one of his army nicknames, "Chaplain," because "he's always fighting someone's battles."[60] Given that the thirty-one-year-old Skelton was ten to thirteen years older than most recruits, they also affectionately called him "Pops.")

GI Skelton was doing so many military camp shows around the United States that Stillwell's 1944 Christmas gift to her ex-husband was a "cross-indexed gag-file of 80,000 jokes" that conveniently fit into a leather carrying case.[61] Skelton might have continued this ongoing domestic base tour until war's end, but he lobbied strongly to go overseas. The comedian wanted to entertain closer to the real conflict. Otherwise, his service only seemed like he was playing at war. In fact, Skelton kiddingly implied just that in a well-published comment (including an appearance on the front page of the *Vincennes Sun-Commercial*) he made to a high-ranking officer: "General, it seems I'm doing much better than [the antiheroic] Private Hargrove."[62] This was a tongue-in-cheek reference to Marion Hargrove's comic memoir of army life, *See Here, Private Hargrove* (1942), sort of a print version of cartoonist George Baker's comic strip about another antiheroic soldier, *The Sad Sack*, which also debuted in 1942. Skelton made his crack shortly after *See Here, Private Hargrove* (1944) had become a hugely successful film. (And this would be followed by the cinema sequel, *What Next, Corporal Hargrove?* 1945.)

As the old axiom suggests, "be careful what you wish for" because you might receive it. The Atlantic crossing was an ordeal for Skelton. He later wrote *Los Angeles Herald Express* columnist Harrison Carroll, "I was so sick [on the troopship USS *General Altman*] the face of my watch turned green"[63] With Skelton's direct ties to the *Herald Express*, and his detailed scrapbooks, the first stateside announcement that he had left the country was probably an April 17, 1945, article in that publication: "Red Skelton Now In Overseas Area."[64]

However, in a seven-page longhand letter to "Little Red" (his nickname for second wife) dated March 28, 1945, Skelton states he has been in Naples, Italy, for six days.[65] This lengthy letter covers a myriad of topics, beginning with a backbreaking performance schedule. The comedian had already done "41 shows in six 6 days, about 8 a day." Still, he had been able to play tourist. With an assist from the armed forces brass giving him a navy driver and military police clearance to take pictures, the amateur shutterbug snapped shots throughout Naples and the surrounding area, including a visit to the ruins of Pompeii. The military section of Skelton's 1945 scrapbook showcases many of his Naples pictures, revealing a good sense of composition.[66]

· While Skelton's first two wives both took credit for getting him interested in painting, the letter to "Little Red" documented an already discerning critic. This was his comic take on the potential audience for the work of one Naples street artist: "a blind coal miner in Pittsburg[h]." (Maybe such mediocrity helped encourage his painting tendencies.) Ironically, given that this correspondence is to Skelton's bride, he makes reference to some local prostitutes: "I saw a few Italian girls putting on more make-up [than] they had [in] all of Max Factor's … they like to make people think they are younger." Maybe his lapse is explained by a later letter admission, "I think the Booz[e] Has Hit Me."

A further letter paradox, given Skelton's frequent entertaining at the White House, was Skelton's belief that President Franklin D. Roosevelt and the Democrats had put one over on the public by masking Roosevelt's poor health during the previous year's (1944) election: "I just saw a picture of Roosevelt [and] he don't [*sic*] look good. I wonder what the people would say if they knew how [Democratic National Committee Treasurer] Ed Pauley and [Democratic National Chairman Robert E.] Hannegegan took him [Roosevelt] out in the sun before the last election to make him look healthy … I got a feeling [Vice President Harry] Truman is going to be President of [the] U.S." Roosevelt died two weeks later.

Skelton's letter to "Little Red" even had a touch of pathos near the close. Unbelievably, the comedian's accommodations aboard the troopship, even after docking in Naples, were general quarters for enlisted men. He literally had no downtime. An inordinate number of GI shows was one thing, but when he tried to get some privacy, generally just for sleep, there were nonstop demands for autographs, solo and/or small group performances, and soldiers wanting to talk. Without ever stopping his advocacy for the rank and file, the comedian needed some rest.

Luckily, one of the ship's cooks came up with a brilliant solution—an extra pantry off the main galley was free, and Skelton had a secret hideaway: "This little closet I sleep in is sure nice; they can't find me for autographs ... I'd go on deck for some air but some bastard [officer] would rank [order] me into a show." Here is a major movie and radio star, ever so thankful for a hole-in-the-wall hideaway. As an addendum to Skelton's "bastard" reference, after the war the comedian was famous for the seemingly self-deprecating line, "Guess I'm the only celebrity who entered the Army as a buck private and came out the same way. I dood it."[67] But remaining a private was actually a point of honor for Skelton. During the course of his military career, officers had so overworked and under appreciated Skelton, the last thing he wanted was to join their ranks.

The comedian's nervous breakdown occurred shortly after reaching Italy, because he was already on a ship going home in April 1945. History has not recorded an exact date for the "crack-up," but it must have been sometime between the March 28 letter, written six days after landing, and some disturbing diary-like notes Skelton penned on April 12—the day Roosevelt died. Skelton observed, in part: "They say it was a massive cerebral hemorrhage. He had that in February [at the Yalta Conference] when he and [British Prime Minister] Churchill gave China and other concessions in the Far East to [Soviet Union dictator Joseph] Stalin."[68]

Skelton's ugly diatribe against Roosevelt continues along these lines. He seems to be parroting the faulty period views of the reactionary right. As historian Arthur M. Schlesinger Jr. later wrote, "Some critics have written as if Roosevelt and Churchill had perpetrated a 'betrayal' at Yalta. They have contended that Poland, Rumania, and China were 'sold down the river.' A glance at the text of the Yalta agreement makes it hard to sustain such charges. Far from things having been made easy for Stalin at Yalta, he was obliged thereafter to *break* the pledges he made there in order to achieve his aggressive purposes."[69]

Be that as it may, while Skelton's remarks seem overly harsh, especially for a former Roosevelt insider, they are still perfectly lucid. One might best explain them as an after effect of Skelton's nervous breakdown. Or, the comedian's darkly comic take on the president's death could be called emblematic of the general depression the comedian was undoubtedly working through at the time. The breakdown can be seen as more a case of depression, brought on by a combination of stress and exhaustion, with an army doctor cutting the comedian some bureaucratic slack by providing a diagnosis that sent him home more quickly. (Stress and exhaustion hospitalized Skelton on several occasions in the postwar 1940s and early 1950s.)

Skelton's stateside recovery took place at Camp Picket in Blackstone, Virginia. In a series of recent interviews with the grandson, David Rulf, of a social worker, Jack Wolfe, on the comedian's C-21 psychiatric ward, a darker picture emerges.[70] The reason the comedian was brought to this closed ward was that he represented a possible suicide threat, having threatened to take a hidden stash of pills. After two days, no one believed Skelton was serious about suicide. Still, the pills needed to be found and confiscated. Wolfe was elected to befriend Skelton and find the drugs.

Once the barbiturates were uncovered (hidden behind the lens of a camera), a real friendship developed between Wolf and Skelton. The young psychiatric social worker felt Skelton was more angry than depressed. The comedian believed the army was not fully utilizing him as an entertainer, while holding him to his other duties as a private. Yet the irony here was that Skelton had initially asked the army to assign him to regular duty, *without* special attention being given to his performer status. As in other situations, Skelton often said one thing, and expected others to guess what he really meant.

As an outpatient, Skelton was able to socialize with Wolfe and his wife, Julie. Between dinners at the Wolfes' home and a local hotel, the couple found being with the comedian a pure joy. They were, however, somewhat startled at how quickly he could shift into "entertainer mode" when in public. Skelton gave the couple one of his first oil paintings, a depiction of Blackstone, Virginia. The picture was signed: "To Jack and Julie. Best of luck to real people folks. May you always be happy and successful. You dood it, Red Skelton, nut ward 1945."

Skelton's former spouse, Stillwell, and his second wife, Davis, made the news by traveling together from the West Coast to visit the comedian. One article subtitle proclaimed: "Red Skelton's Bride and Ex Real Pals."[71] (One must add that such reports of their friendship were greatly exaggerated.) Shortly after their visit, patient Skelton again made the newspapers by helping two comedians (Buddy Baer and Ish Kabibble) entertain at the base. He had initially disrupted their act by pretending to be a disgruntled patient. Skelton had shouted from his ward bed, "I can't stand it any longer!"[72] Skelton had come full circle, back to his initial phrase for entertaining the troops, "laugh therapy."

Discharged from the army in September 1945 after a lengthy convalescence, Skelton spent a month at Davis's parents' ranch in Great Falls, Montana.[73] (Davis had been responsible for bringing paints to Camp Picket to help in Skelton's recovery, and the comedian continued his artwork in Montana.)

Despite the December resumption of Skelton's radio program to glowing reviews, 1945 had been relatively low-key for the returning veteran.[74] But other pivotal people to the comedian turned up in the news *and* in his Stillwell-maintained scrapbook. During July the *Chicago Times* reported: "Now actress Muriel Morris [the Skelton fiancée who had jilted him] changes her mind again ... [only] this time, after marriage."[75] The article went on to document her brief three-month marriage to another Hollywood player, and sympathetically implied Skelton had been one of her victims.

In October the *New York Times* did a feature article on an MGM director Skelton greatly admired, George Sidney, who had directed the comedian in *Thousands Cheer* and *Bathing Beauty*.[76] Sidney also directed Skelton's performance of "Guzzler's Gin" for the *Ziegfeld Follies* (1946). Skelton never blamed Sidney for the decision to focus more on Williams in *Bathing Beauty*, feeling it was a decision of studio officials—a group he placed on the same low level as army officers. Skelton also enjoyed Sidney's sense of humor, which was on display in the *Times* piece: "I came out here [Hollywood] weighing 160 [pounds] and now I weigh 280—so I must be a success."[77]

On November 25, shortly after Thanksgiving, Skelton's writer/ manager and former wife, Stillwell, married Oscar-winning director

Frank Borzage. The union was an impromptu decision, to the point of the bride borrowing her mother's wedding ring before a brief ceremony in Las Vegas.[78] As noted earlier, Borzage had directed Skelton's MGM screen test, as well as the comedian's first picture for the studio, *Flight Command* (1940). The director had remained close to both Stillwell and Skelton since that time. This sophisticated Noel Cowardish lifestyle continued after the war, with both the Skeltons and Borzages living, for a time, in the same luxurious apartment complex (one of Stillwell's investments for Skelton). Moreover, the couples also occasionally socialized together. But despite these appearances, the ongoing working relationship between Skelton and Stillwell put strains upon both new marriages.

For the time being, the comedian busied himself with being one of America's favorite clowns, with a silent-comedy legend sometimes providing a significant but shadowy influence.

9

Resuming a Film Career:
The Buster Keaton Factor

"Buster and Red were very fond of each other, and
Red would take almost any suggestion Buster made."[1]
ELEANOR NORRIS, KEATON'S WIDOW

Returning home from World War II, Red Skelton had a double
cushion with which to resume his film career. First, while his home
studio (Metro-Goldwyn-Mayer) had not always utilized Skelton to
his full potential prior to his military service, the comedian had still
achieved major star status during the war. Second, though Skelton
was returning from sixteen months in the army, Hollywood's movie
production glut during the war guaranteed that Skelton was still
highly visible in America's theaters. That is, with *Bathing Beauty* (1944)
continuing to play in many 1945 markets, and the *Ziegfeld Follies* (shot
1944, released 1946) having not yet opened, it was as if Skelton had
never been away. Moreover, the comedian did not just show up in these
two pictures; he performed some truly classic material. *Bathing Beauty*
showcased two seminal sketches addressed in the previous chapter: the
Buster Keaton-orchestrated ballet bit, and the Edna Stillwell-penned
routine about a woman getting ready in the morning.

In the true variety show format that was the *Ziegfeld Follies*,
Skelton's screen time was limited to a single sketch. But it was the
proverbial doozie. Here is the *Hollywood Reporter*'s sneak preview
(1945) take on the routine: "Red Skelton does his celebrated amusing

television ['Guzzler's Gin'] sketch."[2] Once the movie went into its all-important East Coast release (March 1946), the bit was being called a *Follies'* high point. For example, the *New York Times* stated, "The film's best numbers" are Skelton's sketch and Fanny Brice's "A Sweepstake Ticket" routine.[3] This was quite the accolade, as critics were describing the *Ziegfeld Follies* as a "gorgeous, massive, spectacular revue."[4]

Given this platform, MGM was less than imaginative with Skelton's first postwar assignments: *The Show-Off* (1946) and *Merton of the Movies* (1947). Both properties were hoary with age. The former film was based upon George Kelly's durable 1924 play, which had been adapted to the screen three previous times: 1926 (with Ford Sterling), 1930 (with Charles Sellon and renamed *Men Are Like That*), and in 1934 (with Spencer Tracy). *Merton* was drawn from the hit 1922 George Kaufman and Marc Connelly play, embellished from Harry Leon Wilson's *Saturday Evening Post* story. Prior to Skelton's screen version of *Merton*, the property had appeared in film form in 1924 (with Glenn Hunter) and 1932 (with Erwin Stuart and renamed *Make Me a Star*).

In *The Show-Off* Skelton plays a boastful railroad clerk seemingly obsessed with both the sound of his voice and a pretty neighbor (Marilyn Maxwell). As with his blabbermouth character in *Maisie Gets Her Man* (1942), Skelton's *Show-Off* braggart eventually reveals a good heart. The character's ability to be irritating, especially early in the picture, seems entirely alien to the basic Skelton screen persona, be it the goofy radio personality of his *Whistling* trilogy, or the sweetly silly spy of *A Southern Yankee*. To Skelton's credit, he single-handedly manages to make the old material work, after a fashion. And period critics were quick to give the comedian his due. For instance, *New York Herald Tribune* reviewer Joe Pihodna observed, "It is only because of the expert comedy of Red Skelton that situations and [the narrative] line of the old plot achieve some fire."[5]

Though Skelton dodged the bullet with *The Show-Off*, such was not the case with *Merton*. This tale of a star-struck rustic attempting to make it in the silent screen days of 1915 was, in the words of the *Hollywood Reporter*, "dated quite a bit."[6] The *New York Times* bluntly added, "[*Merton*] didn't work out anywhere nearly as swell as anticipated."[7] The *Washington (DC) News* (normally the most critically supportive of cities for Skelton), complained, "if he doesn't get brighter material than he has in 'Merton of the Movies,' people in large numbers will begin to think he's no comedian."[8]

Thanks, however, to what *Variety* called Skelton's "master clowning," some notices for the picture were positive.[9] Thus, the *Los Angeles Times* credited Skelton with having "developed into one of the genuine comedians of the screen," and the *New York Daily News* stated, "Maybe the current 'Merton' is not as funny as it was years and years ago, but Skelton fans are consistently amused by it."[10] Still, such cinema salve from reviewers could not bolster the box office. *Merton* became the comedian's first starring feature to lose money ($367,000—a sizable amount in 1947 dollars).[11]

Of course, potential patrons might have been scared off by bad *Merton* press long before the picture's autumn 1947 release on the East Coast. In February the *New York Times* reported that *Merton* was one of several shelved movie productions awaiting revisions "because studio executives were dissatisfied with the initial results."[12] In May syndicated Hollywood columnist Bob Thomas said, "All is not peaches and cream between Red Skelton and MGM. The comic is still unhappy over 'Merton of the Movies,' which already has undergone considerable re-shooting. He complains the studio is not publicizing him, and is even talking of playing [taking] his film talents elsewhere. 'I've got them licked,' [Skelton claims], pointing to a radio microphone, 'as long as I've got this.'"[13]

"This," for Skelton, meant his radio career, a medium that gave him both more creative control and more money. (Raleigh Cigarettes, his radio sponsor, paid him $1,000 a week throughout his army tour just to ensure his postwar services.[14]) MGM soon realized this was not a bluff on Skelton's part and others within the film industry were supportive of Skelton's need for better scripts. Celebrated funnyman Joe E. Brown included Skelton in his all-time top ten list of screen comedians during the summer of 1947, and "he [Brown] thinks Skelton could be the greatest of them all, if given different material."[15]

Skelton's lobbying for stronger movies, whether directly or via friends (Brown's list just happened to surface in the syndicated column of Skelton crony Bob Thomas), ultimately paid off. In late August 1947 famed Hollywood columnist Louella Parsons wrote, under the headline "Skelton Gets Break He Has Earned," that MGM was teaming the comedian with producer Paul Jones and the writing duo of Norman Panama and Melvin Frank.[16] For 1940s film comedy, this trio represented the gold standard. Jones had produced such Preston Sturges classics as *The Great McGinty* (1940), *The Lady Eve* (1941), *Sullivan's Travels*, and *The Palm Beach Story* (both 1942). He had also been in charge of the best two Bob Hope and Bing Crosby "Road Pictures": *The Road to Morocco* (1942) and *The Road to Utopia* (1946). Jones had also produced such imaginative Hope solo outings as *My Favorite Blonde* (1942) and *Monsieur Beaucaire* (1946). Continuing this Hope connection, writers Panama and Frank started out collaborating on radio scripts for the ski-nosed comedian in 1938. By the time their names were first linked with Skelton in 1947, their most notable successes were the Hope-Jones pictures *My Favorite Blonde* (story), *Road to Utopia* (script), and *Monsieur Beaucaire* (script).

Fittingly, the film on which this comedy trio joined forces with Skelton, *A Southern Yankee*, ultimately proved to be the comedian's best movie. But ironically, a person never mentioned in either *Yankee* press clippings, or even the credits for the picture itself, proved to be the most significant contributor—silent film comedy legend Buster Keaton. And his first connection to Skelton begins several years before with Skelton's favorite film, *I Dood It* (1943).[17]

Ever since critic James Agee's watershed *Life* magazine 1949 essay, "Comedy's Greatest Era," silent comedy's pantheon four have been Charlie Chaplin, Buster Keaton, Harold Lloyd, and Harry Langdon.[18] Strong cases can also be made for countless others, from the well-known antiheroic exploits of Stan Laurel and Oliver Hardy to the more obscure pioneering work of John Bunny in the early 1910s.[19]

But for the serious student of laughter, Chaplin and Keaton are miles
ahead of the comedy pack. The duo also represent a basic comic
dichotomy. Chaplin's alter ego, the Tramp, is a socially conscious
underdog whose plight moves us with old-fashioned *emotion*, as when
his "little fellow" pantomimes the story of David and Goliath in *The
Pilgrim* (1923); this is a footnote to the sources of all Tramp stories.
In contrast, the unchanging Keaton visage, "the Great Stone Face," is
a modern minimalist defense against the absurdities of today's world.
Consequently, one is moved *intellectually* by his stoic deadpan in the
final scene of *Daydreams* (1922), where Keaton is caught in the whirling
boat paddlewheel and climbs ever faster to avoid becoming a comic
victim in this metaphor for the treadmill nature of life.

Ultimately, Keaton and Chaplin dazzle us with their sorties into
the opposing worlds of the mind and heart by contrasting applications
of technology. Chaplin is a student of realism and lets his art unfold

A publicity poster for Skelton's favorite film with his favorite costar, Eleanor Powell—
I Dood It *(1943).*

in long take and long shot. While this is not uncommon for Keaton, he also flirts with formalism, where special effects and camera angles complement the comedy.

Paradoxically, one is more apt to link Skelton and Chaplin, both because Skelton was often prone to personally reference the "little fellow" creator, and Skelton patterned the pathos of his pivotal television character (Freddie the Freeloader) on Chaplin's Tramp. The cinema Skelton, however, thanks to MGM, had much more to do with Keaton. That is, Keaton was sometimes assigned to Skelton's films as an uncredited gag writer. (Keaton's fall from comedy grace was to Skelton's benefit.) Plus, several of Skelton's best pictures were loose remakes of Keaton movies. Thus, even when Keaton was creating new material for Skelton, the younger comedian's most memorable movie moments were often recycled Keaton bits. This was certainly the case with *I Dood It*, an updating of Keaton's *Spite Marriage* (1929).

Both pictures revolve around a lowly pants presser who is infatuated by a beautiful stage actress. Each movie boasts two inventive set pieces that Skelton replicated closely from the Keaton original. Skelton's *I Dood It* leading lady (Eleanor Powell) is the subject of his obsession. But with her heart initially belonging to another, she uses Skelton's character in a revengeful "spite marriage." Having second thoughts about this misuse of Skelton, she decides to slip him a "mickey," a doctored (knockout) drink, on their wedding night. Naturally, she accidentally downs the concoction and is soon comatose.

Despite Powell's inventively minimalist "performance" as so much dead weight, the sketch that evolves from her sudden Sleeping Beauty status is a slapstick showcase for a gentlemanly Skelton—a seemingly simple attempt to put her to bed. Skelton's one-way wrestling match with Powell includes everything from the comic frustrations of just trying to pick up and carry this stately prop, to the trials and tribulations of planting her on a bed and keeping her there. When Skelton then attempts to go the kindly comic extra mile by getting Powell out of an uncomfortable gown for a more restful night, the naïve antihero is ultimately baffled and finally opts to merely cover her with a bedspread.

The wonderful critical response to Skelton's rendition of this Keaton sketch might have encouraged the older comedian to revisit the routine during his acclaimed comeback performance at Paris's Cirque Medrano in 1947. Keaton was rebooked for this famous French circus and other European venues during the next several years. Keaton's return to the putting-the-bride-to-bed bit might also have been an authorship issue. That is, when Skelton's *I Dood It* version was praised, such as the *New York Daily Mirror*'s comment that it was a "howling [comic] sequence," the routine was often called "Chaplinesque"![20]

The second classic Keaton set piece recycled by Skelton in *I Dood It* involved the attempt to fashion a beard for the comic by cutting and pasting on what might be described, with tongue firmly in cheek, as the fuzzy remnants from the nursery rhyme about an "old grey mare." Skelton is replacing an actor playing a Civil War soldier in a play within the film, and Skelton's scissor-happy preparation scene has him accidentally cutting his ear, his real hair (he glues in fake hair), and the left strap of his undershirt, which he corrects by pasting the garment to his chest. Skelton loses his mouth under all the pretend whiskers, and has to go exploring for the opening with a brush. The glue often does not take, so the comic is also amusingly over generous with its application. Moreover, as a comic topper, Skelton periodically pauses during his exercise in self-barbering to admire in the mirror all his less-than-admirable facial hair. *Time* magazine said of this bit, "Skelton's broad and cheerful silliness—notably in one stretch of pantomime, upholstering himself in a false beard—comes so thick and fast that the effect is like being held down and tickled."[21] Skelton later claimed, "no one will ever say anything nicer about me."[22]

In spite of Skelton's effectiveness with these Keaton sketches, as well as the centerpiece for both *Spite Marriage* and *I Dood It*, a melodramatic Civil War play, Skelton remained insecure throughout the production. His director, Vincente Minnelli, later wrote, "he was

unsure of his effectiveness in comedy of the situation. 'I'm not funny,'
he complained to [his manager and ex-wife] Edna [Stillwell] … 'You're
crazy,' she told him. 'You've never been funnier.' Red proceeded to
agonize over all his previous performances. It was a wonder to him that
he'd ever gotten this far."[23]

For all the assistance Stillwell gave Skelton through the years, from
writing signature sketches to bailing him out of walkathon comedy
pranks that turned expensively destructive, her most important ongoing
gift to the comedian was being his number one fan. Even on what
would prove to be his greatest picture, *A Southern Yankee*, he needed
Stillwell as a cheerleader. Skelton asked her to be a special guest on this
set, and in an article written at that time she confessed, "That man kills
me. No matter what he does it's funny to me. I've been laughing at him
for [over] a dozen years. I'll never stop."[24]

Of the Skelton films that rework a Keaton original, *I Dood It*
follows the older comedian's work most closely. Interestingly enough,
certain sequences, such as the spoof of the Civil War melodrama within
the film, probably played even more effectively for Skelton's audience,
given the then recent huge critical and commercial success of *Gone with
the Wind* (1939). This box office juggernaut played in many smaller
markets, after its initial road-show engagements, well into the 1940s.

For all this Keaton influence, there are other common Skelton
threads that run through *I Dood It*, such as Skelton's antihero/wise guy,
first associated with Hope's screen persona. The casually breezy parallels
between Skelton and Hope were also the catalyst for *I Dood It*'s best
verbal gag. Near the picture's opening, Skelton strolls past an elaborate
department store window advertisement for the picture's feature
musicians, Jimmy Dorsey and his orchestra. Skelton casually observes
to a seemingly random sidewalk passer, "Boy that Jimmy Dorsey's really
got a band!" But this mildly amusing Skelton aside is merely a setup
for an in-joke. The passerby turns out to be the bandleader's bigger
name musician brother, Tommy Dorsey, whose orchestra was featured
in the comedian's *Ship Ahoy* (1942) and *Du Barry Was a Lady* (1943).

This surprise laugh is then topped by Skelton's response to yet another passing person, who asks the comic if he has ever heard Tommy's orchestra. With this brother right there, Skelton observes, "Oh sure, too many fiddles, though."

Comedy routines often follow a rule of three, which is what then transpires here. Tommy Dorsey deadpans the following topper, "I like Bob Hope, too." Director Minnelli then milks this inspired

WES D. GEHRING STILLS COLLECTION

Buster Keaton (right) near the close of his starring career at Metro-Goldwyn-Mayer, where he was briefly teamed with Jimmy Durante. Keaton's face mirrors the many problems that derailed his life in the 1930s.

comedy clinic by closing on Skelton's almost poignant expression of surprise. Dorsey's comeback has succeeded on several levels, beyond the entertaining back and forth setups. For example, it presupposes that the viewer is aware that Skelton's shtick is often Hope-like, so there is an "aha factor" going on—a cerebral in-joke, if you will. Plus, by allowing himself to be the butt of this elaborate three-part gag, it makes Skelton's already congenial character even more sympathetic.

Unfortunately, another non-Keaton common component to Skelton pictures was also present in *I Dood It*—the variety show format that distracted from Skelton. The added time for other acts was made possible, in part, by dropping a Keaton subplot aboard a yacht. However, if anything made this phenomenon more acceptable in *I Dood It*, it was the fact that much of the time was filled by the sexy, long-legged dancing brilliance of Powell. Several period critics, such as the *New York Post*'s Archer Winsten, were all but undone by the dancer's provocative allure: "Eleanor Powell, her magnificently sculptured legs showing practically to her lower ribs, can tap in the [perfect] manner to which everyone is accustomed."[25] This attraction carried over to Skelton himself, who later told me she was his favorite costar, which is also implied in a Skelton authored article, "The Role I Liked Best."[26] Years later, after his death, the subject came up in a phone conversation with his private secretary, Anita Mykowsky, and this was her bemused response: "He really liked Eleanor Powell!"[27]

Though the many parallels between *Spite Marriage* and *I Dood It* make this Skelton film arguably his most Keatonesque, the two comedians first worked together on the later *Bathing Beauty*. MGM called Keaton in as a gag writer and story consultant, when the Skelton and Esther Williams portions of the script seemed to be going in opposite directions. Keaton did as much bridging as possible, as well as creating such memorable Skelton bits as the ballet sketch. "Those who were present on the day when Buster met Red Skelton have all commented that there appeared to be immediate rapture between the two men," according to a Keaton biographer. "Buster took to Red the way he did because, as Buster put it many times, 'he reminded me of me at a younger age.' The initial relationship between these two men was like that of a teacher and his star pupil"[28]

While MGM must be credited for bringing the two comedians together, the studio missed the proverbial golden opportunity to make the duo a production team. Keaton so liked Skelton, both personally and professionally, that, as later chronicled by the older comedian's close friend and pivotal biographer, Rudi Blesh, Keaton "went to bat for him [Skelton] as if he were his own son—or an extension of himself from the disastrous past into a restored future. He went straight to [MGM chief Louis B.] Mayer.... In the inner sanctum he surprised himself with an eloquence he had never been able to summon in his own behalf. 'Let me take Skelton,' he said, 'and work as a small company within Metro [MGM]—do our stories, our gags, our production, our direction. Use your resources but do it our way—the way I did my best pictures. I'll guarantee you hits,' he said. 'I won't take a cent of salary until they have proved themselves at the box office.'"[29] A supportive Skelton also "offered to work without salary" (no small task for the money-conscious comedian) if he could team up with Keaton.[30]

Sadly, but not surprisingly, given Mayer and MGM's less-than-enlightened perspective on personality comedy during the 1930s and 1940s (versus a screen-clown friendly studio such as Paramount), the production duo of Keaton and Skelton did not happen. And maybe it would not have worked. In Keaton's 1960 autobiography he expressed frustration over Skelton's lack of passion for pictures, though he leaves the funnyman unnamed: "Another great comic would not even watch the scenes in his pictures that he did not appear in. He was more interested in getting back to his dressing room so he could write jokes for his radio show."[31]

How does one know Keaton was referring to Skelton? His widow, Eleanor Norris Keaton, told me at a later film festival in her husband's honor.[32] Keaton had put a name to this "great comic" in an obscure documentary broadcast after his death: "Skelton's first love was radio and yet nobody could do a better scene on the screen than Skelton without opening his trap.... [But] he'd go to his dressing room on the

Skelton's big smile seems to acknowledge the masterpiece status of A Southern Yankee.

stage between scenes and he wasn't worrying about what he'd do in the next scene. He'd go in there and start writing gags for [his] 'Little Junior' to say, or something for his radio script."[33]

Despite this frustration on Keaton's part, the older comedian's next direct collaboration on a Skelton picture, *A Southern Yankee*, still has the comedy connoisseur bemoaning what might have been. While Skelton preferred radio, one would never know it from his whimsically winning performance in *Yankee*. Since Skelton exercised more control on radio, he was more drawn to writing for that medium. Yet, his execution of the often Keaton-devised sketches for *Yankee* is so effortlessly funny they seem almost improvised. (Ironically, late in Skelton's life, he actually made that improvisational claim about *Yankee*.)

Before examining the surviving evidence of Keaton's influence on this picture, one must note again the importance of writers Panama and Frank, as well as producer Jones, whose greatest gift to a production was simply letting the creative people do their thing, with minimal interference. This trio was brought in by MGM after intensive lobbying for better material by both Skelton and others. MGM was also trying to save face in the film industry, since Skelton's first hit postwar-produced picture, *The Fuller Brush Man* (1948, shot just prior to *Yankee*) had been made on loan out to Columbia. Along similar lines, MGM had been embarrassed a few years earlier when its up-and-coming musical star, Gene Kelly, had first maximized his dance on film potential in *Cover Girl* (1944) in another loan out to Columbia! Consequently, MGM very much wanted to make *Yankee* an in-house critical and box-office hit.

Parody and witty dialogue are at the heart of Panama and Frank material. For example, one of their most celebrated bits was Hope's last-second admonishment to a *Road to Utopia* bartender, after his allegedly tough character had inadvertently ordered a sissified drink (lemonade), quickly demanding it be put in a "dirty glass." This writing team was also a master of tongue-twisting dialogue, including the tricky axiom Skelton's *Yankee* character must remember, "The paper's in the pocket of the boot with the buckle, [and] the map is in the packet in the pocket of the jacket." One could argue that the duo's tongue-twisting prose for Skelton was a warm-up for the even more acclaimed Panama and Frank verbiage Danny Kaye must commit to memory in the watershed parody *The Court Jester* (1956), where "The pellet with the poison's in the vessel with the pestle." (The writing team also directed *Jester*.)

While most story treatments for a picture only run ten to twenty pages, the Panama and Frank contribution to what became *Yankee* is a full seventy pages. Titled *The Spy*, the story's Civil War spoofing tone, about a bumbling secret agent (Skelton), is consistent with the finished film, as well as providing a great deal of the movie's dialogue, such as its "the packet in the pocket" bit. As a tongue-twisting addendum, the story also supplies Skelton with potential comic screwups of this tricky line. For example, "The map's in the packle [*sic*] of the bucket with the jackal! No! No! The jacket's in the buckle of the pocket with the boodle [*sic*]!"[34]

For all the delightful parody of an action adventure movie provided by Panama and Frank, their most imaginative touch, an "alternate ending," went unused. But this was probably because Skelton's antihero would not have gotten the girl, Sally Ann (Arlene Dahl). Panama and Frank had proposed that Skelton's character lose touch with her as the war wound down. Then, a chance encounter at the close finds Ann married to a Mr. Butler—Rhett Butler, with a show-stopping cameo by Clark Gable, as he briefly reprises his *Gone With the Wind* role.

Such a delightfully dizzy deviation had much to recommend it, beyond comic surprise. First, with Skelton often borrowing parody pages from Hope, losing the girl in the final reel to Crosby was often the "Road Picture" norm for the comedian. Second, nothing says parody any faster than cameos by actors associated with the genre being spoofed.[35] In Hope's first independently produced picture, the film-noir parody *My Favorite Brunette* (1947), the comedian cast Alan Ladd, a fixture in noir cinema of the 1940s, in the movie's funniest takeoff on this tough guy detective genre. Third, because both Skelton and Gable were MGM contract players, one would assume something could have

Keaton in his classic silent film The General *(1927).*

been worked out. In fact, Gable's widow would later reveal that Skelton was one of the actor's favorite entertainers.[36] Fourth, as my teaching colleague and *Gone With the Wind* scholar Conrad Lane reminded me, fans of the epic story would enjoy even a playful suggestion of what happened to Rhett Butler. (Along related comic lines, Skelton joked at the time that *Yankee* would be another *Gone with the Wind* and should be called *Back with the Breeze*.)

Despite the inventive Panama and Frank original story foundation and the opportunity to draw from Keaton's own Civil War reaffirmation parody, *The General* (1927), there were creative problems on the *Yankee* production. In Keaton's autobiography, he chronicles being called in as a troubleshooter because the movie "had received disappointing receptions when previewed."[37] Other sources suggest he was diplomatically toiling on the film much earlier, for example, Marion Meade's Keaton biography includes this comment from Dahl: "Whatever ideas Buster had were given sotto voce, so as not to hurt Red's feelings. He [Keaton] was a quiet presence who always knew what worked and what didn't. You never would have imagined he was one of the great comedians of all time."[38] Keaton's early involvement was undoubtedly assisted by the fact that *Yankee* was directed by the comedian's old crony Edward Sedgwick, who megaphoned several of Keaton's MGM films, including the memorable *Spite Marriage*. And when it came to collaborations between Keaton and Sedgwick, film historians tend to give the lion's share of credit to the silent clown.

Keaton's earlier involvement in the production would also explain how the comedian's most inspired contribution to *Yankee*, the two-sided flag scene, is included in Harry Tugend script material prepared for the picture.[39] The Tugend pages were filed *after* the earliest documented Keaton involvement on *Yankee*.[40] But because there are some questions about dates cited on the original *Yankee* script material in the Cinema-Television Library at the University of Southern California in Los Angeles, it is possible that the idea for the battle scene with the two-sided flag and uniform originated with Tugend but was not initially shot. Later, Keaton recognized the scene's significance and orchestrated the material's inclusion in the finished film. Adding further to the confusion is a *Long Island (NY) Star-Journal* article suggesting the scene in question would be shot sometime in February 1948, a date more supportive of crediting Tugend.[41]

Still, this pivotal scene is one of the few *Yankee* contributions for which the otherwise modest Keaton takes credit in his memoir. And like Skelton's first mentor, Clarence Stout, Keaton's chronicling of past events usually rings true, as opposed to Skelton's often "creative" reminiscences. Thus, here is the older comedian's detailed account of the two-sided scene, and why it proved to be such a comedy highlight: "[I] contributed the gag in which Red was shown walking between the Union Army and the Confederate Army, with both armies cheering him madly. The reason was that Red was wearing half of a Union Army hat and uniform on the side facing the Northern soldiers and a Southern hat and uniform on the other. In addition, he had sewed together the flags of the two opposing sides so that the boys in blue saw a Union flag and the Southerners only the flag of the Confederacy. Both sides cheer him wildly until a sudden gust of wind reverses the flag, showing both sides the game he is playing. As Red turns around to straighten the flag they discover his half-and-half uniform [too]."[42]

This scene is easily the most brilliant in the Skelton filmography and merits inclusion in any cinema pantheon of legendary comedy routines. The material is also perfectly consistent with the Keaton oeuvre mapped out earlier, by way of a comparison with Chaplin. That is, Skelton's character's foray into the contested space between the two opposing armies is initially a great success—a success predicated upon the most knee-jerk of responses—blindly jingoistic, flag-waving patriotism. Such rigid behavior is what comedy theorist Henri Bergson refers to as "mechanical inelasticity."[43] This is comedy more reflective of the cerebral Keaton than the heart-directed emotion of Chaplin.

Though the scene was initially conceived as having the two flags sewn together, and was first maybe even shot that way, the Hays censorship office would not allow it—too disrespectful! Consequently, in the finished picture Skelton carries *two* flags between the opposing armies, with both the Union and Confederate soldiers initially seeing only their own flags. (Paradoxically, many viewers "remember" the sequence as having the flags sewn together. In fact, that had been my childhood memory of the bit, until I rescreened the movie for this biography.)

Nevertheless, this Keatonesque *Yankee* scene is predicated upon the older comedian's formalistic tendencies. The special camera angles that make both armies think one of their own is bravely carrying the flag through no-man's land. But Skelton's ruse, to extricate himself from being pinned down between two armies, is short-lived. Yet, even this sudden change is classic Keaton. For Keaton, the absurdity of modern life is often triggered by natural forces, be it the rock slide of *Seven Chances* (1925) or the tornado of *Steamboat Bill, Jr.* (1928). In Skelton's *Yankee* a simple change in the wind wreaks comic disaster. Now, each army sees the enemy's flag, and as Skelton struggles to control these symbols in the wind, the two-sided nature of his uniform becomes apparent, also. "A change in the wind"—what a wonderful metaphor for how easily man's grand plans are derailed.

There are several additional Keaton bits documented in the *Yankee* files at the USC archives. The most entertaining example is an inventive exercise in Keaton minimalism, which is again driven by camera placement—and a small pine cone (another bow to provocative mother nature). After a lengthy horseback ride, Skelton's character stops to dismount: "Aubrey [Skelton] glances around for a place to rest his sore posterior. He spies a tree stump. The minute his rump touches the stump, Aubrey jumps with pain. He needs something softer to sit on. He looks about for a moment then, gathering an armful of pine needles on the ground, he places them on the tree stump for matting. He sits down and this time he fairly flies off [the stump] with pain. As he turns around we see that a pine cone which was concealed in the needles is still stuck to the seat of his pants. Aubrey, feeling about in the pine needles where the cone was concealed, and discovering nothing that should have caused such sharp pain, sits down [on the stump] again. Of course, he sits right on the pine cone. Once again he leaps with pain.

He glances about suspiciously—unable to understand what it is that is causing the trouble."[44]

Skelton's battle with the invisible-to-him pine cone is yet another exercise in Keaton basics. The apparent absurdity of modern life is reduced to a pesky pine cone, out of Skelton's line of vision. As with the two-sided flag and uniform scene, this second Keaton-constructed routine is predicated on the positioning of the camera. Indeed, Red's first pine cone-induced jump off the stump is initially a mystery to the viewer, too, until the comedian turns around. Also, like the "change in the wind" catalyst from the earlier sketch, the pine cone represents Keaton's fatalistic use of Mother Nature to cause a comic character grief. And by having Aubrey/Skelton "suspiciously" looking around, as if there were a conspiracy going on, underlines yet again the psychological/cerebral nature of Keaton's art, as opposed to the emotional/heart-directed orientation of Chaplin's films.

Additional *Yankee* production material by Keaton on file at USC includes sketches in which Skelton seemingly attempts to carry half the luggage available during the Civil War, as well as several routines tied to avoiding enemy capture by way of hiding in a doghouse, and behind linen on a clothesline, and an accidental visit to a dentist. Keaton was also responsible for the scrapping of early *Yankee* footage showcasing Skelton acting like an "imbecile." The older filmmaker explained, "As the comedian and leading man, Red lost the audience's sympathy by behaving too stupidly. If you act as screwy as he was doing, the people out front would not care what happened to the character you were playing … [The scenes were reshot,] toning down Red's nutty behavior."[45]

Thanks largely to Keaton, Skelton's greatest film was a critical and commercial success. The all-important entertainment bible *Variety* stated, "It's as wild and raucous a conglomeration of gags and belly-laughs as Skelton's recent [hit] 'The Fuller Brush Man.' The kiddies, the family and the general film fan will find it bait for the risibility's and respond with hearty ticket window payoff."[46] The *Hollywood Reporter* said, "Skelton, well on his road to becoming a really great clown, makes the most of every line."[47] The *Los Angeles Daily News* observed, "Red Skelton fans are going to love this one. It has everything Skelton does best—the pratfall, the delayed gag, the double-take, the mugging, the [spoofing] cowardice, and all the rest."[48]

Cue, with an intuitive sense of the uncredited Keaton, noted: "With gags borrowed from old time silent movies, and slapstick stunts adapted from his [Skelton's] own and others' comedies, Red Skelton romps dizzily through this wacky Civil War comedy."[49] But the critical pièce de résistance came from *Motion Picture Daily*, which called the film the "fastest, funniest comedy of this or any recent year."[50]

I belabor these superlative reviews both because of Keaton's unique contributions to the film, and the fact that history has done a disservice to *Yankee*'s critical reception. Much of this problem can be attributed to Arthur Marx's Skelton book, the first biography of the comedian, which claimed the *Yankee* critiques were "lukewarm"[51] Worse yet, Marx suggested "lukewarm" was an appropriate take on this neglected masterpiece. Marx had a proclivity to limit his review research to the *New York Times*, a publication that had panned *Yankee*.[52] But a close reading of this *Times* critique reveals more of an ongoing attack on MGM's continued mishandling of Skelton's career than simply a slam of the picture.

Of course, to play devil's advocate, there was a contemporary *Hollywood Reporter* article that suggested *Yankee* had not been well received by New York critics.[53] Yet, there were numerous positive *Yankee* reviews. For example, the *New York Morning Telegraph* said, "For Skelton fans ... this is the gravy train. They'll no doubt go rolling down the aisles with [comic] hysterics."[54] And it was obvious that the general New York viewer was pleased with the picture. The *Motion Picture Herald* documented, "Even when [*Yankee* was] previewed in a hot New York theatre—the air-conditioning engineers were on strike—the sweltering audience had itself a great time as Skelton ... mimicked and drawled his way through 90 minutes of pure fun." The same critique also credited these discerning viewers with fully appreciating the pivotal two-sided uniform scene, resulting in "the theatre howling with uproarious laughter."[55]

Sadly, Keaton never received his much-deserved credit at the time *Yankee* was getting such a plethora of positive reviews. In fact, on the rare occasion when a critic even compared the film to the work of a silent comedian, seemingly everyone *but* Keaton was noted. *Motion Picture Daily* stated *Yankee* "summons up memories of Harold Lloyd … [and] Charlie Chaplin."[56] Even more damaging to Keaton's legacy than neglect, or forgotten files in university archives, is Skelton's later denial that such a collaboration ever occurred. The year before Skelton's death, he did an extensive interview for a New York Public Library oral history project. Betsy Baytos conducted the interview at the comedian's home, and she asked him about Keaton's assistance on his films. Skelton responded, "I didn't know until after I left Metro-Goldwyn-Mayer that he had even done work on these movies."[57] An incredulous Baytos could only reply, "You're kidding?" Unfazed, Skelton goes on to claim that on the seminal *Yankee*, "sixty-five percent of it was ad-libbed by me."

Undoubtedly, one could attribute this to the ego-factor synonymous with most prominent people. I had encountered this firsthand with Skelton, after once prefacing a question to him with some obvious parallels between his Freddie the Freeloader character and Chaplin's Tramp. Skelton had taken this as an apparent affront to his creativity, and it nearly derailed an informal interview/conversation. As the comedian's nephew Marvin L. Skelton told me much later, as a blanket explanation of unusual behavior by his uncle or the famous in general, "They simply live different lives."[58]

The most ironic aspect of Skelton's denial of Keaton, beyond all the previously cited documentation, involves Skelton's appearance on a *This Is Your Life* television tribute to Keaton. Telecast April 3, 1957, the younger comedian praised Keaton for being a major influence on those pictures in which they collaborated. In addition, Skelton claimed to be most bowled over by the modesty of the iconic comedian, who had attempted to make onlookers think these inspired suggestions had originated with Skelton! In light of the later Baytos interview, it seems that Skelton ultimately bought into this falsity, too.

Beyond this paradox, however, one must add that Skelton had a tendency to eliminate from his personal history people who had once creatively influenced him. Thus, Keaton had simply gone the disappearing route that Skelton had by then already applied to Stillwell. Skelton's denial of Chaplin ties was a more tangential phenomenon. While the silent-cinema clown had never directly mentored Skelton, he so revered Chaplin, such as constantly using him as a model for his early goals on television, that Skelton's later protestation of parallels is ultimately his most ludicrous.

Regardless, the Keaton-related Skelton pictures were invariably Skelton at his best. Had some sort of ongoing collaboration between the two been allowed by MGM, Skelton's greatest comedy legacy might just have been in movies instead of television. As it was, Keaton would go on to make valuable contributions to the later Skelton films *Watch the Birdie* (1950) and *Excuse My Dust* (1951). Moreover, *Watch the Birdie* (a loose updating of Keaton's 1928 *The Cameraman*), was invariably superior to the other MGM material being offered to Skelton. While one can never say what might have been, it remains historically significant to reestablish here that Keaton's impact on Skelton was considerable.

10

A Small-Screen Chaplin Wannabe
and the Two Mrs. Skeltons

"Look Out, Television; Here Comes Red Skelton!"[1]
1946 NEWSPAPER HEADLINE

As one sorts through the post-World War II Red Skelton literature leading up to the comedian's first season on television (1951–52), one realizes what Skelton's movie mentor, Buster Keaton, was up against, when he voiced frustration about Skelton's obsession with radio at a time when they were jointly involved in a film production. Indeed, Skelton is quoted in 1947 as saying, "Movies are not my friend. Radio and television are."[2] In 1948 Hollywood columnist Sheilah Graham even reported that Skelton would have liked to limit his Metro-Goldwyn-Mayer filmmaking to one picture a year, in order "to take his [weekly] radio show around the country."[3]

Having noted all this, however, had Skelton been able to work exclusively with his favorite director, S. Sylvan Simon, maybe the comedian would have changed his mind. Simon directed Skelton in his career-making film *Whistling in the Dark* (1941), as well as the picture's two sequels (1942 and 1944). When MGM struggled with Skelton's post-World War II film assignments and a loan out to Columbia was arranged, Skelton made certain Simon was part of the production package.

The comedian was not disappointed. *The Fuller Brush Man* (1948) was Skelton's greatest commercial hit as a screen headliner.[4] Moreover,

A "wigged-out" moment for the enthusiastic novice salesman Skelton in The Fuller Brush Man *(1948) with Don McGuire.*

the movie was one of the top grossing pictures of 1948, even besting Skelton's most inspired film, *A Southern Yankee* (also 1948). Skelton later appeared in two movies with higher box-office returns, *Neptune's Daughter* (1949) and *Around the World in 80 Days* (1956). But the former film had Esther Williams as the top-billed title character, while the latter vehicle was an all-star affair with much of Hollywood surfacing in cameos.

Fuller Brush Man had Skelton mixing the door-to-door salesman trade with a murder mystery—shades of the *Whistling* series. Thanks to Simon, much of the comedy was grounded in the real world of Fuller Brush sales. The director's slice-of-life accent resulted in the company sending out ten thousand questionnaires to its men, "asking them to tell the most humorous incident which has happened to them."[5] Simon ultimately used several documented items in the film, such as Skelton the hairbrush salesman being met at the door by a bald homeowner.

Ironically, Skelton's screen frustrations as a door-to-door salesman also seem to have been drawn from reality. First, Simon had the comedian attend an official Fuller Brush class. Though history has not recorded how this went, phase two of his tutorial (actually going door to door) was a comic bust. The *Los Angeles Daily News's* article on the subject was titled, "Red Skelton Finds He's [a] Flop as [a] Fuller Brush Salesman."[6] A subdued Skelton had frequently gone unrecognized by potential customers. One housewife later confessed to him, "You're such a bad salesman; you know, I was only going to buy your brushes because I thought that other man [Skelton's photographer] was a supervisor breaking you in."[7]

Pity factor or not, Skelton loved Simon's research-oriented approach to comedy, with its foundation in meeting real people. Plus, the comedian appreciated the director encouraging him to ad-lib, or as Simon later described it, "[I] let Skelton have full rein and Skelton took advantage of every opportunity."[8] For example, at one point the script had Skelton innocuously asking an investigating detective lieutenant if he wanted cream in his coffee. Instead, Skelton ad-libbed, and Simon retained it in the final print, "How do you like your cream, Lieutenant, with one or two cups of coffee?" Being part of the creative process meant the world to Skelton. This was at the heart of why he preferred his radio program over filmmaking—greater artistic control. Even months after the release of *Fuller Brush Man*, Skelton told a reporter he was "eternally grateful" to Simon, with the journalist adding, "[Skelton] hasn't yet recovered from the shock of meeting such an understanding. director."[9]

The picture's superlative reviews often hinted at the naturalness of Skelton's performance. The *Washington (DC) Star* complimented Columbia studio's "good idea" of "letting the comedian be himself instead of asking him to play a character dreamed up by one of those so-called writers."[10] Along similar lines, the *Hollywood Reporter* said Skelton was "allowed to run completely wild, perhaps for the first time,

WES D. GEHRING STILLS COLLECTION

An informal moment on the set of The Fuller Brush Man, *as Skelton addresses the subject of a door-to-door salesman meeting a sexy customer, Adele Jergens.*

and is, as a result, a wonderfully funny comedian."[11] Fittingly, Skelton's favorite director was often singled out for praise in the reviews, such as the *New York Post*'s comment, "S. Sylvan Simon, producer and director of the film, here shows himself [a] master of the slapstick finale."[12]

Some critics, such as the *Brooklyn Eagle*'s Lew Sheaffer, entertainingly documented the demonstratively positive response of an *Fuller Brush Man* audience: "The [theater] house must have been full of Red Skelton fans yesterday ... because the laughter was loud, frequent and almost continuous. They obviously thought him a very funny chap."[13] Heartland audiences and critics were equally taken with the film, as documented by this review excerpt from Iowa's *Cedar Rapids Gazette*: "Red Skelton is currently Hollywood's top comedian. The large, howling audiences viewing his hilarious 'Fuller Brush Man' are getting proof of that."[14]

For all the brilliance of this Simon-Skelton collaboration, the movie was also greatly assisted by the writing of Frank Tashlin, who coscripted *Fuller Brush Man* with Devery Freeman. Tashlin's later comedy writing and directing for Bob Hope, Dean Martin and Jerry Lewis, and a solo Jerry Lewis made him the critical darling of the influential French film journal *Cahier du Cinema*. Given that Tashlin's background included being a syndicated newspaper comic-strip artist, as well as later stints with Walt Disney and Warner Brothers' Looney Tunes animation department, his live-action work with various personality comedians often assumed a frantically surrealistic nature. *Fuller Brush Man*'s best example of this is the movie's universally praised closing chase that showcases Skelton and costar Janet Blair fighting off gangsters in a military surplus warehouse. Drawing from Tashlin's inventive script, Simon creates a cartoonish world full of comically inflating dinghies, camouflage netting that doubles as a trampoline, distress flare explosions, and a falling prefab barrack wall. *Time* magazine described the exaggerated scene as "full of the ingenious low-comedy ideas which practically nobody seems to be able to think up these days."[15]

Moving beyond Tashlin's gift for exaggerated physical comedy in live-action settings, *Fuller Brush Man*'s warehouse close also anticipated

Tashlin's satirical skills at lampooning big business, fashion, and advertising in *The Girl Can't Help It* (1956, screenwriter/director/ producer) and *Will Success Spoil Rock Hunter?* (1957, screenwriter/ director/producer). The Skelton teaser for the shape of satirical Tashlin things to come occurs when the comedian and Blair are trying to get help via a warehouse stockpile of walkie-talkies, with their transmissions comically disrupting local radio and television broadcasts. Consequently, after a radio announcer begins a meat commercial with the following pitch, "And this is what a satisfied user of 'Simon Sausage' has to say about 'Simon Sausage,'" Skelton's plea cuts in with "Help, they're killing me," with Blair adding, "We can't hold out much longer."

The warehouse conclusion also inadvertently provides satirical cracks when Skelton and Blair are simply attempting to share tactical ideas over the walkie-talkies. For example, Skelton's suggestion to Blair on how to stop the pursuit of the bad guys involves pulling the inflatable dinghy cords. But this "battle" directive breaks in on a radio program covering current clothing fashions. Just as the broadcaster states, "And now the celebrated [French] fashion designer Jean Louis will give us his opinion of the new longer dresses," Skelton seamlessly interrupts, "Blow 'em up!"

Interestingly, Tashlin's work on *Fuller Brush Man* actually predated the writer's collaborations with Hope. This reversed the normal sequence of events where Skelton, if he was lucky, worked with talent that had originally risen to prominence with Hope. For example, the original story idea for *A Southern Yankee* came from Melvin Frank and Norman Panama, who started out as Hope radio writers. Following *Fuller Brush Man*, Tashlin was an integral part of such Hope hits as *The Paleface* (1948, co-screenwriter), *The Lemon Drop Kid* (1951, co-screenwriter/uncredited codirector), and *Son of Paleface* (1952, co-screenwriter/director).

Paradoxically, as noted earlier in the book, Skelton was *not* a fan of Tashlin's less-than-realistic style, despite the praise for the cartoonish conclusion of *Fuller Brush Man*. Skelton preferred the one-foot-in-reality approach to comedy that was more the hallmark of Simon.

Consequently, while it is hardly surprising that Skelton and Tashlin did not work together again, the fact that Skelton and Simon never again collaborated is a surprise, although this was not for a lack of trying. Syndicated Hollywood columnist Sheilah Graham reported in early 1948, prior to the release of *Fuller Brush Man*: "Red Skelton is interested in director Sylvan Simon's [film biography] project to star him as [Harry] Houdini, the magician."[16]

Skelton and Simon remained close, with the director being a special guest on Skelton's radio program in February 1948. Syndicated filmland columnist Bob Thomas kiddingly wrote of the visit, "Perhaps this is Skelton's revenge," given that the comedian was in charge of his broadcasts, versus Simon's control of the movie set.[17] Still, the director was the Skelton's biggest fan, calling him "probably the greatest living comic. The funniest sequences in all the pictures we've done together have come as a result of his split-second inspirations. He's the only comic I know who can get laughs and heart-tugs from the same audience."[18] Reciprocally, Skelton both appreciated being appreciated and Simon's gift for believable buffoonery. Skelton's allegiance to the director is matter-of-factly articulated in the *Los Angeles Examiner*'s glowing review of *Fuller Brush Man*: "Speaking of gratitude, it's not amiss to mention that Skelton and the rest of us owe a great debt to Sylvan Simon."[19]

As previously suggested, by the proposed Houdini film, the comedian and the director had an understanding that they would first bring any special scenarios to each other. Thus, it was also assumed that a pet project of Skelton and first wife, Edna Stillwell, would be under Simon's direction. That is, the former couple had "cooked up three original stories for him [Skelton] to make at Metro [MGM] ... [And] 'One,' says Red, 'is the story of my life with Edna.'"[20] As with the projected Houdini film, however, the Skelton-Stillwell script went unproduced.

The joint script by the former couple was yet another example of their ongoing post-divorce professional relationship. At the time Sheilah Graham comically mused in print, "I wonder how the current

Mrs. Skelton will like that!"[21] As a footnote to the biographical Skelton-Stillwell script, it should be noted that during the immediate post-World War II period the comedian was especially obsessed with documenting his life. In 1946 veteran Hollywood columnist Hedda Hopper reported that Skelton was writing a book bout his army experiences with the entertaining title, "There's a Skelton in My Closet."[22]

One can then couple this memoir news item with two related stories from early 1948. First, in a syndicated article from yet another filmland columnist, Harold Heffernan revealed, "Red Skelton is working on a partially fictionalized autobiography."[23] What makes this statement especially fascinating is that "fictionalized autobiography" perfectly describes Skelton's tall-tale tendencies in interviews.[24]

Second, shortly after this article appeared, Graham reported that the comedian would appear in the independent film *Redso the Clown* once he completed his MGM contract: "It's a circus story based on his own early life and is now being written by former wife Edna."[25] Like all the previously noted tentative projects, going back to Simon's Houdini script, *Redso the Clown* was never produced. Simon, more than even Skelton mentor Keaton, made filmmaking fun for Skelton, and had Skelton and Simon been able to make some of these unrealized projects, maybe the comedian would not have been so anxious to leave movies for radio and television. Coincidentally, while one might date the death knell for Skelton's film career to the 1951 beginning of his legendary television series, I would link it to another event that year—Simon's unexpected death at age forty-one.

Cinema's Simon and Keaton notwithstanding, Skelton was more drawn to radio and television for several reasons, starting with the greater artistic control it provided. And this was a subject on which the comedian could be downright poignant: "I *want* to be good on television ... In the movies, people still haven't seen *me*. They've seen a [film] writer and a [film] director. My new NBC [television] contract reads that I've got to be the [star and the] director."[26]

Second, Skelton recognized the phenomenal possibilities for television, likening the new small-screen medium to the pioneering days of film. In addition, Skelton was drawn to the informal familiarity of the small screen: "I consider the medium so intimate that I'm going to devote my first [1951 television] show to introducing myself and family. I'll be like knocking at the doors of strangers' homes and asking, 'May I come in?' This is the kind of fellow I am. If you like me, I hope you'll ask me back to your home next week."[27] Fittingly, as corny as this might now sound, Skelton's genuinely heartfelt comment was consistent with a performer who spent an earlier summer touring the United States conducting his own personal radio survey. The brainstorm of his like-minded populist manager Stillwell, the trip allowed the comedian to meet and poll his fans on what they wanted from Skelton's already highly rated program. Traveling in a station wagon equipped for sleeping, they found this to be groundbreaking radio "research," especially given that the star was doubling as the chief fact finder. Consequently, it was perfectly logical for Skelton to metaphorically ask his potential television audience, "May I come in?"

A third very practical reason for Skelton's radio and television preference simply came down to money. While largely forgotten today, the commercial airwaves offered Skelton money that dwarfed even a movie star's pay. For example, while his MGM weekly salary in the post-World War II 1940s was approximately $3,000, Skelton made $7,500 a week on radio.[28] Granted, the comedian received a modest raise from MGM in 1948 after the success of the Columbia-produced *Fuller Brush Man* had the latter studio bidding for his services. That same year, Skelton signed a new six-year radio contract worth $3 million. At $500,000 a year, this figured out to nearly $10,000 a week. Moreover, Skelton's eventual 1951 jump to television produced a $10 million, seven-year contract and banner headlines around the country.[29] While most of the headlines prominently featured that eye-popping monetary amount, one small-market publication offered a succinctly apt summation: "Red Skelton Signs Fabulous Contract."[30] Of course, Skelton's comment was more comically verbose, "Can you imagine anyone giving me that much money? They must be crazy."[31]

The film and television industries, however, were in the midst of a major entertainment war, and like a famous athlete being paid a king's ransom to join a new league, signing a film star like Skelton gave a

Charlie Chaplin as his immortal Tramp character in his greatest film, The Gold Rush *(1925). On the eve of Skelton's televisison career, he constantly referenced Chaplin.*

fledgling medium such as television greater legitimacy. Though the comedian's greatest motivation towards working in radio and television was undoubtedly driven by artistic control, these astronomical salary numbers had to be a factor, especially given Skelton's poverty-stricken childhood and his lifelong fascination with money-making schemes.

Finally, Skelton believed that television gave him the chance to be a small-screen Charlie Chaplin. The creator of cinema's immortal Tramp figure was a huge influence on the television Skelton, from his own Freddie the Freeloader character to Skelton's later purchase and transformation of Chaplin's old studio into a television production house. Appropriately, publications from pivotal 1951 (when Skelton entered television) are peppered with references to Chaplin. One *Kansas City Star* article also provided an especially rich perspective on the multiplicity of ways in which Chaplin citations occur. For instance, after reporting, "Red says he hopes to do for TV what Chaplin did for silent movies," the piece added that prominent entertainment biographer Gene Fowler believed "Red is probably the greatest 'sight' comic since Chaplin."[32] Furthermore, the article noted that Skelton even had copies of all of Chaplin's films.

As if documenting his knowledge of the Tramp filmography, another article from this seminal year for Skelton quoted the comedian as saying, "Kids can smell out a comedian who puts himself *above* his audience. That was the great thing about Charlie Chaplin, who is the master artist of all. There is hunger, pathos, and humbleness in Chaplin."[33] When his television show proved to be an instant hit, critics, such as the *Chicago Tribune*'s Larry Wolters, often compared Skelton to the silent star: "His partisans insist he's the funniest fellow since Chaplin."[34] *New York World Telegram* critic Harriet Van Horne was especially moved by an early Chaplin-like small screen Skelton sketch where he portrayed several types of people who frequent a cocktail lounge (part of the ongoing comedy legacy of Stillwell, who, starting with the donut dunking routine, wrote so many bits anchored to observing everyday people). Van Horn felt "the best of these characterizations was one that very few other comedians could do: the lonely woman who drinks," which inspired her review title: "Skelton Has Chaplin Tragic-Comic Touch."[35]

When yet another television critic asked Skelton how he hoped to maintain the medium's frantic pace, the comedian pulled a biography of Chaplin from his library: "Look at this. Here's a list of all the pictures Chaplin made. You can see that he turned out an average of [one] one-reel comedy every week for several years. Now there's a guy who evidently wasn't short of ideas for material."[36] Though Skelton does not quite get the numbers correct here—only in Chaplin's frenzied first film year (1914, under Mack Sennett) did he even flirt with producing a movie short each week, ultimately totaling thirty-five—the key point is that as Skelton began his television career, he was especially obsessed with the iconic comedian.[37]

Interestingly, while Skelton had always held Chaplin in high regard, even when his best film work had been more reflective of Keaton, late 1940s developments in Skelton's personal life encouraged this Chaplin connection in two ways. First, Skelton's second wife, Georgia Davis, had orchestrated her husband's friendship with the writer Gene Fowler, a close friend and chronicler of such celebrated comedy filmmakers as Mack Sennett and W. C. Fields. Davis believed the much older Fowler could be a supportive father figure and mentor to her husband. This proved to be a fruitful bit of intellectual matchmaking, from Fowler tutorials on Chaplin to the revelation that the hard-drinking Fields had been a huge fan of Skelton's, possibly drawn to Skelton's "Guzzler's Gin" sketch. Indeed, Fowler revealed, "Bill [Fields] often said before he died that no one else but Red could play Fields."[38] (An unrealized Fowler-Skelton project was to make a film biography on Fields, with Skelton playing the classic huckster.)

Second, the pièce de resistance for hero worship comes from a positive encounter with one's special luminary. Through regularly scheduled dinner parties at the home of *Los Angeles Examiner* critic Cobina Wright, the Skeltons were able to occasionally dine with Chaplin and the love of his life, fourth wife Oona O'Neill, daughter of playwright Eugene O'Neill. Skelton's joy over these meetings was

W. C. Fields on the set of Poppy *(1936), a production built upon the Broadway play that made the comedian's career.*

compounded by being able to successfully entertain this comedy master. Davis later confessed, "When he made Chaplin laugh at Cobina's he was so proud."[39] Host and critic Wright was more expansive on Skelton's entertainment skills concerning Chaplin and other comedians: "I have seen that now legendary comic, Charlie Chaplin, hold his sides, doubled over with laughter at Red's antics ... [and] men like Fred Allen and Jack Benny, choking with laughter, tears streaming down their cheeks, have begged him to stop long enough to catch their breath."[40]

One can assume, however, that for all of Skelton's admiration for Chaplin, there was little discussion of politics. As demonstrated earlier in the book, with regard to President Franklin D. Roosevelt, Skelton's political views were decidedly conservative, while the Tramp's alter ego was 180 degrees to the left. In fact, the year after the plethora of Skelton quotes concerning Chaplin, the veteran funnyman's longstanding left-wing politics resulted in his reentry permit to the United States being canceled. The comedian and his family were en route to Europe by ship for the London premiere of his latest picture, *Limelight* (1952). Because Chaplin was still a British citizen, despite a long U.S. residency, any attempt to return would have necessitated an appearance before an immigration board of inquiry. Given that Communist witch-hunting was then in full swing, and Chaplin had already long been persecuted in the conservative American press, he chose to relocate to an estate in Switzerland.

Sadly, through the fear tactics of politicians such as Senator Joseph McCarthy of Wisconsin, many Americans of the early 1950s believed assorted witch hunts were more important than preserving basic civil liberties. The blacklisting of many politically liberal artists sent shock waves through the entertainment industry—fueled by the inquisition-like tactics of the House Un-American Activities Committee. Unfortunately, frightened artists, such as Skelton's close friend Vincent Price, became HUAC "friendly witnesses," naming names of possible Communists in the entertainment industry in order to safeguard their own careers. (Price's leftist political activity as a young actor was the leverage HUAC used to force him into an unfortunate action.)

There was no such Skelton political baggage to be used against the comedian. Moreover, with an established conservative mindset, Skelton was predisposed to say the right thing. Of course, he might have received coaching from one of Hollywood's most rabid anti-Communists—syndicated columnist Hopper. Either way, Skelton's comments in her column also had the patented embellishments so synonymous with his public statements: "The Commies may point to our slums, or take in people who like to think they never had a chance. I could have stayed in these slums and rotted but I didn't. I got out on my initiative. And anybody else with the proper initiative can get out, too."[41]

Despite these rather over-the-top comments about Communism and the alleged slums of Vincennes, I cannot help thinking that Skelton's 1951 proclivity for positive comments about Chaplin was partly driven as a defense of his hero. At a time when political criticism of the silent comedy giant had reached all the way to the halls of Congress, Skelton would not have been the first period artist to attempt to counteract this overblown persecution of Chaplin. For example, in Gene Kelly's Oscar-winning picture *An American in Paris* (1951), Kelly performs a brief homage to the comedian's Tramp, mimicking the "little fellow's" shuffling gate to entertain some Parisian children.

Between the postwar resumption of Skelton's multifaced entertainment career and the 1951 launching of the comedian's television series, he had never been busier. As a late 1947 article in *Silver Screen* magazine stated, "If there's a harder working comedian in Hollywood than Red Skelton, he's crazy, because Red already works twice as hard as he should. His routines are not just chatter. Red invariably knocks himself out all over the place in putting over a gag."[42] Similar to Willie Mays, the Hall of Fame baseball player who worked so hard at his game that he was periodically hospitalized for exhaustion, the conscientious comedian's equally driven work ethic necessitated periodic medical attention, too.

If being a harried helter Skelton movie and radio star were not enough, the postwar private life of the comedian was equally complex.

At the forefront of attention was what *Movieland* magazine, among many other publications, referred to as "The Two Mrs. Skeltons."[43] Skelton was married to second wife Davis, but former wife Stillwell managed his money and produced the comedian's radio program. But beyond that, Skelton felt he owed his career to Stillwell and continued to be professionally insecure without her advice on all major decisions. Mix in Skelton's guilt over leaving this still dedicated Skelton disciple, and one has a lot to cope with if you are the *second* Mrs. Skelton.

Beyond all this, there was the simple fact that Stillwell was either ever present or close by. After the war she had arranged for Skelton and Davis to live in the Wilshire Palms, a luxury apartment complex owned by the comedian and Stillwell. But Stillwell and her husband, former Skelton director Frank Borzage, also lived there. In addition, the equally driven Stillwell often dropped by unannounced to discuss business and/or radio material with Skelton. Georgia found the whole arrangement peculiar—a feeling also shared by Skelton's extended family.[44]

In Stillwell's defense, however, there was a great deal for her to confer with Skelton about, since the two were very proud of what they liked to call their ongoing professional arrangement, Skeltons, Incorporated. Couple this with the fact that Hollywood is all about mixing business with pleasure, and the two Mrs. Skeltons were frequently thrown together. For example, the weekly ritual of dining at the famous Brown Derby restaurant following Skelton's radio broadcast was often an extended "family" occasion involving staff and spouses.

Even Christmas generosity could get Skelton in trouble. One Yuletide Skelton "bought two identical mink coats, in the $5,000 range, and gave one to Edna and one to Georgia. [As *Look* magazine comically noted] this sort of thing is not recommended by marriage counselors."[45] What undoubtedly made the transaction even more galling for Davis was that Stillwell controlled the comedian's purse strings on large purchases—a safeguard against Skelton's susceptibility to hucksters and hard-luck stories. While this made good business sense, having your husband's ex-wife sign off on your Christmas present, which she was also receiving, defused the magic.

Skelton's second wife, Georgia Davis, in costume for a small role in Judy Garland's The Harvey Girls *(1946). Davis retired from films soon after this movie.*

Differences over Stillwell produced some classic donnybrooks between the Skeltons. However, Stillwell was not always the catalyst for their marital discord. Davis found that living with this insecure man-child was not an easy task. She later wrote, "He still is highly changeable in his moods. I never can be certain of them but I know they are caused by a [childlike] lack of a long-run view, by subconscious fears that persist. I know I have to be six jumps ahead in awareness of how he's about to feel."[46]

When Davis was unable to circumvent Skelton's depression, or differences over Stillwell surfaced, arguments often turned ugly. Sometimes heavy drinking further fueled these fights and a pattern soon developed. Skelton would storm out of their apartment and check into an area hotel. In a day or two tempers would cool and all would be forgiven, for a time. Despite this, or maybe because of this, the couple decided to start a family. A daughter, Valentina Marie, was born May 5, 1947. With Skelton anxious for a son, Valentina soon had a baby brother—Richard Freeman was born June 14, 1948. (Skelton's given name was Richard, and Freeman was in honor of an early Skelton agent and adviser, Freeman Keyes.)

Ironically, part of the personal attractiveness of Skelton to both his wives was rooted in a component that also generated problems—his man-child nature. Davis's positive spin on this duality might have been uttered by either woman: "He is a madcap clown, with an appealing helplessness and kindness that opens your heart."[47] Still, whether it was Stillwell having to orchestrate damage control over Skelton's walkathon pranks, or Davis being upset about duplicate Christmas gifts, the comedian just did not always clearly think through his actions.

While both women tried to protect Skelton from himself, late 1940s fans were most aware of Stillwell's attempts to fix the comedian's "kidadult" tendencies. The most glaring period example of this phenomenon also addressed another Skelton weakness—his proclivity for misrepresenting the facts and/or embellishing the truth. The case in point involves Skelton's unhappiness with MGM's handling of his film career. In 1947 there was a flurry of articles about the comedian's claim that he would pay the studio $750,000 to release him from his contract.[48] While armchair critics and pop-culture pundits debated Skelton's deep-pocketed offer, the comedian was soon "red" in the face. A week after his Daddy Warbucks-like pitch, it was revealed that "Red Skelton, who knows more about jokes than high finance, said today he was all mixed up when he told everybody he'd offered MGM $750,000 to let him go. He hasn't, he's discovered, that kind of dough."[49]

How does this happen? Yet again, Stillwell had to come to the rescue. Sometimes an attempt at damage control only made things worse and that seemed to be the case here. Stillwell stated, "We've asked for our release—or an adjustment in salary. What I told Red was that he'd earn about $750,000 during his next four years there. Not—definitely not—that we'd pay them that for our release! But all he remembered from the conversation was the $750,000."[50] Moreover, this embarrassing situation was the catalyst, in the same article, for the comedian's single most telling comment of his public life. A "snickering" Skelton said, "That's my trouble. If you want a good story—talk to me. If you want the facts—talk to Edna." This speaks volumes about Skelton's creative approach to the facts of his life.

Skelton might have been married to Davis in 1947, but crises like this more often linked him to Stillwell in the public's eye. Her high-profile identity with Skelton was also underlined by the fact that she continued to perform spouselike duties for him: "She's on twenty-four-hour call for anything pertaining to his [Skelton's] career, oversees all business investments, and takes care of chores such as looking after his wardrobe and making sure that six suits are in the cleaners and six available to work with."[51] Indeed, when a journalist during this period asked the comedian to see a picture of his baby daughter Valentina, Skelton said, "Hey, Edna, show her a picture of Valentina."[52]

Despite all of the comedian's postwar prophetic comments about the future of television, or his insightful observations about comedy and Chaplin, the late 1940s media often saw Skelton as an overgrown kid. Unlike Stillwell's and Davis's lovingly parental attempts to protect him, critics could be less than kind. For example, syndicated Hollywood columnist Graham was so put off by Skelton's former wife handling everything, right down to his child's baby picture, that she wrote, "One day I'm going to ask Edna to show me a picture of Red Skelton, because he's like a baby, too. That's the way Edna handles him."[53]

Events of the early 1950s put Skelton on a further metaphorical roller coaster with representatives of the fourth estate. A last hurrah to the comedian's film career and a brilliant launching of his much-anticipated television career still made him a popular positive subject of the press. A disastrous second season on the small screen and a public meltdown with Davis, however, led to more questions about the comedian's stability. Events such as these would no doubt trigger Skelton's later frequently noted mantra, "I'm nuts and I know it but as long as I make them laugh they ain't going to lock me up."[54]

11

Racking up the Pressure

"Red is a perpetual worrier. When he got out of the Army he bit his nails and couldn't ever relax. He still has trouble being quiet more than a minute but he isn't as insecure inside as he was."[1]
GEORGIA DAVIS SKELTON, 1952

Sadly, the above quote was overly optimistic. Later that same year, the calamitous opening of Red Skelton's second television season, and the unnerving ongoing pressure to simply create fresh material for this all-consuming "glass furnace," put his health and marriage at risk. Not since Skelton suffered what was sometimes described as a nervous breakdown during his World War II tour of duty in the army had he been brought so low by overwork and day-to-day anxiety. But for the student of Skelton, it is surprising that there had not been more psychological meltdowns in the interim, given his crowded work schedule.

After the war Skelton had continued to headline a popular radio program that had finally decisively beaten Bob Hope—the comedian that had influenced him through the years—in the ratings for the 1949–50 season.[2] Moreover, while the hectic demands of television eventually put the kibosh to Skelton's screen career, he did not wind down gradually. Here is Skelton's filmography following his masterpiece movie *A Southern Yankee* (1948): *Neptune's Daughter* (1949); *The Yellow Cab Man*, *Three Little Words*, *Duchess of Idaho* (cameo), and *Watch the Birdie* (1950); *Excuse My Dust* and *Texas Carnival* (1951); *Lovely to Look*

At (1952); and *The Clown, Half a Hero*, and *The Great Diamond Robbery* (1953). But other than one additional starring vehicle (*Public Pigeon No. 1*, 1957), and a handful of cameos (most memorably in *Those Magnificent Men in Their Flying Machines, or How I Flew from London to Paris in 25 Hours and 11 Minutes*, 1965), Skelton's movie career abruptly ended.

Before exploring the notable rise and fall of those first two television seasons, it is important to closely examine the movies that led up to Skelton's small-screen debut. Ironically, they reveal that MGM was finally getting a better handle on how best to use Skelton. The even greater paradox is that if Skelton had stayed with film and not jumped to television, he would probably now be acclaimed as one of the pantheon screen comedians, instead of a promising movie clown who aborted his big-screen career much too early.

An inspired cameo by Skelton in Those Magnificent Men in Their Flying Machines *(1965)*.

This MGM epiphany concerning Skelton did not, however, happen immediately. After Skelton's major personality comedian hits in 1948—*The Fuller Brush Man* (produced by rival Columbia studio) and *A Southern Yankee*— Skelton's only screen appearance the following year was in support of Esther Williams's title character in MGM's *Neptune's Daughter*. This was a regression to the "cinema vaudeville" of World War II, where Skelton is limited to some entertaining turns in a variety show setting. Plus, unlike his earlier teaming with Williams in *Bathing Beauty* (1944), Skelton is not her love interest. That honor went to Ricardo Montalban, who, with the casting of Xavier Cugat and his orchestra, also reflected another aspect of Hollywood's war mentality— feature Latin American talent in order to pick up new foreign markets and compensate for lost audiences in Nazi Germany-controlled Europe.

Skelton plays a country club masseur who is confused with Montalban's South American polo player. This is an effective catalyst for several Skelton scenes, such as his attempts to mount a polo pony, or a routine in which he pretends to speak Spanish, with the help of a record. Skelton is also funny in a musical duet with underrated comedy character actress Betty Garrett, when they share warbling duties of the Oscar-winning song "Baby It's Cold Outside" with Williams and Montalban.

One might query, "What's the problem?" Skelton had the potential to be one of the premier pantomime-oriented screen clowns of history—a verdict first put forward by no less a legendary film comedian than Buster Keaton. Consequently, why would the studio put someone with such a colossal comedy capacity in a wordy supporting role? Distressingly, this is reminiscent of MGM's misuse/underuse of Keaton himself in the early sound picture *Free and Easy* (1930). As the critic and later filmmaker Pare Lorentz said of Keaton's performance in that movie, "[He] not only talks; he sings and dances. He does them all well but ... there are thousands who can do his tricks just as well.... He is no longer the enigmatic [silent] personality."[3] Lorentz might have been speaking of Skelton in *Neptune's Daughter*.

Moving on to Skelton's high visibility 1950, his first feature outing was more in line with what a major personality comedian should be doing. Skelton was the title character of *The Yellow Cab Man*—a loopy inventor who becomes a cabbie in an attempt to sell his nonbreakable "elastiglass" to the company. *Cab* is an entertaining mix of both old-school clown comedy and some new parody twists. The former trait is best characterized by the picture's parallels with the comedy world of W. C. Fields.[4] Despite Fields's ever-so distinctive voice, a flowery drawl of honey-toned hucksterisms, his work is often visual in nature, especially when he plays an inventor.

Coincidentally, one of Fields's zany screen visionaries, from the silent *So's Your Old Man* (1926), also creates an unbreakable windshield. Indeed, a pivotal scene in both this movie and *Cab* involved the special glass being switched just prior to an all-important sales demonstration, with each comedian's character then being comically mortified when his unbreakable glass shatters. Interestingly enough, another Fields film might also have contributed to Skelton's *Cab*. When Fields remade *So's Your Old Man* in the sound era as *You're Telling Me* (1934), the invention changed from unbreakable glass to a puncture-proof tire. When Fields tests his tires by firing a pistol at them, he also wears a baseball glove with which to catch the ricocheting bullets; and this is precisely how Skelton checks his unique glass in *Cab*.

These Skelton links to Fields might have been an outgrowth of Skelton's close friendship with writer Gene Fowler, one of the late Fields's favorite drinking companions. Skelton was also enough of a Fields fan to have acquired, through Fowler's assistance, several of the older entertainer's comedy props. These included some oddly shaped cues and irons from signature Fields sketches involving a pool table and golf. Along related lines, early in Skelton's tenure in television he added a Fields-like figure to his cast of comedy characters. Going by the name of San Fernando Red, this smooth-talking con artist was very much in the tradition of Fields's huckster persona, including selling a "talking dog" to a sucker in *Poppy* (1936).

Cab was not, however, just a retro personality comedy. The picture also applied parody to the period's most up-to-date developments, such as that new genre of the 1940s, film noir. A more user friendly phrase would be "pulp fiction's tough-guy detectives," forever synonymous with such hardboiled detectives as Dashiell Hammett's Sam Spade and Raymond Chandler's Philip Marlowe. The film-noir hero, or antihero, might be tough but because he frequently is victimized by hard blunt objects and/or knockout drugs, he often finds himself in a surrealistic dream/nightmare state. For example, in Edward Dmytryk's screen adaptation of Chandler's *Farewell My Lovely* (*Murder, My Sweet*, 1944), Dick Powell (as Marlowe) blacks out so frequently it becomes a darkly comic component of the picture.

The film-noir element in Skelton's *Cab*, complete with mind games, is anchored in Walter Slezak's portrayal of a mobster out to get Skelton's secret formula for elastiglass. By doubling as a psychiatrist, Slezak can get at the inner inventor by simply hypnotizing the comedian

Skelton being victimized by Walter Slezak (right) and J. C. Flippen in The Yellow Cab Man *(1950).*

into a trancelike state. Since Slezak's shrink has Freudian overtones, given his psychological attempts to take Skelton back to childhood, this noir dreamlike state segues naturally into broad comedy, such as a brief sketch with Skelton playing both himself as a child and a battling twin. But sometimes the movie's sense of the surreal has more to do with Skelton's character being a goofy inventor. For example, his multifaceted alarm system has so many moving parts and assorted noisemakers that the *Motion Picture Herald* described it as "Rube Goldbergish," which merely means a contraption that performs a simple task with a maximum amount of energy/action being spent.[5]

Of course, the greatest drawing card for any personality comedy picture is the highlighted clown himself. This is a genre driven by a beloved characterization, a cinema friend with whom one is so minutely familiar that the fan simply wants to reconnect through laughter. Iconic clowns got that way by tapping into the universal in the particular, such as Chaplin using the victimization of his Tramp character by the neighborhood cop as yet another metaphor about the plight of the individual in modern society. Overt change to the personality comedian is not popular. Audiences simply want variations upon the same comedy shtick. Thus, when Chaplin abandoned the vulnerable Tramp for a murderous French Bluebeard in the brilliant *Monsieur Verdoux* (1947, a title character that assumes society's victimizing role), audiences stayed away.

Skelton's antiheroic persona embraces a philosophy of feel-good populism—a study in comedic humanism that celebrates the persevering good of the common man. Skelton was consistent to this characterization throughout his complete oeuvre (stage, screen, radio, and television), without even a threat of a *Verdoux*-like detour. The best encapsulation of Skelton's persona came from a *Cab* review by *Los Angeles Times* critic Philip K. Scheuer: "Skelton always comes up smiling, quick to forgive and ready to believe the best of his fellow men. He is the servant of the people, the courteous Yellow Cab Man."[6]

As a related *Cab* footnote, personality comedians often acknowledge their special link with fans through direct address—breaking the fourth wall and playing directly to the camera/audience. Invariably, the clown is the only one in the cast with this playful awareness of the story's pretend nature, which further cements his bond with the equally artifice-conscious audience. Fittingly, Skelton's *Cab* opens with the comedian giving a direct address tip of his hat to viewers—a fan connection gesture further underlined by then holding that clown image in a friendly freeze frame.

Appropriately, *Cab* was a major critical and commercial hit, with a profit margin double that of Skelton's greatest picture, *A Southern Yankee* ($545,000 to $263,000).[7] (While both movies had roughly the same domestic box office, *Cab* cost less to produce and attracted a larger foreign audience.) Of the picture's many positive reviews, the *Motion Picture Herald*'s critic was most magnanimous: "'The Yellow Cab Man' is as wonderful a bit of Red Skelton zany business as has ever come off the Metro [MGM] lot."[8]

In playing a cabbie or a Fuller Brush man, Skelton's comedy had benefited from having one foot in reality. In fact, Skelton's *Fuller Brush Man* director (S. Sylvan Simon) actually drew movie material from real company surveys. With that thought in mind, Skelton's film follow-up to *Cab* takes the process one step further; Skelton plays a real person, songwriter Harry Ruby. The biography picture in question, *Three Little Words*, chronicles the career of Ruby and his writing partner, Bert Kalmar, played by Fred Astaire.

Normally, one might have misgivings about derailing an up-an-coming personality comedian into a biography film. But *Words* presents several extenuating circumstances. First, Ruby is an often comic character, especially as related to his obsession with baseball. Through the songwriter's friendship with Washington Senators pitcher Al Schact, Ruby frequently worked out with the players. These amusing segments in the movie provide Skelton with physical comedy opportunities that draw upon reality. That is, besides Ruby's less-than-major-league skills, his diamond friend Schact later became more famous as the "Clown Prince of Baseball." Plus, Ruby's favorite team then occupied a belovedly antiheroic position most synonymous today with the Chicago

Cubs. The following is a popular baseball axiom about the luckless Senators: "Washington, first in war, first in peace [pause], and last in the American League."

A second extenuating reason for the appropriateness of casting Skelton in the movie was his pre-established comedy connection with baseball. This came courtesy of Skelton's inspired shenanigans in *Whistling in Brooklyn* (1944), when he did comic battle with another revered bunch of baseball losers—the Brooklyn Dodgers. Add to this Skelton's occasional baseball references in other pictures, such as catching ricocheting bullets with his glove in *The Yellow Cab Man*, and the national pastime seems the perfect setting for Skelton's comedy.

A final justification for Skelton turning up in this film biography is that while Kalmar and Ruby's music might be most associated with romance, such as the haunting "Three Little Words," which doubles as the movie's title, comedy connoisseurs gravitate towards their funny

Vera-Ellen and Fred Astaire are fascinated by Skelton and a canine friend in Three Little Words *(1950).*

musical numbers. These comic songs included: "Hooray for Captain Spaulding," *Animal Crackers* (1930, the Marx Brothers, and later Groucho's theme song), "Everyone Says 'I Love You'" and "I'm Against It," *Horse Feathers* (1932, Marx Brothers), and "The Country's Going to War," *Duck Soup* (1933, Marx Brothers). Kalmar and Ruby also wrote Helen "boop-boop de-doop" Kane's signature song "I Wanna Be Loved by You." And Woody Allen creatively reprised "Everyone Says 'I Love You'" throughout his charming musical comedy of the same name (1996). Moreover, though often forgotten today, Kalmar and Ruby provided music and scripts for pivotal pictures by other important 1930 comedians, such as Eddie Cantor (*The Kid From Spain*, 1932), Bert Wheeler and Robert Woolsey (*Kentucky Kernels*, 1934), and Joe E. Brown (*Bright Lights*, 1935). While *Three Little Words* did not fully address Kalmar and Ruby's comedy legacy, its mere existence further legitimized the casting of Skelton as Ruby.

Three Little Words scored highly with both the public and critics. As one of 1950s top box office pictures, it grossed nearly as much as the year's critically acclaimed *All About Eve*, which won the Academy Award for Best Picture, as well as a then unprecedented thirteen nominations in other categories.[9] Skelton's reviews for *Words* were yet another exercise in superlatives, with even the hard-to-please *New Yorker* waxing poetic about his understated performance, "Red Skelton does splendidly as Mr. Ruby."[10] The *Hollywood Citizen News* credited Skelton's "surprising performance … [which] proves that he has the stuff for weightier efforts than his slapstick films."[11]

After this excursion into film biography, Skelton returned to the familiar landscape of clown comedy, starring in *Watch the Birdie*, a loose remake of Keaton's *The Cameraman* (1928). In *Birdie* Skelton orchestrates a comedy trifecta, as he plays cameraman Rusty Cammeron, as well as the character's father and grandfather. His multiple role trick might have been encouraged by the previous year's *Kind Hearts and Coronets* (1949), the British dark-comedy hit in which Alec Guinness plays eight comic victims. Regardless, critics were taken with Skelton's comedy cloning. The reviewer for the *Los Angeles*

Examiner observed, "Red continues to grow in stature as an actor with each succeeding effort on the screen. This time, in a brave challenge, he does it by way of three distinct roles."[12] This triple-threat Skelton also won over new fans. The *Los Angeles Mirror* critic normally found Skelton "predictable," but in the comedian's playing of the father and grandfather, "he becomes an actor. He concentrates on the humor inherent in the characters, and he's much more amusing."[13]

Skelton's sensitive *Birdie* portrayal of father/grandfather figures is reminiscent of comedian Brown's comparable playing of senior family figures in his movies of the 1930s and early 1940s, especially in *The Circus Clown* (1934).[14] While both Brown and Skelton had a tendency to make their main characters over the top, they often reined in these older types to an almost poignant minimalism. Appropriately, Skelton further honed his senior figures as he aged, often highlighting them on the pantomime portion or "silent spot" of his long-running television show. Three of his most age-related pantomimes, which were invariably featured in his later post-television one-man-shows, were: "Old man watching parade," "Old man playing golf," and "Old man smoking pipe."[15] Of course, in a broader context, Skelton's playing of multiple figures in a 1950 movie seemed to be a sneak preview for his character-laden television series.

The most entertaining interaction of *Birdie* Skeltons occurs when "Grandpop" gives shy grandson Rusty a cinema tutorial on romance. This scene also allows MGM to promote two of its biggest contract stars, Clark Gable and Robert Taylor, by having Skelton "study" Gable's *Boom Town* (1940) and Taylor's *Johnny Eager* (1941). The topper to this—beyond two Skeltons interacting—is that Grandpop encourages Rusty to mimic the now politically incorrect rough-with-the-ladies style of Gable and Taylor. Not surprisingly, timid young Skelton asks old Skelton, "What if she slaps back?" A knowing Grandpop comically answers, "That, my boy [chuckling pause], is marriage." But this somewhat cracked crackerbarrel wisdom is consistent for a character that amused viewers with this senior axiom on romance: "Let the ladies beware, let the music begin, there's many a good tune in an old violin."

Skelton battles with Mike Mazurki in the dressing-room scene from Watch the Birdie *(1950).*

There are, however, a wealth of funny *Birdie* scenes that do not
depend upon Skelton's older characters. The two best are actually lifted
from Keaton's *Cameraman* original. The first is a sight gag where a
camera-carrying Skelton risks the proverbial "life and limb" to board
a speeding fire truck in hopes of scooping the competition on some
newsworthy disaster. Holding precariously to the side of the emergency
vehicle, Skelton's bravado immediately involves the viewer in this race
for provocative film footage. Where will the fire truck take him/us?
Soon the destination is clear—the fire truck is simply returning to the
station!

The second Keaton bit showcased in Skelton's remake was even
comically footnoted in the *Birdie* script treatment: "Here we steal a
scene from 'The Cameraman.' The ... [routine] where Buster Keaton
and another man change clothes in a dressing room hardly big enough
for one midget."[16] Unfortunately, while the new version is funny, the
laugh quotient of the original is much higher. Keaton later dissected
the problem in his autobiography: "[MGM used] Mike Mazurki, the
huge, ex-wrestler as the other man in that undressing scene. In my
opinion, the audience just did not believe that Mazurki would not have
thrown Red Skelton out the moment he got annoyed enough. [Keaton's
dressing-room nemesis was more his size.]"[17]

This lack of creative tweaking notwithstanding, *Birdie* was another
critical and box-office hit. As with *Cab*, the hosannas began with
Birdie's opening credits. *Film Daily* observed, "A cleverly contrived
credit sequence, with Red Skelton joking about the cast and crew of
his latest comic endeavor, starts the laugh-chain reaction which lasts
throughout the footage."[18] *Variety* added, "[Skelton's] followers will
like it and others will find much to chuckle at."[19] As an addendum to
this rosy reception, MGM had possibly helped to garner goodwill for
the film during production with witty press releases centering upon
Skelton's multiple *Birdie* roles. For example, the studio assigned the
comedian *three* dressing rooms, and each day *three* Skelton scripts were
delivered to the set. How this affected the reviews is anyone's guess,
but it certainly generated a great deal of affectionately amusing free
publicity, such as the *New York Telegraph* article, "Red Skelton Is 'The

Third Man,'" which punningly referenced the previous year's acclaimed
noirish thriller from Britain, *The Third Man* (1949).

Skelton's string of hit movies continued with *Excuse My Dust*
(1951), which opened the summer before the autumn debut of his
small-screen series. *Dust* is an amalgamation of Skelton's then recent
film successes. Like *Cab* and *Birdie*, the picture is a personality comedy.
Because *Dust* is a period piece, about a small-town automotive pioneer
from Skelton's home state of Indiana, the movie is a more restrained
clown comedy. Thus, the *Hollywood Reporter* felt "It's a Skelton more
like that of 'Three Little Words' than in his days as a broad buffoon—
and the metamorphosis is all to the good."[20]

Paradoxically, for all this high praise of a low comedian, *Dust's* most
acclaimed sequence is its slapstick finale, a race of vintage automobiles.
Even the staid *New York Times*, a publication often unimpressed by
Skelton, was moved to comment: "[The] old-fashioned cross-country
[horseless carriage] race … is a frantically funny affair, well worth the
time given to it."[21] Fittingly, a segment that was called "a socko 'third-
act'" by *Variety*, came courtesy of Keaton.[22] Ironically, this *Dust* finale,
constructed by Keaton and fellow gagmen Roy Royland and George
Wells, also represented the last time Keaton teamed with Skelton on
a picture.[23] Since Skelton was always more interested in radio and
television than film, to the utter frustration of Keaton, how appropriate
that their closing collaboration occurred on the very eve of Skelton's
television series.

Besides showcasing the comedy talents of Skelton and Keaton,
Dust also charmed viewers with its nostalgic Technicolor homage to
yesteryear. The title of the *Washington (DC) Star* review said it all,
"'Excuse My Dust' Recalls How Nice It Was in 1900."[24] The *Star's*
Americana perspective on *Dust*, moreover, found time to highlight the
Indiana setting for the film, implying that the Hoosier State was almost
a universal backdrop for amusingly wistful pop culture time tripping to
the past.

Be that as it may, Skelton's wave of positive *Dust* reviews, which,
in the presaturation booking days correlated to regional opening dates
stretching from spring until midsummer, meant his biggest news

An informal moment on the set for Skelton with Monica Lewis, the comedian's costar in Excuse My Dust *(1951).*

competition was himself—articles about his new autumn television show. Even before *Dust* opened, Skelton agonized in print about failing on the small screen: "I think the campaign saying I'll be great was started by my enemies. They're giving me the big build-up so the people will expect too much and I'll lay an egg. Please print that I'll probably stink."[25]

This "campaign saying I'll be great" was largely generated by the string of Skelton hit movies that led up to his television debut. Here was a *major* movie star coming to the small screen. Prior to this, hit television personalities were performers who had either washed out of film, such as Milton "Mr. Television" Berle, or merely had been B movie stars, such as *Hopalong Cassidy's* cowboy William Boyd. Skelton was something unique, with a huge $10 million contract to prove it! The underlying pressure to succeed, however, was huge—star status in *two* media was at stake. Fail on television and kiss the movies goodbye, too.

Skelton further helped rack up the stress by the frequent analogies he made between the great Chaplin and himself concerning Skelton's small-screen aspirations. Of course, this connection went beyond Skelton just wanting to be the best television clown possible (à la Chaplin's Tramp). Intuitively, Skelton seemed to sense what might be called the "blank page phenomenon." When one is talented *and first*, you not only establish the quality standards, you also write the rules. Historical timing (a window to immortality), and a great gift, allowed Chaplin to forever become screen comedy's gold standard. Skelton entered television early to achieve a comparable status on the small screen.

Skelton also contributed to a pressure situation by his obsessive preparation. With one of his many hobbies being amateur filmmaking, the comedian spent a fortune shooting test footage at home of potential sketches and costumes for his series. In a particularly detailed article titled "Fantastic Capers by Red Skelton Are a Prelude to His TV Show," readers essentially receive a ticket to the comedian's own "backyard movie set."[26] The shooting of these short films further fueled Skelton's thoughts of the early Chaplin, whose first movie "shorts" were only one or two reels in length (ten to twenty minutes). Plus, as a pertinent point of reference, Skelton's forthcoming series was in a half-hour time slot. When one subtracts the commercial breaks, the program that remains is roughly two reels in length.

While Skelton's persistent insecurities made him anything but confident on the eve of his television debut, the general public could be forgiven for thinking the funnyman was all but bulletproof. This is because, in addition to Skelton's recent string of movie hits and all the ballyhoo about his future on the small screen, a series of unexpected events was about to qualify the comedian as a real-life hero. Skelton had been booked to play London's prestigious Palladium in July 1951. Other stops on this European visit for Skelton and Georgia Davis Skelton (the children remained at home) included entertaining American troops at bases in West Germany and France, and an audience with Pope Pius XII. But the flight from Rome to the London engagement was almost the last thing the Skeltons ever did.

The couple's commercial airliner had mechanical problems in three of the four engines while flying over the Alps. With the pilot jettisoning fuel in order to compensate for lost altitude and to minimize fire and/or explosions during a forced landing, desperation gripped the fifty-four multinational passengers, many of whom were children. Among the people traveling with the Skeltons was the Jesuit priest Father Edward Carney. Turning to the comedian he said, "Okay, Red, you take care of your department, and I'll take care of mine."[27] As Carney gave last rites to passengers, Skelton went through what *Time* magazine called "35 minutes of juggling, shadow-boxing, and pantomime gags until the plane made an emergency landing in Lyon [France]."[28] As reported by *Newsweek*, Skelton credited it as being "the performance of his life."[29]

To borrow a line from America's then most prominent novelist, Ernest Hemingway, Skelton had exhibited "grace under pressure," though the often improvising comedian might have called it "humor under pressure." (While much was deservedly made of the comedian's emergency pantomiming, he later confessed to also segueing to his "mean widdle kid" character Junior, too.) Regardless, the darling of early 1950s film criticism had now upped the celebratory ante to embrace most of the fourth estate. The title of the *Los Angeles Herald Express*'s coverage nicely summarized the comedian's new heroic status with the media: "Red Skelton Hailed for Averting Panic on Crippled Airliner over Alps."[30] Some headlines even hinted at the extraordinary mix of comedy and the potential for tragedy inherent in Skelton's very real incident of "whistling in the dark." For example, *Newsweek* labeled its piece "Laugh Clown," à la the title of silent star Lon Chaney's pathos-driven *Laugh, Clown, Laugh* (1928), where a funnyman sacrifices himself for the love of another.

Though a near-death experience quickly puts the superficial world of reviews into perspective, Skelton's subsequent Palladium engagement was a triumph. The *London Times* stated, "Mr. Skelton ... does more than many of his fellow-visitors from the American screen. His patter, of course, is as smoothly sophisticated, but he has a very pretty talent for pantomime which is all his own. He can twist that large, mobile, and deceptively naïve face into the semblance of quite different faces, those of two ill-matched boxers and the referee, or the face of a man deeply moved by a film while engaged in eating an ice [cream]."[31] In contrast, the *Los Angeles Examiner*'s critique keyed upon the response of the Palladium audiences. For example, it documented everything from the crowd's frequent "roars of laughter," to "the conclusion of each show [when] there were ... cries of 'Bravo.'"[32]

On a more personal level, Davis was euphoric about her husband's Palladium success: "Red has simply won London. He's been doing three shows daily and every performance is a sell-out."[33] The comedian's friend and then current mentor, writer Gene Fowler, also part of Skelton's travel entourage, was equally positive about Skelton's Palladium run, as well as upset about a slight to his friend by entertainer Danny Kaye. Fowler told the *Chicago Tribune*, "Skelton is a big hit ... not withstanding all manner of handicaps [such as] Danny Kaye failed to introduce him [as is the hitherto unbroken tradition] on Danny's last night at the Palladium."[34]

This slight might seem like small potatoes to an American. In the hallowed tradition of this celebrated setting, however, it was considered a major insult. Custom long dictated that the star in residence introduce the next headliner from the stage. With Skelton and Davis seated in a balcony box, surrounded by friends, posed for Kaye's acknowledgement, the reigning star closed his act with no mention of Skelton. Even Kaye's definitive biographer, Martin Gottfried, later wrote of the incident: "An audible gasp [came] from the audience ... The slur of Skelton was unmistakable—and terrible. Georgia Skelton began to cry. Helen Parnell [wife of the Palladium's managing director] whispered aloud, 'What is the matter with that man? It's tradition! That's never been done!'"[35]

Sadly, another event during Kaye's final show foreshadowed the entertainer's conscious decision to slight Skelton. Kaye unexpectedly added a comic drunk routine to his act, as if to preempt the impact of Skelton's signature "Guzzler's Gin" routine. No real explanation has ever come forth on why Kaye had it in for Skelton. Most speculation centers on the fact that Kaye was a hopeless Anglophile—to the point that period insiders used to joke he actually thought he was English. Skelton's then recent wave of hit films had also been popular in Great Britain, and his live show at the Palladium was highly anticipated, fueled all the more by Red's brave turn aboard the troubled airliner. Thus, it is possible that egotistical Kaye was fearful of losing his status as favored American performer in Britain to the upstart Skelton. Fittingly, when Bob Hope played the Palladium that same season, he comically skewered Kaye's English-tinged vanity with jokes like, "Danny Kaye visits me when he comes to America. You should see his dressing room here [in London]—two mirrors and a throne."

Whatever caused Kaye's pettiness, it did nothing to derail Skelton's hit status in London. Indeed, the insult might have assisted the comedian's Palladium run with a sympathy factor. One might even interpret a line from the *London Times* review—"Mr. Skelton ... does more than many of his fellow-visitors from the American screen"—as a veiled knock against Kaye. Whereas today this probably would have descended into a game of celebrity bashing, Skelton took the high road and let it drop. Consistent with this attitude, in an unrelated article a few years later, he observed, "I don't like to steal from Will Rogers but I've yet to meet the human being I didn't like."[36]

Skelton's critical acclaim continued through the fall, with arguably the biggest debut in television's young history. The *Hollywood Reporter* declared, "Move over, Mr. Berle—Mr. Skelton has arrived ... the new medium has found its newest—and perhaps greatest—comedy star."[37] The *New York World Telegram* said, "[Skelton] has an India rubber face and an apparently unbruisable body ... There is a kind of joyous lunacy in Mr. Skelton's work. And for this reason I've always thought he'd do better in television than most radio performers in transition."[38] All-important *Variety* opined, "[Skelton's] a terrif bet for TV [and he] seemed completely at ease before the lenses. His material was good and he tossed in what seemed to be some ad libs in fine style."[39] One might simply summarize the critiques by recycling the *Los Angeles Herald Express*'s review headline: "Red Skelton TV Debut Brings Down House."[40]

Still, the comedian's tour-de-force material that night would have been familiar to either period viewers or to fans from much later in Skelton's career. To illustrate, while he introduced all his characters that night, the most praised sketch involved his oldest and most Hoosier-anchored antihero, the beloved Clem Kadiddlehopper. There was also a decidedly Edna Stillwell tone to his opening comedy. His first wife/writer had penned such signature Skelton routines as "Guzzler's Gin" and the donut dunking bit that segued into various later "how to" sketches. Consequently, Skelton's initial small-screen program featured both different "tipsy types" and a tutorial on various ways servicemen hitchhike.

By Emmy time in February of 1952, Skelton must have felt like he could walk on water. As his own producer, he took home the statuette for Best Comedy Show. Plus, Skelton was selected as television's Best Comedian. Award night also saw him garner more kudos for modesty. In beating out Lucille Ball for the latter Emmy, he said, "I don't like this. I think it should go to Lucy." Several critics, such as the *Los Angeles Herald Express*'s Owen Collin, were impressed: "This is where Skelton endeared himself in our hearts forever."[41] Couple all this short-term video acclaim with his remarkable run of hit movies leading up to the series, not to mention his real-life heroics aboard the crippled plane, and the Palladium triumph, and one has almost an unprecedented string of high-profile success. Moreover, just after his television debut, MGM had the East Coast premiere of the comedian's latest picture, *Texas Carnival* (1951). The future box-office hit was praised in a manner reminiscent of his recent small-screen reviews. The *Los Angeles Examiner* declared "that irrepressible clown ... [is] in nearly every scene, so that's quite a lot of fun."[42] (According to the studio's records for 1951–52, *Texas Carnival* proved even more profitable than MGM's classic 1952 film *Singin' in the Rain*.[43])

Flash forward to the following fall and, shock of shocks, the wheels suddenly came off the Skelton success bus. The comic who could do no wrong for so long was almost universally panned at the start of his second television season. As the media critic for the *Washington Star* summarized less than two years later, "Skelton turned to the movie camera for his [video] shows and almost plummeted right out of television."[44] What does that mean? Skelton's program was "live" the first season and the stress nearly killed him. In fact, when his sponsor demanded the comedian return to that format early in the disastrous second season, Skelton said, "He can either have a live comedian on a filmed show or a dead comedian on a live show."[45] Underlining the seriousness of this statement, the quote appeared in a syndicated article titled, "Red Skelton May Quit Television."

Unfortunately, while it was healthier for Skelton to film his series in advance, popular thinking was that live comedy had the edge, as well as pushing the performer's creativity. As the darkly comic *Los Angeles Mirror* critic so entertainingly put it in an analogy that seemingly equates race-car crashes with comedy, "Red Skelton is on film now and has lost his magic touch.... Before we wondered if he was going to break his neck [through slapstick]. Now we know he won't because with the film being made ahead of time we would have heard about it."[46]

Worse yet, without a studio audience, one must deal with the patented artificiality of a laugh track.

In addition to the stress of live television, a 1950s small-screen series was much more grueling. Here is Skelton's frank realization following his first season: "After 39 weeks before the camera [today's season is roughly half that length] I can honestly say that for the first time in my life I've found out how utterly exhausted a human being can be."[47] In addition, Skelton was involved in nearly every behind-the-scenes facet of the program. On top of that, he was still doing his radio program that necessitated its own original material each week.

Of course, the plus side to his train wreck of a second season was that 1950s television programming had more stability. A series was not canceled so quickly back then, especially if a network and/or a sponsor had a great deal invested, as was the case with Skelton. Today the comedian would have been history almost immediately. What became Skelton's greatest legacy, that twenty year small-screen reign, would have been nipped in the second year. It literally took Skelton *years* to return to his 1951–52 top-four rating status.[48]

The irony here is that his very successful movies were *filmed*, and like the beginning of his second television season, they also did *not* have an audience. The difference was that Skelton was doing too much on his program, and unlike the movies, he needed a finished product *every* week. His sponsors (Proctor and Gamble) and NBC brainstormed, with suggestions ranging from a new format (more of a variety show) to a revisionist "live" program. The latter course won.

The shooting of Skelton's show now involved what the industry calls a "stop-and-go" method. The individual scenes were live, but there were breaks between segments. These allowed Skelton adequate time for the various comic costume changes, as well as giving him a brief respite before morphing into a different character. There was also a new studio that was more audience friendly. As much as Skelton liked to perform for a crowd, he had vetoed an audience when filming his second season because all the equipment made spectator viewing haphazard at best, especially since Eagle Lion Studio had *not* been designed for an audience. That was to change. His show was not fixed yet, but important corrections had been made.

Sadly, there were bigger personal problems with which to deal. Skelton was near meltdown mode, not unlike his nervous breakdown during the war. Performers need more validation than most people. As the stereotype goes, that is why entertainers are so quick to kiss and embrace when meeting. Well, these needs seemed doubled for Skelton. Long after he left television, an interviewer asked how he would like to be remembered, with most of the options as a variation on being a great clown. After a pause, Skelton said, "I think I'd just like to be remembered as a nice guy."[49]

With this in mind, the broadside of bad reviews for his second television season were devastating for Skelton, especially after the amazingly unmitigated successes of the first season. Granted, anyone would be upset, but for man-child Skelton, who had had so much of his career orchestrated by motherly first wife, Stillwell, criticism was extremely hurtful. Keep in mind that entertainment was all but a religion for Skelton. The field of laughter, to paraphrase poet Donald Hall, was Skelton's Bible, Koran, Plato and Aristotle, Euclid, Thomas Aquinas, and *Boy Scout Handbook*.[50] Among his voluminous unpublished private papers is a folder labeled "The Critic." Here is a telling observation on being a critic: "A godless being, that hasn't discovered that the theatre does as much good as the church and that those in the theatrical world are as dedicated as the most devout monk."[51]

Worse yet, 1952 was the year Skelton and Stillwell parted company professionally. Though long divorced, she had guided Skelton's career into the 1950s, watching over every detail, from producing his radio program to standing in the wings with a fresh shirt when he came off wet with sweat. More importantly, she was his primary cheerleader. For example, during any free moment of a program they had a special ritual: "'Okay?' he would ask anxiously, 'Okay,' she would say smilingly."[52]

In a series of articles about Stillwell in the late 1940s, her ongoing significance to her ex-husband had been underlined yet again. However, along more disturbing lines, there was the suggestion that her single-mindedness towards making Skelton's career work had been the cause of her second marriage failing. Thus, in early 1951 she took a leave from her multidimensional position with Skelton, though he told the press, "Edna will be back with me when my TV show starts in October."[53]

Although she was said to have logged some low-profile work during Skelton's first small-screen season, she was definitely gone, and gone permanently, during the second. Indeed, many industry insiders, such as influential Hollywood columnist Louella Parsons, blamed Skelton's fall from television grace, in part, on Stillwell's absence. While this was probably a factor, the more debilitating component for Skelton was simply her being gone. After all, she had been metaphorically holding his hand since the walkathon days of the early 1930s.

History still has yet to reveal the ultimate catalyst for Stillwell's exit, but the general consensus is that Davis was responsible. When the Skeltons had the most public of temporary splits in late 1952, Stillwell and the disappointing series were again in the news. Parsons suggested the domestic donnybrook was caused by the couple's disagreement over Skelton's desire to bring Stillwell back to save the sinking series.[54] (Skelton was always sensitive to claims that Davis wore the pants in the family, and he had even written Parsons the previous year, 1951, to explain that Stillwell's initial leave had been health related.[55])

Regardless, the Skeltons' 1952 fight provides the most revealing window into their marriage—one that often sounds like the comedian's union with Stillwell. Exhibit one would be Skelton as the "kidult," beginning with the fact he actually called syndicated columnist Earl Wilson, saying "I had to get away because I'm ruining my life ... There are 12 guys [gag writers] in this room trying to stop me from telling about it but it's definite—Georgia and I are getting a divorce."[56] By late-edition papers of the same day, such as the *Seattle Times*, he was reconsidering those divorce plans, claiming "I'm so much in love it's pitiful."[57] The only real point of contention to hit the papers seemed to reaffirm Skelton's man-child tendencies. Davis told the *New York World*, "He'd come in at four o'clock in the morning—he often worked very late at night—and want to play with them [the children]. Then they'd have terrible colds. I finally told him, 'Red, I'll have to lock my [bedroom] door [the children's rooms were through her suite]. I can't allow my babies to get up at that hour.'"[58]

Conversely, Georgia often played parent to Skelton, as quoted in the *Los Angeles Herald Express*: "I've had plenty of trouble with this boy, only before it just never got into the papers. If I was going to quit, I would have quit a long time ago."[59] Still, as had Stillwell, Davis invariably spent more time defending Skelton: "He deserves a little happiness—he makes so many other people happy. It's true we don't get along. But maybe a guy with that much pressure on him doesn't get along with anybody in the world."[60]

As Stillwell often put a comic slant on her differences with Skelton, so did Davis. The *San Francisco News* reported her sardonic comment on a reconciliation: "He may come back home [soon], since he left his gag files behind."[61] The most curiously sad parallel between the two Mrs. Skeltons involved a Davis comment that almost exactly parroted a Stillwell quote cited earlier. Each woman felt a need to defuse negative behavior and even become a "whipping boy" (Stillwell's phrase[62]), all for the sake of his gift. This is Davis's take on the phenomenon: "He gets this way [being difficult] because he's artistic. He's a high-strung genius and he gets emotionally upset so he tees off on the person nearest him, and that's me."[63] Such is the hidden cost of art. Of the many comedians I have profiled, rare was the one without such private demons. In fact, the cynic might say Skelton was just emulating yet another facet of his comedy hero—the brilliant, but mercurial, Chaplin.

While the media would have undoubtedly moved quickly to another story—this being Hollywood, after all—headlines about the Skeltons' spat were soon replaced by *two* unlikely new developments in the comedian's life, a health danger and an artistic risk. He seems to have been a candidate for reality television decades before its development.

12

Triumph and Tragedy in the 1950s

Under the headline, "Skelton Wows 'Em at Las Vegas Club:
Just Like Atomic Blast," the Los Angeles Herald Express *stated,*
"Few comedians—if any—have received the rousing ovation accorded Red."[1]
LOS ANGELES HERALD EXPRESS, JULY 15, 1953

The hit opening alluded to in the above quote, embellished with
a period reference to atomic testing in the desert, was the beginning
of Red Skelton's television resurrection. Of course, the comedian's late
1952 very public feud with his second wife, Georgia Davis Skelton, was
old news by then, helped along by a reconciliation through a medical
emergency. The comedian had needed surgery for a diaphragmatic
hernia—a condition in which the stomach is constricted at the
center and presses against the heart and lungs. The procedure was
successfully performed on December 12, 1952, with Skelton generating
some positive press with the adhesive tape note he stuck to his chest
just before the operation: "Do Not Open Till Christmas."[2] Almost
simultaneous to the surgery, the holiday film release of Skelton's hit *The
Clown* (though often listed as a 1953 film) had also given him some
critical balm after the painful panning of his second season.

Despite this "sophomore jinx," rival CBS was interested in luring
Skelton from NBC. CBS was in the midst of a power struggle with
NBC (ABC was then a distant third in importance.) Stories of Skelton's
drinking during the comedian's 1952 meltdown, however, had CBS
executives second-guessing this inclination. Writer Marty Rackin, a

Skelton friend since the 1930s, convinced Skelton that he could turn everything around with a showcase of his best material in a Las Vegas act. CBS representatives could come and see a sober Skelton knocking the audience in the proverbial aisles.

Rackin arranged a July 1953 booking for Skelton with the Sahara nightclub and helped him select material. Moreover, when Skelton wanted to back out at the eleventh hour, Rackin all but kidnapped him to America's gambling capital, or as comics like to describe it, "The place where you get nothing for something." His act was a smashing success, including everything from his cast of comedy characters to a revival of Skelton's parody of how stars such as James Cagney die in the movies. Ironically, for someone trying to demonstrate his sober discipline, Skelton's pièce de résistance was the "Guzzler's Gin" sketch. *Variety*'s review even keyed on the sketch and how it produced "continuous roars of laughter."[3] Before the end of July, the comedian had signed a lucrative contract with CBS.[4] Amazingly, the comedian who by all rights should have been bounced off the tube for the previous season's abysmal reviews, now would be making $12,000 a week.

A new direction at CBS involved returning to a totally "live" show, with the comedian exercising less control behind the scenes in terms of directing and producing the program. Unfortunately, Skelton's binge drinking and unstable tendencies, such as playing with his extensive (always loaded) gun collection while under the influence, continued into the new television season. Though stress was the catalyst for much of this unstable behavior, Skelton had become a fan of alcohol in the 1940s, undoubtedly fueled in part by his hard-drinking friend Gene Fowler (crony to such celebrated imbibers as W. C. Fields and John Barrymore) and Skelton's alcoholic wife, Davis. Indeed, the Skeltons' daughter, Valentina Skelton Alonso, later recalled: "There was a lot of drinking going on with Fowler and his wife Agnes. My parents would always come back [from the Fowlers' home] drunk."[5] Along related lines, Skelton's father had been an alcoholic, with the prevailing feeling in the family being that he had drank himself to death. During this period of excess, Skelton operated at cross purposes with novelist

Gustave Flaubert's famous axiom for artists—live the quiet bourgeois life and save one's wildness for the work. But conversely, maybe Skelton's passion for his comedy craft was driven, in part, by the release it provided him from his private demons.

A possible window into these dark days comes from an unusual insider source, a novel by former Skelton writer Ben Freedman. Called *Lootville* (1957), Freedman's book, coauthored with his wife Nancy, sympathetically tells the tale of a self-destructive redheaded television clown named Zane Cochrane. Here are the most obvious parallels with Skelton, besides being set in 1953: a former MGM star obsessed with making people laugh, double Emmy winner in 1952, alcoholic tendencies, struggling to maintain television career, father of a young daughter and son, collects guns, suffered a mental breakdown during World War II, had an attractive alcoholic wife, and was a personable people person.

Given this obvious fictional link to Skelton, what kind of possible insights are provided by the Freedmans' *Lootville*? First, when Skelton's program was floundering, one suggested solution from NBC was to put him in a situation comedy. The phenomenal success of *I Love Lucy* had made this genre the answer to any network problem. Coincidentally, the character of Zane Cochrane is being asked to consider a sitcom format, and his entertainingly stressful rant sounds a great deal like Skelton, "It doesn't matter to them [the network] that situation comedy is not what I do. I'm a clown. I'm wild, nutty, fruity, a low comic, that's what I am. I don't know from situation comedy. It's what they call *believable*. Like Lucy gets dressed up like an Egyptian belly dancer and Desi doesn't recognize her. With that show if Desi ever recognizes her, they're dead … [And this is believable?] That's their [network] principle—take what's selling and go it one better."[6]

Second, Freeman also amusingly addresses a comic paradox between Skelton's favorite drink (vodka) and his paranoia about Communism. Thus, Zane observes, "Damn Communist drink. [I] have a revolution in my guts every time I pour it down."[7] (Fittingly, an undated passage in Skelton's unpublished private papers suggests his fears about

Putting on a happy face, Skelton and his family: wife Georgia, Richard, and Valentina (circa mid-1950s).

Communism probably originated with his fatherly drinking companion Fowler. The comedian wrote of Fowler, "As a newspaperman, he saw the government from the inside as well as the outside and learned the profoundly important truth ... conquer the disease of Communism."[8])

Third, *Lootville* paints the beautiful alcoholic wife of its comedian as being oversexed to the point of nymphomania. While that would be an unfair assessment of Davis, Skelton was frequently suspicious of his wife's relationships with any number of other men. According to Arthur Marx's biography of Skelton, which drew upon the writer's industry insider status as the son of Groucho Marx, Skelton's anxiety was grounded in fact. The comedian had caught Davis in bed with a member of their personal staff. Marx wrote: "'I know it's true,' says [Skelton producer Seymour] Berns, 'because Red personally told me the story of coming home and catching them in the act. [Skelton business manager] Bo Roos told me the same story. He knew about it because Red made him do the firing.'"[9]

As a footnote to Skelton's milquetoast nonconfrontational behavior (even in such an inflammatory situation), the comedian generally avoided conflict. Along similar lines, I will later address the often daily "love letters" he wrote to Davis in the 1960s, and how they were sometimes more admonishments—written admonishments I am convinced he never shared with her. Or, one could also backtrack to an argument between the Skeltons about late-night access to the children that was quickly defused by the comedian's sudden flip-flopping epiphany, "I'm so much in love [with Davis] it's pitiful."[10] Here was the spirit of an arrested child in search of affection, and as Valentina even said, "Mom would refer to Dad as her 'man/child.'" Plus, while Skelton could have many moods, the marital spats with Davis were invariably precipitated by minor details—the tantrums of a child. Skelton avoided major confrontations.

Consistent with the mild-mannered Skelton, here is how the narrator of the Freemans' *Lootville* ultimately describes their fictional comedian: "A guy not out to save the world but neither particularly anxious to harm anyone, who liked to laugh and hear other people

laugh and wasn't too highbrow about how he got those laughs."[11]
Though Skelton was initially embarrassed by the suggested revelations
in the novel, maybe it helped save his life through greater self awareness.
The tragic conclusion to *Lootville* has the central character committing
suicide, a victim of his own pent-up anger. This novel-writing couple
were not disasterizing for their art. Throughout the 1950s, many
members of the Hollywood entertainment industry saw Skelton
as a walking time bomb. As late as 1963, the mainstream Sunday
supplement magazine *Parade*, in a positive cover story on the comedian,
included the following jaw-dropping disclosure, "Two years ago one
shrewd veteran observer told me, 'Every morning I pick up the paper
I expect to read about Red Skelton's suicide.' Another former Skelton
employee told me: 'This man has so much hostility within him ... but
no way of releasing it. He's going to blow his top.'"[12] (Ironically, years
earlier, *Parade* had run an article on Skelton that related how he had
once staged a rather theatrical suicide for his first wife, Edna Stillwell, in
order to demonstrate his unhappiness, and encourage her to give him a
divorce.[13] Hyperbole, or the truth? It was hard to tell with Skelton.)

Though the comedian's marriage to Davis was a work-in-progress
during the 1950s, the greatest stress early in the decade was still
Skelton's struggling television program. The calamitous ratings of
1952–53 continued through the next two seasons. But as one pores over
the program's press coverage during this time, a curious phenomenon
begins to surface—call it a grassroots empathy for a beloved clown.
For example, a critic for the *San Diego Evening Tribune* described the
opening of Skelton's 1953–54 season as a disappointment, yet he went
on to poignantly add, "There isn't another personality on video screens
who has the same standing with audiences that Skelton seems to have.
Almost everyone sympathizes with him, wants him to have hit shows
and suffers for him when the entertainment isn't up to par."[14]

What was it about Skelton that could elicit such an audience
connection? Growing up in a 1950s household that *always* watched
his program, I remember that my dad once insightfully described the
attraction as Skelton's apparently "genuine sincerity," though my father

found the comedian's sign-off line, "And may God bless," bordering upon the mawkish. Of course, for many conservative viewers in the 1950s, that particular phrase probably sealed the deal all the more as proof of Skelton's sincerity. Years later television critic John Heisner elegantly fleshed out Skelton's neighborly appeal. In an article treating Skelton as "probably the most interesting of all the TV institutions," Heisner wrote, "His forte has got to be the great warmth that oozes from the man and reaches across the normally vast gulf separating the performer from the living room. Skelton probably comes as close as anybody ever has … to creating and maintaining the feeling that he is indeed right there in your home, talking directly to you, and telling you those corny jokes."[15]

Skelton would later pooh-pooh his poor ratings during the early 1950s, suggesting that when one just barely falls out of the hallowed top ten everyone yells catastrophe. But *Washington Star* critic Harry MacArthur was closer to the truth when he stated that Skelton had "almost plummeted right out of television."[16] At one point during this attempted comeback period Skelton's program had dropped to eighty-sixth in the ratings. Just as Skelton's sympathetic fan base was rooting for him to recover, reviewers, such as MacArthur, were moved to put a positive spin on his personal problems.

Although the sad clown is a stereotype hoary with age and countless exceptions, it is more than applicable to the often troubled Skelton. Given Skelton's natural tendencies toward pathos, television critic MacArthur suggested that "Skelton should include in his show a sketch on the order of Jackie Gleason's silent, heart-breaking Poor Soul. There is more to this man Skelton … than a falling-down-drunk ["Guzzler's Gin] act and the country rube [Clem Kadiddlehopper] with straw in his hair."[17]

This wise comedy counsel had actually already been acted upon by Skelton, though the character had not yet fully registered with fans and reviewers. Arguably, the only positive to come out of Skelton's abysmal second season was the introduction of his now most acclaimed and beloved figure, Freddie the Freeloader. This inspired character, sort of a cross between Charlie Chaplin's Tramp and Emmett Kelly's Weary Willie, was the most fully realized figure in Skelton's eccentric menagerie. Like Gleason's Poor Soul, Freddie was silent and predisposed to tragedy, though Skelton eventually let his character speak.

When considering the various comedy characters played by both Skelton and Gleason, beyond Freddie and the Poor Soul, one key difference often noted in the 1950s, to the detriment of Skelton's show, was that Gleason's figures were more realistic. As early as the start of Skelton's second season, *San Francisco Examiner* critic Dwight Newton wrote, "unlike Skelton's characters, Gleason's have a natural, true-to-life ring. Everyone knows a 'loud mouth' as Gleason portrays him, everyone has met a 'Poor Soul,' everyone has, imagined a [vain, pompous Reggie] 'Van Gleason, III.' When, as the *Honeymooners*, he [Gleason as Ralph Kramden] says: 'I haven't done one thing right since I have been married,' there's a genuine touch of pathos in his performance."[18]

So why was a more realistic approach preferable on the small screen? In entertainer and author Steve Allen's watershed book on television comedians of the 1950s, *The Funny Men* (1956), he noted, "It is an axiom of the TV-comedy business that the less realistic you are the bigger your jokes have to be. If you're not being at least a little true to life, your script has to blast a laugh out of the audience every few seconds because their emotions are not much involved. But, if the audience is intensely interested in *what happens* to your characters, they will laugh amiably at almost any little joke you sprinkle the story line with."[19] As with the *San Francisco Examiner* critic Newton, Allen also uses the Skelton-Gleason comparison when discussing realistic small-screen figures.

One should hasten to add that no one was saying Skelton's characters were not as funny—simply that they were more high maintenance. Thus, this was one explanation as to why Skelton's ratings had dropped off, eclipsed, for a time, by Gleason. Ironically, Skelton had established himself in vaudeville with several brilliant slice-of-life sketches, starting with the donut-dunking routine, all

Jackie Gleason (center) and Honeymooners *regulars Art Carney and Audrey Meadows.*

scripted by Stillwell. These were largely "how to?" pantomimes based in observational (realistic) humor.

Appropriately, when CBS brought in Sherwood Schwartz to turn around Skelton's ratings, the new head writer said the comedian's old shows were 80 percent verbal and 20 percent pantomime—numbers he thought should be reversed.[20] Skelton doing pantomime was more realistic. Of equal importance, Schwartz had Skelton appearing as just one of his characters each week. Previously, the comedian had been flirting with over exposure by parading several figures through every installment of the show. Coupling this more focused programming with a single theme also had the advantage of further encouraging viewer identification, even if Skelton's characters were more exaggerated than those of Gleason's.

These changes made all the difference. Skelton's first season (1955–56) with Sherwood, later kiddingly referred to as "Robin Hood's rabbi," put the comedian back among television's top-rated programs. Skelton continued to generate impressive numbers through the 1969–70 television season, logging in as high as number two (behind the Western *Bonanza*) in 1966–67.[21] Schwartz stayed with Red for eight seasons before creating such hit television programs as *Gilligan's Island* (1964–67) and *The Brady Bunch* (1969–74). Though both of these shows were miles away from delineating anything lofty and poetic, they perfectly demonstrate what Schwartz brought to Skelton's program—an uncanny ability to "read" public tastes. The modest Schwartz, who never worked directly with Skelton (a mutual preference by both men), simply saw himself as a Skelton facilitator: "We didn't make him any funnier—we just created a format to maximize his possibilities."[22]

As a postscript to the relative realism of Skelton's comedy characters, I suggest they represent more of a middle ground in believability. If Gleason's Ralph Kramden equals the realistic gold standard of 1950s television comedy, the opposite end of the spectrum would be owned by the iconoclastic Ernie Kovacs, undoubtedly the most original comic mind of his day. His theater of the absurd characters included the cockeyed poet Percy Dovetonsils and the Nairobi Trio—three men in ape masks, trench coats, and bowler hats miming the strange musical number "Solfeggio." Two apes pretended to play instruments (piano and drums), while the nominal leader conducted. Given that leadership counts for little in the absurd modern world, the "crowning" achievement was that in a moment of distraction, the drummer pounded on the conductor's head. After several subterfuge-driven repetitions of this darkly comic drumstick violence, the ape conductor wraps the routine with a vase to the head of his musical nemesis. Compared to such Kovacs characters, Skelton's comedy troupe is just this side of Italian neorealism.

Skelton saw a great of realism in his characters, claiming: "They're based on different people I've met—I see something funny, yet tragic."[23] Certainly this is true of his oldest and arguably most important early figure, Clem Kadiddlehopper. As noted earlier, Skelton appeared to have based Clem on childhood friend, Carl Hopper, whose severe hearing loss as a youngster made it difficult for him to communicate, sometimes suggesting he had a learning disability. Yet, by redefining this figure as what American humor would call a "wise fool," Kadiddlehopper is often allowed to succeed. This wise fool moniker also applies to Skelton's punch-drunk fighter, Cauliflower McPugg. During the 1950s, Skelton wrote, "But for all his inane antics, Cauliflower is basically an honest and sympathetic character. Like Clem, he dearly loves people, but he too does the wrong thing at the right time [the hallmark of the wise fool]."[24]

Significantly, Skelton believed a certain degree of comic distortion/distraction was necessary to facilitate laughter. He believed comedy was triggered by an innate "emotional outburst. People see themselves in the same situation or know someone like that. By exaggeration it becomes funny, yet it's tragic."[25] One might build a tragic foundation to Freddie the Freeloader, since Skelton sometimes called the character a tribute to his grocer father, who Skelton desperately wanted to believe was a world-famous clown. Yet, as examined earlier, Freddie's classic material is more apt to be borrowed from Charlie Chaplin's Tramp. When Skelton "appropriated" material, he often attributed it to his father.

For example, *New York Herald Tribune* critic John Crosby took Skelton to task in 1952, noting: "Last Sunday … he did a pantomime of a girl dressing in the morning—a bit, he assured us, his [circus] father did … fifty years earlier. This was illuminating information since the ensuing pantomime was, almost to a gesture, an exact replica of Sid Caesar's famous burlesque on the same subject. I suppose this lays Caesar open to the charge of stealing Skelton's father's material fifty years ago which seems hardly likely. Caesar wasn't around that long ago."[26]

I am not overly bothered by borrowed material. After all, just a few months after the Crosby column, Lucille Ball did her celebrated "Vitameatavegamin" sketch (*I Love Lucy*, May 5, 1952), which is clearly lifted from Skelton's "Guzzler Gin" routine. The routine was written by Stillwell, who had taken the idea from a Fred Allen radio program. Obviously, there is very little that is original, however, giving material fake origins, based upon a sketchy father figure, only seems to compound the falseness. Skelton would have been on much more solid ground if, in prefacing the sketch examined by critic Crosby, "a pantomime of a girl dressing in the morning," Skelton had simply said, "I first did a variation of this routine back in the 1930s, when I was a vaudeville headliner. Originally conceived by Edna Stillwell, I hope you enjoy my new rendition of this material."

As a biographer, however, one constantly needs to reframe a problematic action by one's subject. Biographer Marc Pachter offers the challenge, "how much can be learned about an individual from the facts he invents about himself?"[27] Let us briefly examine the smokescreen created by Skelton when he credited the morning ritual routine to his father. First, since he never knew his father, it adds to the common legacy he has already established for them—being clowns. Second, Skelton wore his heart on his sleeve, and he would have intuitively recognized the added poignancy the routine would generate with a sentimental backstory. Third, Skelton had a comic gift, but he was insecure about his lack of an education. His press releases and concert programs were miniresumes about the sheer volume of the comedian's creativity, tabulated on a daily basis. Consequently, if Skelton had knowingly lifted elements of the sketch from Caesar, as suggested by the period critic, Skelton quite possibly would have worried that he needed a personal footnote to safeguard his credibility as a creative, educated person. These are just some *hypothetical* suggestions as to what might have motivated his actions. Of course, the simplest explanation might be that, as the consummate storyteller, the raconteur par excellence, Skelton was merely trying to tell a better story.

Before leaving the subject of Skelton's competing comedians, I would like to backtrack briefly to the subject of Kovacs's entertainingly disturbing Nairobi Trio. While their surrealistic silliness was from a different comedy planet than that occupied by Skelton, one wonders if the comedian ever picked up a basic metaphorical life lesson from the Trio. That is, years later the darkly comic humorist Jim Knipfel wrote the memoir, *Quitting the Nairobi Trio* (2000). Like Skelton, he went through some troubling psychological times before he came up with an unorthodox but effective mindset to fight depression. As the title of his book suggests, Knipfel came to equate the ultimately destructive repetitive nature of life with being stuck in a nightmare version of a favorite television comedy routine. The secret to survival was to: "Recognize the skit I was in before I got too far into it. Figure out who—or what—was holding the drumsticks over my head early enough so I could dodge them, before they caved in the back of my skull."[28]

Skelton also managed to put his personal demons at bay, for a time, by the mid-1950s. I am reminded of a pertinent comment later made by Wade Boggs upon his 2005 induction into the Baseball Hall of Fame: "Our lives are not determined by what happens to us, but how we react to what happens."[29] Skelton had soldiered through a difficult time. By the end of the 1950s, another memoir spoke directly to the comedian's greatness. No less a laughter legend than Groucho Marx wrote, "I think the logical successor to Chaplin is Skelton. Red, to my mind, is the most unacclaimed clown in show business." Marx was especially impressed that the redhead did not need funny clothes and/or special make-up: "The last time I watched Skelton perform in a theatre, he came onstage in an outfit that could conceivably have been worn by … [anybody]. With one prop, a soft battered hat, he successfully converted himself into an idiot boy, a peevish old lady, a teetering-tottering drunk, an overstuffed clubwoman, a tramp, and any other character that seemed to suit his fancy."[30]

Marx's hat perspective is well taken. Despite Skelton's minimalist needs as a performer, he was lost without headgear. Indeed, Red once claimed, "I couldn't get into character without the right hat."[31] When his one-person stock company is examined, each character is defined by his lid apparel. Freddie the Freeloader's suggestion of a fall from grace (or is that a dream of better things?), comes by way of wearing a battered top hat. Oddball Clem tries for normalcy by wearing a fedora, but the headgear's rakish angle and folded-up brim suggest "he hasn't a clue." The boastful San Fernando Red and Sheriff Deadeye both wear broad-brimmed Stetsons, as if to embellish their attempts at being larger than life. A later addition to Skelton's comedy troupe, the henpecked husband Mr. Appleby, tries for a modicum of dignity by wearing a derby (à la the often henpecked antiheroes Stan Laurel and Oliver Hardy). The "mean widdle kid" Junior wore a ribboned porkpie hat, and boxer Cauliflower McPugg, Skelton's closest character to a street person, accents that fact by wearing a newsboy's cap. Otherwise, when Skelton was running through more generic figures, the fedora became his all-purpose prop. For example, when he performed the "Guzzler's Gin" sketch, his inebriated television pitchman's fedora gets increasingly smashed down on his head, as he becomes progressively more "smashed" with each subsequent commercial. But between times Skelton also played a poet reciting his work. As this sober literary type, Skelton wore the same fedora upside down, making it resemble an academic mortar board cap. No wonder Marx was impressed.

When Skelton was not making news as television's favorite comeback comedian of the 1950s, his private and professional life still generated headlines. What follows are a subjective list of ten memorable Skelton-related news stories from that decade. Arranged chronologically, save the last one, some stories begin with Skelton, while others simply draw him into a bigger picture. But taken as a whole, they represent a Skelton mosaic of the 1950s. The first, involving Johnny Carson, was completely involuntary. At that time, Carson was an up-and-coming young comic who had had some local success with a Los Angeles-based Sunday afternoon television program called *Carson's Cellar*. With no budget to speak of, Carson got by with wit and moxie, such as an episode on which he "announced that Red Skelton was the show's 'special guest star.' A lone figure then raced across the stage. That, Carson said, was Red Skelton."[32] As luck would have it, Skelton just happened to catch his fleeting "appearance" and was charmed. The comedian ended up "really" appearing on the program with Carson several times. When *Carson's Cellar* was canceled in the early 1950s, Skelton hired the young comedian as a monologue writer and a sketch participant.

Flash forward to August 18, 1954. The two-hundred-pound Skelton, once described as "show business' answer to [bruising football pioneer] Bronco Nagurski," was rehearsing a routine shortly before airtime that involved crashing through a breakaway door that did not break away. Briefly knocked out, Skelton was unable to go on that night. As if borrowing a plot twist from *42nd Street* (1933), where an unknown subs for the disabled lead and becomes a star overnight, Carson replaced Skelton on the show.

The former Nebraska disc jockey, calling himself "the poor man's Red Skelton," garnered across the board rave reviews, such as, "[Carson] ad-libbed the entire Skelton show, doing what network executives enthusiastically claimed was a great job."[33] (Though Carson's gift for impromptu humor undoubtedly played a part in maximizing this break, a goodly portion of his "ad-libbing" that night was a recycling of his comedy act, such as Carson's Robert Benchley-like "lecture" on the economics of television.) Regardless, a number of big-name comedians, besides Skelton, weighed in with praise, such as Jack Benny's kudos, "The kid is great, just great."[34] Shortly after the broadcast, Carson confessed, "I could tell the studio audience was disappointed when they saw me instead of Red [before the show]. But I just told them: 'Look,

I'm in a spot—and we're all in this together.'"[35] Carson also added that the suddenness had been a blessing, "If they [had] told me a week ahead of time I'd have to replace Red Skelton, I'd have gotten the shakes for sure. But there wasn't time to think or get nervous. I was in a daze."[36] He was also pleased that Skelton was so happy with the turn of events, prompting him to kid that he had sent Skelton a "stay sick card." In less than two weeks, with an assist from Benny, Carson was signed to an exclusive contract with the network.[37] The following season (1955–56) Carson even had a short-lived prime time comedy variety show.

Though Carson's style was more in the tradition of Benny, the young comedian "did adapt Red's 'anything for entertainment'

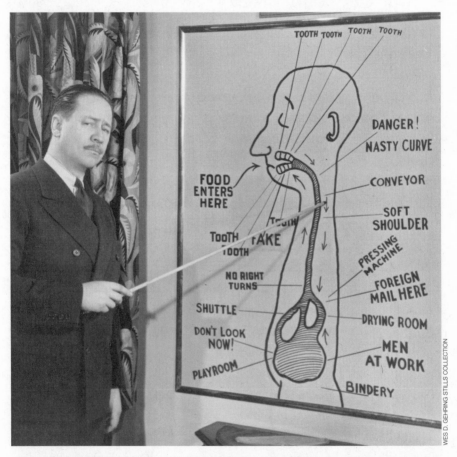

Robert Benchley's "lecture" approach to comedy influenced both Skelton and Johnny Carson. In this publicity shot, Benchley examines The Romance of Digestion *(1937).*

fearlessness in stunts. Over the years Johnny has placed his life in more jeopardy than any comic, Skelton included ['breakaway' doors notwithstanding]."[38] Carson's troupe of comedy characters was also often reminiscent of Skelton's, particularly the parallels between their two hucksters, San Fernando Red and Art Fern, the Tea Time Matinee Movie host. Plus, with both Skelton and Carson coming from the Midwest, there was generally an amicable tone to their humor. Thus, the following description of Carson during his early years on *The Tonight Show* would not be out of place in a Skelton biography: "a gentle, almost shy host who seems to want everyone to have a good time, and no feelings hurt."[39]

Skelton's second memorable 1950s news event involved a television phenomenon in the midst of all its proverbial glory. During the 1954–55 season Walt Disney first came to the small screen with an anthology program initially titled *Disneyland*, an ongoing commercial for his soon-to-open amusement park of the same name. *Disneyland* the program was an immediate hit for ABC, the third place network's first major success. But the episodes that really launched *Disneyland* were from the anthology's "Frontierland" segment (more tie-ins to the park), featuring the adventures of real-life frontier hero Davy Crockett (Fess Parker). The Davy Crockett segment was an overnight sensation that spawned a merchandising bonanza in the mid-1950s—coonskin caps, comic books, fringed leather jackets, shirts, shorts, pajamas, soap, dolls, lunch boxes, tents, bedspreads, draperies, and so on. Reporters in Washington, D.C., even gave President Dwight D. Eisenhower a Davy Crockett necktie for his 1955 birthday.[40] The *New York Times* projected that Crockett merchandise totaled a staggering $300 million in sales by the end of 1955.[41] For many baby boomers, including this author, the Davy Crockett craze was a defining part of early childhood.

Like the rest of the country, Skelton and his baby-boomer children (eight-year-old Valentina and seven-year-old Richard) were huge Crockett fans. Because of the power of celebrity, Davis was able to organize a joint birthday bash for the children with Crockett (Parker) and his sidekick George Russel (Buddy Ebsen) as special guests. Davis, however, had a hidden agenda: "It was the only way I could get Red to stay [with several dozen youngsters]—tell him Davy Crockett was coming."[42] While one article covering the party was titled, "Kids Can't Get at Davy; Skelton Monopolizes Him," the comedian amusingly spread the blame, noting, "it was like the [new] electric train at Christmas—the kids couldn't get to Crockett because of the parents."[43]

For those who might call this tale "cute but inconsequential" and question its inclusion, there is a pertinent back story. As so often happens with anything popular, there eventually was a modest backlash against Crockett. Some revisionist historians debunked the real Crockett, suggesting he was little more than an alcoholic braggart who doubled as his own press agent. This really angered Skelton, and he responded to these critics through the syndicated column of his friend James Bacon. After the then current controversies associated with the Korean War and the Communist witch hunts tied to Senator Joseph McCarthy, Skelton stated, "Davy Crockett has made it popular to be an American again. What's wrong with that?"[44] Long a missionary-like advocate for the power of comedy, Skelton celebrated the crackerbarrel humor inherent to the Crockett stories, while naively implying such programming was a blow against a problem new to the 1950s—juvenile delinquency: "To see our children laugh—to see ourselves laugh with our children because of Davy Crockett is one of the greatest forces for good this country has had in years.... [But] the greatest good to come out of the Crockett craze, is that it has taken kids off the streets and put them in the backyard under Davy Crockett tents."[45]

While I applaud Skelton's enthusiastic spirit here, especially given my own youthful ardor for all things Crockett, I would be remiss if I did not point out that Skelton's pooh-poohing of actual facts about the frontiersman (in favor of the legend) is precisely how he constructed his own life story. Granted, for a Disney children's program such as Crockett, excising a possible notion of "clay feet" is perfectly understandable. But in the adult biography realm, tweaking one's personal history, though a common human temptation, can jettison the most interesting part of the story.

A third 1950s event that provided entertaining headlines for Skelton was boxer Rocky Marciano's guest appearance on the show in the fall of 1956. The only undefeated heavyweight champion in history, Marciano had retired with great fanfare earlier that year, including a front-page story in the *New York Times*.[46] Moreover, when Marciano was on a visit to the nation's capital to receive a "man of the year" award, President Eisenhower said the boxer had demonstrated "qualifications of sportsmanship, courage, character and citizenship."[47] (This was still a time when boxing, after baseball, remained the most closely covered sport in America.) Given Marciano's still young age, comeback stories frequently peppered the sports section of newspapers across the country. Consequently, that was the comedy slant taken for his visit to Skelton's program—a "comeback" against Cauliflower McPugg.

In a special *Los Angeles Examiner* article titled "Rocky vs. McPugg," the former champion played it straight and said, "If I can get on my bicycle [keep moving away from my opponent] and last the distance with Cauliflower, then I've had it."[48] Besides allowing Marciano to have some fun with sportswriters, his high-profile visit to Skelton's program is emblematic of another improvement to the show by the mid-1950s—better guest stars.

While one could argue that tactic would improve any program, it was especially helpful for sidekick-free Skelton. Many of the other pivotal small-screen comedians during that decade had a memorable teammate or two: Jackie Gleason had Art Carney and Audrey Meadows; Jack Benny had Eddie "Rochester" Anderson and Don Wilson; and Sid Caesar had Carl Reiner, Imogene Coca, and Howard Morris. The overkill of too much Skelton and less than notable guests (when he even had guests) had probably contributed to the poor ratings of the early 1950s. A judicious rotation of Skelton's comedy characters, and special guests such as Marciano, however, had changed all that by mid-decade.

Indeed, at the time of Marciano's visit to Skelton's show, the champ even seemed imbued with the populist spirit of a Skelton character. In a much-noted interview earlier that year, Marciano recalled winning the title from Jersey Joe Walcott: "I started to holler," he said in his soft, gentle voice, and I wanted to whoop it up because I was so thrilled at winning. But when I looked at him [on the canvas] all I could think of was, 'Gee, he must feel awful.' I just didn't have the heart to do it [celebrate]."[49]

Just how synonymous to Skelton's mid-1950s show a famous guest had become can be gauged from an episode of Gleason's *The Honeymooners* (1955–56). These acclaimed original thirty-nine episodes rarely make note of other television programming, with the exception of Ed Norton's (Art Carney) obsession with the children's show *Captain Video*. But in the *Honeymooner* installment, "Here Comes the Bride" (first broadcast February 25, 1956), two comic references are made to Skelton and guest Boris Karloff. The catalyst is Ralph Kramden's (Gleason) advice to a soon-to-be-married friend about not moving in with his in-laws: "Sure they seem like nice people. *Now*, they seem like nice people. Boris Karloff seems like a nice guy when he's dancing on the *Red Skelton Show*, too. Did you ever see him in *Frankenstein*? That's the real Karloff. And you'll meet the real relatives when you move into that house." What accents this Skelton guest star phenomenon all the more is that when this *Honeymooner* episode was broadcast, Karloff had yet to appear on Skelton's show! But the reference works because viewers had become used to famous Skelton guest stars doing the unusual, such as a Karloff dancing, or a real heavyweight champion fighting Cauliflower McPugg.

The year 1956 also saw several news articles related to Skelton's writing. The focus was on two projects: a biography of writer Fowler and a screenplay titled *Redso, the Clown*. (References to *Redso* had initially begun to appear in 1948, but at that time authorship was credited to Stillwell.[50]) These and other previously mentioned Skelton writing projects have fallen through the cracks of time. Yet, they were very real and important goals to the comedian, though he seldom shared that significance with the public. One rare exception occurred with writer James Bacon: "Skelton admits that his lucrative life as a clown has gotten in the way of a secret desire to be a writer."[51] For

Skelton as boxer Cauliflower McPugg (circa 1956).

the Skelton biographer, however, his "desire to be a writer" is sadly documented by boxes and boxes of unpublished tales, essays, and story fragments in Vincennes University's Red Skelton Collection.

The comedian reveals in one autobiographical piece that Fowler helped give structure to his passions "When he discovered that I, in a very primitive way, took a blank sheet of paper and ... [wrote daily,] he was more than surprised. 'Course, I was more surprised than he when he sat me down and calmly said: 'You have talent in the writing field but God knows you have a lot to learn.' So I tried. He became my teacher. His lessons and criticisms were love, fun. The most serious of all subjects, life itself, became fun to jot down."[52]

What makes such tutelage fascinating for a Skelton biographer is that Fowler's approach to writing would have reinforced Skelton's predisposition to entertainingly mix fact and fiction in pursuit of telling a better and often more sentimental story. Fowler, a longtime journalist, was best known after 1930 as a scriptwriter and best-selling biographer of show-business personalities. A pivotal insight to this later Fowler writing canon comes from the fact that his first significant newspaper job was under the sponsorship of the legendary Damon Runyon, who was famous for his colorful, slang-filled tales about New York and/or Broadway characters with big hearts, strange names, and imaginative styles of speech. Films showcasing his wonderful characters were very popular at the time of the Fowler-Skelton friendship, and included *The Lemon Drop Kid* (1951), *Stop, You're Killing Me* (1952), and *Guys and Dolls* (1955).

Given that hyperbolic "anecdotes in the best *Front Page* [journalism] tradition" were still being told about Fowler years after he left the newspaper business, and that his apocryphal writing style often embraced earthy "gutter terms," one could even argue he achieved a certain Runyonesque status himself.[53] Granted, Fowler's biographies are more anchored in fact than a Runyan short story, but Fowler still had a tall-tale component he brought to his profiles. For example, as a young reader of Fowler's biography of pioneering screen comedy producer Mack Sennett, *Father Goose* (1934), I remember thinking the book was

aptly titled, since the author seemed very "creative" (fairy tale-like) with
the facts. Consistent with that, the *New York Times*'s positive review
did include the following observation: "Most of the book is written in
a style that befits its cinema relationship, a slapstick, dramatic, tinseled,
vulgar, incredible yarn that is often, apparently, short on facts and long
on imagination and invention. It runs over with anecdotes about movie
actors and producers, that the reader can believe or not, as he thinks
best. But they are always effectively told."[54]

Fowler's later biographies, such as his group portrait of the alcoholic
quartet—John Barrymore, W. C. Fields, painter John Decker, and poet
Sadakichi Hartmann—*Minutes of the Last Meeting* (1954), are obviously
more grounded in fact. Nevertheless, Fowler's longtime drinking
friendship with this foursome, as well as the subjects of several other
books, could lead to hyperbolic tendencies. One might call it a trade
off, exaggeration mixed with insight, such as his poignant verdict that
the quartet's knowing embrace of substance abuse made them "their
own executioners."[55]

Regardless, Skelton's study of Fowler's writing, which the comedian
diligently pursued, would have renewed Skelton's tendencies toward
tall tales in his personal life. Moreover, an examination of the Skelton
essays and short stories at Vincennes University also suggest that the
Fowler influence even muddied an interpretation of Skelton's fiction,
which is often peppered with real people and places. Thus, one has both
exaggerated autobiographical writing on one hand, and what might
be called "Red's take on historical fiction" on the other. Sadly, neither
Skelton's projected biography of Fowler, nor Fowler's planned volume
on Skelton, were ever realized. They might have revealed a great deal
more about their teacher-student relationship.

Skelton's fifth memorable 1950s news story involves the remnants
of his movie career. Despite film's constant second-class status in the
comedian's pecking order, behind radio and then television, Skelton was
a major film star into the early 1950s. Ironically, even during the midst
of Skelton's universally panned second television season, *The Clown*
was a critical and commercial hit. Unfortunately, the remainder of his

sporadic 1950s screen work has been unfairly denigrated, starting with *Half a Hero* (1953). Skelton and Jean Hagen, the actress with the glass-shattering voice from *Singin' in the Rain* (1952), play a young couple who cannot afford a move to the trendy suburbs. Skelton biographer Arthur Marx, the one and only source on the comedian for years, mistakenly implied that *Hero* opened to uniformly bad reviews.[56] Marx's only research on the subject seems to have been a funny but inaccurate crack Skelton was fond of making for years after *Hero*'s release. As late as 1956, Skelton told the *Los Angeles Mirror* critic, "[The movie was so bad] they were afraid to show it at the Chinese [Grauman's] Theater for fear the [movie star] footprints [in cement] would get up and walk away."[57]

In point of fact, Skelton the actor received excellent notices for *Hero*. *Variety* stated, "Skelton's subdued comedy comes over very well in aiming at the heart more than the funny bone."[58] The *Hollywood Reporter* called the film "a warm, mirthful domestic comedy presenting Red Skelton at his best."[59] Under the headline, "Timid Skelton Does Fine Job," the *Los Angeles Examiner* said, "Both Red and Jean let the story provide the laughs by remaining in character throughout, and with their combined flair for comedy, there's no dearth of fun."[60] A less manic Skelton probably lessened the box office, yet MGM records document that *Hero* showed a profit.[61] This was no small accomplishment in a television-driven decade, with ever-dwindling box office receipts.

So why did Skelton kid about the film's lack of success? There are several possible answers. It was not a monster hit, like so many of his earlier movies. *Hero* also came at a time when he was essentially closing down a career in pictures. Consequently, implying it was a bomb represented an easy explanation as to why he focused on television. Mainly, the "anti-*Hero*" crack is symptomatic of what self-deprecating comedians do. For example, Jack Benny mocked his movie *The Horn Blows at Midnight* (1945) for years, maybe to the detriment of his film career. Yet, this often inspired comedy-fantasy, with Benny as an angel sent to destroy earth, is a delightful departure for him. Finally, Skelton might have used the line because he liked old jokes. The Grauman cement footprints walking away was a bit he had first used in the early 1940s, after getting his own shoe size so honored. Except at that time, the only famous footprints threatening to leave were those of his hero, Chaplin.

Paradoxically, Skelton's last MGM picture, the *Great Diamond Robbery* (1953, though it had been on the shelf for some time), would have been a more fitting target of his comic ire. Skelton plays a diamond cutter patsy in a robbery. Though not without some kudos (*Time* magazine enjoyed the movie's "keystone kop finish"[62]), the *Hollywood Reporter* was more on target: "Skelton does as well as possible in an inane role that gives him little opportunity to demonstrate his genuine acting ability so well displayed in 'Half a Hero.'"[63] Yet even here, note the critic's kindly defense of Skelton, and praise for *Hero*.

The rest of Skelton's 1950s film appearances were fleeting, starting with entertaining cameos in *Susan Slept Here* (1954, a Frank Tashlin-directed comedy) and producer Michael Todd's epic version of Jules Verne's *Around the World in 80 Days* (1956). In fact, Todd's spectacle could be called the ultimate cameo movie, showcasing a who's who of Hollywood in bit parts. Thus, for Skelton's drunk routine to often be featured in reviews was a special accomplishment, given all that star power, and the fact that *Eighty Days* went on to win the Oscar for Best Picture.

Public Pigeon No. 1 (1957) was Skelton's last feature film in which he starred. He played another dumb bunny victimized by criminals, and reviews were mixed. The *Washington (DC) News* critic said, "Being a confirmed Skelton fan I was pleased with his nit-witted efforts … and managed a few hearty laughs."[64] The *Hollywood Reporter* added, "Red Skelton has some hilarious scenes in RKO's … [picture] and shows again that he can be one of the top clowns of our day."[65] The *New York Times*'s pan also underlined the time difficulties of juggling small screen/big screen stardom in the 1950s: "Red Skelton movie fans who wish television hadn't swallowed the comedian may change their minds after seeing 'Public Pigeon No. 1.'"[66]

What was unfair, however, about the *Times'* review was that Skelton had already played this part to great acclaim on television as an installment of the dramatic anthology program *Climax* (1954–58). There had been so many calls for a rebroadcast that Skelton had bought the rights to the story and made it the first project for his new production company; it was released through RKO. (Skelton's earlier drinking problems are usually given for the reason MGM did not renew its option on the comedian.) Therefore, the box office for the *Pigeon* movie might have been hurt by its small-screen exposure. Regardless, coverage of both versions generated a great deal of Skelton press during 1956 and 1957.[67]

Skelton's sixth notable news story for the decade involved the sudden 1957 fourth-estate awareness that, despite all his early video struggles, he was a comedy survivor. Syndicated television critic Walter Hawver wrote, "Sid Caesar, Carl Reiner, Howard Morris, Jackie Gleason, Art Carney, Wally Cox, Herb Shriner all have fallen by the wayside. But Red Skelton, whose appeal seems to be eternal, will be back again with his gallery of characters."[68] Hawver might also have added Milton Berle and Red Buttons to that list of prominent comedians then on hiatus from the small screen. What made Skelton's durability all the more impressive was that most of these comedy figures had been, at one time, phenomenally popular on television. Of course, the student of Skelton has an immediate topper to this achievement— he was just getting started, as he appeared on television for another thirteen consecutive years. Periodically during that time journalists made that longevity rediscovery, such as a two-part *TV Guide* article from 1961, "Television's Greatest Clown," marking Skelton's first video decade.[69]

Still, Skelton always maintained his modesty, treating his success like a comic conundrum, and wishing he could share the humor wealth. In 1957 he had observed, "All around me comics are biting the dust. Why they are out I don't know. Neither does anyone else. I know this though. If I had any formula for the success of a comedy show, I'd gladly share the secret with the comics. There's certainly room for lots of laughs in this old world of ours."[70]

Seventh, the year 1957 also provided another news events with special ties to Skelton. Although television Westerns had been popular since the medium's early days, blockbuster hits such as *Hopalong Cassidy* (1949–51, then syndicated) and *The Lone Ranger* (1949–57) were directed at children. Starting with the joint appearance of *Gunsmoke* (1955–75) and *The Life and Legend of Wyatt Earp* (1955–61), there was soon a mushrooming number of adult Westerns on the small screen. By the late 1950s there were more than thirty video Westerns on in prime time! "There are so many television Westerns," joked Bob Hope, "I have to brush the hay off my set before I can turn it on!" (The genre's popularity was equally strong at the theater, where approximately one in four American films was a Western in the 1940s and 1950s.)

During the 1957–58 television season, this six-shooter parade first began to make its presence known in the ratings, with five of the top eight ranked programs being Westerns: *Gunsmoke* (number one), *Tales of Wells Fargo* (number three, 1957–62), *Have Gun Will Travel* (number four, 1957–63), *Wyatt Earp* (number six), and *The Restless Gun* (number eight, 1957–59).[71] Overall, there were four other Westerns in the top twenty-five, with Skelton's show logging in at number fifteen. With this much sagebrush product out there, it was only a matter of time before there would be a tongue-in-cheek backlash. By late 1957, a series of nationally syndicated articles appeared that claimed television comedians were planning to spoof the genre off the small screen.

Given that one of Skelton's comedy characters was a cowboy, Sheriff Deadeye, the comedian seemed to be, as one headline stated, "Caught In [a] Cross Fire."[72] Wanting to be fair, this same syndicated piece presented the positions of "both" entertainers. Skelton stated, "Cowboys have taken over, and there's hardly a minute of air time left for us comedians. There's gonna be a range war, if we can ever find the range." But Deadeye countered, "Shucks, Pardner, them comics been squattin' on open rangeland too long. Let 'em declare war on us. We'll head 'em off at the pass. We'll make 'em smile [à la *The Virginian*] when they say that, stranger."

Ultimately, Skelton's alter ego, Deadeye, proved the more insightful. Television Westerns were even more dominant in the years to come, which guaranteed Deadeye would continue to be a prominent figure in Skelton's one-person stock company. And though his comic cowboy took a backseat to Freddie and Clem in overall importance among Skelton figures, Deadeye represented an important line of continuity with Skelton's screen career-making character Wally Benton in the 1940s *Whistling* trilogy. That is, like Wally, Deadeye's dual focus persona fluctuates between being a smart aleck and a cowardly antihero.

Despite this throwback connection, Deadeye also doubles as Skelton's only topical 1950s figure—a character that parodies the decade's most popular television genre. A timeliness moniker was unusual for Skelton's gallery of goofy figures, since many period critics still found his humor a corny regression into a yesteryear entertainment tradition. But two developments the following year brought critical raves about the comedian's versatility.

Skelton's range is defined through two well-publicized accomplishments in 1958 that dovetail into another pivotal story about the amazing sweep of his talent. In August Skelton opened at Las Vegas's Riviera Hotel to reviews that rivaled the comedian's notices from his last appearance in the desert community in 1953. *Variety* said, "[Skelton] proves without a doubt that he is one of the great clowns of modern times. The romp is a decathlon of comedy."[73] The *Los Angeles Herald Express*, under the headline "Red Skelton Big Vegas Hit," added, "For an incomparable 90 minutes ... the rangy redhead gave a sold-out-in-advance opening night audience ... the spectacle of the art in human comedy."[74]

One of Skelton's many scrapbooks is devoted to a more personal slant on this 1958 triumph.[75] The numerous photos and telegrams document a show business love fest for the comedian, with stars such as Bing Crosby, Carol Channing, and Debbie Reynolds in attendance.

Gunsmoke star James Arness sat with Davis opening night and was later the recipient of a gift from Skelton—a gun the comedian had found during a recent visit to Japan. (As an avid gun collector himself, Skelton thought the Western star would appreciate the present.) Stars sending telegrams included Benny, Eddie Fisher, George Gobel, Frank Borzage, and Elvis Presley and his manager, Colonel Tom Parker. A note from Danny Thomas was the most personal. It read: "Thank God you're back where you belong—making people happy. Have fun."

Contrast this big boisterous 1958 cabaret success, anchored in broad renditions of such classic material as the "Guzzler's Gin" sketch, with Skelton's special Thanksgiving 1958 episode of his television series that was entirely devoted to the holiday trials and tribulations of Freddie the Freeloader in pantomime. As television historian Wesley Hyatt later wrote, "He got glowing reviews … [and television critics] began to realize that maybe, just maybe, this comedian that they had written off a few years earlier as being unable to handle the medium or had come back just due to lucky scheduling had more talent and versatility to offer than they thought."[76]

A ninth memorable Skelton news item from the 1950s involved a celebrated appearance on someone else's television program. Guest spots were something Skelton seldom did. They had to be heartfelt for the comedian, like his 1956 visit to the show of fellow Hoosier Herb Shriner. In a very honest *TV Guide* interview/article from 1960, Skelton also confessed, "I don't do very many guest shots. Frankly, nobody asks. I don't like those swap deals where you do my show and I do yours. They're contrived, they're not spontaneous—and I think the audience senses it."[77]

These comments notwithstanding, the previous year Skelton had made a very popular appearance on the *Lucille Ball-Desi Arnez Show*, which was a series of one-hour specials showcasing the continued misadventures of the *I Love Lucy* cast after that program ceased weekly production. Playing upon the recent statehood of Alaska, the story involved a bad land deal and was called "Lucy Goes to Alaska." As

with most personality comedian-driven entertainment, the plot did
not get in the way of a charming Freddie the Freeloader duet between
Skelton and Ball, as well as a slapstick plane ride. For viewers with good
memories, this teaming of television's favorite redheads brought back
memories of their rousing "Friendship" finale number from *DuBarry
Was a Lady* (1943).

The episode took an added significance in later years when Skelton
kept his old programs out of the marketplace, and "Lucy Goes to
Alaska" was one of the few quality examples of Skelton's television work
readily available to fans. As a final footnote to this episode, Ball did
not enjoy Skelton's ad-libbing tendencies during the shoot. She was a
strictly by-the-script performer and found any variations thereof to be
less than professional. In contrast, Ball's *I Love Lucy* costar, William
Frawley (Fred Mertz), had gotten along famously with Skelton when
he had supported the comedian in the 1958 Freddie the Freeloader
Thanksgiving program.

Sadly, the final notable news story from the decade dwarfs all the
others, as is invariably the case when the unthinkable occurs. The
Skeltons lost their nine-year-old son Richard to leukemia in 1958.
Like a work of tragic literature, the calamity played itself out in five
acts. First, there was simply shock—how could this happen to a little
boy that close friends of the family described "as a carbon copy of his
father, and a comedian in his own right?[78] Less than two weeks after the
January 1957 diagnosis, the comedian thanked the public for their great
outpouring of support and "Skelton said the boy knows he is seriously
ill with leukemia. He was listening when a television commentator
broke the story. 'Perhaps it is better that he does know,' Red added.
'Now he will cooperate better with the doctors. We are not giving
up hope. All of us, including Richard, are praying hard. He's a good
boy.'"[79] (Ironically, Skelton friend Humphrey Bogart died of cancer the
same month Richard was diagnosed.)

Act two involved what came to be called the "See It All Tour,"
where the comedian "plans to pack a lifetime of adventures for his
young son into less than four months this summer."[80] Richard, though

on medication, was still able to lead a relatively normal life, so the exploration of East Coast historic sites began. The many stops ranged from seeing Philadelphia's Liberty Bell to steering a ferry to New York harbor's Statue of Liberty. Soon Skelton decided, "The little fellow got such enjoyment out of that [American] trip—and no ill effects—that we decided to show him the rest of the world."[81]

Richard essentially remained in remission, and medical specialists said the child was fit to travel overseas, however as a precaution during the family's tour of Europe, Richard underwent periodic checkups. In addition, Skelton hoped that all this contact with international specialists might trigger some sort of breakthrough. The family spared no cost, and there was even a plane "standing by at all times to take Richard home ... in case of an emergency."[82] Initially, the European trip went well, including a private audience with the pope, where Richard received a silver medal, and a visit to the ruins of Pompeii—both special

WES D. GEHRING STILLS COLLECTION

Skelton and his family on the way home from their "See It All Tour," July 1957.

highlights for the boy. Even reports of a squabble between the Skeltons had a comic family-on-vacation tone to them. That is, the couple argued about touring in a Volkswagon van: "Mrs. Skelton was afraid of his driving on the twisting, narrow European roads and living off the beaten track in a foreign country."[83]

Both Richards (the child was named after his father) also provided intended comedy. When the boy asked the comedian why the Mona Lisa was smiling, Skelton replied, "Because everyone's looking at her."[84] But the article's author reported the crowd was really looking at the Skeltons. Moving from Paris to London, young Richard showed a dark sense of humor at the airport when he dryly asked a reporter, "I say, how is the Skelton boy?"[85] That was the trip's last bit of levity.

The catalyst for act three (nasty criticism of the tour) came from a press conference at the Skeltons' London hotel, the Savoy. *London Daily Sketch* columnist Simon Ward wrote of the gathering, "I found myself in the middle of a nauseating jamboree. Publicity men, looking like mourners, were gravely handing out printed copies of Red Skelton's life story. Waiters were bringing in trays of drinks."[86] Ward felt little Richard was a frightened victim of a publicity stunt staged by the comedian. Ward's perspective, however, was an aberration. A more typical response to the press conference can be found in the title of John Camsell's syndicated *New York Journal American* article, "Little Dick Skelton Looks at Death—And It Has No Terror For Him."[87] Moreover, American journalists were quick to point out that it was customary in the United States for background material to be handed out at news conferences.

Still, Skelton told the *London Daily Mail*, "I'm furious. People have been very unkind. This is not a publicity stunt."[88] The Skeltons' tour continued with a short visit to Scotland, but a damper had fallen on their trip, and they soon left Europe for home. Yet, "Despite their troubles, Skelton said the entire family thought the trip was a success. 'The kids had a lot of fun. Probably we would still be there but both of them are anxious to see their little friends back home.'"[89]

In the United States there was a backlash against the British press accusation, with this excerpt from a *Los Angeles Herald Express* editorial being a typical response: "The cruel implication that Red Skelton might be interested in obtaining personal publicity through his son's incurable ailment during this tour was acid poured on wounds in the heart."[90] Indeed, the outcry was such that the British Consulate issued a diplomatic denial that London newspapers "insulted" Skelton.[91] The consulate's case in print again laid the blame on the aforementioned *London Daily Sketch* columnist.

Skelton let the issue drop and soon returned to the challenge of being funny on a weekly basis. One of the most difficult aspects of doing the television program was maintaining his habit of periodically mentioning his children in the monologue. Prior to Richard's diagnosis, Skelton had sometimes even used his son as a surrogate Junior character. But when he stopped talking about Valentina and Richard, his son complained. Consequently, heart-rending or not, back they went into the monologue.

The original prognosis for Richard was only five months. But even then, Skelton and Davis were in denial. When their son was still alive a year later, however, they could not help hoping maybe he could beat the disease. Paradoxically, the parents were now themselves having health issues. Skelton almost died in December from a severe asthma attack, brought on by stress, and in January Davis was hospitalized for exhaustion. Richard's condition started to deteriorate in April, and he began to spend an increasing amount of time at the University of California at Los Angeles Medical Center. Readmitted in early May, he suffered through daily blood transfusions and died the evening of May 10, less then two weeks before his tenth birthday.

Skelton and Davis had taken a room in the medical center near Richard's, spending as much time with him as possible. That final day's activities included watching one of his favorite Saturday morning cartoons, *Mighty Mouse*, and talking about his upcoming birthday. The couple and Valentina had then left briefly for supper, only to be immediately called back when Richard took a turn for the worse. Fittingly, for a little boy who was a "carbon copy of his father," Richard managed to impart his last minutes with a darkly comic pronouncement. Sensing his death was near, he requested a final kiss from his mother, father, and sister. A few days later Skelton recalled, "He asked Valentina to pull up a stool [for added height] and give him a kiss, too. [But she was slow to respond to this dying wish. And] I remember Richard said, 'Hurry up, Valentina, I haven't got all day.'"[92] (Of course, given the comedian's hyperbolic tendencies, one cannot help wondering if this was one of his many embellishments.)

This fourth act, the death of their son, left the Skeltons inconsolable. A sense of their extreme grief is suggested in one of two telegrams from composer/actor/author Oscar Levant, "Please bear up for our sake. My deepest sympathy and love."[93] (At the Forest Lawn funeral three days later, neither parent could walk without assistance, and they spent most of their time in a room adjacent to the main chapel.) The sympathy cards and telegrams filled a huge scrapbook and part of another. Mamie Eisenhower wrote, in part, "The President joins me in sending our heartfelt and deepest sympathy to you both. Having lost our first little boy, we both know the empty place it leaves in your heart."

Several letters poignantly, though indirectly, praised the Skeltons' special travel tour for Richard. For example, General George Marshall wrote, in part, "He was a brave little fellow and, as parents, you did a most noble thing by pouring into his life all that time would allow." J. Edgar Hoover, head of the Federal Bureau of Investigation, even provided a firsthand memory of the tour: "I recall so vividly your visit [to Washington, D.C.] last year. He was such a happy and courageous little fellow and a regular little trouper. I deeply regret this tragic loss to you."

Probably the two most eloquent letters received came from Sammy Davis Jr. and Academy Award-winning actor Paul Muni. The latter wrote, "Your goodness, courage and wisdom throughout your ordeal has inspired a world and somehow resounded to the credit of all in our profession. My wife and I know from personal experience what you have lived through.... May the concentrated thinking of millions who love you be of solace to you and yours."

Appropriately, among the who's who of entertainers chronicled in the funeral scrapbooks, comedians are especially well represented. Their numbers, listed in the order by which the cards and telegrams are arranged, included: Jackie Coogan, Edward Everett Horton, Harold Lloyd, Cantiflas (Mario Morena Reyes), Jack Carson, Marion Davies, Red Buttons, Wonderful Smith (one of Skelton's radio sidekicks). Sterling Halloway, Henny Youngman, Gleason, Charles Ruggles, Thomas, George Burns and Gracie Allen, Benny and Mary Livingstone, Ed Wynn, Lucille Hardy (the widow of Oliver Hardy), Eddie Cantor, and Steve Allen.

As luck had it, Allen's card also serves as an unintended ironic segue to act five—life after one's loss. Allen's note said, "As a writer I could think of some appropriate words to say to you at this difficult time but as a father I know that words in themselves couldn't bring you any comfort. Only time can do that."[94]

13

The Skeltons in Palm Springs: Paradise or Prison?

*"It seems to me that ever since we moved to Palm Springs [1962],
things have straightened out."*[1]
RED SKELTON, 1967

Losing one's child goes against the natural order of things. Red
and Georgia Davis Skelton believed they could never recover from the
1958 death of their son Richard Skelton. Some people, however, find
reservoirs of strength when coping with tragedy. In time, Red Skelton
turned a corner on his grief, claiming that his son's death "gave him
an understanding of pain and feeling for people who were suffering."[2]
Coupled with this, he suddenly had a newfound joy in the simple
things of life. This is clearly an example where Skelton's personal
history lends itself to one of biography's basic precepts—showcasing
"the evolution of an individual."[3] I am also reminded of the axiom,
"Our lives are not determined by what happens to us, but how we react
to what happens."[4] Regardless, Skelton's resilience was undoubtedly
assisted by the demands of getting back to a weekly television series.

Davis did not have a comparable distraction. Plus, one of
the idiosyncrasies of Skelton's recovery handicapped his wife's
improvement. The comedian felt the need to turn parts of the Skeltons'
Bel Air mansion into a memorial to Richard. Skelton decided that
everything in the boy's room had to remain exactly as it was when
he was alive—wherever the toys were last played with, or discarded.

Indeed, even bags of fan mail sent to Richard during his long struggle with leukemia remained on the floor of the child's room. Skelton also had a glass cabinet full of Richard mementoes placed in the hall outside the room.

These things only served to further depress Davis, especially since she was home all day, every day. Moreover, Richard's room and the mourning cabinet were in her wing of the home, making them harder to ignore, and despite her protestations this remained the status quo for years. Skelton seemed to need these artifacts to better communicate with his son. As in a populist film by director John Ford, in which the grave of a loved one frequently becomes a comforting catalyst for regular monologues with the deceased, Skelton recurrently talked to Richard in the boy's bedroom.

Ironically, while their son's death worsened Davis's alcoholism and addiction to prescription drugs, Skelton stopped drinking hard liquor. Like many individuals with great discipline, he did not always understand how others were incapable of just stopping addictive behavior. For example, in a rough draft of a letter Skelton wrote to Davis in the 1960s, he shared a story about an "anonymous" alcoholic woman and the problem-solving lessons to be drawn from classic literature: "so many lovely ladies became old—ugly—half asleep all day [and] they drink the nite unto sunrise. What happiness [Daniel] Defoe tried to give to the world with the simple story of Robinson Crusoe learning the value of self without becoming bored, uninspired."[5]

Paradoxically, for all that discipline, Skelton avoided confrontation, so it is unlikely that Davis ever saw this teaching epistle. In fact, another bit of correspondence included with this letter begins, "In going over letters I have never given to you."[6] Also, two additional fallacies about Skelton's wifely correspondence merit addressing at this point. First, though the comedian enjoyed telling reporters he wrote a love letter every day to Davis, "love" is probably not the best term. While many are quite romantic, "reflections" would better describe them. Under the latter moniker, their tone ranges from the philosophical parable (such as the previously cited Defoe example), to outright anger. This is evidently how the nonconfrontational comedian worked out his aggression, since his target person did not see the written complaint.

This sounds like a perversion of something Skelton might have acquired in therapy, where patients are sometimes encouraged to write a purging letter to a source of frustration who is no longer alive. Or, this venting correspondence might have represented another example of the comedian's own peculiar brand of Eastern mysticism. After several 1950s visits to Japan, Skelton became fascinated by that country's culture, everything from Buddhism to bonsai trees. On more than one occasion Skelton told me about a ceremony he and his then third wife (Lothian Toland, whom he married after his 1973 divorce from Davis) performed if someone had wronged them.[7] The ritual involved lighting a candle, saying something nice about the individual and then totally erasing that person's existence from their lives. As with the "love" letters, there was no direct confrontation.

This rite was not unlike Skelton biographer Arthur Marx's description of a phenomenon already addressed—the comedian's ability to simply not acknowledge someone (like first wife Edna Stillwell or Buster Keaton) once they were no longer part of Skelton's life. Marx christened this Skelton's "way of mentally burying people."[8] Along related lines, Toland also became the target of biting Skelton letters that were never delivered.[9]

A second fallacy about Skelton's daily love letters to his wife is that they were written throughout their marriage. To the contrary, in a *Boston Globe* article from 1969, Davis revealed that this homegrown correspondence only began after their 1962 move to Palm Springs.[10] This is borne out by the previously mentioned Skelton Collection at Vincennes University, with the often bound letters beginning in 1962. This is yet another example of Skelton's proclivity for always trying to tell a better, in this case, a more romantic, story.

In that same *Globe* article, Davis seconds the sentiments expressed by Skelton to open this chapter—by moving to Palm Springs they "found peace and tranquility."[11] So what motivated this seemingly positive move? Several factors were at play, starting with the mental health of the couple's daughter, Valentina Skelton. In 1970 she revealed that at the time of her brother's death, "I thought my parents loved him more than they loved me ... I was so silly, I was jealous, but then I was only eleven at the time."[12] Consistent with that understandable but misguided perspective, Valentina's claim that the move came on the advice of her doctor, as a way to curb the girl's ongoing feeling of inferiority, gives great credence to this being the primary reason for exiting Los Angeles.[13] More recently, Valentina has added an addendum to this position, indicating that her parents were also anxious to get her away from some young people they believed were a bad influence on the fifteen-year-old.[14]

A second explanation for the move is a general consensus among Skelton friends and professional colleagues that the mansion as memorial was finally getting to Skelton by the early 1960s, too, making him more receptive to Davis's and/or Valentina's need for change. Third, the near loss of their Los Angeles home in 1961 to one of Southern California's intermittent brush fires somehow made the subject of moving more palatable. Fourth, with so many of their entertainment friends and acquaintances already comfortably ensconced in Palm Springs, celebrities such as Bob Hope, Frank Sinatra, and Indiana-born bandleader/comedian Phil Harris, the desert community had become a tempting second home for Hollywood types such as the Skeltons.

Each of these elements no doubt played a factor in the Skeltons move to Palm Springs. At this point, however, I am tempted to quote a line writer Jean Strouse posits as the central task of the biographer. Originally attributed to American financier J. P. Morgan, the statement reads, "There are two reasons why a man does anything. There's a good reason and there's the real reason."[15] Years later, Skelton would see the "real reason" for the move entirely tied to his wife's instability. In a 1968 rough draft of a rambling letter to Georgia he writes, "For 7 years now I have tried to live on the desert ... [and] help bring you back.... We [still] have a beautiful home in Bel Air you don't like—I need the feel of the city to be creative."[16] Almost ten years later, after the Skelton's divorce and Davis's subsequent suicide, Skelton gave a similar story to the *New York Times*. Again, he claimed to dislike the Palm Springs desert and blamed the move on Davis's assorted demons: "She had a problem with alcohol and pills and fear. [And] she thought we could get away from … freeloaders."[17]

So what is the real reason behind the relocation to Palm Springs? I would still emphasize the first four points, starting with the mental health of the Skeltons' daughter. After losing one child, I cannot imagine anything else taking precedence over the well-being of their only surviving child. Moreover, Skelton's bitter-sounding revisionist perspectives only surface much later, starting with a time when Davis's addiction problems were at their worst. Of course, the most basic explanation is to simply quote a fundamental biography axiom credited to Claire Tomalin, "Like most people, he gave different accounts of what he believed at different times."[18] Still, after sifting through mountains of Skelton material at archives across the country, there is just too much evidence chronicling how creative *and* happy he was in their desert getaway, Davis's problems notwithstanding. But before exploring some of this documentation that reveals how Skelton became a sort of Palm Springs Renaissance man, one must first address the strange development associated with the selection of their house in the desert.

Wealthy Palm Springs, located approximately a hundred miles east of Hollywood, has been kiddingly called "the sandbox of society," but Hope's application of a recycled line from the *Road to Morocco* (1942) is funnier: "This must be the place where they empty all the old hourglasses." The community offered year-round sun, clean air, and beautiful golf courses, especially the trendy Tamarisk Country Club. While Skelton had given up the sport years before, after a brief trial run during his marriage to Edna Stillwell, he liked the idea of a home along one of Tamarisk's fairways. As someone who did little socializing, he planned to keep up with friends as they golfed by.

The only problem, however, was that none of the available houses did anything for the Skeltons. This all changed by the sixteenth fairway, when the couple saw a small but attractive U-shaped home accenting a swimming pool. But it was neither the setting nor the architecture that sold the place. This is where things get a little mystical, yet several reputable sources, including Marx's 1979 biography of the comedian, reveal, "As Red and Georgia looked toward the place, they both simultaneously thought they saw the ghost of Richard playing and laughing on the grass in front of the house."[19] When I recently asked Valentina about the incident, she did not recall hearing the story. But she said it was consistent with Skelton's mindset, adding, "My dad was very psychic."[20]

There is more than a little irony involved in leaving one home, in part, because it has become too much like a memorial shrine to a dead son, only to select another house based upon seeing that son's ghost. For some, such a ghostly event would bring to mind that previously noted Steve Allen quote: "I have never known a successful comedian who was not somewhat neurotic. The unsuccessful ones must be in even worse condition."[21] Yet as Valentina suggested, Skelton's sighting of his son's ghost was not the comedian's only paranormal experience. Three years later, Skelton was credited with editing a collection of scary stories with the punning title, *A Red Skelton in Your Closet* (1965). The comedian confessed in his foreword, "Sometimes, just before I go on stage the ghost of the greatest pantomimist [Joseph Grimaldi] whispers in my ear."[22]

In fairness to Skelton, as well as being consistent with Allen's blanket statement about crazy comics, many laughmakers have had mystical beliefs. But what makes the Skelton story about Grimaldi especially intriguing is how much it resembles an often told tale by Peter Sellers. He believed that the spirit of Dan Leno, one of the most revered comedians of the Victorian age, guided his career: "He follows me around everywhere [in my mind]. For years I felt his help, especially with my timing. ... He has given me some wonderful advice ... it's as though somebody is speaking inside your head, which is why many people dismiss it, dismiss spiritualism as being dotty [crazy]."[23]

Of course, by the 1960s, such Skelton/Sellers mystical confessions not only sounded strange, they also were out of touch with that era's darkly comic approach to such subjects. For example, here are two now classic jokes from one of the decade's pivotal stand-up comedians,

Woody Allen: "I was thrown out of NYU. On my metaphysics final I looked within the soul of the boy sitting next to me…. [Actually] I don't believe in the afterlife but I am bringing a change of underwear."[24] Regardless, before leaving the subject of mystical-like parallels between Skelton and Sellers, one must cite their compulsive need to escape into various characterizations. They likened themselves to empty vessels, before a given personality took over. Interestingly, Skelton's "multitude of humanity within me," to borrow a phrase from poet Walt Whitman, even stretched beyond his one-man band of comedy characters. According to Guy della Cioppa, the first chief of Skelton's Van Bernard Productions (formed when Skelton's television show expanded to an hour in 1962), "[The comedian] always thinks of himself as two people.

WES D. GEHRING STILLS COLLECTION

Woody Allen and frequent costar Diane Keaton relax on the set of the 1973 comedy Sleeper.

The offstage Skelton is Red. The fellow who performs *on*stage he always refers to in the third person as 'Victor Van Bernard.'"[25] (Bernard was Skelton's middle name. But by adding the upper class "Van," the name is reminiscent of Jackie Gleason's pompous character Reginald Van Gleason III.)

Moving beyond ghosts and Skelton's multiple characters, how did Palm Springs become a creative retreat for the comedian? First, Skelton seemed to be in a better state of mind. This is probably best symbolized by dismantling the funeral parlor aspects of their Bel Air mansion shortly after the move to the desert. (They retained both residences, because Skelton stayed in Los Angeles two or three nights a week when his television series was in production.) Two years after the move, Skelton told syndicated Hollywood columnist Hedda Hopper, "Georgia and I have always done everything together—painting, swimming, shopping—and she's a great audience for testing [the comedy] material I write. We're happy with our home in the desert and the life we lead there when I'm not working. We get to bed early and get up early; we like regular hours."[26]

Second, by physically getting away from any and all distractions, Skelton was able to devote more time to his numerous hobbies, especially painting. Although he had been dabbling in this area for years, the Palm Springs move finally made him get serious about his art. Skelton's wife, a former art student, was the catalyst for this interest. Shortly after their move to the desert, he told a reporter, "Georgia taught me painting 20 years ago. She's very good."[27]

A *Screenland* article from more than ten years earlier, however, more fully fleshes out Davis's art-instructor influence on her husband. The original goal was just to use painting as a way of getting him to relax. When Skelton struggled at first, she encouraged him to paint what he knew, which is how his focus on clowns began. "I called each [Skelton] painting a step into control of his imagination," said Davis.[28] Skelton's first wife, Stillwell, is also on record for strongly supporting the comedian's beginning artistic efforts, which would have paralleled the managing portion of her career with him.

Skelton and his wife Davis early in their marriage with one of the comedian's earliest hobbies—a train set.

Valentina said that her father was a very prolific artist. "The paintings would stack up," she remembered. "Dad did tons and tons of Freddies [Freddie the Freeloader] and people—celebrities—in clown form."[29] A broad spectrum of entertainers bought Skelton's work, ranging from Hope to Burt Reynolds. Valentina noted a certain irony in her father's success as an artist. Skelton was so needy of attention that he had a smothering effect on Davis, to the point where Valentina believed her mother was "losing her identity." The added paradox for Valentina was that Davis was the trained artist, yet ultimately, "Dad overshadowed her there [in art], too."[30]

When discussing painting, Skelton the raconteur often enjoyed telling an apocryphal story about an abstract exhibition he had once seen in, of all places, a large urban department store (the city and date frequently changed.). He supposedly asked the price of one prominent painting in this modern art collection. When the clerk answered, "10,000 wouldn't buy that one," Skelton comically replied, "And I would be one of the 10,000." After this, he decided to try painting. Though it is unlikely this comic exchange ever took place, the construction of the story reveals a great deal about Skelton. First, even though the comedy comes from a play on words, Skelton, as a child of poverty, was greatly impressed with anything costing $10,000. Second, as the most practical of people, at some level one can assume he might have thought, "If an abstract painting can be priced that high, why couldn't I make even more money with representational art? Third, Skelton's story also clearly places him with the masses (one of ten thousand) on his rejection of modern art. And though some of Skelton's later canvases fetched tens of thousands of dollars, he was always most pleased with making his art affordable to the general public by way of poster and plate reproductions.

Thanks to his increased activity as a Palm Springs painter, Skelton had his first art show in June 1964. The exhibition was at Las Vegas's Sands Hotel, where Skelton was entertaining. The public was charmed by this revelation about a clown painting clowns, and it generated a great deal of publicity, including a color photo spread in *Look* magazine.

Even the manner in which Skelton's art was showcased produced kudos. The upper portion of a wall covered by rows of his clown paintings included a window-like opening that allowed Skelton, made-up as a clown, to pose from the other side, as if he were yet another painting.

The comedian knew he had arrived when major art collectors in show business, people such as Maurice Chevalier and Frank Sinatra, wanted a Skelton original. Despite this success, Skelton remained self-deprecating about his painting, such as the revelation, "I work on ... [two paintings simultaneously] until I can figure out what's wrong with the first one. Sometimes I don't find out for weeks. Sometimes I just don't find out."[31] Trying to stay cool in the desert heat, Skelton also found that painting in the shallow end of his pool presented certain problems, as in oil and water do not mix: "You ought to see the pool after one of my painting sprees. It's an olympic-sized palette."[32] But consistent with his revisionist history tendencies, once someone was out of his life, after his divorce from Davis and her subsequent death, she ceased to be credited with introducing him to painting.

Skelton painting in his Muncie, Indiana, hotel room prior to his one-man-show at Ball State University in 1977.

By his final years Skelton had spun a story that sounds apocryphal in nature: too poor for supplies, he fashioned a brush from a lock of his hair, which was somehow attached to a pencil. Paint was scrounged from discarded school supplies. Skelton was nothing if not a good storyteller. When I ran all these art stories by Valentina she further fleshed out her mother's art resume.[33] Davis was going to be an illustrator for the *Denver Post* but it did not work out. She attended the Art Center School in Los Angeles and qualified for a commercial degree but there was little work available. Georgia then drifted into modeling and was soon signed by MGM. Valentina's final adjunct to the art story, however, was that while she had never heard her father's homespun yarn about a brush from his hair and so on, he had done some early painting. That is, Skelton had once gifted her with a painting he dated from his teenage years. (In Skelton's last years, when health problems kept him from performing, his painting gave the comedian great comfort, allowing him to continue to be creative.)

Besides the comedian's full embrace of painting during the Palm Spring years, Skelton divided his free time among several other hobbies. His interest in gardening resulted in buying the vacant lots on either side of the Palm Beach residence. They were soon transformed into formal Italian and Japanese gardens, with Skelton's favorite horticulture activity being the care and maintenance of his bonsai trees—the small, ornamental shrublike plants whose size and shape are severely restricted by the grower. In the Japanese garden Skelton also had an elaborate teahouse constructed that ultimately might have doubled as a guesthouse. This building became hobby central, with Skelton working here on his musical compositions and short stories, not to mention his paintings.

While his music skills were never in a class with his paintings, which eventually generated millions of dollars for the comedian, several Skelton compositions were published by sheet-music companies, such as "The Kadiddlehopper March" and "Red's White and Blue March." His writing skills, despite the tutelage by Gene Fowler, never really panned out. There was a charming children's book, *Gertrude and Heathcliff* (1971), about his two comic seagull characters, but that volume's success is a product of Skelton's humorous drawings. In fairness to Skelton, he seldom tried to market these tales, other than a handful sold with his artwork, such as his short story about "The Ventriloquist" or "Old Whity" (a horse). He simply preferred to stockpile them, as a someday legacy to his family. There are literally thousands of these Skelton stories, and story fragments, in Vincennes University's Red Skelton Collection. As he demonstrated in his relationship with the press concerning an inventive take on his life history, Skelton's writing often mixes fact and fantasy at random. Though many Skelton pieces show promise, the vast majority suffer from a lack of attention. Writing is essentially about rewriting. But Skelton seems to have been more concerned with daily numbers—one short story, five tunes, a love letter to Davis, and whatever else he included in this rigorous schedule.

Why did he turn what were essentially hobbies into such a daily grind? First, Skelton had always been blessed (cursed?) with a midwestern work ethic, and it had served him well through the years. I am reminded of critic Joan Acocella's comment, "What allows genius to flower is not neurosis but its opposite ... ordinary Sunday-school virtues such as tenacity and above all the ability to survive disappointment."[34] By reducing his television work week to two intense days, he had never had so much free time, and it was soon arranged like a work schedule.

A second explanation for this hobby intensity, especially as it embraced the arts (painting, musical composition, writing), was probably tied to creative respectability. Skelton used to regularly complain to his production company chief, Guy della Ciappa, "Most people think I'm just a cheap vaudeville clown. I get no respect from anybody."[35] Third, many of Skelton's entertainment heroes through the years had worn many creative hats, from his Vincennes mentor Clarence Stout to the ultimate in multitasking, Charlie Chaplin.

At some level, Skelton undoubtedly felt a true artist does it all. Consequently, with the extra time and creative isolation made possible by his Palm Springs getaway, Skelton's artistic flowering was the 1960s.

Now, what boded well for Skelton the Renaissance man was not necessarily ideal for family and loved ones. Though he and Davis were at home more, and the comedian enjoyed talking about the couple doing things together, the truth of the matter was that Skelton tended to be off in his own creative world. Even before the move, the comedian had become something of a reclusive artist. What follows is a telling Skelton revelation, made two years prior to Palm Springs: "We stay home a lot, Georgia and I. When I'm not working, I stay in my room upstairs and write. Sometimes I don't leave the room all day."[36] Ironically, while the title of the *TV Guide* interview/article this quote is drawn from, "It Hasn't All Been Laughs," is meant to document the dark side of being a clown, it also doubles as an apt description of life, in general, for this clown's wife. Davis's situation reminds me of the Chekhov adage, "If you are afraid of loneliness don't marry." This was worse than the Eleanor Rigby variety of loneliness, because in Davis's case, her alleged soul mate was there but often missing in creative action.

If the situation was less than ideal for Davis, it was worse for the extended family. The comedian's nephew, Marvin L. Skelton, told me that when Skelton and Davis moved to Palm Springs it was like they "dropped off the earth."[37] According to Marvin, while they were never a close family, there had been regular contact, though usually on his uncle's terms. For example, Marvin's father lived close to Skelton's home studio (MGM), and the comedian sometimes stopped by after work. Plus, there were occasional special birthday parties for the family star. This all but ceased after the Palm Springs move. As a bit of back history, Marvin suggested that Skelton's family ties were directly related to whom he was married. Calling Edna Stillwell a "great gal," he said there was "lots of family contact when he [Skelton] was married to her."[38] Marvin believed Davis was always a bit standoffish and that often characterized the comedian's family attitude during that marriage. Regarding Skelton's third wife, Toland, Marvin hesitated to say anything, then, exhibiting some of the earthy humor favored by his uncle in private, he said, "She goes around like she has a chapped ass."[39] Needless to say, there was little family connection during Skelton's third marriage.

Even in the 1960s, Marvin's main link with his uncle was by way of the woman the public thought of as the comedian's mother, Ida Mae Skelton. Years before, Skelton had given her a home near MGM, where she lived with her husband, Gustave Soderstrom. After Skelton's stepfather died, the comedian bought Ida Mae a house in Palm Springs. Through summer visits to his grandmother's desert home, Marvin managed to maintain some affinity with his famous uncle, who lived just a few miles away. Though Skelton had largely let the family network slip away, he remained loyal to his adoptive mother. Marvin recalled, "Red was always giving her gifts. When she died [1966] there were stacks of $100 bills taped to the bottom of her bathroom floor mat. She didn't care about material things; she was just happy to have a nice home."[40] Though she was in some ways overwhelmed by her son's success, Marvin affectionately described her as, "a funny old gal that liked to drink beer and have a good time."[41]

Ida Mae was also the catalyst for an eye-opening letter Skelton wrote to his daughter Valentina. The two had visited the octogenarian in the hospital, the year before she died. Valentina would have been approximately eighteen years old at the time, and presumably still at home. Thus, even before examining the document, one ponders the necessity of writing such a note. The answer, however, seems present in the loving but formal tone of the letter, which might have been penned in the Victorian era:

> It was most generous and kind of you to accompany me to
> Bel Air and to the hospital to visit your Grandmother
> Mur [Skelton's pet name for Ida Mae]. Most teenagers
> are less polite towards Mothers and Dads and age itself.
>
> I sure was proud to be in the company of such a well-

disciplined lady and happy to hear of the love you
revealed toward your dear Mother.

The respect you gave me will add to our [Davis and
Skelton's] prayers that the blessing of God may attend
you in all your endeavors ... I'll bet He must find
it difficult to get more material to make another you.

Love,

Your Dad[42]

One would hope Skelton's one-on-one time with his daughter was
not so rigid, though the letter itself was still a convoluted "I love you"
to Valentina. Skelton felt a need to quantify all aspects of his life—from
bound-in-leather letter collections to the women *he lived with*, to the
assorted stockpiles of art projects he kept turning out. Like a whirling
dervish, Skelton's professional side sometimes became mixed up with
his personal, and his personal with professional. The result could be a
parental note that sounds more like a "well done" commendation from
a Dickens headmaster.

Valentina has indicated she has little memories of these at-home
letters from her father.[43] Consequently, as sometimes occurred with
Skelton's undelivered in-house correspondence to his second (Davis)
and third (Toland) wives, writing became an end in itself. If there was
a complaint, the undelivered letter seemingly became cathartic, or, if
such a note was complimentary, one supposes Skelton was stockpiling
documentation of his love.

Since the highlighted letter to Valentina discussed her paternal
grandmother, I asked Skelton's daughter if her father had shared with
her his controversial private belief that his biological mother had really
been a prostitute. Surprisingly, Valentina said he had, and replicated
much of what was discussed earlier. This was yet another enigma of the
man, often secretive and prone to compartmentalization, here he could
share the most provocative of suggestions with his daughter.

Before moving from this complex puzzle of a private life back to
Skelton's more familiar public persona, there is one more transition

hobby to examine—watching and studying television. For most of his twenty consecutive years on television, Skelton was a regular video junkie. This went beyond research for his program, though given his workaholic tendencies, at some point he probably justified it along those lines. More correctly, he was, like most pioneering television viewers, totally mesmerized by the phenomenon. After all, this was a pop culture development that even changed America's eating habits, introducing such new terms (and customs) as the "TV dinner" and the "TV tray"—eliminating the need for family small talk at dinner.

Given Skelton's television insider status and his unlimited resources, the comedian had video recording capabilities at home decades ahead of the general public. At one point, he also had a bank of three television sets (for yesteryear's three main networks) so that he could monitor all programming simultaneously. Though Skelton only had the sound on for one focus show, if something else of interest appeared on the competition, he was ready to tape. (His fascination with television-related technology was merely an updated example of Skelton's longtime interest in gadgetry that began with photography and later included assorted tape recorders, which is how the comedian did his "writing.")

For all Skelton's artistic activity in the desert, 1960s America still knew him as its favorite television clown. What is more, for someone who had struggled so long to turn his ratings around in the 1950s, his Nielsen numbers from the 1960s are truly amazing. For most of the decade he was in the top ten, charting as high as the third-ranked show during the 1962–63 season (behind *The Beverly Hillbillies* and *Candid Camera*) and rising to number two in 1966–67 (behind *Bonanza*).[44]

Impressively, Skelton accomplished all this on essentially a hectic, two-day schedule. On Sunday the comedian would drive one of his Rolls Royces the hundred miles from Palm Springs to his Bel Air estate in Los Angeles. (For a short time after the move to the desert, a private plane flew him between the two cities.) Davis only joined him sporadically on these trips, though after the mid-1960s, it meant more time with Valentina, who had moved back to the Bel Air residence to attend college in Los Angeles and escape the reclusiveness of her parents' desert lifestyle.

Mondays and Tuesdays represented multiple run-throughs and rehearsals, with the actual taping of the show on Tuesday night before a studio audience of two hundred for broadcast three weeks later. (For much of the decade Skelton's time slot for his program was from 8:30 p.m. to 9:30 p.m. on Tuesday.) During Skelton's intense two-day production period, he slept little and ate less. "Except for an occasional candy bar or 10-cent package of soda crackers, he would consume nothing except a large and explosively hot jar of peppers. ('They're the hottest obtainable,' he was to explain later. [They] help kill the desire for food. No use to eat. I couldn't keep it down,')" *TV Guide* reported.[45] After the taping, the magazine added, "Red is exhausted—a beat, trembling man. His clothes are wet enough to wring out."[46] Skelton then rehashed the program with his producer, had a bite to eat, cleaned up, and drove back to Palm Springs all that same night.

As the comedian's "after-shows" became famous to radio insiders of the 1940s, Skelton's blue television rehearsals had achieved notoriety among CBS employees by the 1960s. Often referred to as the *Red Skelton Dirty Hour*, the comedian's producer, Seymour Berns, recalled of Skelton's routines, "We let him do it because we really had to let him get it out of his system before we let the audience in.... While Red was doing a 'snatch' joke, we'd be in the control room trying to figure out what would go in that spot that would be clean."[47]

The paradox here, of course, is that Skelton always prided himself on being a clean comic, but a provocative explanation comes from the comedian, no less, in a 1960s *TV Guide* article. Revisiting the split-personality approach noted earlier in this chapter (where the off-stage person is Red, and the performer is Victor Van Bernard), Skelton confessed, "I picture him [Bernard] as someone who is afraid to offend anyone. I am myself [blue comedy and all] at rehearsals but I'll be Victor Van Bernard on the show."[48] It represents an odd defense, sort of like one is interviewing a comedic Sybil.

In Skelton's defense, what constituted a "dirty hour" in the mid-1960s now plays as pretty tame in the post-*Aristocrats* (2005) twenty-first century. But even in the 1960s, when his blue rehearsals were discussed in mainstream publications, they were given inventive justifications. For example, here is another *TV Guide* article on the subject: "Frequently he [Skelton] will embroider a [rehearsal] joke with colorful phraseology not usually considered ideal for the living room. The idea is to lead the victim [that week's costar] right up to air time, making her think he is actually going to say it, then cut off the remark in mid-flight, turning it into a mild reference to, say, the girth of her elbow."[49] The end result was often a certain comic tension in the taped program, as Skelton's guest performer might entertainingly stumble and/or snicker through his/her exchanges with Skelton. The viewer either enjoyed the seemingly fun, partylike atmosphere, or was perturbed by missing out on some inside joke.

Regardless, there is a certain hypocrisy in Skelton's double-standard on provocative humor, not to mention the strange split personality explanation. In contrast, I am reminded of stage and screen comedian Joe E. Brown. Brown was also famous for his clean comedy advocacy.[50] There were no exceptions, however, for the older comedian, even if it was a nonpaying informal setting—the type of arena that brought out Skelton's, to quote *TV Guide*, "randy character who tosses off unexpected blue lines and makes gestures never seen in polite company."[51] Indeed, during World War II, Brown received kudos from the parents of GIs whose sons had written home praising the veteran comic's classy shows, despite settings that might have encouraged ribald riffs.

To paraphrase *New York Times* critic Manohla Dargis, a strong whiff of piety is not a bad smell, but there's often more to it than that.[52] Applied to Skelton, this means his often extremely Rabelaisian nature in private life seemed to push him into overly sanctimonious statements about public humor. But as the line from *Hamlet* instructs, always be wary of those who "doth protest too much." What follows is a classic case of Skelton's bawdy private wit. The setup is that Davis's promiscuous tendencies, coupled with questions of infidelity, often meant Skelton gave his wife bitingly comic paybacks. The Skeltons were at a large Beverly Hills party hosted by John Wayne. The comedian and his wife were with Humphrey Bogart when an extremely sexy foreign actress sauntered by, attracting the attention of every man in the room. When Skelton asked Bogart who she was, he answered, "I don't know her name but Ty[rone] Power says she's the best cocksucker in town." With that, Skelton patted his wife's head and told Bogart, "Aw, now you've gone and hurt Georgia's feelings."[53]

Part of the comedy conundrum that was Skelton went beyond basic contradictions such as clean humor versus the *Red Skelton Dirty Hour*. Sometimes Skelton was bothered by comedy elements of rivals that were more than a little present in his own work. For example, he was a big fan of the *Jackie Gleason Show*, the rotund comedian's comeback variety hour, which ran from 1962 to 1970. "Dad would even imitate some of Gleason's pet lines around their house, like 'And away we go,'" according to Valentina.[54] But Skelton had problems with Gleason's Joe the bartender sketches, because they featured Frank Fontaine's nonsense ramblings as the less-than-bright lush Crazy Guggenheim. Skelton felt the character bordered too much on being mentally deficient. Now granted, Skelton was always proud of his comedy sensitivity, forever noting how even as a child he was bothered by the films of cross-eyed silent film comedian Ben Turpin. Still, Crazy Guggenheim came from the same humor gene pool as Skelton's Clem Kadiddlehopper and Cauliflower McPugg. Plus, as Valentina insightfully added, when I shared this story with her, part of Guggenheim's comic problems were also brought on by drink, "and Dad was famous for his 'Guzzler's Gin' routine"—another comic victim of drink.[55]

In fact, when one does the comedy genealogy on Guggenheim, a composite of an early Gleason friend and a punch-drunk figure from Fontaine's act, the background is reminiscent of Kadiddlehopper's origins—drawn from a Skelton childhood buddy. Moreover, since part of Guggenheim's eccentricity can be blamed on drink, one could argue

Skelton as the henpecked antihero George Appleby, caught in a compromising situation by his wife, Virginia Grey (left).

that Kadiddlehopper and McPugg are the more disturbing duo. I am reminded of the scene in *It's a Gift* (1934) when W. C. Fields's character is called a drunk and he responds, "Yeah, and you're crazy. I'll be sober tomorrow and you'll be crazy for the rest of your life!"

Though Skelton's sensitivity issue with Fontaine's Guggenheim character merely had Skelton changing the channel when the Joe the bartender sketches came on, the liberal political humor of the *Smothers Brothers Comedy Hour* (1967–69) put Skelton on a soapbox, "I watched the Smothers Brothers a time or two," he said. "That's not humor. It's not even satire. Anytime you have to shock people into a laugh or to get their attention, you're wrong. It's not advanced humor at all. If they lived in the Middle Ages, they'd get their heads chopped off."[56]

For the time, the Smothers Brothers' program was a very irreverent variety hour that attacked the Vietnam War, right-wing politicians, and a host of youth-orientated bugaboos. Though Skelton's comments sound reactionary today, they would have resonated with a number of people in 1969 who also found the show too controversial. This conservative coalition included Skelton's own network (CBS), which canceled the program after two-and-a-half seasons. So where is the inconsistency with Skelton, whose politics always leaned right, anyway? Over a decade earlier, in a *San Francisco Chronicle* article titled, "Skelton Razzes Network Ban on Political Jokes," the comedian sang a different song: "According to Red, when a nation loses its ability to laugh at its leaders it gives up an important element of democracy." Then, quoted directly, Skelton added, "But they [political leaders] aren't the only sacred cows. There are hundreds of other things you could laugh about ten years ago that are taboo today. [It's] getting so you step on some toes or hurt somebody's feelings these days any place you turn."[57]

While Skelton's politics had usually been conservative, there had also often been a liberalness of spirit, as demonstrated by those *San Francisco Chronicle* comments. By the late 1960s, however, a certain rigidity had formed about what constituted entertainment for Skelton. He might have been forewarned by one of his own file jokes on aging: "You know how to tell when you're getting old? When your broad mind changes places with your narrow waist."⁵⁸ Although the Smothers Brothers show did not last long, it was a harbinger of things to come.

In a move to attract a younger urban audience, CBS dropped Skelton's show at the end of the 1969–70 season, despite the program coming in at number seven in the Nielson ratings.⁵⁹ It was an unprecedented action by a network, making Skelton a victim of demographics. His audience numbers, though high, skewered too small town/rural and old. The comedian was not alone in his victimization. CBS executed what might be called a purge of its populist programming. *Petticoat Junction* (1963–70), which had been a Tuesday night staple with Skelton, was canceled the same year. The following season, CBS dropped its two other high-profile rural situation comedies, *The Beverly Hillbillies* (1962–71) and *Green Acres* (1965–71).

Skelton's sacking was a shock, especially since it had largely been a decade of television achievements for him, beyond the ratings. What follows is a brief look at the most memorable episodes of his program during this period. Easily the most acclaimed 1960s show was his "Concert in Pantomime," which costarred internationally acclaimed mime Marcel Marceau and was broadcast on February 2, 1965. Hosted by Maurice Chevalier, the program included Skelton and Marceau performing before a black-tie studio audience of prominent guests. The two men each alternated with four solo sketches, before combining for a mimed version of *Pinocchio*. This was the first time most of America had seen the French mime. Appearing as his clown-tramp character Bip, with white face and pants and striped tight shirt, Marceau performed the signature routines, "The Tug of War," "Bip the Dice Player," "Bip the Skater," and his pièce de résistance, "Bip as a Mask Maker." The *New York Daily News* observed, "It's as the mask maker that his great genius is best displayed"—where once the hideous mask is removed, the true person is revealed.⁶⁰

In contrast, Skelton's broader pictorial style was applied to "A Girl Dressing in the Morning," "Mixing the Salad," "The Drunken Doctor in Surgery," and "The Old Man Watching the Parade." With the exception of the latter sketch, Skelton often managed to transform gross elements into comedy, such as sneezing into the salad. While reviewers tended to give Marceau the higher artistic marks, Skelton seemed to play more effectively for homegrown viewers. Thus, the *Hollywood Reporter* said, Skelton's segments, "at least for U.S. audiences, seemed far the most enjoyable."[61]

Skelton silence was golden in the 1960s for several other reasons, too. For many fans, the highlight of the comedian's show was the "Silent Spot," which he fittingly saved for last. In this pantomime

Skelton appears as his greatest character, Freddie the Freeloader (circa 1965).

he tended to play an everyman, such as the "Old Man Watching the Parade," and his entertaining attention to detail was a continuation of the slice-of-life routines Edna Stillwell had penned for him back in the 1930s. There were also some additional 1960s Skelton shows where much or all of the program was keyed to silence, starting with Harpo Marx's guest appearance on September 25, 1962. The mad mute played the guardian angel to Skelton's henpecked antiheroic character, George Appleby. Skelton also did another all-pantomime show on February 27, 1968. Called "Laughter, the Universal Language," Skelton traveled from Los Angeles to New York to perform at the United Nations. Vice President Hubert Humphrey opened the program with a special taped introduction.

Though Skelton's Freddie the Freeloader character is often mistakenly now remembered as silent, he was entertainingly verbal by the 1960s. Regardless, he was Skelton's most universal figure and deserves special recognition. If one Freddie episode from the decade were featured, pivotal Skelton writer Larry Rhine would nominate the December 22, 1964, Christmas show that costarred Oscar winning actress Greer Garson. In correspondence with the author, Rhine was eloquent in his celebration of Skelton's tramp: "Freddie was our [the writers'] favorite. There was depth to this lovable rogue. Chaplinesque. A have-not but in his mind a have-everything. A soul in a discarded tin can. Whereas Clem is one joke, a bonehead; Appleby a henpecked spouse … [and so on]; Freddie is a poet, philosopher, make-doer."[62]

Another unique Skelton show that decade was his "Pledge of Allegiance" broadcast of January 14, 1969. Dropping his monologue that week, the comedian did a narrative on what the pledge meant— an insight inspired by one of Skelton's childhood educators. As television historian Wesley Hyatt later noted, Skelton's timing was perfect: "Following a year filled with assassinations [Martin Luther King Jr. and Robert Kennedy], public protests gone violent and the endless unproductive military campaign in Vietnam, Red's 'Pledge of Allegiance' struck a chord with … [viewers] about patriotism and what's right with America despite what had gone on previously."[63] The

"Pledge" became a résumé item for Skelton, from spawning a minor hit spoken record, to sometimes being included in his concert material. As a conservative having trouble coping with an emerging liberal movement, the popular support generated by his interpretation of the "Pledge" meant a great deal to the comedian.

One of Skelton's unique special guests during the decade was American icon John Wayne (October 28, 1969). The distinctiveness of his appearance went beyond just a perennial box office champ/movie star—Wayne was the face of America's defining genre, the Western. Consequently, he gave remarkable comic resonance to Skelton's Deadeye spoof of sagebrush land. Plus, Wayne allowed himself to be an affectionately targeted extension of the genre. For example, one of the Skelton sketch's best lines that night asked the ultimate cowboy, "Hey, where'd you get that walk?" Compounding the comedy was the fact that Wayne rarely appeared on television, let alone variety programs.

These were some notable Skelton small-screen appearances during yet another volatile decade for Skelton. Though the comedian later questioned his 1962 move to the desert, his multifaceted artistry in assorted media seemed to negate that verdict. Gauging the Palm Springs relocation on Davis is more problematic. While she was on record as praising the move, her mid-1960s shooting "accident" (which was really a suicide attempt), and the Skeltons' early 1970s divorce, seemed to put that all in question. The next and final chapter will further flesh out these wheels-off-the-bus events. And Skelton's last act plays just as enigmatically as the journey leading him there.

14

The Last Act

Decades before another Hoosier comedian, David Letterman, announced his casual comedy style as, "it ain't brain surgery," Red Skelton had embraced a similar philosophy, "even if we fluff a few [comic lines], who cares? We aren't the United Nations in a debating session. We're just having fun."[1]

Even if this nonchalant manner used to bug that other golden age of television redhead (Lucille Ball), Red Skelton was still the consummate professional. Moreover, Skelton's twenty consecutive years in nighttime television were unprecedented in comedy (only to later be broken by one of his protégées, Johnny Carson). Thus, Skelton was shocked by CBS's 1970 cancellation of his show. Despite Skelton's high ratings, the network felt his demographics were too small town/rural and old. CBS was out to attract a younger, urban-based audience. The comedian, however, did receive a year reprieve, as the NBC network picked up Skelton's program for the 1970–71 season. Nevertheless, in the network moving the program from its longtime Tuesday night slot to Sunday evening and cutting its length from sixty minutes to a half hour, Skelton lost a good portion of his old audience, which still skewered as less than ideal for youth-orientated Madison Avenue. Skelton was canceled yet again.

While anyone would be upset at this professional rejection, Skelton maintained a bitter attitude toward CBS for the remainder of his life. Part of the comedian's ire was grounded in a statement he had made several years before: "I only come to life when there are people watching

[me entertain]."[2] Performing was everything to Skelton, and the
network took away his greatest stage—television. A second component
in Skelton's anger towards CBS was about respect. This was a pivotal
word with Skelton. The term came up all the time with the comedian,
from conversations to correspondence, such as the letter to his daughter
cited in the previous chapter.[3] But maybe his most telling respect
reference occurred in a syndicated 1969 article the year before CBS
dropped him when he said, "You only get respect in this world through
your own creative ability."[4] With regard to the network, he had given
CBS years of "creative ability" through quality popular programming,
and it had unceremoniously fired him. For Skelton, this translated as no
respect.

In a Las Vegas curtain call the following year, Skelton said, "My
heart has been broken [by the cancellation of the television show]."[5]
The first high-profile display of his lingering bitterness, however,
occurred in an exclusive 1974 interview he with the supermarket
tabloid *National Enquirer*: "I was thrown off TV because I didn't think
rape and abortion and murder were funny. My producers insisted I deal
with 'adult material' but I just wanted to be Red Skelton."[6] Yet, this is
a misleading indictment of television. Here are the top five programs
during Skelton's last season: *Marcus Welby, M.D.* (1969–1976), *The Flip
Wilson Show* (1970–74), *Here's Lucy* (1962–74), *Ironside* (1967–75), and
Gunsmoke (1955–1975).[7] Other than Wilson, these were shows with a
direct link to the 1950s. Indeed, *Gunsmoke* and *Here's Lucy* were 1950s
programs, with the latter show just pared down to the title character
of *I Love Lucy* (1951–57). Former *Father Knows Best* (1954–60) star
Robert Young transferred his crackerbarrel wisdom to another fatherly
title character in *Marcus Welby, M.D.* Along similar recycled lines,
Perry Mason (1957–66) star Raymond Burr continued to fight crime in
Ironside, a title drawn from his character being confined to a wheelchair.

Granted, Wilson broke new ground as the first black entertainer
to achieve major success as the host of a primetime variety series. But
even here, once the race card was played, Wilson was very much in
the tradition of so many multitalented 1950s comedians, excelling

at playing a host of comedy characters such as Geraldine Jones and Reverend LeRoy. In fact, sassy Geraldine's signature crack, "The devil made me do it," is reminiscent of Skelton's Junior character proudly flaunting being naughty, "I dood it!" Indeed, a young Wilson had had the most practical Skelton-related epiphany about his career, noting, "the comedians who have done characters have had the longevity. Gleason, Skelton had characters to help them carry the weight on TV."[8]

Skelton's rant in *National Enquirer* was more about a television comedy phenomenon that started the year *after* his series was canceled—a sitcom called *All in the Family* (1971–79). This controversial comedy changed television history, embracing reality like no series had ever done before. While Skelton liked to think the networks were forcing this type of provocative material on the American public, *Family* reigned as the number-one rated program for five consecutive seasons from 1971 to 1976.[9] Ironically, for all the provocative topics showcased by *Family*, even here there was a connection with one of Skelton's favorite 1950s rivals, Jackie Gleason's seminal 1950s character Ralph Kramden. Both Kramden and *Family*'s Archie Bunker (Carroll O'Connor) were reactionary loudmouths who were capable of a metamorphosis into a vulnerable everyman, considerably broadening their audiences.

Regardless, Skelton never let go of his CBS-directed anger. For example, when the Academy of Television Arts and Sciences gave him the Governor's Award for lifetime achievement at the 1986 Emmy Awards, he told the audience, after a standing ovation, "I want to thank you for sitting down. I thought you were pulling a CBS and walking out on me." Why belabor Skelton's acrimony? Sadly, it was the catalyst for a decision that essentially negated Skelton's great television legacy. The comedian owned the rights to his programs and never allowed them to be rebroadcast in syndication.

In contrast, the two most celebrated figures from early television history are now considered to be Ball and Gleason. But this lofty status is not based upon comedy brilliance alone. *I Love Lucy* and *The Honeymooners* have remained on the small screen in nearly continuous reruns since the 1950s. This mix of high-quality comedy and familiarity has cemented the unique pop culture status of Lucy and Kramden. (Repeated television broadcasts have also worked the same magic on *The Wizard of Oz*, 1939, and *It's a Wonderful Life*, 1946.) Skelton merits equal pantheon status with Ball and Gleason. But by bitterly keeping his television shows out of circulation, he denied himself that special recognition. That was not the worst of it, by sitting on these programs and minimizing his cooperation (not providing clips) for documentary producers chronicling the early years of television, Skelton inadvertently erased himself from video history.

This, however, is getting ahead of Skelton's story. On the eve of the comedian's exit from prime-time television he was still living the good life in Palm Springs. There were cracks in the façade, however, as best demonstrated by the events that transpired on the night of July 20, 1966. Skelton was entertaining at Las Vegas's Sands Hotel. Skelton had been accompanied by his wife Davis, daughter Valentina, and her college boyfriend, Art Coleman. During Skelton's midnight show, Davis "accidentally" shot herself with a .38-caliber handgun in the bedroom of the entertainer's suite. Valentina and Coleman were the first on the scene, though Coleman would not let Valentina enter the bedroom. They had been preparing something to eat in the suite's kitchen when they heard Davis moaning in the bedroom. Coleman investigated and had Valentina call the hotel doctor.

Alhough treated as an accident by the authorities, the family knew it was a suicide attempt. In an interview, Valentina shared some insights about that night and her parent's "screwy marriage"—insights that reveal a lot about living with a workaholic artist.[10] Valentina said her mother was suffering from depression and feels today Georgia would have been diagnosed as having a bipolar disorder.

On the night in question, Valentina said there were two possible catalysts for her mother's suicide attempt. First, Skelton had insisted upon introducing Davis onstage during an earlier show. Davis was unhappy about this, feeling she had gained weight and did not look her best. Not only had Skelton insisted, but he also proceeded to make a comic crack about her appearance. Second, Valentina had also heard that her mother was having an affair with the president of the Sands Hotel, and that relationship had taken some melodramatic turn.

Valentina's first take on the possible cause of the suicide attempt is closest to previous accounts of the incident. In Arthur Marx's biography, Skelton is upset about a low-cut gown Davis wore that evening. Marx quoted writer/producer Bob Schiller as saying, "Red didn't like the dress, and he bawled the hell out of her [privately] for wearing it. He really was furious, like only Red can be."[11] Of course, both items probably fueled the shooting. As was established in the previous chapter, Davis's promiscuity often triggered a mean streak in Skelton's humor.

A final wild card that night in Vegas was that Georgia was on Valium and assorted prescription pills. And though she was an alcoholic, it is unclear whether Davis had also been drinking. Naturally, this further clouds the issue as to just what pushed her over the line. Also, in any big-picture overview of her parents' "screwy marriage," Valentina is adamant about her father's controlling nature: "He really messed her [Davis] up. Dad wanted her attention 24-7. She had no life of her own. He would even wake her up [with attention needs, such as his writing]. She couldn't sleep—so that got her into more pills. I think mother had spunk when they first met but he was so very demanding that he broke her spirit. I would tell her, 'You've lost your identity doing everything for Dad.'"[12]

Paradoxically, while there is an abundance of evidence to support Valentina's claims about her father being controlling, the original citations are couched in language that grants Skelton a childlike innocence, without suggesting the debilitating long-term impact on Davis. Thus, a 1961 *TV Guide* reported, "Before a show he is a frightened man who desperately needs comfort and clings to Mrs. Skelton. 'It's fear of not being liked, I guess,' Red says. 'The fear of not being good.'"[13] One is reminded of earlier references to how Skelton's first wife and writer, Edna Stillwell, always had to be visible in the theater wings when he performed. The need for a comforting presence was not limited to show time, as the *TV Guide* article went on to note, "Skelton is a lonely man, sentimental, brooding, sensitive. 'When I go out to the hairdresser or shopping, that is a big minus for Red,' says Mrs. Skelton [Davis]. 'He wants me around all the time.'"[14]

Valentina's poignant comment about her mother's original "spunk" is well taken. Among Skelton's private papers is a folder containing a childhood memoir Davis composed in 1934 when she was twelve years old. While the comments one makes when the world is young often resonate with proverbial "piss and vinegar," Davis sounds like quite a feisty handful: "My father ... is always telling me what to do and I fly into him like a fox after a chicken, then the fight is on. All of a sudden my mother appears ... and I pity my dad. That's the way it goes. I boss [my younger sister] Maxine and daddy around and mother bosses us all. Maxine and I have grand fights together and sometimes she gets a bloody nose.... It seems like one of us ought to be a prize fighter."[15]

The young, spirited Davis also demonstrated a wonderful sense of comic irony in this memoir, as well as linking her passion to the red hair she shared with an equally animated mom: "My mother came from a family that was pretty well off and from the way she still buys things I guess she thinks she still is. You don't want to even be around when the bills come in 'cause she and daddy just raise old ned [à la "raise Cain," cause a disturbance]. She has red hair like mine and hazel eyes."

There is even a passage in the autobiography that hints at the flirtatious young woman Skelton fell in love with a decade later: "I like to be noticed like other children, so I am always trying to attract someone, often ... by making wisecracks but I don't get very far with it." Combine this lively nature to Davis's eventual drop-dead beauty as a 1940s starlet (likened to "a young Rita Hayworth," according to Valentina), and one can understand the attraction for Skelton.[16] Therefore, it is gut-wrenching to move from Davis's bubbly autobiography to the next item in the folder—a newspaper article about her 1976 suicide. Where had that little "prize fighter" gone?

Valentina believes that if there had been something like the Betty Ford Clinic back in the 1960s, maybe her mother's life could have turned out differently. Davis did see a psychiatrist once or twice after her 1966 suicide attempt. "Dad decided she didn't need any more sessions, saying 'She'll just fool them anyway,'" Valentina recalled.[17] As noted earlier in the text, Skelton felt his innate sense of discipline was something of which anyone should be capable. Persons of great accomplishments often have this blind spot, even when it involves loved ones. I am reminded of similar comments made about Bing Crosby by his son Gary, when the latter was promoting his *Mommie Dearest*-like book, *Going My Own Way* (1983). Even Skelton was not completely oblivious to his martinet tendencies as a husband/father, because late in life he asked Valentina if she, too, planned a *Mommie Dearest* type tome about him.

While the pop-culture stereotype of the clown has long implied a sad private life, the often equally somber plight of their spouses is a neglected subject. But being married to a comedian is frequently less than amusing, for example, in writing two books on the Marx Brothers, I was amazed that each of Groucho's three wives became an alcoholic.[18] Just as a reference was made earlier to the Steve Allen comment about rare is the nonneurotic comic, the vast majority of my many comedian biographies document failed relationships.[19] Moreover, Davis not only found herself in a suffocating marriage, but there was also a precedent in her family for taking an early exit from life. Two of her uncles had already committed suicide, and studies suggest that once a family antecedent exits, follow-ups are more likely.

Despite all these sad musings on the marital front, it would be unfair to neglect some of the comedian's positive daily letters to his second wife. In an undated note from the late 1960s, he equates love with that all-important "r" word (respect): "Now that Valentina's birthday has passed, I feel I should thank you for all you have given me. I love you and Valentina … there is nothing about us unblessed. Love and respect was so noticeable last night it was almost noisy."[20]

In a comic letter from 1967, Skelton sounds like a self-deprecating "New Age" Shirley MacLaine: "We console ourselves that, if we come back in the next life, we'll come back as a dog or a cat or a ghost and haunt some bastard. Not me. I was royalty in my last life. I come back [this time] as one of two things: a love bug or a jackass 'cause I am happy and won't carry more than my load too long."[21]

The initial catalyst for a lengthy 1969 letter is the televised movie the Skeltons had watched in bed the previous night, a British courtroom drama titled *Man in the Middle* (1964). But Skelton soon segues into an affectionate chronicle of their life, actually qualifying this writing for the phrase the comedian so loosely applied to all his in-house correspondence—"love letters": "But we were safe in our beds, free to talk, laugh and grumble a bit, to read and have a cold glass of milk with an oatmeal cookie. My, we sure live it up. It's for sure, if anyone says we are hokey, they had better add 'and healthy, too.' You have never been more understanding, more lovable, more kind. When we go over our notes [to each other] … we will find not one cross word … How we are blessed with love. It's like love should be, not talked about or read about but lived."[22]

To paraphrase a line from Ernest Hemingway, no subject is more complicated than man. How else does one mesh these just cited sweet and amusing Skelton ramblings with the other difficult and often unappealing sketches of him previously noted? But to muddy the waters all the more, sometimes Skelton's daily letters to Davis neither praise nor disparage his spouse. Instead, they retreat into the world of political paranoia. In a 1968 letter he claimed, "The Cuban Missile Crisis [1962] joke was to get Democratic governors elected under [President] Kennedy. I wonder why the U.S. news agency has never told the people about Russian fishing boats that unloaded off the coast of Big Sur, Cal., twenty atomic bombs which were placed in aircraft—seven to be exact, and they took off to different parts of the U.S. But where?"[23]

Earlier in the book Skelton's conservative questioning of President Franklin D. Roosevelt's negotiations with the Soviet Union were addressed. But there is little to prepare one for such a crackpot claim that the Cuban Missile Crisis was a Democratic scam. Paradoxically, though his letter questioned the legitimacy of the Cuban incident, he frequently stockpiled canned goods in the years after the crisis, convinced that a nuclear Armageddon was inevitable. The comedian's nephew recently shared a conversation he once had with Phil Harris, the Hoosier-born bandleader/comic who lived near his uncle's Palm Springs home. All a mystified Harris could say about Skelton was, "That guy is weird."[24] But Marvin could not get Harris to embellish his comments. My guess is they simply talked a little politics.

Though a global apocalypse never came to pass, a series of events at the end of the 1960s precipitated Skelton's own personal meltdown. In 1969 the twenty-two-year-old Valentina married Carlos J. Alonso, a bouncer at a private membership-only Los Angeles nightclub called Climax. "Dad was totally against him," said Valentina. "He was not up to their [my parents'] standards, and he was not American, being European." Although Skelton went on to get Alonso a job at CBS's local film department, Valentina soon felt "ostracized as a black sheep," a relationship status with her father that characterized much of his remaining years.[25] The Skeltons had wanted their daughter to marry a wealthy captain of industry, and had even tried to play matchmaker with the millionaire oil man Ed Pauley. Valentina, who today sees her rebelliousness as akin to the independent young Davis, had other ideas. Combine this with a lack of interest in show business and "my parents were very disappointed in me," Valentina said.[26]

Coupled with this, CBS canceled Skelton's television program at the end of the 1969–70 season, and the subsequent move to NBC also failed. As often happens in all walks of life, when a career is in crisis, so goes the personal life, too. Almost twenty years before, when Skelton's television show last struggled, the comedian's marriage had gone through its most publicized problem period. This time neither the show nor the marital union survived. But the failed marriage was further fueled by another 1969 development—Skelton met Lothian Toland, the daughter of famed cinematographer Greg Toland, who pioneered the deep-focus technique synonymous with *Citizen Kane* (1941).

The thirty-two-year-old Toland (Skelton was fifty-six) was the secretary/girlfriend of composer Frederick Loewe, who collaborated with lyricist Alan Jay Lerner on such hit Broadway musicals as

Brigadoon, *Paint Your Wagon*, *My Fair Lady*, and *Camelot*. With
the Skeltons and Loewe being members of Palm Springs's Tamarisk
Country Club, they were soon socializing. Davis, who soon nicknamed
Toland the "nymphet," later told one of Skelton's television producers,
"You wouldn't believe how that girl went after Red."[27]

According to Valentina, the relationship between the Skeltons and
Toland "started out as a happy friendship but Lothy was aggressive
and she and Dad soon had a phone code—three rings meant it was
her. It was so obvious, so very Hollywood. There's a movie there."[28]
Davis's health issues, often related to or exacerbated by her alcoholism,
meant she was frequently hospitalized, providing numerous rendezvous
possibilities for Skelton and Toland. In addition, Skelton essentially had
a separate residence in his teahouse/office.

Eventually, any pretense was dropped, and Skelton spent most
nights at Toland's nearby condominium, returning each day to his
Palm Springs estate to hole up in the teahouse and work on his various
artistic projects. Presumably, there were no more daily love letters to
Davis, though they lunched together. Ironically, Davis kept writing
to him. The bound letters to Skelton during their last year (he filed
for divorce in November 1971) provide a harrowing window into the
life of a desperate woman. Her often pleading tone is sensitive to the
"respect" the comedian found so important. In an undated letter from
1971 she described finding some old love notes to her husband and
offered them to him as homage/proof of her love: "I would be honored
if you would keep them. Perhaps ten years from now you may see the
blinding brilliance of my love and respect for you down through our
lives together. You so dwell now on only the unhappy days and forget
our joyous ones. You say your daughter believed we gave her no proper
childhood, yet the films [home movies] and remembrances of happy
times prove her wrong.... [These surviving] letters to you, dear, dear
Big Red [Skelton] ... prove my deeply sustained powerful devotion,
admiration and respect for you all this time."[29]

On May 19, 1971, at five in the morning, Davis wrote: "My
dearest, beloved Big Red, please, please read my note. I humbly ask
your forgiveness for what it is I have done to contribute to your losing

faith in yourself [his program would have recently been canceled] and in our precious holy love. Again, may I ask your forgiveness for the apparent disrespect I've shown you for not paying more attention to your physical agonies [years of pratfalls would eventually necessitate that Skelton wear leg braces]."[30]

By the time of Davis's October 5, 1971, letter, there was general resignation (even about Toland), as Davis savored what time they had together and prayed for the renewal of his creative gift: "My heart's spirit wants to give you every happiness possible during the hours you remain with me, to bring you and us, just us, happiness and joy as we have always known it during our good times together—and there always were so many, if we truthfully look introspectively.... Please, always remember my heart is yours forever, and my love and respect for you only grows more magnificently with each bright new dawn. May God bless your friend [Toland] who loves you so and wishes with all her heart and soul she might take wing with your spirit and soar.... Then the God-given creative flow in you will [again] well up to overflowing."[31]

Before becoming resigned to the divorce, Davis had used some very unorthodox actions to get Skelton back, including having a lover move into the Skeltons' Palm Springs home in hopes of making her husband jealous. After the couple's divorce, according to Valentina, her mother had no kind words to say about Toland. Moreover, she continued to "escape" through various affairs, including a lesbian liaison.[32] Years later, after the 1973 marriage of Skelton and Toland and the 1976 suicide of Davis, the comedian glossed over these events, and added some patented Skelton embellishments: "I pushed her [Toland] in a baby buggy when she was little. I'd visit her father [Greg Toland] when she was just a little thing. My wife Georgia, to whom I was married for 26 years, was dying of cancer, and she said to Lothian, 'If you see your way clear, you kind of take care of Red because you know him better than anyone.'"[33]

As a rebuttal witness once remarked, "Where to begin." One might start by repeating a quote already noted in the book, with Skelton saying in 1947: "That's my trouble. If you wanta good story—talk to

me. If you want the facts—talk to Edna [Skelton's former wife and
then manager]."[34] Skelton's story about a dying Davis implied that
they were still married at the time of her death and Toland only came
in *later* for the passing of the marital baton. As the previous pages
have documented, this was obviously not the case. Plus, according to
Valentina and period press coverage of Davis's suicide, she was *not* dying
of cancer.[35]

Pushing Toland in a baby carriage is an interesting touch and
certainly not the kind of admission most people would make about
their May-December relationship. But it is consistent with Skelton's
enjoyment of comic surprise, despite an equal fondness for old jokes.
Yet, maybe part of the shock involved is a cover for the unlikelihood
of it occurring. Toland was born in 1937, at a time when Skelton and
Edna Stillwell were nomadic vaudevillians entertaining in the eastern
half of the United States. Other than one brief stop in Hollywood
for Skelton's small role in *Having Wonderful Time* (1938), the couple
did not relocate to the film capital until the early 1940s. Thus, while
the carriage story is possible, given Skelton's "creative" track record,
one cannot be blamed for questioning it. Even his only grandchild,
documentary filmmaker Sabrina Alonso, questions the baby-carriage
story. During a lengthy interview she told me, "I'm sure he [Skelton]
made it up. It was probably a big joke for him."[36]

Before exploring the whys and wherefores for all this invention,
Skelton's tale of Davis's death has another apocryphal element. He
was fond of saying, "on the day that our son died of leukemia, my
wife couldn't stand the pain from her own cancer any longer. So she
took her life at the very hour that he passed away. And she left a note:
'The reason I chose this day was so you wouldn't feel bad twice in one
year.'"[37]

Davis did commit suicide on the anniversary (May 10) of her
son's death. But besides the fact that she was not dying of cancer,
press coverage at the time was adamant about there not being a
suicide note. However, maybe one turned up later, like the fascinating
case of director James Whale, whose mysterious death long puzzled

Hollywood, until it was discovered years later that his Catholic housekeeper had hidden the suicide note to save him from the damnation of the church.[38]

In Davis's case, I do not think there was a note. But I am not questioning the veracity of Skelton's claim. By killing herself on the same day her son died, Davis's troubled mind might have believed this would minimize the family's future suffering. But this bit of Skelton storytelling demonstrates yet another facet of the comedian's tall-tale tendencies. Whereas the please "take care of Red" spiel was self-serving, both covering up a messy affair and probably placating a sense of guilt over abandoning such an unstable woman, Skelton's yarn about Davis's stoic suicide is every bit as romantically noble as the sacrificial suicide of Norman Maine (James Mason) at the close of *A Star Is Born* (1954). Skelton is trying to soften and recast a harsh act.

Yet these are just two extremes (the self-serving versus the noble) of Skelton's tendency to reverse reality to mold his own personal mythology. The greatest catalyst to his mythomania was seemingly quite simple—the need to tell a better story. Earlier I paraphrased an Ernest Hemingway comment about man being the most complicated of all subjects. But it is even more pertinent to reference the novelist's Skelton-like proclivity for self-invention. Literary scholar Jeffrey Meyers wrote, "Hemingway always tended to exaggerate and embroider the events of his life.... [He] combined a scrupulous honesty in his fiction with a tendency to distort and rewrite the story of his life. Given his predisposition to mythomania, his reluctance to disappoint either his own expectations or those of his audience, and the difficulty of refuting or verifying the facts of his life, he felt virtually forced to invent an exciting and imaginative alternative to commonplace reality."[39]

All these comments are equally applicable to Skelton, whose art brilliantly tells the truth through comedy (especially his miniaturist's eye in amusingly capturing so many human foibles), but whose personal history is a crazy quilt of invention, from claims that his father was a world famous clown and a college professor, to Skelton later erasing the influence of Stillwell and Buster Keaton from his life. Like

Skelton enjoys himself at Ball State University upon receiving an honorary doctorate from the institution.

Hemingway, there was also a "reluctance to disappoint either his own expectations or those of his audience." For example, when the comedian reveals in his private papers the belief that his mother was actually a prostitute in his grandmother's brothel, he adds, "Such a story will rock the foundation of my career."[40] And while Skelton felt that it should come out, he never got around to telling his true life story, despite the fact that his career is peppered with announcements about forthcoming autobiographical books and films.

I am reminded of a relevant story by one of Skelton's favorite comedians—W. C. Fields.[41] Fields was famous for his hyperbolic approach to his own personal history, especially when he played center-stage raconteur at dinner parties. Late in life Fields had an increasing reluctance to enter into these biographical tall tales, confessing concern about getting caught in a network of entertainingly conflicting whoppers. Something very much like this might have played out in Skelton's mind, too. So instead, to borrow another analogy from Meyers, "The scholar concerned with the truth finds himself lost in rumor and—proved fact, in conflicting statements and pure fantasy."[42] While Skelton never published a memoir, he continued to write and stockpile stories somewhere between fact and fiction. Or, to lift a phrase from literary criticism, these were tales seeped in "non-fiction fiction." Examining these unpublished stories allows the Skelton biographer to experience the traditional benefit to be derived from autobiographical musings, as defined by *New York Times* critic Danielle Trussoni, "The real pleasure of reading a memoir lies not in the consumption of confessions but in watching a writer grapple with the reality that shaped him."[43] Skelton grappled more than most.

Though Skelton never got over his dismissal from television, it fueled the comedian's active return to live performances, especially playing numerous college campuses. He wanted to prove the network demographic gurus wrong. Skelton seemed to have accomplished this in 1978, when he was awarded the College Comedian of the Year Award. The governing board that selected him, the National Entertainment Conference, represented 460 colleges and universities. But Skelton also played various other venues, with the pièce de résistance being two acclaimed shows at Carnegie Hall in 1977. The *New York Times* said, "He is as hilariously rubbery as ever, nimble legs, facile hands, plastic-putty face and expressive eyes."[44]

The *New York Daily News* critic wished that the not quite sixty-four-year-old comedian had featured his Mean Widdle Kid in his Carnegie material, but insightfully added, "Junior still lurks behind every Skelton move. The man watching the drive-in movie alone—who finally gives up on the film to eyeball the [sexual] action in the next car—is simply the mean widdle kid at middle age."[45] Even when the *Daily News* reviewer had problems with Skelton's act, such as calling the comedian's "Pledge of Allegiance" routine "patriotic camp," the criticism was still perceptive—"[Skelton's] main malady; his brain is still in his heart."[46]

The most telling critical remarks about this Carnegie engagement, however, came from the *Hollywood Reporter*. This publication focused on the extremely warm reception Skelton received from his audience. Like Stan Laurel and Oliver Hardy, I think of Skelton as more a comedian of the people, and best appreciated, even revered, by the people. The audience response chronicled by the *Reporter* was repeated in numerous heartland appearances by Skelton. The *Reporter* stated there was a standing ovation *before* the concert began, followed by the most responsive of crowds: "The audience reacted with hilarity to the stories and applauded his mimicry vociferously."[47] Along similar lines, the *New York Daily News* even noted the post-Carnegie show emotion: "lots of people were milling [around] with tears in their eyes. A man told his wife that he wished Skelton had stayed on stage longer."[48] This was the typical response of a Skelton audience, whether it was New York or Muncie, Indiana.

Besides reconnecting with live audiences and winning the College Comedian of the Year Award, there were many other honors in Skelton's final years. These prestigious acknowledgements included: the Golden Globes' 1978 Cecil B. DeMille Award for "outstanding contributions to the entertainment industry," the aforementioned 1986 Emmy for lifetime achievement, a 1987 Screen Actors Guild Award for career

achievements, his 1989 induction into the Television Academy's Hall of
Fame, and his 1993 admission into the Comedy Hall of Fame. Skelton's
many diverse regional honors ranged from a 1964 homecoming to
Vincennes, Indiana, for the dedication of a Wabash River bridge named
in his honor, to a 1986 honorary doctorate bestowed upon him by Ball
State University.

Despite all this love, or maybe partly because of it, Skelton's rancor
over his television cancellation continued. But his bitterness seemed
to take on an unstable note in a 1980 interview with *People* magazine:
"Skelton has directed that the original kinescopes and tapes of his TV
programs be burned upon his own death. 'I worked hard to make
them, and they're not going on the market for someone else to use.'"[49]
Not surprisingly, several of his former television writers took Skelton
to court to block such an action, citing possible loss of income from
syndication rights. Later that year, Skelton told *Variety* it had all been a
misunderstanding, yet he still seemed combative: "Would you burn the
only monument you've built over 20 years? ... [But] how can they [the
writers] sue over something in a will anyhow? Nobody knows what's in
a man's will until he dies and it goes through probate. But the burning's
not in my will."[50]

The court was not convinced: "Myrna Oliver of the *Los Angeles
Times* reported that one former writer, Jack Ritchard, submitted a
sworn statement that he had heard Skelton say, 'I have in my will that
when I die, all my tapes will be burned.... I figure if I wasn't important
enough during my lifetime for the networks to do something with the
reruns, there's no reason to leave these things for anyone else to profit
from.'"[51] In September 1980 Skelton agreed to preserve roughly eight
seasons of his small-screen show.

Television historian Wesley Hyatt strongly suggests that this bizarre
case, coming so soon after Arthur Marx's provocative 1979 Skelton
biography, "no doubt formed a prejudice within the industry about
using Red for any [future] television work. His eccentricities now were
public knowledge and damaging to him. Who needed to work with
someone so crazy that he would try to destroy his own hard work as

well as that of hundreds of other people?"[52] Interestingly, Skelton's
sanity question was not helped by its similarity to silent screen legend
Mary Pickford's earlier expressed desire to have her films burned upon
her death for fear young viewers would now find them to be laughable
museum pieces. Thankfully, people within the industry convinced her
otherwise. But the crackpot nature of such a scheme, largely blamed
upon the infirmities of Pickford's old age, were now deposited upon
Skelton's doorstop.

In 1984 Skelton attempted to end the estrangement with his
daughter by helping her open an art gallery that featured reproductions
of his work. (Valentina's 1969 marriage had ended after three years,
but it did produce a daughter, Sabrina Alonso.) Though Valentina
appreciated the gesture, she had no experience in the field and felt
overwhelmed by the gallery. Inexplicably, she was given little access to
her father and had to work through his secretary. Because Valentina
was not allowed to handle her father's original paintings, she had to
scramble to maintain the gallery by featuring local artists. After a year
she had had enough and retired from the operation. According to
Valentina, her father, who had been "totally self-absorbed" up until
this point, then "had a fit and shunned her." This distancing continued
"until the last three years of his life, other than meeting at a restaurant
once a year for Thanksgiving."[53]

At one of these subsequent Thanksgivings, probably in 1990,
Valentina said, "Dad and Lothy [Toland] had been upset at how
casually [the now grown] Sabrina was dressed, despite the long drive she
had made to be there. How you dressed was a big thing with Dad. Even
if your outfit was just a little different, he would really kid you." (Years
before, Davis had said of her husband, "He has a clothes complex—
won't wear old ones because they bring back the memories of when he
was so poor."[54])

For whatever reason, maybe the teasing, this was also the
Thanksgiving in which Sabrina came out to Skelton and Toland.
According to Valentina, while the homophobic Skelton "was kind to

Sabrina's face, he verbally stabbed her behind her back. Dad was just down on homosexuals. He made fun of them." Valentina is fiercely proud of Sabrina, who went on to graduate from UCLA and is now a documentary filmmaker in San Francisco.

Sabrina's take on this Thanksgiving is slightly different from her mother's, remembering that her gay background came out just *before* she arrived. Moreover, Sabrina has a balanced biographer-like take on Skelton: "My grandfather was a very conservative man. Things had been strained [between us] but I think we did have closure at the end. He had just grown up in a different era. It was what it was. But I really don't think he was homophobic. [Gay comedian] Rip Taylor was one of his good friends. I think Lothian was the homophobic one."[55]

Unfortunately, the voluminous Skelton holdings at Vincennes University contain little concerning the relationship of Skelton and Sabrina, although two drafts of letters he wrote to her suggest it was a work in progress. The first is undated, though it sounded like it might have been composed after the volatile Thanksgiving: "I am sorry about our relationship and the attitudes of all concerned. When you were a child I looked forward to the name Grandfather. But it seemed it was all one-sided, no real affection.... I know nothing about your lifestyle, for you have never confided in me or Lothian.... I never received word on a very expensive camera [presumably a gift from photography hobbyist Skelton] which I had used only 3 times.... I am proud of the fact you're willing to work—I wish you all the success that comes."[56]

The second letter is in response to correspondence Skelton had received from Sabrina in 1991. Skelton's granddaughter was in Scotland as part of a college program abroad, and she had appeared in a production of Gogal's *The Overcoat*. Skelton's correspondence is much more chatty than his previous letter, with pertinent insights, such as telling her Marcel Marceau had appeared in a staging of this story, too. Skelton then affectionately added, "I wish I could see you on stage. I remember how good you were when we saw you while in school here. There is an old saying 'Play to the Gallery'—face them with confidence."[57] Other fleeting references to Sabrina in the Vincennes holdings suggest that Skelton and his granddaughter had moved on to an affectionately positive relationship.

Ultimately, Sabrina said of Skelton, "I loved my grandfather. I think of him all the time…. His TV show, especially the early black and white programs are great. I'm glad a scholarly press is interested [in his work]. His influence in comedy is not being addressed. Grandfather is a good subject." Sabrina's complaint was more with the "controlling" Toland. For example, in the same interview, Sabrina told me, "Her [Toland's] treatment of me near the time of grandfather's death was appalling. I could not really see him [in the hospital]. But thanks to a sympathetic nurse, who saw what was going on, I got in to see him [when Toland briefly left] and grandfather was able to acknowledge that he loved me."[58] In Skelton's last years, he and Valentina reached an understanding of sorts, too. But as she told me towards the end of a three-hour interview, "While Dad was open and warm with fans, there was always a lot of secrecy going on with the family."[59]

As with the comedian's first two wives, Stillwell and Davis, Toland had to wear many hats but mainly her role boiled down to being a motherly cheerleader. For example, here is her note on an undated birthday card to her husband: "My dreams and hopes are for you to realize all your dreams and hopes, that you shall be the writer, author, painter, composer and homemaker *you* have at some time dreamed of. I'll be yours and proudly so."[60]

Also like Skelton's previous wives, Toland demonstrates almost a savage loyalty to her husband. As sometimes happens in an interview, one of my questions actually came back in testimonial form. But in its own way, it speaks volumes about the zealousness Skelton could inspire: "I would've defended him to the death, and I would do the same thing for him after [his] death. I'm fiercely loyal. He's the finest person I ever knew."[61] One can imagine Stillwell or Davis saying the same thing, which is another tribute in itself.

Skelton had been in poor health for several years when he died of pneumonia on September 17, 1997. (His condition had been

made worse by legs battered from years of slapstick. Thus, Skelton
was susceptible to blood clots and accompanying infections.) Toland
decided to keep the funeral small, and according to Valentina, only
a trio of celebrities made it a point to be there: Bob Hope, Milton
Berle, and Steve Allen. Each of these three had long been on record
as champions of Skelton. Indeed, Allen's chapter on Skelton in *The
Funny Men* (1956) remains the best word-for-word analysis of Skelton
yet written.[62] But my favorite tribute on Skelton comes by way of
Hope, and it has a Hoosier footnote. Years ago Hope played Ball State,
and in asking management what other comedians had appeared at
the university, Skelton's name kept coming up. Hope then said, "He's
a great performer. I had him on my show [the comedian's periodic
television specials] one time but never again. He's too funny. He stole
the show. I'm not going to have someone on my show who steals it, and
he did."[63] Not a bad compliment, given Hope's status as arguably the
twentieth century's most influential performer.

Ultimately, Skelton was an inspired comedian despite a myriad of
personal problems with the most imaginative biography this side of
Dizzy Dean. He was a self-made man who was not as well-made as he
might have been. While most of us traffic in small self-deceptions to
help us survive, Skelton needed an industrial-strength variety to soldier
his way through life. Still, he persevered his way to comedy greatness.
The miracle is that so much laughter could be born of so much personal
torment. One can only hope that this modern-day Grimaldi was able to
recognize even part of the joy he gave others. Regardless, to paraphrase
author Ruth Prigozy, Skelton remained faithful to his comedy dream,
and we are the "fortunate beneficiaries of his enduring legacy."[64]

Filmography

Features

1938 *Having Wonderful Time* (71 minutes).
    Director: Alfred Santell. Screenplay: Arthur Kober, from his play. Stars: Ginger Rogers, Douglas Fairbanks Jr., Peggy Conklin, Lucille Ball, Lee Bowman, Eve Arden, Dorothea Kent, Richard (Red) Skelton.

1940 *Flight Command* (116 minutes).
    Director: Frank Borzage. Screenplay: Wells Root, Commander Harvey Haislip. Stars: Robert Taylor, Ruth Hussey, Walter Pidgeon, Paul Kelley, Nat Pendleton, Shepperd Strudwick, Red Skelton.

1941 *People vs. Dr. Kildare* (78 minutes).
    Director: Harold S. Bucquet. Screenplay: Willis Goldbeck, Harry Ruskin. Stars: Lew Ayres, Lionel Barrymore, Laraine Day, Bonita Granville, Alma Kruger, Red Skelton.

1941 *Whistling in the Dark* (77 minutes).
    Director: S. Sylvan Simon. Screenplay: Robert MacGunigle, Harry Clark, Albert Mannheimer, based upon a play by Lawrence Gross and Edward Childs Carpenter. Stars: Red Skelton, Conrad Veidt, Ann Rutherford, Virginia Grey, "Rags" Ragland, Henry O'Neill, Eve Arden.

1941 *Lady Be Good* (111 minutes).
    Director: Norman Z. McLeod. Screenplay: Jack McGowan, Kay Van Riper, John McClain. Songs: George and Ira Gershwin, Jerome Kern, Oscar Hammerstein II, Roger Edens, Arthur Freed. Stars: Eleanor Powell, Ann Sothern, Robert Young, Lionel Barrymore, John Carroll, Red Skelton, Virginia O'Brien.

1942 *Ship Ahoy* (95 minutes).
    Director: Edward Buzzell. Screenplay: Harry Clark. Stars: Eleanor Powell, Red Skelton, Bert Lahr, Virginia O'Brien, Tommy Dorsey and his orchestra.

1942 *Maisie Gets Her Man* (85 minutes).
    Director: Roy Del Ruth. Screenplay: Betty Reinhardt, Mary C. McCall Jr. Stars: Ann Sothern, Red Skelton, Allen Jenkins, Donald Meek, Walter Catlett, Fritz Feld, Ben Weldon, "Rags" Ragland.

1942 *Panama Hattie* (79 minutes).
    Director: Norman Z. McLeod. Screenplay: Jack McGowan, Wilkie Mahoney, based upon a play by Herbert Fields and B. G. DeSylva. Songs: Cole Porter. Stars: Red Skelton, Ann Sothern, "Rags" Ragland, Ben Blue, Marsha Hunt, Virginia O'Brien.

1942 *Whistling in Dixie* (74 minutes).
    Director: S. Sylvan Simon. Screenplay: Nat Perrin, additional dialogue by Wilkie Mahoney. Stars: Red Skelton, Ann Rutherford, George Bancroft, Guy Kibbee, Diana Lewis, Peter Whitney, "Rags" Ragland.

1943 *DuBarry Was a Lady* (101 minutes).
    Director: Roy Del Ruth. Screenplay: Irving Brecher, adaptation Nancy Hamilton, additional dialogue Wilkie Mahoney, based upon the play by Herbert Fields, B. G. DeSylva. Songs: Cole Porter. Stars: Red Skelton, Lucille Ball, Gene Kelly, "Rags" Ragland, Zero Mostel, Donald Meck, Tommy Dorsey and his orchestra.

1943   *Thousands Cheer* (126 minutes).
        Director: George Sidney. Screenplay: Paul Jarrico, Richard Collins. Stars: Kathryn
        Grayson, Gene Kelly, and all-star appearances that include: Mickey Rooney, Judy
        Garland, Red Skelton, Eleanor Powell, Ann Sothern, Lucille Ball, Virginia O'Brien,
        Frank Morgan, Lena Horne, Marsha Hunt, Donna Reed, Margaret O'Brien.

1943   *I Dood It* (102 minutes).
        Director: Vincente Minnelli. Screenplay: Sig Herzig, Fred Saldy, a remake of Buster
        Keaton's *Spite Marriage* (1929), with additional gags by Keaton. Stars: Red Skelton,
        Eleanor Powell, Richard Ainley, Patricia Dane, Jimmy Dorsey and his orchestra.

1943   *Whistling in Brooklyn* (87 minutes).
        Director: S. Sylvan Simon. Screenplay: Nat Perrin, additional dialogue by Wilkie
        Mahoney. Stars: Red Skelton, Ann Rutherford, Jean Rogers, "Rags" Ragland, Ray
        Collins, Henry O'Neill, Leo Durocher and the Brooklyn Dodgers.

1944   *Bathing Beauty* (101 minutes).
        Director: George Sidney. Screenplay: Dorothy Kingsley, Allen Boretz, Frank Waldman,
        additional gags by Buster Keaton. Stars: Red Skelton, Esther Williams, Basil Rathbone,
        Ethel Smith, Harry James and his Music Makers.

1946   *Ziegfeld Follies* (110 minutes).
        Director: Vincente Minnelli. (A revue). Songs: Harry Warren, Arthur Freed, Ira and
        George Gershwin, Ralph Blane and Hugh Martin, Kay Thompson and Roger Edens.
        Stars: Fred Astaire, Gene Kelly, Lucille Bremer, Lucille Ball, Fanny Brice, Judy Garland,
        Kathryn Grayson, Lena Horne, James Melton, Red Skelton, Esther Williams, William
        Frawley, Virginia O'Brien, William Powell.

1946   *The Show-Off* (83 minutes).
        Director: Harry Beaumont. Screenplay: George Wells, based upon the play by George
        Kelly. Stars: Red Skelton, Marilyn Maxwell, Marjorie Main, Virginia O'Brien, Eddie
        "Rochester" Anderson, George Cleveland, Leon Ames.

1947   *Merton of the Movies* (82 minutes).
        Director: Robert Alton. Screenplay: George Wells, Lou Breslow, based upon the novel
        by Harry Leon Wilson and the play by George S. Kaufman, Marc Connelly, additional
        gags by Buster Keaton. Stars: Red Skelton, Virginia O'Brien, Gloria Grahame, Leon
        Ames.

1948   *The Fuller Brush Man* (93 minutes).
        Director: S. Sylvan Simon. Screenplay: Frank Tashlin, Devery Freeman. Stars: Red
        Skelton, Janet Blair, Don McGuire, Hillary Brooke, Adele Jergens.

1948   *A Southern Yankee* (90 minutes).
        Director: Edward Sedgwick. Screenplay: Harry Tugend, from a story by Melvin
        Frank, Norman Panama; loosely based upon Buster Keaton's *The General* (1927), with
        additional gags by Keaton. Stars: Red Skelton, Brian Donlevy, Arlene Dahl, George
        Coulouris.

1949   *Neptune's Daughter* (93 minutes).
        Director: Edward Buzzell. Screenplay: Dorothy Kingsley, additional dialogue by Ray
        Singer, Dick Chevillat. (Buster Keaton provided additional material.) Stars: Esther
        Williams, Red Skelton, Richardo Montalban, Betty Garrett, Keenan Wynn.

1950   *The Yellow Cab Man* (85 minutes).
        Director: Jack Donohue. Screenplay: Devery Freeman, Albert Belch. Stars: Red Skelton, Gloria de Haven, Walter Slezak, Edward Arnold, James Gleason.
1950   *Three Little Words* (102 minutes).
        Director: Richard Thorpe. Screenplay: George Wells, based on the lives and songs of Bert Kalmar and Harry Ruby. Stars: Fred Astaire, Red Skelton, Vera-Ellen, Arlene Dahl, Keenan Wynn.
1950   *Duchess of Idaho* (98 minutes).
        Red Skelton has a cameo in this Esther Williams feature.
1950   *The Fuller Brush Girl* (85 minutes).
        Inspired by Red's *Fuller Brush Man*, Skelton has a cameo in this Lucille Ball film.
1950   *Watch the Birdie* (70 minutes).
        Director: Jack Donohue. Screenplay: Ivan Tors, Devery Freeman, a loose remake of *The Cameraman* (1928), with additional gags by Buster Keaton. Stars: Red Skelton (three parts), Arlene Dahl, Ann Miller, Leon Ames.
1951   *Excuse My Dust* (82 minutes).
        Director: Roy Rowland. Screenplay: George Wells, with additional gags by Buster Keaton. Stars: Red Skelton, Sally Forrest, MacDonald Carey, William Demarest, Monica Lewis.
1951   *Texas Carnival* (77 minutes).
        Director: Charles Walters. Screenplay: Dorothy Kingsley. Stars: Esther Williams, Red Skelton, Howard Keel, Ann Miller, Paula Raymond, Keenan Wynn.
1952   *Lovely to Look At* (105 minutes).
        Director: Mervyn LeRoy. Screenplay: George Wells, Harry Ruby, additional dialogue Andrew Solt, based upon the musical comedy *Roberta*, from the novel by Alice Duer Miller, book and lyrics Otto A. Harbach (additional and revised lyrics Dorothy Fields), music by Jerome Kern. Stars: Kathryn Grayson, Red Skelton, Howard Keel, Marge Champion, Gower Champion, Ann Miller, Zsa Zsa Gabor.
1953   *The Clown* (91 minutes).
        Director: Robert Z. Leonard. Screenplay: Martin Rackin, a remake of *The Champ* (1931). Stars: Red Skelton, Tim Considine, Jane Greer, Loring Smith.
1953   *Half a Hero* (71 minutes).
        Director: Don Weis. Screenplay: Max Schulman. Stars: Red Skelton, Jean Hagen, Charles Dingle.
1953   *The Great Diamond Robbery* (69 minutes).
        Director: Robert Z. Leonard. Screenplay: Laslo Vadnay, Martin Rackin. Stars: Red Skelton, Cara Williams, James Whitmore, Kurt Kasznar.
1954   *Susan Slept Here* (98 minutes).
        Red has a cameo in this Dick Powell-Debbie Reynolds comedy.
1956   *Around the World in Eighty Days* (167 minutes).
        Skelton has a cameo, as does a who's who of Hollywood, in producer Michael Todd's epic version of Jules Verne's story.
1957   *Public Pigeon No. 1* (79 minutes).
        Director: Normand Z. McLeod. Screenplay: Harry Tugend, from a teleplay by Devery Freeman. Stars: Red Skelton, Vivian Blaine, Janet Blair, Jay C. Flippen.

1960   *Ocean's Eleven* (127 minutes).

Red has a cameo in this Frank Sinatra Rat Pack movie.

1965   *Those Magnificent Men in Their Flying Machines, or: How I Flew From London to Paris in 25 Hours and 11 minutes* (132 minutes).

Skelton's cameo steals the show in this international comedy extravaganza.

Notes

Preface

1. Virginia MacPherson, "Mischievous Red Skelton Tangled Up in Red Tape," *Alameda (CA) Times Star*, November 28, 1947.

2. Claire Tomalin, quoted in Thomas Mallon's review, "Thomas Hardy's English Lessons," *New York Times*, January 28, 2007.

3. Marc Pachter, "The Biographer Himself: An Introduction," in *Telling Lives: The Biographer's Art*, Marc Pachter, ed. (Philadelphia: University of Pennsylvania Press, 1985), 14.

4. Jeffrey Meyers, *Hemingway: Life into Art* (New York: Cooper Square Press, 2000), 134.

5. Valentina Skelton Alonso, interview with author, March 5, 2007.

6. Various court records, starting with the January 1893 indictment from the Daviess Circuit Court of Indiana: "State of Indiana vs. Ella Cochran [formerly Ella Richardville]" for "Keeping a House of Ill-Fame"; and the Red Skelton folder "Memories By Red," both are in the "Personal Legal Documents/Papers" box, Red Skelton Collection, Vincennes University, Vincennes, Indiana.

7. Wes Gehring, *The Charlie Chaplin Murder Mystery* (Shreveport, LA: Ramble House Press, 2006).

8. Skelton Collection.

9. Tom Hiney, *Raymond Chandler: A Biography* (New York: Grove Press, 1997), vii.

10. Groucho Marx, *Groucho and Me* (1959; reprint, New York: Manor Books, 1974), 136.

11. Alonso interview, February 27, 2007.

12. Steve Allen, *The Funny Men* (New York: Simon and Schuster, 1956), 145.

13. Wes Gehring, *Seeing Red ... The Skelton in Hollywood's Closet: An Analytical Biography* (Davenport, IA: Robin Vincent Publishing, 2001).

14. Bill Davidson, "'I'm Nuts and I Know It,'" *Saturday Evening Post*, June 17, 1967, p. 69.

15. The culmination of Red Skelton's Ball State University visits was the school awarding him an honorary doctorate on September 18, 1986. The author gave the keynote address on this occasion.

16. Carl Rollyson, *A Higher Form of Cannibalism? Adventures in the Art and Politics of Biography* (Chicago: Ivan R. Dee, 2005), 4.

17. David Wild, "Steve Martin: The 'Rolling Stone' Interview," *Rolling Stone*, September 2, 1990, p. 90.

18. Cheech Marin, conversation with the author, January 31, 2004.

19. John A. Williams and Dennis A. Williams, *If I Stop I'll Die: The Comedy and Tragedy of Richard Pryor* (1991; reprint, New York: Thunder's Mouth Press, 2006), 41.

20. Ibid., 45.

21. Frank Friedrichsen, "The Short Tragic Life of Jimmy Dean," *Movie Star Parade*, December 1955, p. 42.

22. Alonso interview, March 5, 2007.

23. Dwight Garner, "Sontag, Late and Early," *New York Times*, March 11, 2007.

24. Mark Twain, *The Selected Letters of Mark Twain*, Charles Neider, ed. (1982; reprint, New York: Cooper Square Press, 1999), 245.

Prologue

1. Red Skelton, interview with author, Muncie, Indiana, September 18, 1986.

2. "Hoosier Comedian Makes Good in Films," *Indianapolis Star*, August 31, 1941.

3. Red Skelton, "I'll Tell All" (part 5), *Milwaukee Journal*, December 12, 1941.

4. Paul Murray Kendall, *The Art of Biography* (1965; reprint, New York: W. W. Norton and Company, 1985), 130.

5. Frederick C. Othman, "Ex-Usherette Leads Skelton to Success," *New York World Telegram*, August 14, 1941.

6. Sally Jefferson, "The Skelton in Hollywood's Closet," *Photoplay*, July 1942, p. 38.

7. Skelton, "I'll Tell All."

8. Arthur Marx, *Red Skelton* (New York: E. P. Dutton, 1979), 54.

9. The best single overview was from "Capitol, Wash.," *Variety*, March 10, 1937, p. 50.

10. Nancy Lee, "At the Riverside," *Milwaukee Journal*, June 20, 1937.

11. John G. Cawelti, *Adventure, Mystery, and Romance: Formula Stories as Art and Popular Culture* (Chicago: University of Chicago Press, 1976), 166.

12. Leo McCarey, "The Could-Be Quality," *Hollywood Reporter*, October 28, 1939. See also Wes Gehring, *Leo McCarey: From Marx to McCarthy* (Lanham, MD: Scarecrow Press, 2005).

13. Betty Baytos, "Interview with Red Skelton," Dance Collection Oral History, New York Public Library at Lincoln Center, February 20, 1996.

14. Ibid.

15. G. E. Blackford, "'Whistling in the Dark' Shown at Loew Criterion," *New York Journal American*, August 28, 1941.

16. Robert Coleman, "Red Skelton Gets $35,000," *New York Daily Mirror*, November 10, 1938.

17. Blaud Johaueson, "Ate 12,000 and Each Made 'em Roar," *New York Daily Mirror*, July 13, 1938.

18. John Chapman, "Mainly About Manhattan," *New York Daily News*, July 8, 1938.

19. Red Skelton, interview with author, September 18, 1986.

20. Jay Dee, "Red Recalls Great Days in Milwaukee," [1947], incomplete citation, in Red Skelton Scrapbook #12, May–September 1947, Red Skelton Collection, Vincennes University, Vincennes, Indiana.

21. Valentina Skelton Alonso, interview with the author, March 5, 2007.

22. Joe E. Brown, as told to Ralph Hancock, *Laughter is a Wonderful Thing* (New York: A. S. Barnes and Company, 1956), 202.

23. "His Heavy (Eating) Role Fits Joe Brown Exactly," *New York World Telegram*, May 6, 1933.

24. Wes Gehring, *Seeing Red … The Skelton in Hollywood's Closet: An Analytical Biography* (Davenport, IA: Robin Vincent Publishing, 2001).

25. Barbara W. Tuchman, "Biography as a Prism of History," in *Biography as High Adventure*, Stephen B. Oates, ed. (Amherst: University of Massachusetts Press, 1986), 94.

26. Wes Gehring, *"Mr. B" or Comforting Thoughts about the Bison: A Critical Biography of Robert Benchley* (Westport, CT: Greenwood Press, 1992) and *Film Clowns of the Depression: 12 Memorable Movies* (Jefferson, NC: McFarland and Company, 2007).

27. James S. Pooler, "Mickey Rooney Steals Show as Cabin Boy in 'Slave Ship,'" *Detroit Free Press*, July 3, 1937, and "Humorist Ready with a New Farce," *Detroit Free Press*, July 3, 1937.

28. "All the World Loves a Dunker," *Pic* magazine, August 23, 1938, p. 24.

29. Ibid.

30. "Indiana Boy's Doughnut Dunking Hit on Stage," *Indianapolis Star*, June 27, 1937.

31. Hilton Als, "Shining Hours," *The New Yorker*, May 22, 2006, p. 87.

32. Caroline Latham, *The David Letterman Story* (1987; reprint, New York: Berkley Books, 1988), 112.

33. Holland Cotter, "Pollock on Paper: A Magician Flinging Swirls and Pixie Dust," *New York Times*, May 26, 2006.

34. Martin Gottfried, *Nobody's Fool: The Lives of Danny Kaye* (New York: Simon and Schuster, 1994), 52.

Chapter 1

1. "Red Skelton, TV and Film's Quintessential Clown, Dies," *Los Angeles Times*, September 18, 1997.

2. Letter to Red Skelton from researcher L. Ross, February 14, 1964, in "Personal Legal Documents/Papers" box, Red Skelton Collection, Vincennes University, Vincennes, Indiana.

3. *State of Indiana vs. Joseph Earhart*, October 1891, ibid.

4. Robert "Gus" Stevens (Vincennes historian) conversation with the author, Vincennes University's Lewis Historical Library, 1999, Vincennes, Indiana.

5. For example, see, "North End Grocer Dies Suddenly," *Vincennes Western Sun*, May 30, 1913.

6. *State of Indiana vs. Ella Cochran" (formerly Richardville)*: Indictment for "Keeping a House of Ill-Fame," January 1893, "Personal Legal Documents/Papers" box, Skelton Collection.

7. Valentina Skelton Alonso, interview with author, March 5, 2007.

8. "Memories by Red" folder, [undated], in "Private Papers Box," Skelton Collection.

9. *State of Indiana vs. Ella Cochran*: Indictment for "receiving and concealing stolen goods, May 1894, "Personal Legal Documents/Papers" box, Skelton Collection.

10. *State of Indiana vs. William Cochran*: Indictment for "premeditated malice … to kill and murder, December 7, 1900, ibid.

11. *Ella Cochran vs. William Cochran* (divorce granted), January 1903, ibid.

12. *State of Indiana vs. Joseph Eheart and Ella Cochran*: Indictment for "assault and battery," March 1901, ibid.

13. *State of Indiana vs. Joseph Eheart*: Found guilty of "obstructing the view of his saloon room," March 1901, ibid.

14. Various sources, including interviews with Valentina Alonso (February 27, March 5, 13, 2007) and Marvin Skelton (December 12, 14, 2006, and February 6, 2007).

15. "Autobiography by Red Skelton," transcribed October 8, 1975, in "Autobiography" file, in Writing Box 9, A-B-C, Skelton Collection.

16. Ibid.

17. Eileen Creelman, "Red Skelton of 'Having Wonderful Time,' Discusses His Hollywood Debut," *New York Sun*, July 6, 1938.

18. Wesley Hyatt, *A Critical History of Television's "The Red Skelton Show," 1951–1971* (Jefferson, NC: McFarland and Company, 2004), 6.

19. "North End Grocer Dies Suddenly," Skelton Collection.

20. Glen Elsasser, "We Remember Red," *Indianapolis Star Magazine*, August 26, 1962.

21. Edward L. Sebring, "Birth Records Index Says Ehart but World Knew Him As Skelton," *Vincennes Sun-Commercial*, September 18, 1997.

22. Brenda Hopper, interview with author, February 6, 1994, Indianapolis, Indiana.

23. Andy Soltis, "Good Night and God Bless," *New York Post*, September 18, 1997.

24. Wes Gehring, *Joe E. Brown: The Baseball Buffoon* (Jefferson, NC: McFarland and Company, 2006).

25. Ruth Prigozy, *F. Scott Fitzgerald* (New York: Overlook Press, 2001), 15.

26. Wes Gehring, *Charlie Chaplin: A Bio-Bibliography* (Westport, CT: Greenwood Press, 1983).

27. Daniel Wallace, *Big Fish* (New York: Penguin Books, 1998), 22.

28. Joe E. Brown, as told to Ralph Hancock, *Laughter is a Wonderful Thing* (New York: A. S. Barnes and Company, 1956), 7.

29. Arthur Marx, *Red Skelton* (New York: E. P. Dutton, 1979), 7.

30. "Red Skelton," *Current Biography 1947*, Anna Rothe, ed. (New York: H. W. Wilson Company, 1948), 580.

31. Red Skelton, "I'll Tell All" (part 1), *Milwaukee Journal*, December 8, 1941.

32. David W. Jackson, "Vincennes' Famed Comedian Drops in for Visit to His Old Home Wednesday," *Vincennes Sun Commercial*, October 30, 1962.

33. Robert Schultheis, "Stark Account of Skelton's Life in Vincennes Rings True," *Vincennes Valley Advance*, October 9, 1979.

34. Red Skelton, interview with author, September 18, 1986.

35. Ross Wetzsteon, "Red, the Renaissance Goof," *Village Voice*, March 14, 1977.

36. Ibid.

37. "Tribute by Red Skelton Would Embarrass Teacher," *Indianapolis News*, March 18, 1969.

38. Hopper interview.

39. Wes Gehring, "Red Skelton and Clem Kadiddlehopper," *Indiana Magazine of History* 92 (March 1996): 46–55.

40. Wes Gehring, *Laurel and Hardy: A Bio-Bibliography* (Westport, CT: Greenwood Press, 1990).

41. Wes Gehring, *W. C. Fields: A Bio-Bibliography* (Westport, CT: Greenwood Press, 1984) and *Groucho and W. C. Fields: Huckster Comedians* (Jackson: University Press of Mississippi, 1994).

42. See especially, Walter Blair, *Native American Humor* (1937; reprint, Scranton, PA: Chandler Publishing, 1960).

43. Ring Lardner, *You Know Me Al: A Busher's Letters* (1914; reprint, New York: Collier Books, 1991).

44. Ben Yagoda, *Will Rogers: A Biography* (1993; reprint, New York: HarperCollins, 1994), 224.

45. Wes Gehring, "Kin Hubbard's Abe Martin: A Figure of Transition in American Humor," *Indiana Magazine of History* 78 (March 1982): 26–37.

46. Kin Hubbard, *Abe Martin's Barbed Wire* (Indianapolis: Bobbs-Merrill Company, 1928), 17.

47. Fred C. Kelly, *The Life and Times of Kin Hubbard: Creator of Abe Martin* (New York: Farrar, Straus and Young, 1952), 167.

48. John Crosby, "Radio and Television," *New York Herald Tribune*, January 6, 1952.

49. "Red Skelton, TV Clown, Dead at 84," Microsoft Internet Explorer site visited September 30, 1997.

50. Hal Humphrey, "Red Skelton Comes Back to TV and Brings Along an Old Buddy [Ed Wynn]," *Los Angeles Mirror*, March 15, 1961.

51. Red Skelton, "I'll Tell All" (five parts), *Milwaukee Journal*, December 8–12, 1941.

52. "Red Skelton," 580.

53. Wes Gehring, *Seeing Red … The Skelton in Hollywood's Closet: An Analytical Biography* (Davenport, IA: Robin Vincent Publishing, 2001).

54. Kin Hubbard, *Abe Martin's Almanack [for 1909]* (Indianapolis: Abe Martin Publishing Company, 1908), 39.

55. Janice Thompson Dudley, letter to the author, July 10, 1991, Evansville, Indiana.

56. Dudley letter to the author, January 20, 1998, Evansville, Indiana.

57. Ibid.

58. Hopper interview.

59. David L. Smith, *Hoosiers in Hollywood* (Indianapolis: Indiana Historical Society Press, 2006), 87.

60. Marcus Stuckey, interview with the author, December 8, 2006.

61. George McCormack, "Red Skelton Started Clowning in Vincennes," *Evansville Sunday Press*, August 26, 1962.

62. "Skelton, Ida" (1923) and "Albia, Ida" (1924), Vincennes Public Schools (RHC #370), Enumeration–District 2 (May 1 each year).

63. Kin Hubbard, *Abe Martin of Brown County, Indiana* (Indianapolis: Levey Brothers, 1906), 48.

64. Elsasser, "We Remember Red," 33.

65. Donald C. Manlove, ed. *The Best of James Whitcomb Riley* (Bloomington: Indiana University Press, 1982), 69.

66. Kelly, *Life and Times of Kin Hubbard*, 52.

67. Hubbard, *Abe Martin's Almanack [for 1909]*, 103.

68. Brown, *Laughter is a Wonderful Thing*, 30.

69. Bruce Handy, "Bad Vibrations," *New York Times*, July 23, 2006.

Chapter 2

1. Robert Schultheis, "Stark Account of Skelton's Life in Vincennes Rings True," *Vincennes Valley Advance*, October 9, 1979.

2. David L. Smith, *Hoosiers in Hollywood* (Indianapolis: Indiana Historical Society Press, 2006), 88.

3. Wes Gehring, "The Mentor and The Clown: Clarence Stout and Red Skelton," *Traces of Indiana and Midwestern History* 12, no. 4 (Fall 2000): 32–41.

4. Clarence Stout, letter to music publishing executive Lou Levy, October 31, 1947, Clarence Stout Papers, Lewis Historical Library, Vincennes University, Vincennes, Indiana.

5. Robert Schultheis, "Vincennes' Composer Had His Own Tin Pan Alley," *Vincennes Valley Advance*, October 5, 1967.

6. Robert Schultheis, "Stout's Minstrel Shows Gave Start to Lad Called Red," ibid., October 19, 1967.

7. Richard Day, *Vincennes: A Pictorial History* (Saint Louis: G. Bradley Publishing, 1988).

8. "City Prepares Homecoming for 'Red' Skelton," *Vincennes Post*, February 15, 1939.

9. Edna and Red Skelton, letter to Inez and Clarence Stout, February 27, 1939, Stout Papers.

10. Ibid.

11. "City Greets Red Skelton, Famous Entertainer at Reception Sunday, Civic Dinner Monday," *Vincennes Sun-Commercial*, February 20, 1939.

12. Clarence Stout, letter to Thomas Gerety, April 18, 1947, Stout Papers.

13. A. A. Mercey, "Bag of Tricks Unloaded at 'The Minstrel-Revue,'" *Vincennes Commercial*, May 14, 1929.

14. Ibid.

15. Harold Williamson, "Minstrel Revue Scores a Hit," *Vincennes Sun*, May 14, 1929.

16. "Skelton Out of the Closet: Red Skelton's Film Masterpiece Has Never Grossed a Dollar," *Baltimore Sun*, October 12, 1941.

17. Ibid.

18. Williamson, "Minstrel Revue Scores a Hit."

19. Carl Sandburg, *Abraham Lincoln: The Prairie Years and the War Years* (1926; reprint, New York: Harcourt, Brace and World, 1966), 385.

20. Red Skelton, "I'll Tell All" (part 2), *Milwaukee Journal*, December 9, 1941.

21. Arthur Marx, *Red Skelton* (New York: E. P. Dutton, 1979).

22. Stout letter to Levy.

23. Schultheis, "Stout's Minstrel Shows Gave Start to Lad Called Red."

24. Red Skelton, telegram to Clarence Stout, March 15, 1937, Stout Papers.

25. Richard Schickel, *D. W. Griffith: An American Life* (New York: Simon and Schuster, 1984), 215.

26. "The Evolution of Richard Hofstadter," *New York Times*, August 6, 2006.

27. John M. Blum, "Retreat From Responsibility," in *The National Experience: A History of the United States*, John M. Blum, ed. (New York: Harcourt Brace, 1968), 640.

28. "Ku Klux Klan Initiation" advertisement, *Vincennes Morning Commercial*, February 20, 1924.

29. "Clarence A. Stout, Composer, Friend of Red Skelton, Dies," *Vincennes Sun-Commercial*, October 30, 1960.

30. Betty Baytos, "Interview with Red Skelton," Dance Collection Oral History, New York Public Library at Lincoln Center, February 20, 1996.

31. Red Skelton Scrapbook, Lewis Historical Library.

32. Ibid.

33. John Strausbaugh, *Black Like You: Blackface, Whiteface, Insult and Imitation in American Popular Culture* (New York: Penguin, 2006), 24.

34. Ibid., 72.

35. Schultheis, "Stout's Minstrel Shows Gave Start to Lad Called Red."

36. Bound letters to Georgia, Box 10, R. R. S. Letters to Friends, August 15, 1967, and Red Skelton letter to Godfrey Cambridge, Skelton Collection.

37. "Our Dear Sweet Beloved Richard," Funeral Scrapbook (I), May 1958, Sammy Davis Telegram, ibid.

38. Douglas Wissing, "Red Skelton: The Last Vaudevillian," *Traces of Indiana and Midwestern History* 10, no. 1 (Winter 1998): 12.

39. Glen Elsasser, "We Remember Red," *Indianapolis Star Magazine*, August 26, 1962.

40. "Red Skelton," in *Current Biography 1947*, Anna Rothe, ed. (New York: H. W. Wilson Company, 1948), 580.

41. Baytos, "Interview with Red Skelton."

42. For example, see David W. Jackson, "Vincennes' Famed Comedian Drops in for Visit to His Old Home Wednesday," *Vincennes Sun Commercial*, October 30, 1962.

43. Marx, *Red Skelton*, 9.

44. Skelton, "I'll Tell All."

45. Ibid.

46. "1929 YMCA Circus Scores Biggest Hit," *Vincennes Sun*, April 19, 1929.

47. Wes Gehring, *Seeing Red ... The Skelton in Hollywood's Closet: An Analytical Biography* (Davenport, IA: Robin Vincent Publishing, 2001).

48. Frederick C. Othman, "Ex-Usherette Leads Skelton to Success," *New York World Telegram*, August 14, 1941.

49. Virginia MacPherson, "Mischievous Red Skelton Tangled Up in Red Tape," *Alameda* (CA) *Times Star*, November 28, 1947.

Chapter 3

1. Frederick C. Othman, "Ex-Usherette Leads Skelton to Success," *New York World Telegram*, August 14, 1941.

2. Wes Gehring, *Charlie Chaplin: A Bio-Bibliography* (Westport, CT: Greenwood Press, 1983).

3. "Skelton Out of the Closet: Red Skelton's Film Masterpiece Has Never Grossed a Dollar," *Baltimore Morning Sun*, October 12, 1941.

4. Betsy Baytos, "Interview with Red Skelton," Dance Collection Oral History, New York Public Library at Lincoln Center, New York, New York, February 20, 1996, pp. 27–28.

5. Arthur Marx, *Red Skelton* (New York: E. P. Dutton, 1979), 23.

6. Red Skelton, "I'll Tell All" (part 2), *Milwaukee Journal*, December 9, 1941.

7. Ibid.

8. "Success Story," *CUE*, September 20, 1941.

9. For example see, Marx's *Red Skelton* or Wes Gehring, *Seeing Red ... The Skelton in Hollywood's Closet: An Analytical Biography* (Davenport, IA: Robin Vincent Publishing, 2001).

10. Red Skelton, "I'll Tell All"; Edna Stillwell Skelton (as told to James Reid), "I Married a Screwball," *Silver Screen* (June 1942).

11. John Branch, "60 Years and 1,000 Tales Since 14 Were Ejected," *New York Times*, July 6, 2006.

12. Red Skelton, "I'll Tell All."

13. Sally Jefferson, "The Skelton in Hollywood's Closet," *Photoplay* (July 1942): 71.

14. Edna Stillwell Skelton, "I Married a Screwball," 22.

15. David L. Smith, *Hoosiers in Hollywood* (Indianapolis: Indiana Historical Society Press, 2006), 87.

16. Edna Stillwell Skelton, "I Married a Screwball," 22.

17. Television Academy's Salute to Red Skelton, Beverly Hills, California, October 21, 1998.

18. Hedda Hopper, "Yes, Red Skelton's Always That Way," *Los Angeles Times*, November 3, 1946.

19. William Eagle, "Out of Love into Business," *American Weekly*, July 27, 1947, p. 9.

20. "Hollywood's Newest Funny Man," *Vincennes Sun-Commercial*, September 5, 1941.

21. "Capitol, Wash.," *Variety*, March 10, 1937, p. 50.

22. Edna Stillwell Skelton, "I Married a Screwball," 22.

23. Othman, "Ex-Usherette Leads Skelton to Success," 2.

24. Red Skelton, "I'll Tell All" (part 1), *Milwaukee Journal*, December 8, 1941.

25. Edna Stillwell Skelton, "I Married a Screwball," 23.

26. "Red Skelton," *Current Biography 1947*, Anna Roth, ed. (New York: H. W. Wilson Company, 1948), 580.

27. Red Skelton, "I'll Tell All" (part 3), *Milwaukee Journal*, December 10, 1941.

28. Ibid.

29. Red Skelton, "I'll Tell All" (part 4), *Milwaukee Journal*, December 11, 1941.

30. Ibid.

31. Jefferson, "The Skelton in Hollywood's Closet," 39.

32. Edna Stillwell Skelton, "I Married a Screwball," 61.

33. James Thurber, *My Life and Hard Times* (1933; reprint, New York: Bantam Books, 1947).

34. Manohla Dargis, "Guess Who's Coming to Dinner (and Staying)?," *New York Times*, July 14, 2006.

35. Frank Capra, *The Name Above the Title* (New York: Macmillan, 1971), 59–72.

36. Marx, *Red Skelton*, 204.

37. Jefferson, "Skelton in Hollywood's Closet," 70.

38. Edna and Red Skelton, letter to Inez and Clarence Stout, May 28, 1937, Clarence Stout Papers, Lewis Historical Library, Vincennes University, Vincennes, Indiana.

39. Ibid.

40. Skelton to Stouts (February 27, 1939).

41. Steve Allen, "Red Skelton," in *The Funny Men* (New York: Simon and Schuster, 1956), 266.

42. Conrad Lane, "Famed Novel Doesn't Deserve a Racist Epithet," *Muncie Star Press*, July 16, 2006.

43. Skelton to Stouts (1937).

Chapter 4

1. Edna and Red Skelton, letter to Inez and Clarence Stout, May 28, 1937, Clarence Stout Papers, Lewis Historical Library, Vincennes University, Vincennes, Indiana.

2. Josh Rottenberg, "The Piracy Debate," *Entertainment Weekly*, July 14, 2006, p. 41.

3. "Capitol, Wash.," *Variety*, March 10, 1937, p. 50.

4. Nelson B. Bell, "'Maid of Salem,' on the Screen, and 'Red Skelton,' on Stage, Capitol Hit," *Washington Post*, March 6, 1937.

5. "Capitol, Wash.," 50.

6. Capitol Theatre advertisement, *Washington Post*, March 4, 1937.

7. "Capitol, Wash.," *Variety*, March 17, 1937, p. 50.

8. Nelson B. Bell, "'Red' Skelton, Who Opens His Second Week at the Capitol Today, Begins Ascent to Top of the Heap," *Washington Post*, March 12, 1937.

9. *Red Skelton: America's Greatest Clown* (Eugene, OR: Brentwood, 2005), "G. I. McPugg" DVD episode, undated.

10. "Loew's, Montreal," *Variety*, April 7, 1937.

11. Royal Alexandra, "Shea's Stage," *Toronto Daily Star*, April 10, 1937.

12. "At Loew's Theatre," *Montreal Gazette*, April 3, 1937.

13. "Loew's, Montreal."

14. "At the Riverside," *Milwaukee Journal*, June 20, 1937.

15. "1929 Y.M.C.A. Circus Scores Biggest Hit," *Vincennes Sun*, April 19, 1928.

16. Tom Bronzini, "Red Skelton's Former Wife, Edna, Dies: Married 12 Years, She Wrote Some of Comedian's Best Material," *Los Angeles Times*, November 19, 1982.

17. "'Big Town Girl' Proves Diverting Comedy," *Philadelphia Inquirer*, December 4, 1937.

18. Steve Allen, "Red Skelton," in *The Funny Men* (New York: Simon and Schuster, 1956), 271.

19. Frederic Raphael, *Eyes Wide Open: A Memoir of Stanley Kubrick* (New York: Ballantine Books, 1999), 47.

20. Mark Twain, *A Connecticut Yankee in King Arthur's Court* (1889; reprint, Scranton: Chandler Publishing Company, 1963), 54.

21. "Capitol, Wash.," *Variety*, July 14, 1937, p. 60.

22. "Loew's State, N.Y.," *Variety*, August 18, 1937.

23. John Crosby, "Radio and Television: Mr. Skelton's Middle Phase," *New York Herald Tribune*, October 24, 1951.

24. Red Skelton's Christmas Dinner review, *Variety*, January 1, 1986.

25. *Red Skelton's Greatest Clown* (Eugene, OR: Brentwood, 2005); "Clem and the Dalton Girls," DVD episode, 1962.

26. Skeltons to Stouts (May 28, 1937).

27. "Indiana Boy's Doughnut Dunking Hit on Stage," *Indianapolis Star*, June 27.

28. Skeltons to Stouts (May 28, 1937).

29. "NEW ACTS: Red Skelton," *Variety*, June 15, 1937, 50.

30. John Dunning, *On the Air: The Encyclopedia of Old-Time Radio* (New York: Oxford University Press, 1998), 593.

31. Skeltons to Stouts (May 28, 1937).

32. "'Red' Skelton Tells of City in Radio Debut," *Vincennes Sun-Commercial*, August 13, 1937.

33. Arthur Marx, *Red Skelton* (New York: E. P. Dutton, 1979), 65.

34. Ibid., 64–65.

35. Henry Jenkins, *What Made Pistachio Nuts? Early Sound Comedy and the Vaudeville Aesthetic* (New York: Columbia University Press, 1992), 72.

36. David L. Smith, *Hoosiers in Hollywood* (Indianapolis: Indiana Historical Society Press, 2006), 249.

37. "Red Skelton to Pursue Feud with Joe Cook on Air Tonight," *Vincennes Sun-Commercial*, August 26, 1937.

38. Ibid.

39. Irving A. Fein, *Jack Benny: An Intimate Biography* (1976; reprint, New York: Pocket Books, 1977), 57.

40. Ibid., 58.

41. In order of appearance: "The Skunk Trap," from the record album *The Best of W. C. Fields* (Columbia CG 34144); "Children" and "Feathered Friends," both from the record album *W. C. Fields on Radio: With Edgar Bergen & Charlie McCarthy* (Columbia CS 9890).

42. Walter Winchell, On Broadway, *Indianapolis Star*, August 24, 1937.

43. "Red Returns to Radio by Popular Demand," *Vincennes Post*, August 27, 1937.

44. "Wave Lengths," *Indianapolis News*, August 25, 1937.

45. Eileen Creelman, "Red Skelton of 'Having Wonderful Time,' Discusses His Hollywood Debut," *New York Sun*, July 6, 1938.

46. Edna Stillwell Skelton (as told to James Reid), "I Married a Screwball," *Silver Screen* (June 1942): 61.

47. Creelman, "Red Skelton of 'Having Wonderful Time,'" 17.

48. "Red Skelton," in *Current Biography 1947*, Anna Rothe, ed. (New York: H. W. Wilson Company, 1948), 581.

49. Edna Skelton, "I Married a Screwball," 61.

50. Kristopher Tapley, "The (Tinsel) Town That Ate Superman," *New York Times*, August 20, 2006.

Chapter 5

1. Edna Stillwell Skelton (as told to James Reid), "I Married a Screwball," *Silver Screen* (June 1942).

2. Frank S. Nugent, *Having Wonderful Time* review, *New York Times*, July 8, 1938.

3. *Having Wonderful Time* review, *Variety*, June 15, 1937.

4. Nugent, *Having Wonderful Time* review.

5. Ginger Rogers, *Ginger: My Story* (New York: Harper Collins, 1991), 190.

6. Ibid.

7. "Loew's State, N.Y.," *Variety*, August 18, 1937.

8. Pandro S. Berman, interview with author, Beverly Hills, California, June 1975.

9. Edna and Red Skelton, letter to Inez and Clarence Stout, March 30, 1938, Clarence Stout Papers, Lewis Historical Library, Vincennes University, Vincennes, Indiana.

10. "RKO Takes 'Lady' Off Shelf For Lens," *Hollywood Reporter*, October 28, 1937.

11. Eileen Creelman, "Red Skelton of 'Having Wonderful Time,' Discusses His Hollywood Debut," *New York Sun*, July 6, 1938.

12. Ibid.

13. Dwight Whitney, "'A Clown Is a Warrior Who Fights Gloom … and Red Skelton Fights Harder Than Anyone," *TV Guide* (August 20, 1966).

14. "'Having Wonderful Time' OK Summer Camp Life Comedy," *Hollywood Reporter*, June 11, 1938.

15. "Richard Skelton Given Comedy Spot in 'Time,'" September 7, 1937, ibid.

16. Paul Harrison, "Red Skelton's Screen Test Which Won Him Film Role, So Funny It May Be Made a Short" (syndicated column), *Vincennes Sun-Commercial*, December 18, 1940.

17. Edna and Red Skelton, postcard to Clarence Stout, November 21, 1937, Stout Papers.

18. YMCA Circus program/ad, *Vincennes Sun*, April 18, 1929.

19. Glen C. Pullen, "'Red' Skelton Funnier in His New Palace Act," *Cleveland Plain Dealer*, February 12, 1938.

20. Skeltons to Stouts (March 30, 1938).

21. Red Skelton, "I'll Tell All" (part 5), *Milwaukee Journal*, December 12, 1941.

22. Betsy Baytos, "Interview with Red Skelton," Dance Collection Oral History, New York Public Library at Lincoln Center, New York, New York, February 20, 1996.

23. Ibid.

24. Edna and Red Skelton, telegram to Inez and Clarence Stout, December 15, 1938, Stout Papers.

25. Harrison B. Summers, ed. *A Thirty-Year History of Programs Carried on National Radio Networks in the United States, 1926–1956* (New York: Arno Press, 1971), 75.

26. Edna Stillwell Skelton, "I Married a Screwball."

27. For example, see Skeltons to Stouts, May 28, 1937, Stout Papers.

28. "City Prepares Homecoming for 'Red' Skelton," *Vincennes Post*, February 15, 1939.

29. "City Greets Red Skelton, Famous Entertainer, at Reception Sunday, Civic Dinner Monday," *Vincennes Sun-Commercial*, February 20, 1939, and "Vincennes Takes Delight in Honoring Popular 'Red' Skelton," *Vincennes Post*, February 21, 1939.

30. "City Prepares Homecoming For 'Red' Skelton."

31. "Vincennes Takes Delight In Honoring Popular 'Red' Skelton."

32. "Truant from the Midway," *New York Times*, June 8, 1941.

33. "'Red' Skelton Homecoming Starts at 10:12 Today," *Vincennes Post*, February 19, 1939, and welcome home advertisement for Red Skelton, ibid.

34. "'Red' Skelton Homecoming Starts at 10:12 Today."

35. Ibid.

36. Red Skelton, interview with author, September 18, 1986, Muncie, Indiana.

37. Red and Edna Skelton publicity still, *Vincennes Post*, February 19, 1939.

38. "Red Goes Back to School, but Not to Study," *Vincennes Sun-Commercial*, February 21, 1939.

39. "Vincennes Takes Delight in Honoring Popular 'Red' Skelton."

40. Ibid.

41. Skeltons to Stouts (February 27, 1939).

42. Hermione Lee, "Casting a Cold Eye," *New York Times*, November 21, 1999.

43. Edna Stillwell Skelton, "I Married a Screwball."

44. "Chicago," *Variety*, September 6, 1939.

45. Arthur Marx, *Red Skelton* (New York: E. P. Dutton, 1979), 109–11.

46. "Paramount, N.Y.," *Variety*, March 20, 1940, p. 46.

47. Hedley Donovan, "President's Birthday Balls Draw 20,000 Here," *Washington Post*, January 31, 1940.

48. Cobbett Steinberg, *Reel Facts: The Movie Book of Records* (New York: Vintage Books, 1978), 404.

49. Marx, *Red Skelton*, 3.

50. "Red Skelton, Conferral of the Degree Doctor of Humanities, honoris causa," Muncie, Indiana, Ball State University, September 18, 1986.

51. Baytos, "Interview with Red Skelton," 56.

52. "Paramount, N.Y." *Variety*, April 17, 1940, p. 48.

53. Baytos, "Interview with Red Skelton," 56.

54. Harrison, "Red Skelton's Screen Test Which Won Him Film Role, So Funny It May Be Made a Short."

55. "Skelton Out of the Closet: Red Skelton's Film Masterpiece Has Never Grossed a Dollar," *Baltimore Sun*, October 12, 1941.

56. Marx, *Red Skelton*, 72.

57. "Paramount, N.Y.," *Variety*, April 17, 1940, p. 48.

58. "Red Skelton," in *Current Biography 1947*, Anna Rothe, ed. (New York: H. W. Wilson Company, 1948), 581.

59. This has been my Academy experience in researching twenty-eight film-related books.

60. Richard L. Coe, "'Oscar' Awards and 'Typhoon' Click at Earle: Dorothy Lamour, Bob Preston in Feature; Skelton Continues," *Washington Post*, May 18, 1940.

Chapter 6

1. Fred D. Cavinder, *The Indiana Book of Quotes* (Indianapolis: Indiana Historical Society Press, 2005), 215.

2. "Skelton, Back Home from Hollywood, Reveals He Has Gone Serious in New Film," *Vincennes Sun-Commercial*, October 14, 1940.

3. Paul Harrison, "Red Skelton's Screen Test Which Won Him Film Role, So Funny It May Be Made a Short," *Vincennes Sun-Commercial*, October 18, 1940.

4. "Swings Hammer," *Vincennes Post*, October 15, 1940.

5. *Flight Command* review, *Film Daily*, December 23, 1940.

6. "MGM's 'Flight Command' Clicks from All Angles," *Hollywood Reporter*, December 17, 1940.

7. Archer Winsten, "'Flight Command' Zooms into Capitol Theatre," *New York Post*, January 17, 1941.

8. Robert Francis, "'Flight Command' at the Capitol," *Brooklyn Eagle*, January 17, 1941.

9. Leo Mishkin, *Flight Command* review, *New York Telegram*, January 17, 1941.

10. Edna Stillwell Skelton (as told to James Reid), "I Married a Screwball," *Silver Screen* (June 1942): 62.

11. "Ragland Gets Workout," *Hollywood Reporter*, June 2, 1941.

12. "Skelton Sees 'Dr.,'" ibid., June 5, 1941.

13. Wanda Hale, "Dr. Kildare Is Back, Showing at Criterion," *New York Daily News*, May 8, 1941.

14. "Slight Dip in High Average for Series," *Hollywood Reporter*, April 30, 1941.

15. Gilbert Kanour, "'The People vs. Dr. Kildare' Now Showing at New Theater," *Baltimore Evening Sun*, May 9, 1941.

16. Arthur Marx, *Red Skelton* (New York: E. P. Dutton, 1979), 77.

17. Red Skelton, interview with author, Muncie, Indiana, September 18, 1986.

18. "Harvey Makes 'Sage' Out of Joe E. Brown," *Indianapolis News*, February 16, 1948.

19. At this time, the daily *Hollywood Reporter* would list, once a week, which films were in production. The movies in question first appeared in this section during the following weeks in 1941: *Lady Be Good* (March 14), *Dr. Kildare's Wedding* (June 6, listed as "untitled"), and *Whistling in the Dark* (June 27).

20. "Skelton 'Whistling' First MGM Break," *Hollywood Reporter*, June 12, 1941.

21. Eric Lax, *Woody Allen: A Biography* (New York: Alfred A. Knopf, 1991), 25.

22. Maxine Arnold, "Clown in Civies," *Photoplay* (February 1948): 89.

23. Wes Gehring, *The Marx Brothers: A Bio-Bibliography* (Westport, CT: Greenwood Press, 1987) and *Groucho and W. C. Fields: Huckster Comedians* (Jackson: University Press of Mississippi, 1994).

24. Gehring, *W. C. Fields: A Bio-Bibliography* (Westport, CT: Greenwood Press, 1984) and *Film Clowns of the Depression: 12 Memorable Movies* (Jefferson, NC: McFarland, 2007).

25. "Red Skelton Scores in First Starring Role," *New York Morning Telegram*, August 28, 1941.

26. "Comic Hailed as Bright New Star," *Hollywood Reporter*, July 30, 1941.

27. Irving Hoffman, "Red Skelton Hailed as New MGM Star," *Hollywood Reporter*, September 2, 1941.

28. William Boehnel, "Red Skelton Terrific in Funny Picture," *New York World Telegram*, August 28, 1941.

29. Edith Werner, "Skelton's 'Whistling in Dark' Clicks as Laugh-Thriller," *New York Mirror*, August 28, 1941.

30. Bosley Crowther, *Whistling in the Dark* review, *New York Times*, August 28, 1941, 23.

31. "Meet Red Skelton, Hope of the B's," *PM*, August 28, 1941.

32. Herbert Cohn, "Red Skelton Arrives as a Comedy Star," *Brooklyn Daily Eagle*, August 28, 1941.

33. Wanda Hale, "Red Skelton Clicks in First Big Role, *New York Daily News*, August 28, 1941.

34. "Meet Red Skelton, Hope of the B's."

35. "'Whistling in the Dark' Bowls 'Em Over at Capitol," *Washington Post*, undated [1941], Red Skelton Scrapbook Number Two, 1941–42, Red Skelton Collection, Vincennes University, Vincennes, Indiana.

36. *Whistling in the Dark* picture caption, *New York World Telegram*, August 28, 1941.

37. "Skelton Wins New Deal and 'DuBarry,'" *Hollywood Reporter*, October 30, 1941.

38. Metro-Goldwyn-Mayer Legal Department Records, Special Collection File, 1941–43, Margaret Herrick Library, Academy of Motion Picture Arts and Sciences, Beverly Hills, California.

39. Eileen Creelman, "Red Skelton of 'Having Wonderful Time,' Discusses His Hollywood Debut," *New York Sun*, July 6, 1938.

40. Wanda Hale, "New Kildare Movie May Be Last of Series," *New York Daily News*, September 18, 1941.

41. *Lady Be Good* review, *New York Times*, September 19, 1941.

42. Red Skelton, "I'll Tell All" (part 5), *Milwaukee Journal*, December 12, 1941.

43. Jim Knipfel, *Slackjaw* (1999; reprint, New York: Berkley Books, 2000), 180.

44. "Look Out, Television; Here Comes Red Skelton!" *Long Beach (CA) Press Telegram*, February 13, 1946.

45. Ibid.

46. Mark Haddon, *The Curious Incident of the Dog in the Night-Time* (New York: Vintage Books, 2003), 90.

47. "Benny's Wit Called Best By 300 Editors in Poll," *Hollywood Reporter*, December 23, 1941.

48. John Dunning, *On the Air: The Encyclopedia of Old-Time Radio* (New York: Oxford University Press, 1998), 593.

49. "Red Skelton," *Variety*, October 15, 1941, p. 26.

50. All Hooper radio rating numbers were drawn from Harrison B. Summers, ed., *A Thirty-Year History of Programs Carried on National Radio Networks in the United States, 1926–1956* (New York: Arno Press, 1971), 99.

51. Red Skelton, "I'll Tell All" (5 parts), *Milwaukee Journal*, December 8–12, 1941.

52. Ibid. (part 1), December 8, 1941.

Chapter 7

1. "Moves to Divorce Red Skelton," *New York Times*, December 30, 1942.

2. Edna and Red Skelton, letter to Inez and Clarence Stout, February 27, 1939, Clarence Stout Papers, Lewis Historical Library, Vincennes University, Vincennes, Indiana.

3. Arthur Marx, *Red Skelton* (New York: E. P. Dutton, 1979), 89–90.

4. Jordan R. Young, *The Laugh Crafters: Comedy Writing in Radio and TV's Golden Age* (Beverly Hills, CA: Post Times Publishing, 1999), 263.

5. Edna Stillwell Skelton (as told to James Reid), "I Married a Screwball," *Silver Screen* (June 1942): 63.

6. Ibid.

7. Vivian Cosby, "Edna Skelton's Lasting Loyalty," *American Weekly*, November 13, 1949, 4.

8. William T. Vollman, "The Constructive Nihilist," *New York Times*, August 14, 2005.

9. "Red Skelton," *Variety*, October 15, 1941.

10. Ozzie Nelson, *Ozzie* (Englewood Cliffs, NJ: Prentice-Hall, 1993), 166.

11. Ibid., 164.

12. Harrison B. Summers, ed., *A Thirty-Year History of Programs Carried on National Radio Networks in the United States, 1926–1956* (New York: Arno Press, 1971), 37.

13. Paul Cooley, interview with author, September 21, 2000, Muncie, Indiana.

14. "New Acts: Red Skelton," *Variety*, June 16, 1937.

15. John Dunning, *On the Air: The Encyclopedia of Old-Time Radio* (New York: Oxford Press, 1998), 59.

16. "Doolittle Dood It," *Los Angeles Herald Express*, May 19, 1942.

17. "'Red' and the Famous Headline" (picture), *Los Angeles Herald Express*, May 21, 1942, in "Red Skelton Scrapbook Number 2, 1931–42, Red Skelton Collection, Vincennes University, Vincennes, Indiana.

18. "4 Days of Storm Vex Los Angeles," *New York Times*, February 23, 1944.

19. Wesley Hyatt, *A Critical History of Television's "The Red Skelton Show," 1951–1971* (Jefferson, NC: McFarland and Company, 2004), 12.

20. Skelton, "I Married a Screwball," 61.

21. Verna Felton, "Love That Red-Head," *Radio Mirror*, January 1948, 46.

22. Arthur Frank Wertheim, *Radio Comedy* (1979; reprint, New York: Oxford University Press, 1992), 377.

23. John Whitehead, "Red Skelton as the 'Little Brat,'" *Radio Life*, April 12, 1942, p. 3.

24. John R. Franchey, "Ex's Can Be Friends," *Screenland* (September 1943): 31.

25. See the September 1943 section, Red Skelton Scrapbook Number 3, 1942–43, Skelton Collection.

26. Franchey, "Ex's Can Be Friends," 78.

27. "Radio Warm-Ups #3," *Radio Life* (August 29, 1948): 34.

28. Betty Baytos, "Interview with Red Skelton," Dance Collection Oral History, New York Public Library at Lincoln Center, February 20, 1996, p. 70.

29. Franchey, "Ex's Can Be Friends," 78.

30. Maxine Arnold, "Clown in Civies," *Photoplay* (February 1948): 89.

31. Ibid.

32. "Red Skelton Waits Outside Court as Wife Divorces Him," *Los Angeles Times*, February 12, 1943.

33. Ibid.

34. For Skelton caricature and note to Edna, see the August 1941 section, Red Skelton Scrapbook Number 2, 1931–42, Skelton Collection.

35. Sidney Skolsky, "The Gospel Truth," *Chicago Sun*, [1941], in Red Skelton Scrapbook Number 2, 1931–42, Skelton Collection.

36. Kitty Callahan, "Redheaded Comet," *Family Circle*, July 31 [1941], ibid.

37. Louella Parsons, "'Rationing,' MGM Comedy," *Los Angeles Examiner*, January 15, 1943.

38. Ibid.

39. Jennifer Adams, "Why the Skeltons Parted," *Movieland* (March 1943): 64.

40. Ibid.

41. "Red Skelton Waits Outside Court as Wife Divorces Him."

42. "Red Skelton to Marry," *New York Times*, April 7, 1944.

43. "Red Skelton Practically Left Waiting at Altar," *Los Angeles Times*, April 11, 1944.

44. "Red Skelton Tangle Grows," *Los Angeles Examiner*, April 12, 1944.

45. Ibid.

Chapter 8

1. John R. Franchey, "Ex's Can Be Friends," *Screenland* (September 1943): 78.

2. Leonard Maltin, *The Great Movie Comedians: From Charlie Chaplin to Woody Allen* (New York: Crown, 1978), 207.

3. Theodore Strauss, *Whistling in Dixie* review, *New York Times*, December 31, 1942.

4. "MGM 'Whistling in Dixie' Full of Audience Howls: Skelton Picks Up Note of First Hit," *Hollywood Reporter*, November 4, 1942, p. 3.

5. *Whistling in Dixie* review, *Variety*, October 28, 1942.

6. Special Collection: Metro-Goldwyn-Mayer Legal Department Records, 1941–43, Margaret Herrick Library, Academy of Motion Picture Arts and Sciences, Beverly Hills, California (hereafter cited as MGM Legal Department Records); For ticket prices, see Cobbett Steinberg, *Reel Facts: The Movie Book of Records* (New York: Vintage Books, 1978), 368.

7. MGM Legal Department Records.

8. "Skelton Whistles Again—In Brooklyn," *Hollywood Reporter*, August 27, 1942.

9. Theodore Strauss, "A Hollywood Safari into Darkest Flatbush," *New York Times*, April 11, 1943.

10. Arthur Frank Wertheim, *Radio Comedy* (1979; reprint, New York: Oxford University Press, 1992), 377.

11. Thomas M. Pryor, *Whistling in Brooklyn* review, *New York Times*, March 24, 1944.

12. This is based upon the author's film memorabilia collection.

13. Thomas M. Pryor, "By Way of Report," *New York Times*, September 12, 1943.

14. "The Quips Fall Where They May as Skelton and Durocher Meet," *New York Herald Tribune*, March 19, 1944.

15. *Whistling in Brooklyn* review, *Variety*, September 29, 1943.

16. Neil Rau, "Red Skelton Comedy Corn, but Hilarious," *Los Angeles Examiner*, December 3, 1943.

17. MGM Legal Department Records.

18. "Powell at Her Best to Dorsey Rhythms," *Hollywood Reporter*, April 17, 1942.

19. Rose Pelswick, "Present 'Ship Ahoy' at Capitol Theatre," *New York Journal American*, June 26, 1942.

20. *Ship Ahoy* review, *Daily Variety*, April 22, 1942.

21. Archer Winsten, "'Ship Ahoy' Docks at Capitol Theatre," *New York Post*, June 26, 1942; *Ship Ahoy*, review, *Showman Trade Review*, April 18, 1942.

22. "Skelton Out of the Closet: Red Skelton's Film Masterpiece Has Never Grossed a Dollar," *Baltimore Sun*, October 12, 1941.

23. Herbert Cohn, "'Ship Ahoy' at Capitol a Fast, Funny Show," *Brooklyn Daily Eagle*, June 26, 1942.

24. Kate Cameron, "Abundance of Fun, Rhythm at Capitol," *New York Daily News*, June 26, 1942.

25. Jerry Gaghan, "'Ship Ahoy' Hit with Jitterbugs," *Hollywood Reporter*, May 27, 1942.

26. Lee Mortimer, "'Ship Ahoy' Is for Swingsters and Skelton Fans," *New York Daily Mirror*, June 26, 1942.

27. Robert Bianco, "Critic's Corner," *USA Today*, August 24, 2006.

28. For example, see Harnet T. Kane's "'Maisie' Picked as Public Favorite," *Hollywood Reporter*, August 14, 1941.

29. "Draws of Co-Stars Can Get Film By," *Hollywood Reporter*, May 27, 1942.

30. Edith Werner, "'Maisie Gets Her Man' at the Criterion," *New York Daily Mirror*, July 16, 1942.

31. Archer Winsten, "'Panama Hattie' Opens at the Capitol Theatre," *New York Post*, October 2, 1942; Edgar Price, *Panama Hattie* review, *Brooklyn Citizen*, October 2, 1942.

32. "Musical Ignores Plot to Score Hit," *Hollywood Reporter*, July 22, 1942.

33. *Panama Hattie* review, *The New Yorker*, October 3, 1942.

34. Bosley Crowther, *Panama Hattie* review, *New York Times*, October 2, 1942.

35. Price, *Panama Hattie* review.

36. *Panama Hattie* review, *Variety*, July 22, 1942.

37. *Panama Hattie* review, *Newsweek*, October 5, 1942.

38. Crowther, *Panama Hattie* review.

39. Edgar Price, *Du Barry Was a Lady* review, *Brooklyn Citizen*, October 7, 1943.

40. *Du Barry Was a Lady* review, *Variety*, May 5, 1943.

41. "Demure Du Barry," *Newsweek*, June 28, 1943.

42. John U. Sturdevant, "Skidding into History on a Mickey Finn," *New York Journal American*, June 27, 1943.

43. *Du Barry Was a Lady* review, *Hollywood Reporter*, May 5, 1943; *Du Barry Was a Lady* review, *New York Times*, August 20, 1943.

44. *Bathing Beauty* review, *New York Times*, June 28, 1944.

45. Leo Miskin, "Astor Film Good Hot Weather Fun," *New York Morning Telegraph*, June 28, 1944.

46. "'Bathing Beauty' at the Astor Just Right for the Warm Days," *Brooklyn Daily Eagle*, June 28, 1944.

47. Steinberg, *Reel Facts*, 405.

48. Lowell E. Redelings, "Red Skelton Highlights New Musical," *Hollywood Citizen News*, July 28, 1944.

49. Ibid.

50. Otis L. Guernsey Jr., "'Bathing Beauty'—Astor," *New York Herald Tribune*, June 28, 1944.

51. Alton Cook, *Bathing Beauty* review, *New York World Telegram*, June 27, 1944.

52. Georgia Davis Skelton, "Do Comics Make Good Husbands?" *Screenland* (June 1952): 23.

53. Ibid., 22.

54. Red Skelton, "Glamour Will Get Me Nowhere," *Movieland* (August 1952): 27.

55. Ibid.

56. Jack Holland, "The Army and Red Skelton," undated and uncited source in Red Skelton Scrapbook Number 8, January to December 1945, Red Skelton Collection, Vincennes University, Vincennes, Indiana.

57. "Everyone's a Kid is Basis for Skelton's Philosophy," *McGuire Banner*, February 1, 1945, ibid.

58. "GIs Perplexed Red Skelton Reveals," *Hollywood Press Times*, May 13, 1945.

59. Wes D. Gehring, *Joe E. Brown: Film Comedian and Baseball Buffoon* (Jefferson, NC: McFarland and Company, 2006).

60. Holland, "Army and Red Skelton."

61. Harrison Carroll, "Christmas Tree Fire in Star's Home," *Los Angeles Harold Express*, January 8, 1945.

62. "Red Just Listens Now," *Vincennes Sun-Commercial*, August 9, 1944.

63. Harrison Carroll, "Red Skelton Sees Last Italy Drive," *Los Angeles Herald Express*, May 8, 1945.

64. "Red Skelton Now in Overseas Area," *Los Angeles Herald Express*, April 17, 1945; see also the service section of Skelton Scrapbook Number 8, January to December 1945, Skelton Collection, Vincennes University.

65. Red Skelton World War II letter to Georgia Davis Skelton, March 28, 1945, Red Skelton Collection, Archives and Special Collections, Western Illinois University Library, Macomb, Illinois.

66. Skelton Scrapbook Number 8, January to December 1945, Skelton Collection, Vincennes University.

67. For example, see the article, "Red Skelton Out of Army; Learns 'Lots of New Words,'" *Portland Journal*, September 30, 1945.

68. Red Skelton's comments on the occasion of President Franklin Roosevelt's death, April 12, 1945, Skelton Collection, Archives and Special Collection, Western Illinois University Library.

69. Arthur M. Schlesinger Jr., "The World in Flames," in *The National Experience: A History of the United States*, John M. Blum, ed. (New York: Harcourt Brace, 1968), 753.

70. David Rulf, telephone interview with author, November 6, 11, 2007.

71. Harrison Carroll, "Carroll," *Philadelphia News*, June 16, 1945.

72. Louella Parsons (syndicated), "Myrna Loy Signs Three Year, One Picture a Season, Contract with Studio [and Related Hollywood News]," *Sacramento Bee*, June 29, 1945.

73. "Skelton in Hollywood after Army Discharge," *San Diego Union*, September 29, 1945.

74. For example, see *Red Skelton [radio] Scrapbook* review, *Variety*, December 12, 1945, 36.

75. "More Than a Word," *Chicago Times*, July 25, 1945, Skelton Scrapbook Number 8, January to December 1945, Skelton Collection, Vincennes University.

76. Barbara Berch, "Directed Subtly by George Sidney," *New York Times*, October 28, 1945, ibid.

77. Ibid.

78. Louella Parsons, "Edna Skelton, Borzage Wed," *Los Angeles Examiner*, November 26, 1945, Skelton Collection, Vincennes University.

Chapter 9

1. Eleanor Norris Keaton, letter to the author, late 1980s.

2. "'Ziegfeld Follies' Gorgeous, Massive, Spectacular Revue," *Hollywood Reporter*, August 14, 1945.

3. *Ziegfeld Follies* review, *New York Times*, March 23, 1946.

4. "'Ziegfeld Follies' Gorgeous, Massive, Spectacular Revue."

5. Joe Pihodna, *The Show-Off* review, *New York Herald Tribune*, March 20, 1947.

6. "'Merton' Parades Skelton," *Hollywood Reporter*, July 18, 1947.

7. Bosley Crowther, *Merton of the Movies* review, *New York Times*, November 7, 1947.

8. Tom Donnelly, "Letting Down to an Awful Build-Up," *Washington (DC) News*, October 4, 1947.

9. *Merton of the Movies* review, *Variety*, July 23, 1947.

10. Philip K. Scheuer, "Red Skelton Tickles Ribs as Merton," *Los Angeles Times*, October 4, 1947; Wanda Hale, *Merton of the Movies* review, *New York Daily News*, November 7, 1947.

11. Metro-Goldwyn Mayer Legal Department Records, 1946–47, Margaret Herrick Library, Academy of Motion Picture Arts and Sciences, Beverly Hills, California.

12. Thomas F. Brady, "Hollywood Agenda," *New York Times*, February 9, 1947.

13. Bob Thomas, "Hollywood," *Burlingame Advance*, May 26, 1947.

14. "Radio Notes," *Newsweek*, September 24, 1945, 26.

15. Bob Thomas, "Ten Best Film Comic Picked by Joe E. Brown," *Long Beach (CA) Press Telegram*, August 20, 1947.

16. Louella Parsons (syndicated), "Skelton Gets Picture Break He Has Earned," *San Diego Union*, August 22, 1947.

17. Red Skelton, "The Role I Liked Best … ," *Saturday Evening Post*, February 28, 1948, 91.

18. James Agee, "Comedy's Greatest Era," *Life*, September 3, 1949, anthologized in *Agee on Film*, vol. 1 (New York: Grosset and Dunlap, 1969).

19. See Wes D. Gehring, *Personality Comedians As Genre: Selected Players* (Westport, CT: Greenwood Press, 1997).

20. Frank Quinn, "Skelton and Eleanor Powell Whoop It Up In 'I Dood It,'" *New York Daily Mirror*, November 11, 1943.

21. *I Dood It* review, *Time*, November 29, 1943, p. 92.

22. Skelton, "Role I Liked Best," 91.

23. Vincente Minnelli, with Hector Arce, *I Remember It Well* (New York: Samuel French, 1974), 128.

24. Harold Heffernan, "Red Skelton Is Funny as a Double Dealing Spy," *Long Island (NY) Star-Journal*, January 29, 1948.

25. Archer Winsten, "'I Dood It' Is Opened at Paramount Theatre," *New York Post*, November 11, 1943.

26. Red Skelton, interview with author, September 18, 1986, Muncie, Indiana, and Skelton, "Role I Liked Best," 91.

27. Anita Mykowsky, phone conversation with author, 2000.

28. Larry Edwards, *Buster: A Legend in Laughter* (Bradenton, FL: McGuinn and McGuire, 1995), 143.

29. Rudi Blesh, *Keaton* (1966; reprint, New York: Collier Books, 1971), 354.

30. Frank Miller, *Leading Men: The 50 Most Unforgettable Actors of the Studio Era* (San Francisco: Chronicle Books, 2006), 115.

31. Buster Keaton, with Charles Samuels, *My Wonderful World of Slapstick* (Garden City, NY: Doubleday and Company, 1960), 261.

32. Eleanor Norris Keaton, conversation with author, Piqua, Kansas (Buster Keaton birthplace), late 1980s.

33. *Telescope: Deadpan (Buster Keaton)*, CBS Canada, broadcast April 14, 1966, video collection of the Museum of Television and Radio, Beverly Hills, California.

34. Norman Panama and Melvin Frank, *The Spy*, August 12, 1947, *A Southern Yankee* script material folder number 1, University of Southern California Cinema-Television Library, Los Angeles, California (hereafter cited as USC Cinema-Television Library).

35. See Wes D. Gehring, *Parody as Film Genre: "Never Give a Saga an Even Break"* (Westport, CT: Greenwood Press, 1999).

36. Kathleen Gable, *Clark Gable: A Personal Portrait* (Englewood Cliffs, NJ: Prentice-Hall, 1961), 79

37. Keaton, *My Wonderful World of Slapstick*, 264

38. Marion Meade, *Buster Keaton: Cut to the Chase* (New York: HarperCollins Publisher, 1995), 239.

39. Harry Tugend, *A Southern Yankee* script material, filed July 19, 1948, *Yankee* script material folder number 1, USC Cinema-Television Library.

40. Buster Keaton and Edward Sedgwick, *A Southern Yankee* "retakes," April 20, 1948, *Yankee* script material folder number 4, USC Cinema-Television Library.

41. Heffernan, "Red Skelton Is Funny as a Double Dealing Spy."

42. Keaton, *My Wonderful World of Slapstick*, 264.

43. Henri Bergson, "Laughter," in *Comedy*, Wylie Sypher, ed. (Garden City, NY: Doubleday and Company, 1956), 105.

44. Buster Keaton and Edward Sedgwick, *A Southern Yankee* "retakes," April 27, 1948, *Yankee* script material folder number 4, USC Cinema-Television Library.

45. Keaton, *My Wonderful World of Slapstick*, 264.

46. *A Southern Yankee* review, *Variety*, August 11, 1948, p. 8.

47. "Top Notch Comedy Won't Miss at B0," *Hollywood Reporter*, August 6, 1948.

48. Darr Smith, *A Southern Yankee* review, *Los Angeles Daily News*, in the *A Southern Yankee* file, Herrick Library.

49. *A Southern Yankee* review, *Cue*, November 27, 1948.

50. William R. Weaver, *A Southern Yankee* review, *Motion Picture Daily*, August 6, 1948.

51. Arthur Marx, *Red Skelton* (New York: E. P. Dutton, 1979), 140.

52. *A Southern Yankee* review, *New York Times*, November 25, 1948, 47.

53. "'Yankee' Verdict Is Generally Negative Among N. Y. Critics," *Hollywood Reporter*, December 1, 1948.

54. Leo Mishkin, *A Southern Yankee* review, *New York Morning Telegraph*, November 25, 1948.

55. Fred Hift, *A Southern Yankee* review, *Motion Picture Herald*, August 7, 1948.

56. Weaver, *A Southern Yankee* review.

57. Betsy Baytos, "Interview with Red Skelton," Dance Collection Oral History, New York Public Library at Lincoln Center, New York, New York, February 20, 1996, p. 59.

58. Marvin L. Skelton, phone interview with author, December 14, 2006.

Chapter 10

1. "Look Out, Television; Here Comes Red Skelton!" *Long Beach (CA) Press Telegram*, February 13, 1946.

2. Bob Thomas, "Red Skelton Will Give Up Films for Television," *Boston Evening Globe*, November 19, 1947.

3. Sheilah Graham, "Red Skelton Hopes Metro Will Ease Contract Terms," *Phoenix Gazette*, February 3, 1948.

4. Cobbett Steinberg, *Reel Facts: The Movie Book of Records* (New York: Vintage Books, 1978), 344.

5. "Fuller Brush Men Help Write Film," *Columbia News*, April 23, 1948.

6. "Red Skelton Finds He's Flop as Fuller Brush Salesman," *Los Angeles Daily News*, September 26, 1947.

7. Ibid.

8. "Red Skelton: Master of Ad-Lib," *Hollywood Lead Sheet*, May 1948.

9. "Red Skelton Makes Survey of Air Show," *Dallas News*, June 22, 1948.

10. Jay Carmody, "Skelton Is His Old Zany Self in Disguise of Brush Man," *Washington (DC) Star*, June 11, 1948.

11. "Skelton Runs Wild in Brilliant Farce," *Hollywood Reporter*, May 7, 1948.

12. "'The Fuller Brush Man' Gives Skelton a Workout," *New York Post*, May 16, 1948.

13. Lew Sheaffer, "Skelton Fans Will Like Red in State's 'Fuller Brush Man,'" *Brooklyn Eagle*, May 15, 1948.

14. Loyal Meek, "Red Skelton's New Comedy Is Hilarious," *Cedar Rapids Gazette*, June 15, 1948.

15. *The Fuller Brush Man* review, *Time*, May 31, 1948, 86.

16. Sheilah Graham, "Hollywood," *Phoenix Gazette*, March 19, 1948.

17. Bob Thomas, "Life in Hollywood," *San Mateo (CA) Times and Leader*, February 24, 1948.

18. Arthur Marx, *Red Skelton* (New York: E. P. Dutton, 1979), 139.

19. Kay Proctor, "Skelton Film Super-Comedy," *Los Angeles Examiner*, June 23, 1948.

20. Sheilah Graham, "Red and Edna Write Life Story," *Hollywood Citizen News*, March 27, 1947.

21. Ibid.

22. Hedda Hopper, "Looking at Hollywood," *Sacramento Union*, January 27, 1946.

23. Harold Heffernan, "Film Folk and Studio Gossip," *Seattle Times*, January 1948, Red Skelton Scrapbook Number 9, January to August 1946, Red Skelton Collection, Vincennes University, Vincennes, Indiana.

24. Red Skelton's Writing, Skelton Collection.

25. Sheilah Graham, "Skelton to Play Own Clown Role," *Hollywood Citizen News*, February 12, 1948.

26. Sid Ross, "Red Skelton … His Plane Was in Trouble," *Parade* magazine, September 23, 1951, p. 9.

27. Hedda Hopper, "Helter Skelton!" *Chicago Tribune*, June 17, 1951.

28. Red Skelton photo showcase with text, *Look* magazine, May 14, 1946, 39.

29. See "10,000,000 TV Pact for Procter and Gamble and Red Skelton," *Long Beach Press Telegram*, May 3, 1951.

30. "Red Skelton Signs Fabulous Contract," *Texarkana Gazette* [May 1951], Skelton Scrapbook Number 11, January to December 1951, Skelton Collection.

31. "Rubber Face on TV," *Life*, October 28, 1951, p. 71.

32. Jack Quigg, "Fantastic Capers by Red Skelton Are a Prelude to His TV Show," *Kansas City Star*, May 13, 1951.

33. Ross, "Red Skelton … His Plane Was in Trouble."

34. Larry Wolters, "Red Skelton TV Comedy Hit of the Year," *Chicago Tribune*, December 2, 1951.

35. Harriet Van Horne, "Skelton Has Chaplin Tragic-Comic Touch," *New York World Telegram*, February 18, 1952.

36. Hal Humphrey, "Skelton Taunts His 'Lazy' Rivals," *New York World Telegram and Sun*, December 8, 1951.

37. See Wes D. Gehring, *Charlie Chaplin: A Bio-Bibliography* (Westport, CT: Greenwood Press, 1983).

38. James Curtis, *W. C. Fields: A Biography* (New York: Alfred A. Knopf, 2003), 488.

39. Georgia Skelton, "Do Comics Make Good Husbands?" *Screenland* (June 1952): 58.

40. Cobina Wright, "Red Skelton Rates as 'Comedian with a Heart'," *Los Angeles Examiner*, May 13, 1951.

41. Hedda Hopper, "Looking At Hollywood," *Oregon Journal*, June 17, 1951.

42. "We Point with Pride to Red Skelton," *Silver Screen* (October 1947): 58.

43. Marva Peterson, "The Two Mrs. Skeltons," *Movieland* (April 1948): 56–57, 88.

44. Marvin L. Skelton, phone interview with the author, December 14, 2006.

45. Leo Rosten, "How to See Red—Skelton That Is" (part 2), *Look*, November 6, 1951, 80.

46. Georgia Skelton, "Do Comics Make Good Husbands?" 58.

47. Ibid., 22.

48. For example, see "Skelton Offers $750,000 for MGM Contract," *Boston Traveler*, October 27, 1947.

49. Virginia MacPherson, "Mischievous Red Skelton Tangled Up in Red Tape," *Alameda (CA) Times Star*, November 28, 1947.

50. Ibid.

51. Maxine Arnold, "Clown in Civies," *Photoplay* (February 1948): 89.

52. Sheilah Graham (syndicated), "Grandma's 'Lickle' Boy Sad with MGM," *Tacoma (WA) News Tribune*, January 4, 1948.

53. Ibid.

54. Bill Davidson, "'I'm Nuts and I Know It'," *Saturday Evening Post*, June 17, 1967, 69. The author also heard Skelton utter this mantra on several later visits to the Ball State University campus in Muncie, Indiana.

Chapter 11

1. Georgia Skelton, "Do Comics Make Good Husbands?" *Screenland*, June 1952, 58.

2. Harrison B. Summers, ed., *A Thirty-Year History of Programs Carried on National Radio Networks in the United States, 1926–1956* (New York: Arno Press, 1971), 165.

3. Pare Lorentz, *Free and Easy* review, *Judge*, May 17, 1930.

4. Wes D. Gehring, *W. C. Fields: A Bio-Bibliography* (Westport, CT: Greenwood Press, 1984) and *Groucho and W. C. Fields: Huckster Comedians* (Jackson: University Press of Mississippi, 1994).

5. *The Yellow Cab Man* review, *Motion Picture Herald*, February 25, 1950.

6. Philip K. Scheuer, "'Yellow Cab Man' Takes Side Street in Chases," *Los Angeles Times*, April 10, 1950.

7. Special Collections, Metro-Goldwyn-Mayer Legal Department Records, 1950–51, Margaret Herrick Library, Academy of Motion Picture Arts and Sciences, Beverly Hills, California (hereafter cited as MGM Legal Department Records).

8. *The Yellow Cab Man* review, *Motion Picture Herald*, February 25, 1950.

9. Cobbett Steinberg, *Reel Facts: The Movie Book of Records* (New York: Vintage Books, 1978), 345.

10. Philip Hamburger, *Three Little Words* review, *The New Yorker*, August 26, 1950, pp. 68–69.

11. Wylie Williams, *Three Little Words* review, *Hollywood Citizen News*, July 22, 1950.

12. Kay Proctor, "Skelton Film at 2 Houses," *Los Angeles Examiner*, January 26, 1951.

13. Tom Coffey, "Red Skelton at Best When Not Himself," *Los Angeles Mirror*, January 26, 1951.

14. Wes Gehring, *Joe E. Brown: Film Comedian and Baseball Buffoon* (Jefferson, NC: McFarland and Company, 2006).

15. See the comedian's one-man-show programs, such as the September 20, 1986, performance notes, "Red Skelton: America's Pantomimist Extraordinaire," for Ball State University's Emens Auditorium, author's collection.

16. Harry Ruskin and Jeanne Bartlett, *Watch the Birdie* treatment, October 18, 1948, 9, in the *Watch the Birdie* script material, Cinema-Television Library, University of Southern California, Los Angeles, California.

17. Buster Keaton, with Charles Samuels, *My Wonderful World of Slapstick* (Garden City, NY: Doubleday and Company, 1960), 263–64.

18. *Watch the Birdie* review, *Film Daily*, November 28, 1950.

19. *Watch the Birdie* review, *Variety*, November 29, 1950.

20. *Excuse My Dust* review, *Hollywood Reporter*, May 23, 1951.

21. Bosley Crowther, *Excuse My Dust* review, *New York Times*, June 28, 1951.

22. *Excuse My Dust* review, *Variety*, May 23, 1951.

23. Buster Keaton, Roy Rowland, and George Wells, *Excuse My Dust* addendum, "NOTES," May 9, 1950, 1-3, in the *Excuse My Dust* script material, University of Southern California Cinema-Television Library, Los Angeles, California.

24. "'Excuse My Dust' Recalls How Nice It Was in 1900," *Washington Star*, July 5, 1951.

25. Erskine Johnson (syndicated), "Erskine Johnson," *Los Angeles Daily News*, February 23, 1951.

26. Jack Quigg, "Fantastic Capers by Red Skelton Are a Prelude to His TV Show," *Kansas City Star*, May 13, 1951.

27. Arthur Marx, *Red Skelton* (New York: E. P. Dutton, 1979), 160.

28. "Red Skelton," *Time*, July 9, 1951, p. 32.

29. "Laugh Clown," *Newsweek*, July 9, 1951, p. 46.

30. "Red Skelton Hailed for Averting Panic on Crippled Airliner over Alps," *Los Angeles Herald Express*, June 28, 1951.

31. "The Palladium: Mr. Skelton," *London Times*, July 3, 1951.

32. Harry Crocker, "Behind the Make-Up," *Los Angeles Examiner*, July 26, 1951.

33. "Skelton Calls from London [and] Lauds Penny Ice Program" (syndicated), *Wichita Beacon*, July 23, 1951.

34. "Gene Fowler Finds Skelton a Big Hit in London Palladium," *Chicago Tribune*, July 12, 1951.

35. Martin Gottfried, *Nobody's Fool: The Lives of Danny Kaye* (New York: Simon and Schuster, 1994), 162.

36. Lloyd Shearer, "Red Skelton: He Never Stops Clowning," *Parade* (May 8, 1955): 30.

37. "Video Reviews: The Red Skelton Show," *Hollywood Reporter*, October 1, 1951.

38. Harriet Van Horne, "Red Skelton Impressive in TV Bow," *New York World Telegram*, October 2, 1951.

39. "Red Skelton Show," *Variety*, October 3, 1951.

40. "Red Skelton TV Debut Brings Down House," *Los Angeles Herald Express*, October 1, 1951.

41. Owen Collin, "Red Skelton Wins 2 'Emmys' at Annual TV Academy Banquet," *Los Angeles Herald Express*, February 19, 1952.

42. Lynn Bowers, "'Texas' Film Lot of Fun," *Los Angeles Examiner*, September 27, 1951.

43. Special Collections, MGM Legal Department Records, 1951–52, Herrick Library.

44. Harry MacArthur, "Red Skelton Is Summer Sub For [Arthur] Godfrey on Wednesdays," *Washington Star*, July 15, 1954.

45. Bob Thomas, "Red Skelton May Quit Television," *Waterbury (CT) Independent*, October 22, 1952.

46. Hal Humphrey, "Hal Humphrey," *Los Angeles Mirror*, October 14, 1952.

47. Red Skelton (subbing for syndicated columnist Erskine Johnson), "TV Proves Toughest Nut to Crack for Entertainment's Funniest Nut," *Bingham Press*, September 4, 1952.

48. Tim Brooks and Earle Marsh, *The Complete Directory to Prime Time Network TV Shows, 1946–Present* (New York: Ballantine Books, 1979), 802.

49. Marx, *Red Skelton*, 313.

50. Donald Hall, "Simple Things: A Poet's Poet," *House and Garden*, September 2003, 164.

51. Red Skelton's Writing, Box 9, ABC, "The Critic" folder, Red Skelton Collection, Vincennes University, Vincennes, Indiana.

52. "How Red Skelton's First Wife Arranged His Second Marriage," *TV Picture Life*, March 1969, p. 56.

53. Erskine Johnson, "Erskine Johnson," *Los Angeles Daily News*, February 23, 1951.

54. Louella Parsons (syndicated), "Red Skelton Moves Out; Ex-Wife Has Role in Row," *Seattle Post*, December 4, 1952.

55. Red Skelton, letter to Hedda Hopper, January 31, 1951, Hedda Hopper Collection, Special Collections, Herrick Library.

56. Earl Wilson, "Red Skelton Phones Earl: I'm Getting a Divorce," *New York Post*, December 3, 1952.

57. "Red Skelton Reconsiders Divorce Plans," *Seattle Times*, December 3, 1952.

58. "Wife Pins Skelton Rift on Dawn Visits to Kids," *New York World*, December 4, 1952.

59. Arline Mosby, "Locked Bedroom Told in Red Skelton Rift," *Los Angeles Herald Express*, December 4, 1952.

60. "Skelton May Get a Divorce," *Los Angeles Herald Express*, December 3, 1952.

61. "Skelton in Tiff with Wife: Interrupts Gag-Writing," *San Francisco News*, December 3, 1952.

62. Vivian Cosby, "Edna Skelton's Lasting Loyalty," *American Weekly*, November 13, 1949.

63. Mosby, "Locked Bedroom Told in Red Skelton Rift."

Chapter 12

1. Jimmy Starr, "Skelton Wows 'Em at Las Vegas Club: Just Like Atomic Blast," *Los Angeles Herald Express*, July 15, 1953.

2. "Ailing," *Newsweek*, December 22, 1952, 57.

3. "Red Skelton," *Variety*, July 22, 1953.

4. Dorothy Beck, "Red Skelton Signs with CBS at Last," *San Francisco News*, July 30, 1953.

5. Valentina Skelton Alonso, telephone interview with author, February 27, 2007.

6. Benedict Freedman and Nancy Freedman, *Lootville* (New York: Henry Holt and Company, 1957), 102–3.

7. Ibid., 87.

8. Red Skelton's Writing, box 11, Gene Fowler Folder, Red Skelton Collection, Vincennes University, Vincennes, Indiana.

9. Arthur Marx, *Red Skelton* (New York: E. P. Dutton, 1979), 217.

10. "Red Skelton Reconsiders Divorce Plans," *Seattle Times*, December 3, 1952.

11. Freedman and Freedman, *Lootville*, 144.

12. Lloyd Shearer, Red Skelton cover story, *Parade* (January 6, 1963).

13. Lloyd Shearer, "Red Skelton Never Stops Clowning," *Parade* (May 8, 1955): 28.

14. David McIntyre, "Skelton's Fans Suffer for Him," *San Diego Evening Tribune*, October 23, 1953.

15. John Heisner, "Red Skelton: TV Institution," *Rochester (NY) Democrat and Chronicle*, October 8, 1967.

16. Harry MacArthur, "Red Skelton Is Summer Sub for [Arthur] Godfrey on Wednesdays," *Washington Star*, July 15, 1954.

17. Ibid.

18. Dwight Newton, "Day and Night," *San Francisco Examiner*, October 8, 1952.

19. Steve Allen, "Red Skelton," in *The Funny Men* (New York: Simon and Schuster, 1956), 270.

20. Sherwood Schwartz (panel speaker), "Salute to Red Skelton," Academy of Television Arts and Sciences, Beverly Hills, California, October 21, 1998.

21. Tim Brooks and Earle Marsh, *The Complete Directory to Prime Time Network TV Shows, 1946–Present* (New York: Ballantine Books, 1979), 803–8.

22. Schwartz, "Salute to Red Skelton."

23. Martha Brian, "Skelton Comedy Taken from Life," *Columbus (OH) Dispatch*, August 23, 1962.

24. Red Skelton (guest columnist for syndicated writer Erskine Johnson), "Red Skelton Writes About 5 Characters Used in His Act," *Muskogee (OK) Times Democrat*, [1956], in Red Skelton Scrapbook Number 26, January-December 1956, Skelton Collection.

25. Brian, "Skelton Comedy Taken from Life."

26. John Crosby, "Radio and Television: Minority Report," *New York Herald Tribune*, January 6, 1952.

27. Marc Pachter, "The Biographer Himself: An Introduction," in *Telling Lives: The Biographer's Art* (Philadelphia: University of Pennsylvania Press, 1985), 14.

28. Jim Knipfel, *Quitting the Nairobi Trio* (2000; reprint, New York: Berkley Books, 2001), 277.

29. Hal Bodley, "Dream Comes True for Duo," *USA Today*, August 1, 2005.

30. Groucho Marx, *Groucho and Me* (1959; reprint, New York: Manor Books, 1974), 136.

31. "Red Skelton: A One-Man Stock Company," *Chicago American*, November 19, 1967.

32. Paul Corkery, *Carson* (New York: Randt and Company, 1987), 67.

33. "'Johnny' of Woodland Hills Wows 'Em with Ad-Libbing as Red Rendered Hors de Combat," *Van Nuys* (CA) *News*, August 22, 1954.

34. Nora Ephron, *And Now … Here's Johnny!* (1967; reprint, New York: Avon Books, 1968), 78.

35. Donald Freeman, "Big Break Comes to Johnny Carson," *San Diego Union*, [August 1954], Red Skelton Scrapbook Number 24, July 1954–October 1955, Skelton Collection.

36. Ibid.

37. Walter Ames, "Carson Signed to CBS Writer-Actor Contract," *Los Angeles Times*, September 3, 1954.

38. Ronald L. Smith, *Johnny Carson* (New York: Saint Martin's Press, 1987), 39.

39. "Johnny Carson," *Current Biography 1964*, Charles Moritz, ed. (New York: H. W. Wilson Company, 1965), 71.

40. W. Granger Blair, "President Enjoys Birthday As World Says 'Get Well,'" *New York Times*, October 15, 1955.

41. "Mr. Crockett Is Dead Shot as Salesman," *New York Times*, June 1, 1955.

42. "Kids Can't Get at Davy; Skelton Monopolizes Him," *Redwood City* (CA) *Tribune*, May 11, 1955.

43. Ibid.

44. James Bacon, "Red Skelton Biggest Fan of Crockett," *Sarasota* (FL) *Journal*, August 8, 1955.

45. Ibid.

46. William R. Conklin, "Marciano Retires from Boxing; Heavyweight Ruler Undefeated," *New York Times*, April 28, 1956.

47. "Marciano Knocks Out End of Retirement Idea," ibid., October 14, 1955.

48. Melvin Durslay, "Rocky vs. McPugg," *Los Angeles Examiner*, [October 1956], Red Skelton Scrapbook Number 26, January–December 1956, Skelton Collection.

49. "Rockabye Baby," *New York Times*, April 28, 1956.

50. For example, see Sheila Graham, "Skelton to Play Own Clown Role," *Hollywood Citizen News*, February 12, 1948;"Skelton to Star in His Biography," ibid., March 23, 1948.

51. James Bacon, "Red Skelton Writes Biography of Biographer," *Las Vegas Sun*, May 24, 1956.

52. Red Skelton's Writing, box 11, Skelton Collection.

53. "Gene Fowler," *Current Biography 1944*, Anna Rothe, ed. (New York: H. W. Wilson Company, 1945), 221.

54. "The Hollywood Scene: *Father Goose*," *New York Times*, October 28, 1934.

55. Gene Fowler, *Minutes of the Last Meeting* (New York: Viking Press, 1954), 104.

56. Marx, *Red Skelton*, 182.

57. Dick Williams, "Skelton Back in Films to Use TV Technique," *Los Angeles Mirror*, May 11, 1956.

58. *Half a Hero* review, *Variety*, July 29, 1953.

59. "Skelton Sparkles in Matt Rapf Prod.," *Hollywood Reporter*, July 29, 1953.

60. Sarah Hamilton, "Timid Skelton Does Fine Job," *Los Angeles Examiner*, September 17, 1953.

61. Special Collections, Metro-Goldwyn-Mayer Legal Department Records, 1953–54, Margaret Herrick Library, Academy of Motion Picture Arts and Sciences, Beverly Hill, California.

62. *Great Diamond Robbery* review, *Time*, February 15, 1954.

63. "'Diamond Robbery' Lets Skelton Down," *Hollywood Reporter*, November 30, 1953.

64. James O'Neill, Jr., "It's All Skelton," *Washington News*, May 24, 1957.

65. James Powers, *Public Pigeon No. 1* review, *Hollywood Reporter*, December 31, 1956.

66. *Public Pigeon No. 1* review, *New York Times*, May 18, 1957.

67. Besides the 1957 reviews for the film version (see notes 64–66), see also: "Skelton Forms His Own Firm," *Los Angeles Herald Express*, February 8, 1956, and Williams, "Skelton Back in Films to Use TV Technique."

68. Walter Hawver, "Durable Red Skelton to Return Next Fall," *Albany (NY) Knickerbacker News*, June 13, 1957.

69. Robert de Roos, "Television's Greatest Clown," *TV Guide*, (part 1), October 14, 1961, 12–15, (part two) October 21, 1961, 26–28, 30.

70. "Skelton's Philosophy: Always Room for One More Laugh," *Los Angeles Times*, June 23, 1957.

71. Brooks and Marsh, *Complete Directory to Prime Time Network TV Shows*, 804.

72. "Skelton Caught in Cross Fire" (syndicated), *Portland (OR) Journa*, December 15, 1957.

73. "Nitery Review: Riviera Hotel," *Variety*, August 6, 1958.

74. Don Bailer, "Red Skelton Big Vegas Hit," *Los Angeles Herald Express*, August 5, 1958.

75. Red Skelton Scrapbook Number 29, August–September 1958, Skelton Collection.

76. Wesley Hyatt, *A Critical History of Television's "The Red Skelton Show," 1951–1971* (Jefferson, NC: McFarland and Company, 2004), 63.

77. "It Hasn't All Been Laughs," *TV Guide*, February 20, 1960, p. 19.

78. "Comedian Red Skelton's Son Victim of Leukemia, Unaware of Condition," *Los Angeles Time*, January 4, 1957.

79. "A Sad Red Skelton Back on TV Tonight," *New York Post*, January 15, 1957.

80. "Skelton, Ill Son in Washington on 'See It All Tour,'" *Albany (NY) Knickerbacker News*, June 28, 1957.

81. "Skelton Family Off for Pompeii to Bring Another Dream to Life," *New York Post*, July 9, 1957.

82. "Red Skelton and His Son Reach Rome, *Buffalo (NY) Courier Express*, July 19, 1957.

83. "Skeltons Squabble on Tour," *Columbus (OH) Citizen*, July 25, 1957.

84. "Show Stolen By Skelton in Paris," *Tri-City (WA) Herald*, July 29, 1957.

85. "'Doomed' Skelton Boy Jokes with Reporter," *Boston Independent*, August 1, 1957.

86. Simon Ward's column is extensively quoted in "Everybody Says I'm Going to Die—That Means Everybody but Me," *Phoenix Gazette*, August 1, 1957.

87. John Camsell, "Little Dick Skelton Looks at Death—And It Has No Terror for Him," *New York Journal American*, August 1, 1957.

88. Red Skelton's comments are quoted in John Camsell, "Red Says London Unkind; Cuts Family's Stay Short," *Cedar Rapids (IA) Gazette*, August 2, 1957.

89. "Skelton Denies Trip with Dying Son Was Just a Publicity Stunt," *Red Wing (MN) Republican Eagle*, August 5, 1957.

90. "Skelton's Homecoming," *Los Angeles Herald Express*, August 7, 1957.

91. "Skelton Insult Denied by British, *Los Angeles Times*, August 13, 1957.

92. Vernon Scott, "Comic Tells of Son's Last Hours," *Indianapolis Star*, May 12, 1958.

93. "Our Dear Sweet Beloved Richard [1]," Funeral Scrapbook, May 1958, Skelton Collection.

94. Both scrapbooks are labeled: "Our Dear Sweet Beloved Richard." See footnote 93. (All celebrity sympathy cards and telegrams, unless otherwise noted; are found in "Our Dear Sweet Beloved Richard [1].")

Chapter 13

1. Gene Handsaker, "The Many Faces and Moods of Red Skelton," *Denver Rocky Mountain News*, October 29, 1967.

2. Ibid.

3. David McCullough, "The Unexpected Harry Truman," in *Extraordinary Lives: The Art and Craft of American Biography*, William Zinsser, ed. (Boston: Houghton Mifflin Company, 1986), 57.

4. Hal Bodley, "Dreams Come True for Duo," *USA Today*, August 1, 2005.

5. Red Skelton, rough draft letter to Georgia Skelton, undated [1960s], in Little Red and Miscellaneous Writing folder, Red Skelton Collection, Special Collections Library, Western Illinois University, Macomb, Illinois.

6. Ibid.

7. Red Skelton, conversations with the author, Ball State University, Muncie, Indiana, during the 1980s.

8. Arthur Marx, *Red Skelton* (New York: E. P. Dutton, 1979), 242.

9. See Red Skelton Collection, Vincennes University, Vincennes, Indiana.

10. Percy Shain, "Skelton Also Composer, Patriot, Loving Husband," *Boston Globe*, April 8, 1969.

11. Ibid.

12. "Money Can't Buy a Daughter's Happiness, *Modern Screen* (September 1970): 88.

13. Ibid.

14. Valentina Skelton Alonso, telephone interview with the author, February 27, 2007.

15. Zinsser, ed., *Extraordinary Lives*, 13.

16. Red Skelton, rough draft letter to Georgia Skelton, December 27, 1968, Little Red and Miscellaneous Writing folder, Skelton Collection, Western Illinois University.

17. Aljean Harmetz, "Skelton: How He Simplified His Life," *New York Times*, March 9, 1977.

18. Claire Tomalin, quoted in Thomas Mallon's review, "Thomas Hardy's English Lessons," *New York Times*, January 28, 2007.

19. Marx, *Red Skelton*, 254.

20. Valentina Skelton Alonso, telephone interview with the author, March 5, 2007.

21. Steve Allen, "Jackie Gleason," in *The Funny Men* (New York: Simon and Schuster, 1956), 145.

22. Red Skelton, ed., *A Red Skelton in Your Closet* (New York: Grosset and Dunlap, 1965), 5.

23. Peter Evans, *Peter Sellers: The Mask behind the Mask* (1968; reprint, New York: Signet, 1980), 194.

24. *Woody Allen: The Night-Club Years, 1964–1968* [long-playing records], United Artists, 9968, 1976.

25. Màrx, *Red Skelton*, 258.

26. Hedda Hopper, "Under Hedda's Hat," *New York Herald Tribune*, March 1, 1964.

27. Gloria Greer, "Red Skelton: At Home on the Desert," *Palm Springs Life*, April 1963, p. 35.

28. Georgia Skelton, "Do Comics Make Good Husbands?" *Screenland* (June 1952): 58.

29. Alonso telephone interview (March 5, 2007).

30. Ibid. (February 27, 2007).

31. "Red Skelton Turns to Art, Scores a Hit," *Chicago Tribune*, August 23, 1964.

32. Ibid.

33. Alonso telephone interview (February 27, 2007).

34. Joan Acocella, quoted in Kathryn Harrison's review, "Lives in the Arts," *New York Times*, February 18, 2007.

35. Marx, *Red Skelton*, 270.

36. Dan Jenkins, "It Hasn't All Been Laughs," *TV Guide*, February 20, 1960, 19.

37. Marvin L. Skelton, telephone interview with the author, December 14, 2006.

38. Ibid. (December 12, 2006).

39. Ibid.

40. Ibid. (February 6, 2007).

41. Ibid. (December 12, 2006).

42. Red Skelton Bound Letters, box 8, Letters to Valentina & Friends, undated letter [1965] to Valentina, Red Skelton Collection, Vincennes University.

43. Alonso telephone interview (March 5, 2007).

44. Tim Brooks and Earle Marsh, *The Complete Directory to Prime Time Network TV Shows, 1946–Present* (New York: Ballantine Books, 1979), 805–8.

45. Dwight Whitney, "The Weekly Ordeal of Red Skelton" (part one), *TV Guide*, April 20, 1963, p. 16.

46. Robert de Roos, "Television's Greatest Clown," *TV Guide*, October 14, 1961, 13.

47. Marx, *Red Skelton*, 278–79.

48. Roos, "Television's Greatest Clown," 13.

49. "The Unflappable Miss Morrison," *TV Guide*, July 11, 1964, 26.

50. Wes D. Gehring, *Joe E. Brown: Film Comedian and Baseball Buffoon* (Jefferson, NC: McFarland and Company, 2006).

51. Roos, "Television's Greatest Clown," 13.

52. Manohla Dargis, "The Imperfect Soul Who Helped Bring an End to the Slave Trade," *New York Times*, February 23, 2007.

53. Marx, *Red Skelton*, 221.

54. Alonso telephone interview (February 27, 2007).

55. Ibid. (March 5, 2007).

56. Wade H. Mosby, "Blue Shows Make Red Redder," *Milwaukee Journal*, March 2, 1969.

57. "Skelton Razzes Network Ban on Political Jokes," *San Francisco Chronicle*, May 11, 1956.

58. Fred D. Cavinder, ed., *The Indiana Book of Quotes* (Indianapolis: Indiana Historical Society Press, 2005), 14.

59. Brooks and Marsh, *Complete Directory to Prime Time Network TV Shows*, 808.

60. Kay Gardella, "A Study of Comedy Styles Is Concert in Pantomime," *New York Daily News*, February 4, 1965.

61. "Parts of 'Red Skelton' Magnificent, Sum Total of Show Sometimes Less," *Hollywood Reporter*, February 4, 1965.

62. Larry Rhine, correspondence with the author, November 16, 1998.

63. Wesley Hyatt, *A Critical History of Television's "The Red Skelton Show," 1951–1971* (Jefferson, NC: McFarland and Company, 2004), 112.

Chapter 14

1. "Right Up There: Red Skelton's Back on Top and Here Are [the] Reasons Why," *TV Guide*, April 28, 1956, p. 6.

2. Noel F. Busch, "Red Skelton—Television's Clown Prince," *Reader's Digest* (March 1965): 145–48.

3. Red Skelton Bound Letters, box 8, Letters to Valentina and Friends, undated letter [1965] to Valentina, Red Skelton Collection, Vincennes University, Vincennes, Indiana.

4. Wade H. Mosby, "Blue Shows Made Red Redder," *Milwaukee Journal*, March 2, 1969.

5. "Red Skelton," *Variety*, January 26, 1972, p. 54.

6. Alan Markfield, "Red Skelton: Why I Was Thrown Off TV," *National Enquirer*, December 10, 1974.

7. Tim Brooks and Earle Marsh, *The Complete Directory to Prime Time Network TV Shows, 1946–Present*, (New York: Ballantine Books, 1979), 808.

8. John A. Williams and Dennis A. Williams, *If I Stop I'll Die: The Comedy and Tragedy of Richard Pryor* (1991; reprint, New York: Thunder's Mouth Press, 2006), 45.

9. Brooks and Marsh, *Complete Directory to Prime Time Network TV Shows*, 808–10.

10. Valentina Skelton Alonso, telephone interview with the author, February 27, 2007.

11. Arthur Marx, *Red Skelton* (New York: E. P. Dutton, 1979), 292.

12. Alonso telephone interview. (All subsequent Valentina quotes in this chapter, are from this session.)

13. Robert de Roos, "Television's Greatest Clown" (part 1), *TV Guide*, October 14, 1961, pp. 13–14.

14. Ibid., 14.

15. Georgia Davis [Skelton], "My Autobiography," 1934, Biography of Red and Georgia folder, Red Skelton Private Papers box, Skelton Collection.

16. Alonso telephone interview.

17. Ibid.

18. See Wes D. Gehring, *The Marx Brothers: A Bio-Bibliography* (Westport, CT: Greenwood Press, 1987) and *Groucho and W. C. Fields: Huckster Comedians* (Jackson: University Press of Mississippi, 1994).

19. Steve Allen, *The Funny Men* (New York: Simon and Schuster, 1956), 145.

20. Red Skelton Bound Letters, box 8, Letters to Georgia and Some to Valentina, undated letter [probably 1969], to Georgia, Skelton Collection.

21. April 2, 1967, letter to Georgia, ibid.

22. August 2, 1969, letter to Georgia, ibid.

23. Red Skelton Bound Letters, box 8, Letters to Georgia & Some to Valentina, August 21, 1968 letter to Georgia, ibid.

24. Marvin L. Skelton, telephone interviews with the author, December 14, 2006, February 6, 2007.

25. Alonso telephone interview.

26. Ibid.

27. Marx, *Red Skelton*, 298, 299.

28. Alonso telephone interview.

29. Undated [1971] letter to Skelton, Letters to Big Red from Little Red (1971), Bound separate volume, Skelton Collection.

30. May 19, 1971, letter to Skelton, ibid.

31. October 5, 1971, letter to Skelton, ibid.

32. Alonso telephone interview.

33. Various sources. For example, see Martin Burden, "Stories of a Funnyman's Romantic Life," *New York Post*, September 10, 1990.

34. Virginia MacPherson, "Mischievous Red Skelton Tangled Up in Red Tape," *Alameda* (CA) *Times Star*, November 28, 1947.

35. Various sources. For example, see "Red Skelton's Former Wife, 54, Takes Own Life," *Los Angeles Times*, May 12, 1976, and Alonso telephone interview.

36. Sabrina Alonso, telephone interview with the author, March 7, 2007. (All subsequent Sabrina comments are from this interview.)

37. Various sources. For example, see Frank Lovece, "Red Skelton: Old Jokes Never Die," *Newsday*, September 12, 1990.

38. See, James Curtis, *James Whale: A New World of Gods and Monsters* (Boston: Faber and Faber, 1998), and Christopher Bram, *Father of Frankenstein* (1995; reprint, New York: Plume, 1996).

39. Jeffrey Meyers, *Hemingway: Life into Art* (New York: Cooper Square Press, 2000), 134.

40. Memories by Red folder, Red Skelton Private Papers box, Skelton Collection.

41. See Wes Gehring, *W. C. Fields: A Bio-Bibliography* (Westport, Connecticut: Greenwood Press, 1984) and *Groucho and W. C. Fields*.

42. Meyers, *Hemingway: Life into Art*, 152.

43. Danielle Trussoni, "Poolside," *New York Times*, March 4, 2007.

44. Richard R. Shepard, "Red Skelton: Gee, He Looks Good," *New York Times*, March 14, 1977.

45. Randall Poe, "Clown Comes to Carnegie," *New York Daily News*, March 14, 1977.

46. Ibid.

47. Charles Ryweck, "Red Skelton," *Hollywood Reporter*, March 16, 1977.

48. Poe, "Clown Comes to Carnegie."

49. Hal Glatzer, "Red Skelton Isn't Clowning Around When It Comes to His Paintings—They Fetch $40,000 Per," *People* (April 28, 1980): 95.

50. Mel Shields, "The Red Tapes Not for Burning," *Variety*, July 30, 1980, pp. 47, 68.

51. Wesley Hyatt, *A Critical History of Television's "The Red Skelton Show," 1951–1971* (Jefferson, NC: McFarland and Company, 2004), 151.

52. Ibid., 152.

53. Valentina Alonso telephone interview.

54. Georgia Skelton, "Do Comics Make Good Husbands?" *Screenland* (June 1952): 58.

55. Sabrina Alonso telephone interview.

56. Undated Skelton letter to Sabrina, Box for Valentina, Letters to Valentina and Sabrina folder, Skelton Collection.

57. September 6, 1991, Skelton letter to Sabrina, ibid.

58. Sabrina Alonso telephone interview.

59. Valentina Alonso telephone interview.

60. Undated birthday card from Lothian Skelton to Red Skelton, Valentina's Personal Items Box, Skelton Collection.

61. Lothian Skelton, telephone interview with the author, December 9, 1998.

62. Steve Allen, "Red Skelton," in *The Funny Men* (New York: Simon and Schuster, 1956), 265-75.

63. Earl Williams, interview with the author, September 24, 1997.

64. Ruth Prigozy, *F. Scott Fitzgerald* (New York: Overlook Press, 2001), 138.

Select Bibliography

Special Collections

Clarence Stout Papers. Lewis Historical Library, Vincennes University, Vincennes, IN.

Metro-Goldwyn-Mayer Legal Department Records. Margaret Herrick Library, Academy of Motion Picture Arts and Sciences, Beverly Hills, CA.

MGM Script Material (Red Skelton). University of Southern California Cinema-Television Library, Los Angeles, CA.

Red Skelton Clipping Files. Margaret Herrick Library, Academy of Motion Picture Arts and Sciences, Beverly Hills, CA.

Red Skelton Clipping Files. Performing Arts Library, New York Public Library at Lincoln Center, New York, NY.

Red Skelton Clipping Files. Vincennes Public Library, Vincennes, IN.

Red Skelton Collection. Archives and Special Collections, Western Illinois University Library, Macomb, IL.

Red Skelton Collection. Vincennes University, Vincennes, IN.

Books

Blair, Walter. *Native American Humor*. 1937. Reprint, Scranton, PA: Chandler Publishing, 1960.

Blesh, Rudi. *Keaton*. 1966. Reprint, New York: Collier Books, 1971.

Bram, Christopher. *Father of Frankenstein*. 1995. Reprint, New York: Plume, 1996.

Brown, Joe E. As told to Ralph Hancock. *Laughter is a Wonderful Thing*. New York: A. S. Barnes and Company, 1956.

Capra, Frank. *The Name Above the Title*. New York: Macmillan, 1971.

Cavinder, Fred D., ed. *The Indiana Book of Quotes*. Indianapolis: Indiana Historical Society Press, 2005.

Curtis, James. *James Whale: A New World of Gods and Monsters*. Boston: Faber and Faber, 1998.

Day, Richard. *Vincennes: A Pictorial History*. St. Louis: G. Bradley Publishing, 1988.

Dunning, John. *On The Air: The Encyclopedia of Old-Time Radio*. New York: Oxford University Press, 1998.

Edwards, Larry. *Buster: A Legend in Laughter*. Brandenton, FL: McGuinn and McGuire, 1995.

Ephron, Nora. *And Now ... Here's Johnny!* 1967. Reprint, New York: Avon Books, 1968.

Evans, Peter. *Peter Sellers: The Mask behind the Mask*. 1968. Reprint, New York: Signet, 1980.

Fein, Irving A. *Jack Benny: An Intimate Biography*. 1976. Reprint, New York: Pocket Books, 1977.

Fowler, Gene. *Minutes of the Last Meeting*. New York: Viking Press, 1954.

Freedman, Benedict, and Nancy Freedman. *Lootville*. New York: Henry Holt and Company, 1957.

Gable, Kathleen. *Clark Gable: A Personal Portrait*. Englewood Cliffs, NJ: Prentice-Hall, 1961.

Gehring, Wes D. *Charlie Chaplin: A Bio-Bibliography*. Westport, CT: Greenwood Press, 1983.

_____. *The Charlie Chaplin Murder Mystery*. Shreveport, LA: Ramble House Press, 2006.

_____. *Film Clowns of the Depression: 12 Memorable Movies*. Jefferson, NC: McFarland and Company, 2007.

_____. *Groucho and W. C. Fields: Huckster Comedians*. Jackson: University Press of Mississippi, 1994.

_____. *Joe E. Brown: The Baseball Buffoon*. Jefferson, NC: McFarland and Company, 2006.

_____. *Laurel & Hardy: A Bio-Bibliography*. Westport, CT: Greenwood Press, 1990.

_____. *"Mr B" or Comforting Thoughts about the Bison: A Critical Biography of Robert Benchley*. Westport, CT: Greenwood Press, 1992.

_____. *Parody as Film Genre: "Never Give a Saga an Even Break."* Westport, CT: Greenwood Press, 1999.

_____. *Personality Comedians As Genre: Selected Players*. Westport, CT: Greenwood Press, 1997.

_____. *Seeing Red … The Skelton in Hollywood's Closet: An Analytical Biography*. Davenport, IA: Robin Vincent Publishing, 2001.

_____. *W. C. Fields: A Bio-Bibliography*. Westport, CT: Greenwood Press, 1984.

Gottfried, Martin. *Nobody's Fool: The Lives of Danny Kaye*. New York: Simon and Schuster, 1994. 🖝

Hiney, Tom. *Raymond Chandler: A Biography*. New York: Grove Press, 1997.

Hubbard, Kin. *Abe Martin of Brown County, Indiana*. Indianapolis: Levey Bros., 1906.

_____. *Abe Martin's Almanack [for 1909]*. Indianapolis: Abe Martin Publishing Company, 1908.

_____. *Abe Martin's Barbed Wire*. Indianapolis: Bobbs-Merrill Company, 1928.

Hyatt, Wesley. *A Critical History of Television's "The Red Skelton Show," 1951–1971*. Jefferson, NC: McFarland and Company, 2004.

Jenkins, Henry. *What Made Pistachio Nuts? Early Sound Comedy and the Vaudeville Aesthetics*. New York: Columbia University Press, 1992.

Keaton, Buster. With Charles Samuels. *My Wonderful World of Slapstick*. Garden City, NY: Doubleday and Company, 1960.

Kelly, Fred C. *The Life and Times of Kin Hubbard: Creator of Abe Martin*. New York: Farrar, Straus and Young, 1952.

Kendall, Paul Murray. *The Art of Biography*. 1965. Reprint, New York: W. W. Norton and Company, 1985.

Knipfel, Jim. *Quitting the Nairobi Trio*. 2000. Reprint, New York: Berkley Books, 2001.

_____. *Slackjaw*. 1999. Reprint. New York: Berkley Books, 2000.

Lardner, Ring. *You Know Me Al: A Busher's Letters*. 1914. Reprint, New York: Collier Books, 1991.

Latham, Caroline. *The David Letterman Story*. 1987. Reprint, New York: Berkley Books, 1988.

Lax, Eric. *Woody Allen: A Biography*. New York: Alfred A. Knopf, 1991.

Maltin, Leonard. *The Great Movie Comedians: From Charlie Chaplin to Woody Allen*. New York: Crown, 1978.

Marx, Arthur. *Red Skelton*. New York: E. P. Dutton, 1979.

Marx, Groucho. *Groucho and Me*. 1959. Reprint, New York: Manor Books, 1974.

Meade, Marion. *Buster Keaton: Cut to the Chase*. New York: HarperCollins Publisher, 1995.

Meyers, Jeffrey. *Hemingway: Life into Art*. New York: Cooper Square Press, 2000.

Miller, Frank. *Leading Men: The 50 Most Unforgettable Actors of the Studio Era*. San Francisco: Chronicle Books, 2006.

Minnelli, Vincente. With Hector Arce. *I Remember It Well*. New York: Samuel French, 1974.

Nelson, Ozzie. *Ozzie*. Englewood Cliffs, NJ: Prentice-Hall, 1973.

Raphael, Frederic. *Eyes Wide Open: A Memoir of Stanley Kubrick*. New York: Ballantine Books, 1999.

Riley, James Whitcomb. *The Best of James Whitcomb Riley*, Donald C. Manlove, ed. Bloomington: Indiana University Press, 1982.

Rogers, Ginger. *Ginger: My Story*. New York: HarperCollins, 1991.

Rollyson, Carl. *A Higher Form of Cannibalism? Adventures in the Art and Politics of Biography*. Chicago: Ivan R. Dee, 2005.

Sandburg, Carl. *Abraham Lincoln: The Prairie Years and the War Years*. 1926, 1939. Reprint. New York: Harcourt, Brace and World, 1966.

Schickel, Richard. *D. W. Griffith: An American Life*. New York: Simon and Schuster, 1984.

Skelton, Red. *Gertrude and Heathcliff*. 1971. Reprint, New York: Charles Scribner's Sons, 1974.

———, ed. *A Skelton in Your Closet*. New York: Grosset and Dunlap, 1965.

Smith, David L. *Hoosiers in Hollywood*. Indianapolis: Indiana Historical Society Press, 2006.

Smith, Ronald L. *Johnny Carson*. New York: St. Martin's Press, 1987.

Steinberg, Cobbett. *Reel Facts: The Movie Book of Records*. New York: Vintage Books, 1978.

Strausbaugh, John. *Black Like You: Blackface, Whiteface, Insult and Imitation in American Poplar Culture*. New York: Penguin, 2006.

Summers, Harrison B., ed. *A Thirty-Year History of Programs Carried on National Radio Networks in the United States, 1926–1956*. New York: Arno Press, 1971.

Thurber, James. *My Life and Hard Times*. 1933. Reprint, New York: Bantam Books, 1947.

Twain, Mark. *A Connecticut Yankee in King Arthur's Court*. 1889. Reprint. Scranton: Chandler Publishing Company, 1963.

———. *The Selected Letters of Mark Twain*. Charles Neider, ed. 1982. Reprint, New York: Cooper Square Press, 1999.

Wallace, Daniel. *Big Fish*. New York: Penguin Books, 1998.

Wertheim, Frank. *Radio Comedy*. 1979. Reprint. New York: Oxford University Press, 1992.

Shorter Works, Including Script Material, Letters, and Interviews

Adams, Jennifer. "Why the Skeltons Parted." *Movieland* (March 1943).

Agee, James. "Comedy's Greatest Era." *Life*, September 3, 1949.

"Ailing." *Newsweek*, December 22, 1952.

Allen, Steve. "Jackie Gleason." In *The Funny Men*. New York: Simon and Schuster, 1956.

———. "Red Skelton." In *The Funny Men*. New York: Simon and Schuster, 1956.

Als, Hilton. "Shining Hours." *The New Yorker*, May 22, 2006.

Arnold, Maxine. "Clown in Civies." *Photoplay* (February 1948).

Baytos, Betsy. "Interview with Red Skelton," February 20, 1996. Dance Collection Oral History, New York Public Library at Lincoln Center, New York, NY.

Bergson, Henri. "Laughter." In *Comedy*. Wylie Sypher, ed. Garden City, NY: Doubleday and Company, 1956.

Blum, John M. "Retreat from Responsibility." In *The National Experience: A History of the United States*. John M. Blum, ed. New York: Harcourt Brace, 1968.

Busch, Noel F. "Red Skelton—Television's Clown Prince." *Reader's Digest*, March 1965.

Cosby, Vivian. "Edna Skelton's Lasting Loyalty." *American Weekly*, November 13, 1949.

Davidson, Bill. "'I'm Nuts and I Know It.'" *Saturday Evening Post*, June 17, 1967.

"Demure Du Barry." *Newsweek*, June 28, 1943.

Dudley, Janice Thompson. Letter to the author, July 10, 1991.

Eisenhower, Mamie. Letter to Red and Georgia Skelton, May 20, 1958, "Our Dear Sweet Beloved Richard" Funeral Scrapbook (1). Red Skelton Collection, Vincennes College, Vincennes, IN.

Engle, William. "Out of Love into Business." *American Weekly*, July 27, 1947.

"Everyone's a Kid is Basis for Skelton's Philosophy." *McGuire Banner* [military hospital publication], February 1, 1945.

Felton, Verna. "Love That Red-Head." *Radio Mirror*, January 1948.

Flight Command review. *Film Daily*, December 23, 1940.

Franchey, John R. "Ex's Can Be Friends." *Screenland* (September 1943).

Friedrichsen, Frank. "The Short Tragic Life of Jimmy Dean." *Movie Star Parade* (December 1955).

The Fuller Brush Man review. *Time*, May 31, 1948.

Gehring, Wes D. "The Gentile Clown [Red Skelton]." *USA Today Magazine*, September 2006.

_____. Interview with Anita Mykowsky, 2000.

_____. Interview with Brenda Hopper, February 6, 1994.

_____. Interview with Cheech Marin, January 31, 2004.

_____. Interview with Earl Williams, September 24, 1997.

_____. Interview with Eleanor Norris Keaton, late 1980s.

_____. Interview with Lothian Toland Skelton, December 9, 1998.

_____. Interviews with Marvin L. Skelton, December 12, 14, 2006, February 6, 2007.

_____. Interview with Pandro S. Berman, June 1975.

_____. Interview with Paul Cooley, September 21, 2000.

_____. Interview with Red Skelton, September 18, 1986. as well as various conversations during his 1980s visits to Ball State University (Muncie, Indiana).

_____. Interview with Sabrina Alonso, March 7, 2007.

_____. Interviews with Valentina Skelton Alonso, February 27, March 5, 13, 14, 2007.

_____. "The Mentor and the Clown: Clarence Stout and Red Skelton." *Traces of Indiana and Midwestern History*. (Fall 2000).

_____. "The Neglected Career of Kin Hubbard's Abe Martin: Crackerbarrel Figure in Transition." *Indiana Magazine of History* (March 1982).

_____. "Red Skelton and Clem Kadiddlehopper." *Indiana Magazine of History* (March 1996).

"Gene Fowler." In *Current Biography 1944*. Anna Rothe, ed. New York: H. W. Wilson Company, 1945.

Glatzer, Hal. "Red Skelton Isn't Clowning Around When It Comes to His Paintings – They Fetch $40,000 Per." *People*, April 28, 1980.

Great Diamond Robbery review. *Time*, February 15, 1954.

Greer, Gloria. "Red Skelton: At Home on the Desert." *Palm Springs Life*, April 1963.

Hall, Donald. "Simple Things: A Poet's Poet." *House and Garden* (September 2003).

Hamburger, Philip. *Three Little Words* review. *The New Yorker*, August 26, 1950.

Hift, Fred. *A Southern Yankee* review. *Motion Picture Herald* (August 7, 1948).

"How Red's First Wife Arranged His Second Marriage." *TV Picture Life*, March 1969.

I Dood It review. *Time*, November 29, 1943.

"It Hasn't All Been Laughs." *TV Guide*, February 20, 1960.

Jefferson, Sally. "The Skelton in Hollywood's Closet." *Photoplay* (July 1942).

"Johnny Carson." In *Current Biography 1964*. Charles Moritz, ed. New York: H. W. Wilson Company, 1965.

Keaton, Eleanor Norris. Letter to the author, late 1980s.

"Laugh Clown." *Newsweek*, July 9, 1951.

Lovece, Frank. "Red Skelton: Old Jokes Never Die." *Newsday*, September 12, 1990.

Loventz, Pare. *Free and Easy* review. *Judge* magazine, May 17, 1930.

McCullough, David. "The Unexpected Harry Truman." In *Extraordinary Lives: The Art and Craft of American Biography*. William Zinsser, ed. Boston: Houghton Mifflin Company, 1986.

"Money Can't Buy a Daughter's Happiness." *Modern Screen* (September 1970).

Pachter, Marc. "The Biographer Himself: An Introduction." In *Telling Lives: The Biographer's Art*. Marc Pachter, ed. Philadelphia: University of Pennsylvania Press, 1985.

Panama Hattie review. *Newsweek*, October 5, 1942.

Panama Hattie review. *The New Yorker*, October 3, 1942.

Peterson, Marva. "The Two Mrs. Skeltons." *Movieland* (April 1948).

"Radio Notes." *Newsweek*, September 24, 1945.

"Radio Warm-Ups #3." *Radio Life*, August 29, 1948.

"Red Skelton." In *Current Biography 1947*, Anna Rothe, ed. New York: H. W. Wilson Company, 1948.

"Red Skelton: Master of Ad-Lib." *Hollywood Lean Sheet*, May 1948.

Red Skelton photo showcase with text, *Look* magazine, May 14, 1946.

"Red Skelton." *Time*, July 9, 1951.

Rhine, Larry. Letter to the author, November 16, 1998.

"Right Up There: Red Skelton's Back on Top and Here Are [the] Reasons Why." *TV Guide*, April 28, 1956.

Roos, Robert de. "Television's Greatest Clown" (two parts). *TV Guide*, October 14 and 21, 1961.

Ross, Sid. "Red Skelton ... His Plane Was in Trouble." *Parade* magazine, September 23, 1951.

Rosten, Leo. "How to See Red—Skelton That Is (Part 2). *Look*, November 6, 1951.

Rottenbery, Josh. "The Piracy Debate." *Entertainment Weekly*, July 14, 2006.

"Rubber Face on TV." *Life*, October 28, 1951.

Schlesinger, Arthur M., Jr. "The World in Flames." In *The National Experience: A History of the United States*. John M. Blum, ed. New York: Harcourt Brace, 1968.

Shearer, Lloyd. "Red Skelton: He Never Stops Clowning." *Parade* magazine, May 8, 1955.

Ship Ahoy review. *Showman Trade Review*, April 18, 1942.

Skelton, Edna Stillwell (as told to James Reid). "I Married a Screwball." *Silver Screen*. (June 1942).

Skelton, Georgia Davis. "Do Comics Make Good Husbands?" *Screenland* (June 1952).

Skelton, Red. "The Role I Liked Best ..." *Saturday Evening Post*, February 28, 1948.

A Southern Yankee review. *Cue*, November 27, 1948.

"Success Story." *Cue*, September 20, 1941.

"The Unflappable Miss Morrison." *TV Guide*, July 11, 1964.

Vincennes Public Schools Records (RHC #370), Enumeration – District 2 (1923 and 1924). Courtesy of a Red Skelton private collector.

Watch the Birdie review, *Film Daily*, November 28, 1950.

"We Point with Pride to Red Skelton." *Silver Screen* (October 1947).

Whitehead, John. "Red Skelton as the 'Little Brat.'" *Radio Life*, April 12, 1942.

Whitney, Dwight. "'A Clown Is a Warrior Who Fights Gloom' … and Red Skelton Fights Harder Than Anyone." *TV Guide*, August 20, 1966.

Whitney, Dwight. "The Weekly Ordeal of Red Skelton" (Part One). *TV Guide*, April 20, 1963.

Wild, David. "Steve Martin: The 'Rolling Stone' Interview." *Rolling Stone*, September 2, 1990.

Williams, John A., and Dennis A. Williams. *If I Stop I'll Die: The Comedy and Tragedy of Richard Pryor*. 1991. Reprint, New York: Thunder's Mouth Press, 2006.

Wissing, Douglas. "Red Skelton: The Last Vaudevillian." *Traces of Indiana and Midwestern History* (Winter 1998).

Yagoda, Ben. *Will Rogers: A Biography*. 1993. Reprint, New York: HarperCollins, 1994.

The Yellow Cab Man review, *Motion Picture Herald*, February 25, 1950.

Young, Jordan R. *The Laugh Crafters: Comedy Writing in Radio and TV's Golden Age*. Beverly Hills, CA: Post Times Publishing, 1999.

Zinsser, William. "Introduction." In *Extraordinary Lives: The Art and Craft of American Biography*, Zinsser, ed. Boston: Houghton Mifflin Company, 1986.

Newspapers (see individual citations in Notes).

Alameda (CA) Times Star, 1947.

Albany (NY) Knickerbocker News, 1957.

Baltimore Sun, 1941.

Bingham (NY) Press, 1952.

Boston Globe, 1947, 1969.

Boston Independent, 1957.

Boston Traveler, 1947.

Brooklyn Citizen, 1942, 1943.

Brooklyn Eagle, 1941, 1942, 1944, 1948.

Buffalo Currier Express, 1957.

Burlingame (CA) Advance, 1947.

Cedar Rapids (IA) Gazette, 1948, 1957.

Chicago American, 1967.

Chicago Sun, 1941.

Chicago Times, 1945, 1951.

Chicago Tribune, 1951, 1964.

Cleveland Plain Dealer, 1938.

Columbia News, 1948.

Columbus (OH) Citizen, 1957.

Columbus (OH) Dispatch, 1962.

Daily Variety, 1941.

Dallas News, 1948.

Detroit Free Press, 1937.

Evansville Press, 1962.

Hollywood Citizen News, 1944, 1947, 1948.

Hollywood Press Times, 1945.

Hollywood Reporter, 1937, 1938, 1940, 1941, 1942, 1943, 1945, 1947, 1948, 1951, 1953, 1956, 1965, 1977.

Indianapolis News, 1937, 1948, 1969.

Indianapolis Star, 1937, 1941, 1958, 1962.

Kansas City Star, 1951.

Las Vegas Sun, 1956.

London Times, 1951.

Long Beach (CA) Press Telegram, 1946, 1947, 1951.

Long Island (NY) Star-Journal, 1948.

Los Angeles Daily News, 1947, 1948, 1951.

Los Angeles Examiner, 1943, 1944, 1945, 1948, 1951, 1953, 1956.

Los Angeles Herald Express, 1942, 1945, 1951, 1952, 1953, 1956, 1957, 1958.

Los Angeles Mirror, 1951, 1952, 1956, 1961.

Los Angeles Times, 1943, 1944, 1946, 1947, 1950, 1954, 1957, 1976, 1982, 1997.

Milwaukee Journal, 1937, 1941, 1969.

Montreal Gazette, 1937.

Muncie Star Press, 2006.

Muskogee Times Democrat, 1956.

New York Daily Mirror, 1938, 1941, 1942, 1943.

New York Daily News, 1941, 1942, 1947, 1965, 1977.

New York Herald Tribune, 1944, 1947, 1951, 1952, 1964.

New York Journal American, 1941, 1942, 1943, 1957.

New York Morning Telegraph, 1944.

New York Post, 1941, 1942, 1943, 1952, 1957, 1990, 1997.

New York Sun, 1938.

New York Telegram, 1941.

New York Times, 1934, 1938, 1941, 1942, 1943, 1944, 1945, 1946, 1947, 1948, 1951, 1955, 1956, 1957, 1977, 1999, 2005, 2006, 2007.

New York World, 1952.

New York World Telegram, 1933, 1941, 1944, 1951, 1952.

New York World Telegram and Sun, 1951.

Oregon Journal, 1951, 1957.

Philadelphia Inquirer, 1937.

Phoenix Gazette, 1948, 1957.

PM, 1941.

Portland (OR) Journal, 1945.

Red Wing (MN) Republican Eagle, 1957.

Redwood City (CA) Tribune, 1955.

Rochester (NY) Democrat and Chronicle, 1967.

Denver Rocky Mountain News, 1967.

Sacramento Union, 1946.

San Diego Evening Tribune, 1953, 1954.

San Diego Union, 1945, 1947.

San Francisco Chronicle, 1956.

San Francisco Examiner, 1952.

San Francisco News, 1952, 1953.

San Mateo (CA) Times and Leader, 1948.

Sarasota Journal, 1955.

Seattle Post, 1952.

Seattle Times, 1948, 1952.

Tacoma (WA) News Tribune, 1948.

Texarkana Gazette, 1951.

Toronto Daily Star, 1937.

Tri-City (WA) Herald, 1957.

USA Today, 2005, 2006.

Van Nuys (CA) News, 1954.

Variety, 1937, 1939, 1940, 1942, 1943, 1945, 1947, 1948, 1950, 1951, 1953, 1958, 1980, 1986.

Village Voice, 1977.

Vincennes Commercial, 1924, 1929.

Vincennes Post, 1937, 1939, 1940.

Vincennes Sun, 1929.

Vincennes Sun-Commercial, 1937, 1939, 1940, 1941, 1960, 1962, 1997.

Vincennes Valley Advance, 1967, 1979.

Vincennes Western Sun, 1913.

Washington (DC) News, 1947, 1957.

Washington (DC) Post, 1937, 1940, 1941.

Washington (DC) Star, 1948, 1951, 1954.

Waterbury Independent, 1952.

Wichita Beacon, 1951.